THE RAYS

Reflections on Islamic Belief,
Thought, Worship and Action

THE RISALE-I NUR COLLECTION

THE RAYS

Reflections on Islamic Belief, Thought, Worship and Action

BEDİÜZZAMAN SAİD NURSİ

Translated by
Hüseyin Akarsu

New Jersey

13 12 11 10 1 2 3 4

Published by Tughra Books
345 Clifton Ave., Clifton,
NJ, 07011, USA

www.tughrabooks.com

Library of Congress Cataloging-in-Publication Data Available

ISBN 978-1-59784-215-0 (hardcover)

Printed by
Numune Matbaacilik ve Cilt San. Ltd. Sti., Istanbul - Turkey
www.numune.com.tr

Table of Contents

THE FOURTH RAY

THE SIXTH RAY

THE SEVENTH RAY

THE NINTH RAY

THE TENTH RAY

THE ELEVENTH RAY

THE TWELFTH RAY

THE THIRTEENTH RAY

THE FOURTEENTH RAY

THE FIFTH RAY

THE FIFTEENTH RAY

Preface

F THE DEFINITIVE HISTORY OF TWENTIETH CENTURY ISLAMIC movements is ever written, one wonders whether its author would be both perspicacious and brave enough to argue a point which, while held in private by many Muslim thinkers and writers, is rarely if ever mooted openly, namely that the 'Islamic resurgence' which is said to have occurred over the past forty or fifty years, should be seen primarily in terms of a *resurgent identity* that has little to do with any surge of interest in, or affiliation to, the faith beneath Islam *per se*. One presumes that Muslims have not suddenly become better believers or more proficient in their outward expressions of submission, although clearly this may have happened in various individual cases. What does appear to have occurred in the Muslim world, however, is a sustained attempt on the part of certain groups to reassert their collective identity in the face of external threats. Some have accentuated their inextricable ties – be they religious, cultural or a mix of the two – to Islam, while others have taken advantage of the centrality of Islam to the socio-political and cultural dynamics of the Muslim world in order to advance their own political and ideological agendas.

The numerous movements of the past 150 years, characterised almost without exception as 'Islamic movements', have had little if anything to do with the resurgence of religious faith as such. Most of these have actually been political movements, with leaders whose underlying goal has been to solve a specific problem: the problem of the perceived backwardness of the Muslim peoples and their subservience, politically and culturally, to the West.

While none of the groups that operate within the definitional matrix of 'Islamic movements' can claim to be identifiable primarily as a faith movement, various individuals have appeared sporadically with the avowed aim of fostering renewal of belief – often to the extent of dedicating their whole life's work to that aim – and around some of these individuals, movements of considerable size and import have accreted. The Turkish Muslim scholar Bediüzzaman Said Nursi (1877/8–1960) is one such individual.

Progenitor of the 'service of belief and the Qur'an' movement, Nursi is arguably the most influential, if woefully under-researched, Muslim thinker of the 20th century. While the 'service of belief and the Qur'an' movement, a faith-based movement consisting of millions of followers worldwide, does not strictly speaking fulfil the definitional criteria of a New Religious Movement, it stands out from other contemporary Muslim religious and ideological groupings not only for its uncompromising focus on the renewal of individual rather than collective faith, but also for its eschewal of any kind of religiously-legitimized violence or militancy for the sake of politico-ideological ends.

Although often stereotyped as the pioneer of reform of an Islam declining under the pressures inflicted on it by the Kemalist secularization policy of the Turkish state, almost half a century after his death, Nursi continues to defy any attempts to locate him precisely within the generally accepted milieu of 'Muslim scholars'. While his *magnum opus*, the *Risale-i Nur*, is for all intents and purposes a commentary on the Qur'an, it is not a work of exegesis in the technical sense of the word, although he was clearly an accomplished exegete. And while Nursi was well-versed in the principles of scholastic theology (*kalām*), devoting the lion's share of the *Risale* to what he claims are rational proofs for the unity (*tawhīd*) of God, it is not a work of traditional theology either.

In fact, on one level, the *Risale* is as resistant to compartmentalization as the Qur'an itself, which it claims to mirror and to elucidate. And if, as Nursi often asserts, the aim of the Qur'an is to guide man to belief, then the teachings of the *Risale* should be seen as consonant with that aim.

> The three supreme matters in the worlds of humanity and Islam are belief, the Shari'a, and life. Since the truths of belief are the greatest of these, the *Risale-i Nur*'s select and loyal students avoid politics with abhorrence so that they should not be made the tool to other currents and subject to other forces, and those diamond-like Qur'anic truths

> not reduced to fragments of glass in the view of those who sell or exploit religion for the world, and so that they can carry out to the letter the duty of saving belief, the greatest duty.

Part of Nursi's appeal lay in his uncompromising belief that it is belief (*īmān*) which must be renewed and protected, and that all other endeavors must be approached with the primacy of belief in mind: the fact that, unlike many of the popular Muslim thinkers of his own epoch, he repudiated the dubious art of politics – and, more importantly, the dubious art of politicking that is buttressed by religion – earned him respect and conferred on him a sense of authenticity that would perhaps be found wanting in so many other Muslim thinkers. Another part of his appeal lay in his shrewd interpretation of the forces ranged against him. For Nursi, unlike many of the Muslim scholars, leaders and ideologues who came later, realized that if there is a conflict between Islam – or belief – and modernity, it is not a conflict fought over issues of government or technology, over science or democracy. As Nursi's own evaluation of the problems facing the Muslim world shows, the conflict is ultimately over transcendence, with the post-Enlightenment experiment claiming a centrality in the universe's affairs for man that Islam, with its emphasis on the dependence of man on God, cannot countenance. Man is faced with a choice: belief in the sovereignty of God or belief in the sovereignty of man, with all that such a choice entails. For Nursi, the way to salvation consists solely in choosing the Other over the self, and it is in the dynamics of this choice that the key to an understanding of Nursi's take on spirituality and man's place in the cosmos may be found.

Renewal and reform, then, do play a central role in the Nursian *Weltanschauung*, but, unlike so many of his coevals, it is the renewal of belief and the reform of the individual that constitute his primary and overriding concern. In this respect, he is one of few Muslim thinkers in the 20th century who has little if anything to say about the socio-economic or political externalia of Muslim life. Over the past century and a half in general, and the last twenty-five years in particular, 'Islam is a complete way of life' has been the mantra of choice for the vast majority of Muslim movements. As a corollary, emphasis has been largely on the 'implementation' of Islam at the socio-political level, with debate and discussion focusing mainly on issues such as Islamic law, Islamic education and the concept of the Islamic state. As such, the lion's share of Muslim movements can be said to adopt an 'externalist' approach to the Islamic revelation, seeing in the strict adherence of Muslims to the *shari'a* – and, where necessary, the imposition of such adherence through legislative means – the key to the formation of the ideal Muslim society. For the 'externalists,' reform has come to mean chiefly the reform of society, the underlying aspiration of which must be to return to the 'golden age' of Islam typified – for the externalists at least – by the community-state of Madina during the lifetime of the Prophet. These 'dreams of Madina', and the concomitant desire to share – or, even, impose – those dreams on others, are responsible in part for the current Western perception of Islam as more political ideology than divinely-revealed religion. The relative merits and demerits of 'Islamism' or 'political Islam' as terms by which to describe this over-politicized approach to Islam need not occupy us here. Suffice to say that in the last analysis, this approach rests on the fulcrum that is the return of 'Islamic rule', the transformation of the Muslim world into an *umma* analogous to the community-state of Madina and, wittingly or otherwise, the reduction of the Islamic revelation to the single issue of governance. While Islam made political and transformed into ideology is a relatively recent phenomenon, the 'externalist' approach to Islam which informs it is almost as old as Islam itself. However, whereas for the likes of 'non-externalists' such as Ghazzali in the 12th century and Mulla Sadra in the 17th it was the nomocentrism of the externalist scholars and the over-emphasis on *fiqh* (jurisprudence) which constituted the greatest obstacles to the health of the Muslim community, for the Ghazzalis and Sadras of today – of whom Nursi is undoubtedly one – it is the over-politicization of religion which is the danger.

Arguably the most important common denominator among Islamic/Islamist groups and leaders of the past fifty to one hundred years has been the tendency to favour the use of force to change 'religiously suspect' regimes in the Muslim world and bring about Islamic revolutions. And it is precisely on this point where one sees a fundamental difference between Nursi and his contemporaries. For not only is Nursi distinguished by his staunch opposition to any kind of uprising or revolution in the name of Islam, but also he stands on account of his aversion to politics in general, and the politicization of Islam in particular. Nowhere is Nursi's ideological departure from the majority of his contemporaries delineated more sharply than on the highly contentious issue of *jihād*. As emphasized above, for

Nursi, the way to salvation consists solely in choosing the Other over the self, and it is in the dynamics of this choice that the key to an understanding of Nursi's take on spirituality and *jihād* may be found.

There are many for whom it is clear that humanity is in a precarious position. We are told on a daily basis that we live under the threat of pollution, global warming, terrorism, famine and a thousand and one different ills. Our time is, we are told, a time of global crisis. Yet few are able to fathom the real cause of this crisis. It is not that we do not understand the problems around us. Our crisis – the crisis of modernity – is that we do not understand ourselves. Indeed, postmodern thought – if such a thing exists and is not really just another name for the confused ideas of late modernity – nurtures a scepticism in which the very possibility of understanding anything is called into question.

Most people, Nursi claims, have been reduced to hardship and misery by the demands and dictates of modern times. Man's innate nobility has also been marred, he says, as the gradual divorce from religious values has opened the floodgates of 'dissipation', encouraging dissolute living and the 'appetites of the flesh.'

Socio-economic inequalities are also the hallmark of this modern civilisation, Nursi adds, with the Western attitude being "So long as I am full, what is it to me that others die of hunger?" and "You work so that I can live in ease and comfort'. By allowing the rift between the classes to widen, the West has engendered so much strife and sedition that it is on the brink of bringing humanity to its knees, giving rise to the struggle between capital and labour – itself the precursor of two World Wars and bloodshed and disorder on a hitherto unknown scale.

One could go on, but surely the point has been made: it was impossible for Said Nursi to approve of a civilisation in which the negative aspects outweighed the positive so decisively. For Nursi, the only way forward for man is to embrace a civilisational form which brings true happiness and prosperity – and if not for all, then at least for the majority.

Human beings are faced with a choice: belief in the sovereignty of God or belief in the sovereignty of man, with all that such a choice entails. For Nursi, the way to salvation consists solely in choosing the Other over the self, and it is in the dynamics of this choice that the key to an understanding of Nursi's take on the 'true civilisation' may be found.

For Said Nursi, for man to be truly human, he must establish for himself not an Islamic state, but an Islamic *state of mind*. If, in secular shorthand, 'civilization' is the highest thing towards which man as a social being can aspire, let us see how Said Nursi redefines the term to make it truly meaningful for limited, impotent man, giving it the ability to 'confront the awesome silence of the grave' in a way that no other civilization is able. Comparing Western civilization with the ideational entity known as Islamic civilization, he locates the source of the former in human artfulness (*daha*) and that of the latter in Divine guidance (*huda*). These sources, he holds, impact in very different ways on society in general and the individual in particular.

Artfulness, writes Nursi, functions in the mind and confuses the heart. It looks to the material and to the corporeal, considering the body and the evil-commanding soul, which it seeks to nurture. It develops the potentialities of the *nafs* while making of the *ruh* a servant or slave. In its love of this world, which is the only world it recognizes, it turns man into a satan, worshipping deaf nature and, in its blindness, drawing a veil of ingratitude over the face of the earth. It sees the bounties before it as ownerless booty, which it usurps like a common thief.

Guidance, on the other hand, works in the heart and lights up the spirit. It develops man's potentialities and spiritual capacities and, in so doing, illuminates nature. It makes of the soul and the body and in so doing produces happiness in this world and the next. It sees Divine art everywhere, and the wisdom and power of God in all things. It worships Allah, the possessor of art and power. It is both seeing and hearing, and as it benefits from Divine bounties, it scatters the light of thankfulness all around it.

In Nursian terms, then, to be truly civilized, man must be truly human, and to be truly human, his goal is not the kind of khilafa that engenders power but the kind of *khilafa* which engenders worship – namely the nurturing of each individual soul into its true state as *khalifat Allah fi al-ard*. This, for Nursi, marks the true civilization to which man should aspire.

With these words in mind I would like to introduce you to one of Nursi's masterpieces, *The Rays*, in which he elaborates upon almost all the points mentioned above in his own inimitable manner.

Colin Turner

University of Durham, June 2010

The Second Ray

The Second Ray

Some fruits of Divine Unity and belief in Divine Unity

In the Name of God, the All-Merciful, the All-Compassionate.

This Ray was written sixteen years ago when, after the release of my friends, I was left alone in Eskişehir Prison. It was written at great speed in my own very deficient hand at a most distressing and disagreeable time: it is, therefore, somewhat lacking in order. However, while editing it recently I realized that in respect of expounding and proving the issues of belief and Divine Unity, it is a valuable treatise that includes forceful arguments.
Said Nursi

What follows is the seventh meaningful point concerning the six Greatest Names of God or God's six Names that have all-comprehensive manifestations, (which have been discussed at the end of *The Gleams*) and which deals with the notion of the Divine Being as *the Unique One of Absolute Oneness* (112:1).

Note: I believe that this treatise is significant for it contains and elaborates many subtle mysteries of belief. I hope God will enable those who read and understand it to rescue their belief. Unfortunately, since I have not been allowed to meet with anyone here, I have been unable to attain a clean copy of it for myself. If you wish to understand the main point of the treatise, begin with The Second and Third Fruits of The First Station. Read them carefully and then study the Conclusion at the end and the matters discussed in the two pages preceding that. When you have done this, go back and peruse the whole of the treatise slowly!

A seventh meaningful point concerning God's six Greatest Names and regarding the fact that "God is the Unique One of absolute Oneness"

In the Name of God, the All-Merciful, the All-Compassionate.

And from Him do we seek help.

What follows here concerns three subtle and beautiful fruits that have grown from an understanding of God's Unity, together with three proofs of His Oneness, which is inspired by a famous oath taken by the Prophet, upon him be peace and blessings, and a particular and extremely impressive meaning of the Qur'anic verse, *And know that there is no deity but God* (47:19).

WHEN TAKING AN OATH, GOD'S NOBLEST MESSENGER, UPON HIM BE peace and blessings, usually said, "By Him in whose hand is Muhammad's life." This oath shows that from the tiniest of its roots, through the incalculable girth of its trunk and all the way to the tips of its innumerable branches, the tree of the universe depends utterly and unequivocally on the Power and Will of the Single, Unique One, both for its being and its continued existence. For if the most distinguished and illustrious of creatures, Prophet Muhammad, upon him be peace and blessings, does not own himself, if he cannot act as he wills and is dependent in all of his actions on the Will of Another, then nothing else in creation—no act, no state, no quality, whether it be universal or particular—can operate outside the sphere of domination and control of that all-encompassing Authority and Will.

What this meaningful oath of Prophet Muhammad, upon him be peace and blessings, indicates is the fact that it is a single, unique Lordship[1] Which dominates the whole of existence. We refer the explanation and numerous clear proofs of this reality to other parts of the *Risale-i Nur*, in this Second Ray we will focus on the three following matters, articulated in three brief "Stations."

In The First Station, out of the numerous subtle, sweet, and precious fruits grown from this extremely important truth of belief, three universal

[1] Lordship or God's being the Lord of the whole creation means that God is the Creator, Sustainer, Maintainer, Raiser, and Director of creation. (Tr.)

fruits will be explained in brief. The emotions, tastes, and experiences which attract my heart to these fruits will also be mentioned.

In The Second Station, three universal facts which both necessitate and explain this sacred truth will be elaborated. These facts, which are also proofs of this truth, have the power of three thousand proofs.

In The Third Station, three signs that indicate the Unity of the Divine Lordship Which dominates the whole of existence will be mentioned. These three signs have the power of three hundred signs and proofs.

The First Station

THE FIRST FRUIT

In Divine Unity and the unity it engenders throughout the universe, Divine grace and beauty and the perfection of Lordship become apparent: if there were no unity, that pre-eternal treasury would remain hidden. It is only in the mirror of or through Unity and in the manifestations of the Divine Names which are concentrated in the faces of particulars at the extremities of the tree of creation that one is able to see infinite Divine grace and perfections, limitless beauties and excellences of Divine Lordship, innumerable gifts and bounties of Divine Mercy, and boundless perfection and grace of God's being the Eternally Besought One.

For example, pure white milk is sent to the aid of a powerless infant from an unexpected place, namely from a source that lies between blood and excrement.[2] When this phenomenon is considered from the perspective of Divine Unity, suddenly the undying grace and beauty in the Mercy of the All-Merciful can be seen in all its splendor through God's wonderful, affectionate sustaining of all infants and His subjugating their mothers to

[2] In 16:66, the Qur'an says: *And surely in the cattle (feeding on the pastures of the revived earth), there is a lesson for you: We give you from that which is within their bodies, (marvelously distinguished from) between the waste and blood, milk that is pure and palatable to those who drink.* This verse describes the process of the production of milk in remarkable detail: the part-digestion of what is ingested as food, the absorption of it, and then a second process and refinement in the glands. Milk is a pleasant source of nutrition for living beings, yet it is a secretion, like other secretions, and it is non-essential for the life of the mother. Despite being a secretion produced from between the dung in the bowels and the blood in the veins, it is one of the most vital and useful foods for living beings. The narration of the process of its production in the Qur'an fourteen centuries ago is one of the countless proofs of its Divine origin. (Tr.)

the needs of their offspring. If we do not consider it from the point of view of Divine Unity, then that grace and beauty remain hidden, while the provision of milk is attributed to "natural" causes, to chance or nature, thus robbing it of all its value and, arguably, even of its very nature.

Another example: if recovery from a dreadful disease is considered from the perspective of Divine Unity, through the act of healing all of the afflicted in the huge hospital—the earth—with remedies and medicines taken from the vast pharmacy of the earth, the grace, beauty and excellences of the affection shown by the Absolutely Compassionate One become apparent in a universal and most amazing fashion. If, however, we do not consider the situation from the viewpoint of Divine Unity, that skilful, expert and conscious act of healing will be attributed instead to the properties of lifeless medicines, to blind forces and unconscious nature, thus stripping the art of healing of both its wisdom and its value, and changing its nature completely.

Because of its relevance, I will explain here a point which has occurred to me concerning the invocation in which one calls down God's blessings and peace upon the Prophet, upon him be peace and blessings. The followers of the Shafi' School of Jurisprudence or Law offer this invocation at the end of the supererogatory glorifications (*tasbih*) which follow each of the five daily canonical Prayers:

> O God! Bestow blessings on our master Muhammad and on the Family of our master Muhammad, to the number of diseases and their cures, and send to him and them Your abundant gifts and favors, and grant them never-ending peace.

This invocation is important because the wisdom in the creation of humanity and the comprehensiveness of human nature require that we entreat our Creator at every moment; it requires that we seek refuge with God and offer Him thanks and praise. Since illness is the most effective whip driving human beings to the Divine Court, and since the sweet bounties which prompt them to give thanks and offer praise with true gratitude and enthusiasm are cures, healing, and good health, this invocation for blessings upon the Prophet has received much appreciation and acceptance. Sometimes when I say "to the number of all diseases and their cures," I see the earth in the form of a hospital and am able to sense the obvious existence of the True Healer—the One Who provides remedies for all physical and spiritual diseases, and answers all needs—and I feel His universal affection and sacred, all-embracing compassion.

Another example: consider someone who, having suffered the terrible spiritual pains of misguidance, has, by dint of belief, received the gift of guidance. If we consider this from the point of view of Divine Unity, we see that an ordinary, impotent mortal has suddenly become an addressee of the Creator and Sovereign of the whole universe, and a worshipper of the All-Worshipped One alone. We see that they have been offered eternal felicity in a vast and most splendid everlasting world. Indeed, all believers will be favored with the same bounty, each according to their degree of belief. The stamp of the eternal Beauty and ceaseless Grace of One Who is All-Munificent and All-Benevolent is seen clearly on this gift of guidance—so much so, in fact, that a single gleam of this Beauty and Grace is enough to make believers love It and to render the elite among them heartsick for It. However, if we do not consider the situation from the perspective of Divine Unity, we become like the imperious and arrogant *Mu'tazilis*[3] and attribute that Divine gift of belief to ourselves or to certain causes. As a result, that sparkling diamond of the All-Merciful, the true price of which is Paradise, will be reduced to nothing more than a shard of glass which no longer reflects the gleam of sacred grace or beauty.

Thus, as these three examples show, Divine Unity—the fact that God is the sole Creator, Deity, Lord and Sovereign of the whole creation—causes thousands of varieties of Divine Grace and Beauty and the perfection of God's Lordship to become apparent in even the most particular states of the most particular beings in the furthermost reaches of the sphere of multiplicity, which is the realm of external existence.

It is because the Divine Beauty, Grace and Perfection are seen by the heart and perceived and experienced by the spirit in Divine Unity that all saints and pure scholars have derived the sweetest of pleasures and the most enjoyable form of spiritual sustenance from the repeated recitation of the

---

[3] The *Mu'tazilis* or *al-Mu'tazila*: The school of the Muslim "rationalists" which accorded creative effect to human will and agency, concluding that it is human beings who create their actions. In addition, this school denies God Almighty attributes, claiming that God is absolutely obliged to reward those who believe and do good deeds, and punish those who disbelieve. (Tr.)

words, "There is no deity but God"—a statement which, more than any other, proclaims the truth of Divine Unity. It is also because Divine Grandeur and Majesty, and the absolute sovereignty of Divine Lordship can be fully perceived in this proclamation of Divine Unity that God's noblest Messenger, upon him be peace and blessings, declared: "Of all the words uttered by me and the Prophets who came before me, the best are 'There is no deity but God.' "[4]

While a small bounty, gift or particle of sustenance, such as a fruit, a flower, or a light, is a tiny mirror in itself, when it is attributed to the One, Single Creator and Lord of the universe, it suddenly joins its fellows and stands shoulder to shoulder with them. In so doing, it becomes part of a large mirror formed of the family to which it belongs and displays some aspect of the Divine Grace and Beauty manifested on its species. Through its short-lived, transient beauty, it points to a Beauty that is everlasting and undying. In accordance with the words of Mawlana Jalalu'd-Din ar-Rumi[5] (in his *Mathnawi*):

> Those illusions are but traps for saints, whereas in reality
> They are the reflections of those with radiant faces in the garden of God.

it becomes a mirror held up to Divine Beauty and Grace. However, if we do not attribute it to Divine Beauty, each particular fruit remains on its own, displaying neither sacred beauty nor elevated perfection. Seen in this way, even the particular gleam within it is extinguished, thus turning what is in reality a diamond into nothing more than glass.

Furthermore, God's Unity—the fact that He is the sole Creator, Deity, Lord and Sovereign of the universe—causes living beings, which are the fruits of the tree of creation, to have a personality that is characterized by their belonging to the Divine; it bestows on them an individuality that bears the stamp of Divine Lordship and a face that reflects Divine Mercifulness, Which comprises the seven key Attributes of God.[6] Again, each liv-

---

4 At-Tirmidhi, *Sunan*, "Da'awat" 123; Imam al-Malik, *al-Muwatta'*, "al-Qur'an" 32. (Tr.)

5 Jalalu'd-Din ar-Rumi, Mawlana (Mevlana/Rumi) (1207–1273): One of the most renowned figures of Islamic Sufism. He was the founder of the *Mawlawi* (Mevlevi) Order of the whirling dervishes, and famous for his *Mathnawi*, an epic of religious life in six volumes. For Western readers, Rumi is a powerful voice among the poets of Sufism. (Tr.)

6 They are Life, Knowledge, Hearing, Sight, Power, Will, and Speech. (Tr.)

ing being displays in concentrated form the manifestations of the Divine Names, and has an identity established by the One Who is addressed by the words *You alone do We worship and from You alone do we seek help* (1:5). However, if we do not consider each living being from the perspective of Divine Unity, then its true personality, individuality, face and identity recede from view and eventually become invisible.

Also, it is clear from our understanding of these living beings that their Maker sees them, knows them, hears them, and does with them as He wills. In other words, the creation and make-up of living beings indicate—especially in the sight of a believer—the One Who has power and will, the One Who hears, sees, and knows. It is especially behind the creation and make-up of humankind that the existence of that One is observed through belief and the mystery of Divine Unity. This is because the manifestation of Divine Attributes, such as Knowledge, Power, Life, Hearing, and Sight, shows itself in humankind more than in any other created beings. Human beings indicate the Divine Attributes through the samples of those Attributes which are manifested in their beings. For example, the fact that a person has eyes shows that the One Who bestows eyes sees both the eyes and what the eyes (will) see or perceive, and then He bestows them. Indeed, an optician who advises you to wear certain glasses knows what kind of glasses you need before prescribing them. Similarly, the One Who gives humans ears surely hears what those ears (will) hear, and then He makes them and bestows them upon His creation. You can draw similar comparisons for other Attributes of the Creator and the human faculties which indicate them.

Also, human beings bear the impresses and manifestations of the Divine Names: through these, people bear witness to the existence of the Names and their manifestations. Again, through the innate weakness, impotence, poverty, and ignorance of the human being, people act as a mirror in a completely different way. That is to say, through our innate weakness and poverty, we bear witness to the Power, Knowledge, Will, as well as the other Attributes of Perfection of the One Who has mercy on our impotence and comes to our aid. Thus, it is because on account of Divine Unity a thousand and one Divine Names are concentrated and can be detected clearly in the tiny missives that are called living beings, which exist in the furthermost reaches of the sphere of multiplicity, the All-Wise Maker extensively multiplies the copies of living beings. He multiplies much more extensively the copies of the species of smaller living beings in particular, and broadcasts them everywhere.

What follows is an account of a personal experience which impelled me to the truth of this First Fruit:

On account of overwhelming feelings of pity, tenderness, and compassion, I found myself exceedingly touched by the plight of living beings, and among these, the plight of intelligent beings and humankind itself, in particular, the oppressed and disaster-stricken. I cried out from the very depths of my heart and soul: "These uniform 'laws' which prevail over the world cannot lend an ear to the woes of these powerless wretches; similarly, those deaf elements which pervade the world do not hear them either. Is there no one who will take pity on them and help them out of their wretched state?" My heart was also crying out with all its strength: "These fine creatures, these valuable assets, these grateful and imploring friends—do they have no owner, no master, no true friend who will be their protector and take care of their business?"

The satisfying answer which came, and which was enough to calm the cries of my spirit and exclamations of my heart, was this: Thanks to the Qur'an and the light of belief, I realized that due to the Divine Unity, the All-Merciful, All-Compassionate Being of Majesty has, outside the sphere of those universal laws, particular favors and special assistance which He directs toward those lovable creatures of His who weep and suffer under the pressure of His universal laws. Through His particular Lordship, He owns, controls, protects, and maintains each and every being in the universe: He Himself directs everything personally and listens to the problems of each being. He is the true Owner, Master, and Protector of everything. As I came to understand this, my seemingly endless despair gave way to limitless joy. In my view, by virtue of being inextricably connected to and completely owned by such an All-Majestic Master, the value and significance of every living being increased a thousand-fold.

Everyone takes pride in the honor, fame, and rank of their master, and in so doing acquires a kind of dignity. Given this, it is clear that through the strengthening of this relation (of beings to their Creator and Owner) owing to the light of belief, a mere ant was able to defeat the Pharaoh. Furthermore, it was able to feel the pride of a thousand heedless Pharaohs, all of whom imagined themselves to be independent and in charge of their own fates, left to their own devices, and who took pride—which was extinguished at the door of the grave—in their forefathers and their dominion over the land of Egypt. Similarly, in the face of the arrogant pride of Nimrod, which changed into torment and shame during his pangs of death, a single fly was able to display the dignity of its relationship with its Owner and Master, thus reducing the pride of Nimrod to nothing.

The verse: *Surely associating partners with God is a tremendous wrong* (31:13) confirms that associating partners with God is an awful and egregious transgression. Associating partners with God is such a heinous crime that it transgresses the rights of all creatures and impugns their honor and dignity. Indeed, it is a crime that only Hell can cleanse.

THE SECOND FRUIT OF DIVINE UNITY AND BELIEF IN IT

While the first fruit relates to the All-Holy Being and Creator of the universe, this second fruit relates to the universe itself and its essential nature.

It is on account of God's being the sole Creator and Lord of the universe and the affirmation of this greatest truth that the perfections of the universe are realized; and the elevated duties of beings are understood; and the purposes behind the creation of beings are realized. It is on account of this that the value of creatures is known; and the Divine purposes underpinning the existence and life of all existent beings come into view; and the wisdom in the creation of animate and conscious beings becomes apparent; and the smiling, beautiful faces of Mercy and Wisdom which lie behind the angry, bitter faces of the violent storms of flux and upheaval are seen. And it is known that the beings which disappear behind the veil of death and decay leave behind many imprints of their existence and consequences of their life in the visible world, such as their identities, natures, spirits, and glorifications.

It is also on account of God's being the sole Creator and Lord of the universe and the affirmation of this greatest truth that it is known that the whole of the universe is a meaningful book of the Eternally Besought One; and all beings, from the depths of the earth to the furthest reaches of the heavens, constitute a miraculous collection of missives written by the All-Glorified One. It is on account of this that all the species of creatures appear as a magnificent, well-organized army of the Lord, and that all tribes of beings, from microbes and ants to rhinoceroses, eagles, and planets, are seen to be dutiful officials of the Pre-Eternal Sovereign. It is on account of this that everything acquires a value thousands of times greater than its own individual worth, thanks to the connection it enjoys with that Sovereign and the fact that it acts as a mirror to Him. It is on account of this that one is able to find answers to enigmatic questions such as: "From where did these vast floods of beings and these endless caravans of creatures come? Where are they going? Why did they come here? And what are they doing, what purposes are they serving?" Were it not for Divine Unity, these elevated perfections of the universe would disappear, and these lofty, sacred truths would be transformed into their opposites.

It is because the crimes of unbelief and associating partners with God are acts of aggression against all of the perfections of creation and its inviolable rights and sacred truths that the universe grows angry with the unbelievers and those who associate partners with God. The wrath of the heavens and the earth descends upon them and the universal elements unite to destroy them, as they did when they drowned the people of Noah, destroyed the 'Ad and the Thamud[7], and obliterated the Pharaoh, all of whom were guilty of associating partners with God. As stated in the verse, *Almost bursting with fury* (67:8), Hell rages and fumes at the unbelievers and those who associate partners with God with such vehemence that it almost bursts apart. Associating partners with God is a tremendous insult to the universe and a monstrous aggression against it. By denying the sacred duties of the universe and demeaning the instances of wisdom in creation, one commits a gross affront to the honor of the universe. To illustrate this, we will mention one example out of thousands.

For example, on account of Divine Unity and the unified character it has bestowed upon creation, the universe resembles a vast, corporeal angel. This angel has as many heads as the number of species of creatures, and each head has mouths to the number of the members of those species. In each mouth there are as many tongues as the number of the organs, parts, and cells of those members. Therefore, the universe is like a wonderful crea-

[7] The 'Ad were the people of Prophet Hud and lived in southern Arabia, and the Thamud were the people of Prophet Salih, living in northwest Arabia. (Tr.)

ture which glorifies its Maker and, with innumerable tongues, declares Him to be the All-Holy, thus engaging itself in worship like the Archangel *Israfil*. The universe is also like an arable field which yields abundant crops for the realms and mansions of the Hereafter; it is like a factory that produces supplies—human deeds, for example—to be dispatched to the various levels of the Realm of Happiness. It is like a movie-camera with thousands of lenses, uninterruptedly taking pictures in this world for the people of the next, including particularly the people of Paradise, to watch. Unbelief and associating partners with God portray this truly wonderful, perfectly obedient and living corporeal angel as a lifeless, decaying, futile, perishing, meaningless and wretched accumulation of things revolving in the turmoil of events, the storms of change and the darkness of non-existence. Also, associating partners with God changes this marvelous, perfectly orderly and most beneficial factory into an idle, disorderly plaything of chance that produces nothing and has no function. It sees and shows it to be the playground of deaf nature and blind force, a place of mourning for all conscious beings and the slaughterhouse of all living creatures.

Thus, in accordance with the verse, *Surely associating partners with God is a tremendous wrong* (31:13, associating partners with God, despite being a single evil, is the cause and source of so many monstrous crimes that it renders those guilty of it deserving of infinite torment in Hell.

What led me to this second fruit was a strange feeling and experience. Once, when I was observing the unfolding of spring, I saw the creatures—in particular, the living ones, and the tiniest of these in particular—enter the sphere of existence, caravan after caravan, and leave it after a short appearance in a flowing torrent displaying hundreds of thousands of examples of the Resurrection.

The scenes of death and decay which appeared in this continuous flurry of activity were so pitiable that they moved me to tears. The more I witnessed the death of those lovely creatures, the more my heart ached. Sighing with pity and regret, I found my spirit in deep turmoil, for life that came to such an end seemed to me to be a torment worse than death.

The living beings of the plant and animal kingdoms, most beautiful and full of precious art, were opening their eyes to gaze on this exhibition of the universe for a moment and were then disappearing. The more I watched, the more pain I felt. I was moved to complain by shedding tears, while my heart asked profound questions such as: "Why do they come and then go away without ceasing?" I saw that these lovely creatures being torn up like rags and thrown away into the darkness of non-existence before my eyes as though they were worthless and without purpose, despite having been created, equipped, and nurtured with so much attention and art and in such valuable forms. And as I saw this, my senses and faculties, captivated as they are by perfection and as attached as deeply as they are to beauty and things of value, began to scream: "Why are these not shown mercy? How pitiful it is! Where do decay and death come from in this bewildering cycle of events to assail these poor beings?"

As I started complaining bitterly about fate because of the painful way the events of these beings' life are governed, indicated by the light of the Qur'an and the mystery of belief, Divine Unity came to my aid as a pure favor of the All-Merciful. It illuminated all those layers of darkness, changing my laments into professions of joy and my pitiful complaints into exclamations, such as "What wonders God has willed!" and "How blessed God is!" It caused me to declare, "All praise and gratitude be to God for the light of belief!" For the unity manifested in creation showed me that Divine Unity causes each created being—and each living creature in particular—to have general benefits and to yield considerably significant results.

For example, each living creature—this ornate flower, for example, or that sweet-producing bee, is such a meaningful Divine ode that innumerable conscious beings study it with great delight. It is such a precious miracle of Power and so great a proclamation of Wisdom that it exhibits the Art of the Maker to countless appreciative observers in a most attractive manner. Another exceedingly elevated result of its creation is that it presents itself to, or is favored with, the gaze of the All-Majestic Originator, Who wills to observe His Art Himself, to look on the grace and beauty of His creation, and view the beauties of the manifestations of His Names in the countless mirrors that are His creatures.

Furthermore, as explained in The Twenty-Fourth Letter[8], it is another elevated duty of the creation of each creature that it in five ways it serves the manifestation of God's Lordship and the demonstration of

---

[8] See *The Letters*, translated by Hüseyin Akarsu, The Light, 2007.

Divine Perfections, which necessitate the infinite activity in the universe. In addition to yielding such results and serving such purposes and benefits, each living being that possesses a spirit (but has no intellect) leaves that spirit behind in this visible realm when it departs. And in countless memories and other "preserved tablets" it leaves behind its form and identity, and in its seeds or eggs it leaves the laws of its nature and a sort of plan for a future duplicate of its life. And in the World of the Unseen and the sphere of Divine Names it leaves the perfections and beauties which it has mirrored, before passing through a veil of death and becoming hidden from worldly eyes through an apparent demise, which is, in reality, a joyful discharge from its duties. I perceived this reality and uttered, "All praise and gratitude are for God!"

These genuine, deeply-rooted, exceedingly powerful, faultless, and infinitely brilliant instances of grace and beauty, which are observable in all the levels of the universe and all the species of creation, demonstrate unequivocally that the extremely ugly, harsh, repugnant, and wretched picture painted by unbelief and associating partners with God is impossible and illusory. For such appalling ugliness could not exist hidden under the veil of such genuine grace and beauty: if it really did exist, then that true grace and beauty would be false, baseless, futile, and illusory. This means that the association of partners with God is not based upon a reality: its way is closed, it has become stuck in a mire, and it is a mere claim or supposition that is impossible to verify. This clearly observable truth of belief has been elucidated with numerous proofs in many parts of the *Risale-i Nur*.

THE THIRD FRUIT

This fruit relates to conscious beings, and particularly to humankind. It is through Divine Unity and belief in it that human beings can be the most valuable fruit of creation, the dearest and most tender of creatures, the happiest and most fortunate of living beings, and the addressee and friend of the Creator of the universe, and they can attain the most elevated of perfections. Indeed, all of the human perfections and their exalted aims find meaning through Divine Unity alone and can be realized only through affirmation of it. Supposing the impossible, were God not the sole Creator, Sovereign, and Ruler of creation, then human beings would be the unhappiest and most wretched of creatures, the poorest of the animals, and the most pained, sorrowful, and suffering of all conscious beings. For together with endless impotence, countless adversaries, boundless desires and countless needs, human beings have been innately decked out with such a large variety of faculties and senses that they feel innumerable kinds of pains and experiences and countless kinds of pleasures. Also, they have such goals and desires that one who does not govern the universe in its entirety could not realize these goals or desires.

For example, human beings have an intense desire for immortality. Only one who has power and control over the entire universe as though it were a palace is able to fulfill this desire—one who can close the door of this world and open the gate of the Hereafter as easily as closing the door of one room and opening that of another. As well as the longing for immortality, human beings have thousands of other desires—some positive and some negative—which spread throughout the world and stretch to eternity. So only the Single, Unique One, Whose absolute Unity has made the entire universe into an integrated entity and Who holds it completely in His grasp, can respond to these desires and heal humanity's two terrible wounds—their innate impotence and destitution.

Furthermore, human beings have such secret and subtle desires pertaining to the satisfaction and ease of their heart, and such vast, comprehensive and universal aspirations for the happiness and immortality of their spirit that only One Who sees the most hidden and imperceptible veils of their heart and does not remain indifferent to this, and hears the heart's most inaudible secret voices and does not leave them without a response, is able to fulfill these desires and bring these aspirations to fruition. That One must also be powerful enough to subjugate the heavens and the earth to His command, as though they were obedient soldiers, and to employ them in the performance of universal tasks.

Also, by virtue of Divine Unity and the affirmation of this greatest truth, all the members and senses of humanity gain an exceedingly high value, whereas unbelief and associating partners with God reduce them to an infinitely low degree. For example, the most valuable faculty of humanity is reason. When Divine Unity is affirmed, reason not only becomes a brilliant key to the sacred treasuries of the Divine, but also to thousands of coffers of the universe. However, if reason falls foul of unbelief and associating partners with God, it becomes an inauspicious instrument of torment which fills the head with all of the grievous pains of the past and all of the dreadful fears for the future.

Also, for example, compassion is the finest and most endearing characteristic of humanity. If the meaning and result of Divine Unity do not come to its aid, this capacity for feeling becomes a burning source of pain and torment that reduces its owner to misery. A mother who has lost her child but, unaware of the truth, supposes that she has lost him forever feels this torturous pain to the full.

Similarly, if the meaning and result of Divine Unity come to the aid of love, which is the sweetest, most pleasurable and most precious of human feelings, it bestows upon miniscule humanity the expanse and breadth of the universe, and makes them tender sovereigns of the creatures. However, if the human being falls into the pit of unbelief and associating partners with God, then—God forbid—love becomes such a calamitous burden that, when they are separated from their loved ones, their heart is torn apart, convinced as it is by these erroneous beliefs that separation through death is eternal. However, vain amusements cause heedlessness and numb the senses, cushioning humanity from feelings of loss.

When you compare the hundreds of other human faculties and senses with these three examples, you will understand the degree to which Divine Unity and the affirmation of it are able to lead the human being to fulfillment and perfection. This third fruit has also been elaborated on in perhaps twenty of the treatises of the *Risale-i Nur*.

What led me to this fruit was the following feeling:

I was standing at the top of a high mountain. During a spiritual awakening that was powerful enough to dispel my heedlessness, the death and the grave appeared to me in their distressing reality, as did painful scenes of mortality and decay. Like everyone else, I found that my innate desire for immortality boiling up and rebelling against death. The tenderness and compassion in my nature also surged up in revolt against the consignment to the grave of the people of perfection, particularly the Prophets, the saints, and the pure scholars, for whom I feel great love and appreciation. I looked in the each of the six directions, seeking help, but found neither solace nor assistance. The past appeared to me as a vast grave; the future seemed to be nothing but darkness. Above me, I saw only horror; beneath my feet, and to my right and my left, all I could perceive was grievous situations and the assault of numerous harmful things. Suddenly, Divine Unity came to my help, drawing back the veil and revealing the face of reality. "Look!" it said.

First I looked in the face of death, which frightened me. I saw that for the people of belief, death was simply a release from their duties: the appointed hour of their demise was their discharge papers. Death was merely a change of abode, the introduction to an everlasting life, and the door opening onto it. I saw that to die was to be released from the prison of this world and to fly to the gardens of Paradise. Upon death, a believer enters the presence of the All-Merciful in order to be remunerated for their service. Death is an invitation to proceed to the realm of bliss. Understanding this with complete certainty, I began to love death.

I then looked at transience and decay, and I saw that they are, like pictures on a movie screen or bubbles on flowing water under the sun, a pleasurable form of renewal and replacement. Coming from the World of the Unseen in order to refresh the exquisite manifestations of the All-Beautiful Names, they undertake an excursion, a tour, in the visible world, with certain duties to perform. They also constitute a wise and purposeful manifestation of the grace and beauty of Divine Lordship, an act of mirroring the eternal Divine Beauty. This I knew with certainty.

I then looked in each of the six directions and, thanks to the truth of Divine Unity, I now saw them to be so bright and beautiful that they dazzled the eyes. The past was no longer a vast grave; rather, having been transformed into the future, it consisted of thousands of enlightened gatherings of friends and thousands of illuminated spectacles. I looked at the true faces of thousands of matters such as these and I saw that they elicited nothing but joy and thanks.

I have described my feelings and experiences concerning this third fruit with proofs, particular and universal, in perhaps forty treatises of the *Risale-i Nur*. They have been explained with particular clarity in the thirteen "Hopes" of the Twenty-sixth Gleam, which is "The Treatise of Hope and Solace for the Elderly." Therefore, here I have cut short this very long story.

The Second Station

There are countless facts that absolutely necessitate Divine Unity and prove it beyond doubt. They also reject the association of partners with God. Since hundreds, and perhaps thousands, of these are demonstrated in detail in the *Risale-i Nur*, here only three of them will be explained in brief.

THE FIRST FACT WHICH NECESSITATES AND PROVES DIVINE UNITY

As testified by the unquestionably wise acts and insightful control and governance observed in the universe, creatures are brought into being through the all-encompassing Attributes and Names of an All-Wise and Perfect Sovereign, including in particular His boundless Knowledge and Power.

It can be inferred and concluded with certainty from the works in the universe that their Maker has sovereignty and authority at the degree of universal Lordship, and grandeur and supremacy or magnificence at the degree of absolute dominion and control. He also possesses absolute perfection, independence, and self-sufficiency at the degree of absolute Divinity, and boundless and unrestrictable command, rule and activity. His sovereignty and grandeur, His perfection, independence, and self-sufficiency, His absolute freedom from any restriction or interference, His infinitude and boundlessness—all of these absolutely necessitate Unity and reject the notion that He has either peers or partners.

The testimony of sovereignty and authority to Unity has been proven with complete certainty in numerous places in the *Risale-i Nur*. A brief summary is as follows:

The essential characteristic of sovereignty is independence and the rejection of outside interference: sovereignty necessitates these. Even when humans, who by their innate weakness are in need of assistance, enjoy a modicum of sovereignty, they reject the interference of others and jealously guard their independence. It is for this reason that there cannot be two kings in a country, two governors in a province, two mayors in a town, or two headmen in a village. If there are two of any of these, it causes chaos, anarchy and rebellion break out, and law and order are destroyed. If the slight sovereignty enjoyed by impotent, helpless human beings rejects the interference and partnership of others to this extent, surely the sovereignty of an absolutely Powerful One, free from all impotence, which is exercised in the form of absolute Lordship, will in no way countenance the partnership or interference of others. Indeed, it most vehemently rejects them, and the absolutely Sovereign One will wrathfully eject from His Court those who attribute partners to Him. It is because of this truth that the wise Qur'an issues severe threats to those who associate partners with God.

As for the testimony of grandeur, supremacy and majesty to Divine Unity, this too has been demonstrated with clear proofs in other parts of the *Risale-i Nur*. What follows is a brief summary of them:

For example, the intensity and splendor of the sun's light leaves no need for other lights in the places where it shines and illuminates; nor does it allow another light to have any effect. Similarly, the supremacy and grandeur of Divine Power leave no need for another force or power, and do not allow it to have any ability to create or any share in creation. It is particularly inconceivable that Divine Power should delegate to others the creation and control of living and conscious beings, upon which the purposes of Divine Power for the existence of the universe are particularly concentrated. It is also in no way possible that Divine Power should leave to other hands the specific or particular states, results and fruits of living beings, which are the points where the Divine purposes for the creation of humanity and the invention of countless varieties of bounties are for the most part manifested. For example, it would be an insult to God's Majesty and the supremacy of His Lordship, and the grandeur of His Divinity and the dignity of His being the absolutely Worshipped One if a living being were to show genuine gratitude or offer adoring praise to anyone other than God Almighty for being healed—even from some minor ailment —or for some particular sustenance or for guidance regarding an insignificant issue.

How perfection points to the meaning and absolute necessity of Divine Unity has also been explained with very clear proofs in other parts of the *Risale-i Nur*. A brief summary is as follows:

The creation of the heavens and the earth self-evidently necessitates an absolute power of infinite perfection. Moreover, the wonderful bodily mechanism of every living being necessitates the same power. The perfection of an absolute power, free from impotence and restriction, most certainly necessitates unity. Were this not so, it would require us to suppose that the perfect was in fact defective, that the unrestricted was in fact restricted, that the infinite was actually finite, that the strongest of powers was actually the most impotent, and that the boundless now had boundaries; all of these are absolutely impossible.

A brief summary of the testimonies to Unity of absolute unrestrictedness, comprehensiveness, and infinity, which has been elaborated in parts of the *Risale-i Nur*, is this: each of the creative and administrative acts observed in the universe show, through the pervasive nature of their acts, effects, and results, that they are comprehensive, unrestricted, and boundless. Now given the fact that partnership and interference would mean placing a restriction on something that is unrestricted and imposing a boundary on something which is boundless, thus destroying their true nature, it is quite clear that partnership in acts which are absolute and comprehensive is impossible. For what is by its very nature absolute and unrestricted spreads and pervades everywhere, even when it concerns itself with something finite, limited, and material. For example, if air, light, heat, and even water had been given an unrestricted nature, they would spread everywhere without let or hindrance. Having an unrestricted nature would grant even a limited being pervasiveness. Given this, it is certain that the true, all-encompassing and immaterial unrestrictedness bestows such all-encompassing pervasiveness on attributes that are infinite, supra-material, unlimited, and free from all defect that this leaves no room whatsoever for the partnership or interference of others. This being so, the sovereignty, grandeur, perfection, comprehensiveness, infinitude, and unrestrictedness of each of the countless Divine Acts and hundreds of Divine Names, Whose works and manifestations are observed in the universe, provide exceedingly powerful proofs of Divine Unity.

An extraordinary force tends to pervade everywhere when it is released, scattering other forces. Similarly, each of the acts of Divine Lordship and each manifestation of the Divine Names display such extraordinary force in their works that if they were not held in check by God's universal Wisdom and absolute Justice, they would overrun the whole creation. For example, is it conceivable that a Power Which creates and nurtures poplar trees all over the world would not take under Its control the odd apple or walnut tree which grows among the poplars? Would that Power delegate the nurturing of that apple tree to the hand of another? The way in which that Power acts in each species, and in each individual creature, shows that It has the ability to invade the entire universe and subjugate all things and beings. Certainly, such a Power could in no way admit any partnership or participation in Its acts.

Also, the owner of a fruit tree will pay great importance not only to the fruit that their tree will bear, but also, bearing in mind its future yields, to the seeds inside the fruit, which are in fact its heart. A sensible owner will not make their ownership count for nothing by handing the fruits over to someone else. Now the universe is like a tree: the elements are its branches, the plants and animals at the tips of the branches are its flowers and leaves, and human beings, who are at the topmost part of the tree, are its fruit. The worship and thanks of human beings are both the purpose for and the outcome of the creation of the tree and its fruit—human beings—and the hearts of the human beings are the comprehensive seeds of the fruit of the tree, while human memories lie at the rear of the heart. This being the case, it is inconceivable that the absolute Owner of the universe would hand over the possession and administration of this tree, with all of its component parts, to other forces, thus negating the sovereignty of His Lordship and negating His fitness to be worshipped.

Again, the aims of Lordship are centered in the particulars, which exist in the outermost reaches of the sphere of contingency and multiplicity, and in the states and circumstances of these particulars. It is from the states and circumstances of these particulars and their states that the thanks, gratitude, and adoration owed to the All-Worshipped One arise, and therefore their Lord would never hand them over to others, thus nullifying His Wisdom or invalidating His Divinity. For the most important purpose of Lordship, as far as the creation of the universe is concerned, is that God should make Himself known to conscious beings, that He should be loved and praised by them, and that He should attract their gratitude to Himself.

It is because of this subtle reality that, in order to demonstrate that the universal and particular acts and favors manifested in the furthest realms of the sphere of multiplicity, such as provision, healing and, in particular, guidance and belief,[9] which in turn give rise to thanksgiving, adoration, gratitude, love, praise, and worship, are the direct works, bounties, gifts, and acts of the Creator and Sovereign of all creatures, the miraculously eloquent Qur'an repeatedly ascribes provision, guidance, and healing to the Neces-

[9] See, for example, 2:22, 60, 142, 168, 172, 213, 272; 3:73; 5:16, 88; 6:71, 88; 26:80....

sarily Existent One. It declares that it is only He Who bestows them and it vehemently rejects the interference of others.

Surely, the One Who bestows the gift of belief, which enables a person to gain an eternal abode of happiness, can only be the One Who creates that abode of happiness and makes belief the key to it. It could only be His favor. No-one else could bestow such a great favor and thereby close the vast window which opens onto the All-Worshipped One; no one could confiscate or steal this most important means of worshipping Him.

In short, the most particular states, circumstances, and fruit on the farthest tips of the tree of creation testify to Divine Unity in the following two ways:

The first: Since the aims of Divine Lordship in the universe are accumulated and centered in these fruits and states, and the manifestations of most of the Divine Names, together with their results and benefits observable in the creation of beings are concentrated in them, each of them declares: "I am the property, act and work of the One Who has created the whole universe."

The second: The human heart and memory—which in a *hadith* is called "the rear of the heart"[10]—are like concise indexes or maps of most species of beings. In addition, they bear the meaning of being the seed of the tree of the universe, and are subtle mirrors held up to most of the Divine Names. Every human being in the world has a similar heart and memory. This fact indicates, with utmost certainty, the One Who holds the whole universe in the grasp of His Power; for each heart and memory declares: "I am the work and art of Him alone."

In conclusion: With respect to its benefits, the fruit indicates the owner of the entire tree. With regard to its seed, it indicates all the parts, members, and nature of the tree. And with regard to the stamp on its face, which also exists on the faces of all its fellows, it demonstrates the similarity between all the fruits of the tree. Together they declare: "We are all the same and have been made by a single Hand. We are the property of a single Being. Whoever has made one of us has made all of us." In exactly the same way, with respect to the stamp on the face of every member, as well as on the faces of all living beings who exist in the furthest reaches

---

10 *al-Bukhari*, "Fadailul-Qur'an" 22; *Muslim*, "Nikah" 76.

of the sphere of multiplicity, and with respect to the fact that humanity is the result and fruit of the tree of creation, with a heart like an inventory of the properties of the tree, humankind directly indicates the One Who holds the entire universe in the grasp of His Power, and humanity testifies to His Unity.

THE SECOND FACT WHICH NECESSITATES DIVINE UNITY

This is that there exists an ease and a facility in unity which renders belief in Divine Unity necessary. Associating partners with God, on the other hand, involves so many difficulties and contradictions that it is simply impossible. This truth has been explained in detail with decisive proofs in many of the treatises of the *Risale-i Nur*—which is also called "The Lamp of Light"—especially in The Twentieth Letter and briefly in The Fourth Part of The Thirtieth Gleam. A brief summary is as follows:

If all things are ascribed to one single Being, the creation and administering of the entire universe become as easy as the creation and administering of a single tree, the creation of a single tree becomes as easy as the creation of a single fruit, the origination and regulation of springtime become as easy as the origination and regulation of a single flower, and organization and nurturing of a whole species become as easy as the organization and nurturing of a single member of that species.

By contrast, when partners are associated with God Almighty and all things are ascribed to (physical or material) causes and "nature," the creation of a single individual becomes as difficult as the creation of a whole species, or indeed of many species. The creation and decoration of a single flower become as problematic as the creation and decoration of a whole spring or many springs, the creation of a single piece of fruit becomes as complicated as the creation of a whole tree, or rather of hundreds of trees, and the bringing into being, nurturing, regulation, and administering of a tree become as hard as, if not harder than, bringing into being the whole universe.

This reality has been demonstrated amply in *The Lamp of Light—The Risale-i Nur*. Since, as we can easily observe before us, there is a superabundance of beings, yet everything is at the highest degree of artistry and value and, despite the fact that each living being is a wonderful mechanism with numerous miraculous components and members, all living beings come into existence in absolute profusion with infinite ease and extraordinary speed, just like striking a match, all of this demonstrates self-evidently that this superabundance and ease arise from unity and the fact that they are the works of a single Being. Otherwise, there would not be this combination of economy, abundance, speed, ease, and value; a piece of fruit that is now bought for five cents could not be purchased for five hundred dollars or would be so rare as to be completely unobtainable. Also, the creation of living beings, which we now see is as easy as setting a watch or operating a mechanism by pushing a button, would be so difficult that it would be impossible. Animals, which come into existence together with all their physical organs and systems in a day, an hour, or a minute, would not be able to come into existence in a year, a century, or perhaps ever at all.

It has been decisively demonstrated in as many as a hundred places in *The Lamp of Light* that if all things are attributed to the Single, Unique One of Unity, their coming into existence is as easy, as speedy, and as economic as a single thing. But if causes and nature are given a role, the creation of a single thing becomes as difficult, as slow, and as expensive as the creation of the whole universe. If you wish to see the proofs of this truth, you may refer to The Twentieth and Thirty-third Letters, The Twenty-second and Thirty-second Words, The Twenty-third Gleam—which is concerned with nature—and The Thirtieth Gleam—which concerns the Greatest Name or the Divine Name that has all-encompassing manifestations; in particular examine The Fourth and Sixth Parts of this, which deal with the Names "the All-Independent Single One" and "the Self-Subsistent by Whom all subsist," respectively. Below we will allude to only one of these hundreds of proofs:

A thing is either created *ex nihilo* or is composed from elements and other things. If it is attributed to a single Being, that Being must have an all-encompassing knowledge and power that prevails over all things. Therefore, the bestowal of external existence on things, which have a kind of immaterial existence within His Knowledge, or bringing them out of apparent non-existence, is as easy and simple as striking a match or spreading a special liquid over a text composed in invisible ink to reveal what has been written, or transposing an image from photographic film to paper. Through the command of *"Be!" and it is*, the Maker brings things into external existence from apparent non-existence.

If a thing is composed from elements or other things, and not created out of non-existence or nothingness, it resembles the members of a regiment who were dismissed to rest being gathered together at the call of a bugle and assembled in orderly fashion. All the movements of the members of the regiment take place under the power, orders, and eye of the commander. Similarly, all the particles or atoms which comprise a certain thing are under the absolute command of the Sovereign of the universe: they move, are mobilized and come together according to the principles of His Knowledge and Determination (Destiny), and in keeping with the laws of His pervasive and prevailing Power. In order to form the body of a living being, they enter and are established in an immaterial mold specified by Divine Knowledge and Determination or Destiny in appointed measures and proportions. All the other things with which they come into contact in this process act as though they were conscious forces, laws, and officials of that Sovereign.

However, if things are ascribed to different agents and causes and to nature, then as all reasonable minds agree, none of these can in any way create something from nothing and from non-existence. For none of them has either an all-encompassing knowledge or an all-prevailing power. Because of this, the non-existence in question would not be only apparent non-existence: it would be absolute. And absolute non-existence can in no way be the origin of existence. Given this, the coming into existence of a being can only be by way of composition. But then, the particles or atoms which constitute the body of, say, a fly or a flower would have to come together from all over the earth and pass through a fine sieve. This would clearly entail innumerable difficulties or impossibilities. Even if we suppose this to be possible, since there would be no immaterial molds appointed by an all-encompassing knowledge to preserve them in orderly fashion without dispersing, there would have to be as many actual material molds as the number of a being's members for the particles or atoms which come together to form its body.

Thus, when attributed to a single Being, the existence of all things is so easy that it becomes necessary; when attributed to numerous causes or origins, there are so many difficulties involved that it is simply impossible. Similarly, when the existence of all things is attributed to the Unique, Single One of absolute Unity, they become valuable, full of art, meaningful, and impressive to the utmost degree, as well as being infinitely economic. But if one takes the way of associating partners with God and ascribes them instead to nature and numerous causes or origins, they immediately lose all value and become totally lacking in art, meaning, and stability, as well as being infinitely costly.

When a man joins the army and becomes affiliated with the commander-in-chief, learning to rely on him, he finds that he can count on the moral support of the army whenever it is needed. Also, since the power of the army is his reserve force, he gains a physical power thousands of times greater than that which he has as a mere individual. Furthermore, since the army as a whole carries the sources of that significant power and ammunition, he does not have to carry them. As a result, since that soldier has attained the power to carry out extraordinary feats, even though he is only a mere private, he will be able to capture an enemy field-marshal, force all the inhabitants of a town to migrate, or seize control of an enemy fort. His works will be exceptional and of great worth. If, however, he leaves the army and remains on his own, he will lose that extraordinary power and moral support: consequently, like a common deserter, the feats he will be able to perform will be in proportion with his personal strength as a single soldier, and will thus be relatively insignificant and of little value.

Similarly, since Divine Unity ensures that everything becomes connected with and relies upon the All-Powerful One of Majesty, an ant is able to defeat the Pharaoh, a fly is able to bring down Nimrod, and a mere microbe is able to fell a tyrant. Also, a seed the size of a fingernail is able to bear on its shoulders a tree the size of a mountain and serve as the source and origin of all the tree's parts and members, as though it were their workbench. The same connection and reliance with Divine Unity also enables all particles or atoms to perform a limitless number of duties in the formation of countless bodies, which are each full of innumerable kinds of arts. The works in which those miniscule officials and tiny soldiers are employed are exceedingly perfect and of the highest art and value, for the One Who produces them is the All-Powerful One of Majesty. He employs them in the production of those works and makes them veils over His Acts. However, if attributed to causes, the works of an ant would be as insignificant as the ant itself, while the artistry in a particle or atom would not have the least value. Everything would become worthless in respect of the meaning it has, as well as physically, and no one would offer as much as a penny for the entire world.

Since this is the reality, and it is clear that everything is exceedingly valuable, full of artistry, flawless, and replete with meaning, there can be no way other than the way of Divine Unity to explain the existence and administration of all things. If there were another way, it would be necessary to change all beings, empty the world into non-existence, and then refill it with meaningless junk, so that a way could be opened up to associating partners with God.

So now you have heard a brief summary of just one of the thousands of proofs for the truth of Divine Unity in the *Risale-i Nur*, which is also called "The Lamp of Light." You may make analogies with this for the others.

The Third Fact Which Necessitates Divine Unity

In addition to the fact that there is extraordinary artistry in the creation of things, and particularly in living beings, there is also the fact that a seed is a small sample of the fruit, containing its meaning and its context in a compact and concise form. Indeed, it is like a small specimen or map of the fruit and the fruit fulfills the same role for a tree; a tree is the same for the species, and the species acts in this way for the universe. Each of these is a comprehensive point or a droplet distilled from the entire universe with principles of Knowledge and scales of Wisdom, and it possesses the capacity of being the origin of the whole of creation. Therefore, the One Who has created any of them must surely have created the entire universe. Certainly, the One Who creates the seed of a melon is self-evidently the same One Who created the melon: it is impossible that it could be any other than He.

We see that all the atoms in our blood perform such a variety of duties that they are not inferior to the stars. All the red and white corpuscles in the blood work to such a degree of consciousness to protect and feed the body that they are more efficient than the most highly-trained and experienced soldiers or guardsmen. All the cells of the body are favored with such orderly processes, incomings and outgoings that their administration is more perfect than the best-run institution or palace. All plants and animals have such a seal on their faces and such mechanisms in their beings that only the One

Who has created all of them could have placed these seals and mechanisms in them. And all the species of living beings have spread over the face of the earth in such an orderly fashion and intermingled with one another in such a way that anyone who is unable to simultaneously create, direct, and raise all these species, unable to weave that most ornate, artistic, living textile with its warp and weft of hundreds of thousands of plant and animal species to cover the face of the earth—one who is unable to do all of these things would not be able to create or direct a single one of these beings. If similar analogies are made for other features of existence, it will be understood that with respect to both the creation and Lordship—raising, managing, nurturing, and sustaining—the universe is a whole that does not admit of division.

This third fact which necessitates Divine Unity has been demonstrated in many of the treatises of *The Lamp of Light*, and particularly in The First Station of The Thirty-second Word. It has been demonstrated so clearly and convincingly that, just as reflections of the sun in transparent things point to the one and only sun, a proof of Divine Unity is reflected and represented in the mirror of every individual entity. These explanations are sufficient and now we cut this long story short.

The Third Station

In this Station three universal signs of Divine Unity will be explained briefly.

The signs and proofs of Divine Unity and Its clear manifestations in the universe are innumerable. Since thousands of them have been elaborated on in *The Lamp of Light*, in this Third Station it will be enough to explain just three of these proofs briefly.

THE FIRST SIGN AND PROOF WHICH LEADS TO THE CONCLUSION THAT "HE IS ONE"

There is a unity in everything and this unity points to one. It is self-evident that a work which displays unity has originated from one maker. What is one certainly proceeds from one. And since there is a unity in all things, this certainly demonstrates that they are the works of a single being.

The universe is like a rosebud, wrapped in thousands a variety of veils of unity. It may even be said that it is a single macro-human, dressed in unities to the number of Divine Names and universal Divine works. One may call it the "tree of *Touba*"[11] of creation, on the branches of which are hung unities to the number of species of creatures.

With respect to how the universe is raised, administered, maintained, and controlled, the universe displays unity in all of its features. The Names and Acts Which operate the universe and cause it to subsist also exhibit unity: each of them encompasses the universe as a whole, or most of it. That is to say, the wisdom at work in the universe is one and the same, the grace observed in the universe is one and the same, the regulation of the universe is one and the same, the provision made for the universe is one and the same, the mercy which hastens to the aid of the needy is one and the same, as is the rain, which is mercy's sweet offering, and the same is true for all of its other features. The sun, that vast furnace of the world, is one and the same; the moon is its lamp and this too is one and the same. Fire is its means of cooking and this is one and the same; the mountains, which are our world's stores of supplies, treasuries, and masts, are one and same. The water suppliers are one and the same and the sponges from which the rain that waters the gardens and vineyards emerges are one and the same, and so on for thousands of other similar features in our world.

All these instances of unity in the world are proofs indicating the Unique, Single One of Unity, and are as clear as the sun. Also, in addition to the fact that all the universal elements and the species inhabiting the earth are of unity, they exist intermixed with one another and help one another. This offers manifest proof that their Master, their Owner and Maker, is one and the same.

THE SECOND SIGN AND PROOF WHICH LEADS TO THE CONCLUSION THAT "HE HAS NO PARTNERS"

This second sign is the fact that throughout the universe, from atoms to stars, there is a faultless, perfect order, a flawless, most beautiful coherence and congruity, and an unblemished, irreproachable balance and justice in all things. A perfect order, coherence, and balance can be possible only through unity. If numerous hands interfere in a work, they cause nothing but confusion.

[11] The tree of *Touba* is the tree of Paradise and is used as a symbol for large, expansive things that have a number of branches. (Tr.)

Come now and see the magnificence of this order: it has made the universe into such a flawless, wonderful palace that each of its stones is as full of artistry as the palace itself; it has made it into such a magnificent city that its limitless goods and boundless bounties and provisions are provided at exactly the right time from places one would not expect, from behind the veil of the Unseen, in a most perfect order. This order has made the universe into such a meaningful and miraculous book that each of its letters has as much meaning as a hundred lines, each of its lines as much meaning as a hundred pages, each of its pages as much meaning as a hundred chapters, and each of its chapters as much meaning as a hundred books. Furthermore, all of its letters, words, lines, pages and chapters refer to one another and are inextricably interconnected.

Now come and look at the perfect decoration and arrangement that is observable within this wonderful order: it has made this vast universe into a perfectly clean city or a beautiful palace which is continuously and carefully cleaned and polished; it has made it into a maiden of the utmost beauty, dressed in layer upon layer of ornate garments, or a rosebud wrapped in numerous delicately embellished petals.

Now come and look at the perfect balance and justice within this order and cleanliness: microscopic organisms which can be seen only through a powerful microscope and stars a thousand times larger than the earth are all weighed on the scales of this balance and are given exactly what they require for their existence, without anything missing or lacking. These miniscule creatures and these vast celestial bodies are equal in the sight of the balance and justice, despite the fact that the largest of the objects in the heavens would, if they were to lose their balance even for a second, destroy the general equilibrium and bring destruction to the world.

Now come and see the extraordinarily attractive beauty within the order, cleanliness, and balance: it has made the universe into a fabulous festival, a rich and remarkably decorated exhibition, a springtime bursting with freshly opened flowers. It has made the vast spring into a beautiful vase of blooms and it has given each spring the form of a marvelous flower with hundreds of thousands of embellishments, which opens every season on the face of the earth. It also has beautified every flower with extremely varied decorations. Through the fine manifestations of the All-Beautiful Names of God, Which have the utmost beauty and loveliness, all the species of beings in the universe, together with each of their individual members, have, in accordance with their innate capacities, been favored with such beauty that Imam al-Ghazzali[12] was moved to remark: "There cannot be a universe more beautiful than the present one." Thus, this all-encompassing, captivating beauty, this all-encompassing, extraordinary cleanliness, this all-pervasive, supremely sensitive balance, this comprehensive order and coherence, miraculous in all of its aspects, provide proofs and indications of Divine Unity that are brighter than the light of the noonday sun.

A CONCISE REPLY TO A TWO-PART QUESTION CONCERNING THIS STATION

The first part of the question: You claim in this Station that beauty, grace, goodness, and justice prevail throughout the universe, but what do you say concerning the ugliness, disasters, illness, tribulations, and death we see around us?

The answer: A single instance of ugliness that results in or manifests numerous instances of beauty is, indirectly, an instance of beauty. Whereas the non-existence or concealment of an instance of ugliness which then causes numerous instances of beauty to remain hidden is not a single, but a manifold, ugliness. For example, if there were no ugliness to function as a unit of comparison or measurement, there would be only one sort of beauty and the numerous varieties and degrees of beauty would remain concealed. For it is through the intervention of ugliness that diverse and increasing degrees of beauty appear. Just as the degrees of heat become apparent through the existence of cold and the degrees of light are perceived on account of the existence of darkness, so too do particular instances of evil, ugliness, harm and impairment cause universal instances of good and beauty and universal benefits and bounties to become manifest. This means that the creation of ugliness is not ugly: it is beautiful because most of its results are beautiful. Rain has so many good and beneficial results that people have called it mercy. Thus, the lazy-minded man who suffers some

---

[12] Imam Abu Hamid Muhammad al-Ghazzali (d. 1111): A major theologian, jurist, and sage who was considered to be a reviver (of Islam's purity and vitality) during his time. Known in Europe as Algazel, he was the architect of the later development of Islam. He wrote many books, the most famous being *Ihyau 'Ulumi'd-Din* ("Reviving the Religious Sciences"). (Tr.)

inconvenience when it rains cannot be a reason for rain to be regarded as evil: he cannot cause mercy to be considered as harm.

As for decay and death, it is demonstrated convincingly in The Twenty-fourth Letter that they are not contrary to universal mercy, to all-embracing beauty, or to all-inclusive good; rather, they are necessitated by them. Even the creation of Satan is good, for he causes people to strive against him and to compete among themselves in order to accomplish good deeds, which are the sources of the spiritual progress of humankind. Also, since unbelievers transgress the rights of all beings and affront their dignity through unbelief, to punish them with the torments of Hell is also good. As this matter has been explained in detail in other treatises, a brief indication here is sufficient.

The second part of the question: We can accept the answer with respect to Satan and the unbelievers from a general point of view, but how is it that the Absolutely Beautiful One, the Absolutely Compassionate One, the Absolutely Good and Self-Sufficient One, inflicts evil, calamities, and ugliness on certain wretched individuals?

The answer: Whatever good, beauty, and bounty exist, they are directly from the treasury of Mercy of that Absolutely Beautiful and Compassionate One and from His particular favor. As for evils and calamities, they are relatively rare occurrences among the numerous outcomes of the general, universal laws of the Sovereignty of the Divine Lordship, which are called "God's usual practice" (*'adatullah*). As these evils represent certain particular results of the implementation of the general or universal laws in question, God the All-Mighty creates these rare occurrences of evil in order to preserve these laws, which are the means to universal benefits. But in the face of these minor evils, He responds to the cries for help of individuals who are afflicted by calamities and tribulations with the special assistance of His Mercy and the particular favors of His Lordship. By demonstrating that He acts in whichever way He wills; by showing that (humankind and jinn have been equipped with free will and are responsible for their decisions and acts); by reminding that whatever takes place in the universe and whatever proceeds from, or is done, by any creature, is through His permission; by making it clear that universal laws are also always subject to His Will, and that an All-Compassionate Lord hears the individuals who cry out under the pressure of these laws and that He comes to their aid with His favors—by demonstrating all of this, not only has He opened up an infinite field for the infinite manifestations of His All-Beautiful Names, but He has also opened the doors of His manifestations of special favor and assistance in the face of His universal laws, thus making Himself loved by His servants.

As this second sign of Divine Unity has been explained in perhaps a hundred places in *The Lamp of Light* (*Risale-i Nur*), this brief indication will suffice.

THE THIRD SIGN AND PROOF, NAMELY THE INNUMERABLE STAMPS OF DIVINE UNITY INDICATED BY THE PHRASES "HIS IS THE DOMINION AND HIS IS THE PRAISE"

There is a stamp on the faces of all things, particular and universal, from particles to the planets, which is such that just as the image of the sun in a mirror indicates the sun in the sky, the metaphorical mirror made up of these innumerable stamps indicates the Sun of absolute Eternity and testifies to God's Unity. Since many of these stamps have been explained in detail in *The Lamp of Light*, here we will briefly indicate only three of them. They are as follows:

Just as a vast stamp of Unity, which comprises mutual help, solidarity, mutual resemblance, and intermingling among the various species of creatures, has been placed on the face of the universe as a whole, so too on the face of the earth there is a similar stamp of Divine Unity, which consists of the fact that the hundreds of thousands of plants and animal species, which make up a magnificent army of the All-Glorified One, are each given particular weapons, uniforms, provisions, and instructions with perfect orderliness and at exactly the right time. On the face of human beings, as on other creatures, there is also a stamp of Divine Oneness, which allows the features of one human being to be distinguished from all others. Similarly, on the head of every creature, whether large or small, or whether a part of a species with numerous members or one with a few, a seal of Divine Oneness has been placed that allows it to be distinguished from all others. These stamps, which have been placed on living creatures, are particularly brilliant; indeed, each living being is itself a stamp of Unity, a seal of Oneness, and a signature of the Eternally Besought One.

All flowers, fruits, leaves, plants, and animals are each such a seal of Divine Oneness and a stamp of the Eternally Besought One that each tree, for example, is a Divine missive, each species a book of the All-Merciful, and each garden a decree of the All-Glorified One. Thus, there are as many stamps as there are individual flowers, as many signatures as there are fruits, and as many seals as there are leaves placed on the missive that is the tree. And in order to show their Scribe, as many stamps as there are members have been placed in the book that is each species of a creature. Similarly, in order to make its Ruler known, as many seals as there are plants, trees, and animals have been placed on the decree that is the garden. Furthermore, there are four other stamps of Divine Unity on each tree: on its origin, at its end, on its outside and in its inside, as indicated by the Divine Names included in the declaration *He is The First, The Last, The All-Outward, and The All-Inward* (The Qur'an, 57:3).

- As the Name *The First* indicates, a seed from which a fruit-bearing tree grows is a tiny coffer which contains the programs, contents, and plans of the tree; it is like a workbench upon which one finds the equipment, systems, and requisites necessary for growth; it is like a machine which produces the small amount of food that is needed at the beginning of its life.
- As the Name *The Last* shows us, the result or fruit of a tree is an instruction sheet which describes the tree's structure, its attributes and stages of existence; it is a proclamation which states its functions, benefits, and special characteristics, and it is a summation that predicts the future peers and progeny of that tree through the seeds in its heart.
- As the Name *The All-Outward* demonstrates, the form and shape in which a tree is dressed is in the form of a skillfully fashioned and embroidered garment, which has been cut out, trimmed, and decorated with such precision that it is an exact fit for the stature of the tree and all of its branches, members, and parts. The tree has been formed so finely, so meaningfully, and with such a sense of proportion that it is an ode, a missive, a book.
- As the Name *The All-Inward* suggests, the workbench operating within a tree is such a factory that it produces all the parts and

> members of the tree and, considering the needs, incomings, and outgoings of these parts and members in exact measures, dispatches and distributes the sustenance required for each with perfect regularity and order. This factory works at the speed of lightning, with the ease of setting a clock, and with the uniformity of giving marching orders to an army.

In short, the origin of a tree is a coffer and a program; its end is an instruction sheet and a sample, while the outside is a skillfully fashioned and embroidered garment and its inside is a factory or workbench. These four aspects are interrelated, and as a whole manifest a supreme stamp, or even a Divine Greatest Name, which self-evidently demonstrates that none other than the Unique, Single Maker of Unity, Who directs the whole universe, could perform these works. Like trees, the origin, end, outside, and inside of every living creature bears a seal of Divine Unity, a stamp of Divine Uniqueness, and a signature of Divine Oneness.

Analogous with the trees in these three examples is spring, which resembles a tree with innumerable blossoms. The seeds and roots entrusted to the hand of autumn bear the stamp of the Name *The First*. The fruits, grains, and vegetables which are poured into the lap of summer and fill its skirts bear the seal of the Name *The Last*. The garments decorated with a hundred thousand designs, which the season of spring wears like a beautiful girl of Paradise, bear the seal of the Name *The All-Outward*. And the factories of the Eternally Besought One which work in the springtime inside the earth, the boiling cauldrons of the All-Merciful, and the kitchens of the Lord in which foods are cooked, all bear the signature of the Name *The All-Inward*.

Every species, for instance the human race, is like a tree. With its roots and seeds in the past and its fruits and results in the future, its life and perpetuation as a species are regulated through certain orderly laws. And in spite of its apparent disorder, its present state, which is governed by the principles of the human individual and social life, bears a stamp of Divine Unity, as well as a hidden, orderly seal of harmony and concord, which in turn indicate the same Unity. In spite of their apparent confusion, the affairs and circumstances of the ordinary human life, over which the principles of Divine Destiny and Decree rule, also bear a seal of Divine Oneness.

CONCLUSION

What follows is a brief reference to the other pillars of belief indicated by Divine Unity.

Come now and consider at least once the three fruits, the three facts that necessitate Divine Unity and the affirmation of it and the three proofs which are explained under the headings of The First, Second, and Third Stations: is it at all possible that the All-Powerful, All-Wise, All-Compassionate and All-Knowing Maker, Who has absolute sovereignty and control over the universe, Who never ignores or overlooks even the smallest cure or the most meager thanks, Who is not indifferent toward even the minutest example of art such as that which is manifested in the wing of a fly, and Who does not delegate it to others, Who attaches to the lowliest common seed as many duties and instances of wisdom as He does to a huge tree, and Who makes His Mercy, Compassion and Wisdom perceivable through all His arts, and makes Himself known through every means and loved through every favor—is it at all possible that He should be indifferent toward the virtues of the Muhammadan Truth,[13] upon him be peace and blessings, his glorifications and the lights of Islam?

Is it at all possible that the Messengership of Muhammad, upon him be peace and blessings, which adorns all creatures and fills them with joy, which illuminates the universe and causes the heavens and earth to resonate with the sounds of happiness and triumph, which has kept almost half of the world and a fifth of humanity under its physical and spiritual rule for fourteen centuries and has perpetuated that glorious rule on account of the Creator of the universe and in His Name—is it at all possible that his Messengership is not one of The Maker's most important purposes for the existence of the universe, or that it is one of His most important lights and mirrors? Is it possible that the other Prophets, who served the same truths as Muhammad, upon him be peace and blessings, should not also have been that Maker's Messengers, friends and officials? God forbid, to the number of the miracles of the Prophet!

---

[13] The Muhammadan Truth is the universal ontological, moral, and spiritual truth or meaning that Prophet Muhammad, upon him be peace and blessings, represents as the Messenger of God. (Tr.)

And is it at all possible that the All-Wise and All-Compassionate Creator, Who attaches a hundred fruits and instances of wisdom to the least significant thing, such as a branch or a twig, and makes His Lordship known and loved through extraordinary instances of His Wisdom and all-inclusive Mercifulness—is it at all possible that He should Himself deny or cause to be denied all His Wisdom and Mercy, and even His Lordship and Perfections, by not bringing about the Resurrection, which is as easy for His Power as the creation of spring, or by not opening up an abode of happiness and eternal permanence? Is it at all possible that He should condemn to eternal annihilation all those creatures whom He loves so much? God forbid, a hundred thousand times! God's Absolute Grace and Beauty are entirely exempt from such an absolute abomination.

A LENGTHY PARENTHETICAL NOTE: A QUESTION CONCERNING THE RESURRECTION

The repeated declarations of the Qur'an, *It is but a single blast* (36: 53) and *The matter of the Hour is but the twinkling of an eye, or even quicker* (16:77) show that the Supreme Resurrection will happen in an instant. Our limited understanding needs a tangible analogy to enable us to concur with and accept such a unique, miraculous event.

THE ANSWER: There are three matters concerning the Resurrection: spirits will return to their bodies, bodies will be reanimated, and bodies will be rebuilt and resurrected.

THE FIRST MATTER: An example for the spirits returning to their bodies: Imagine the soldiers of a highly disciplined army. Having dispersed in all directions in order to rest, they can be summoned back together with one loud bugle blast. The Archangel *Israfil*'s Trumpet is certainly no less powerful than a bugle. In addition, our spirits—each of which responded with "Yes, You are!" to the question "Am I not your Lord?", coming from the direction of pre-eternity when they were in the world of atoms—are more obedient, disciplined and submissive than any soldiers.[14] The Thirtieth

[14] God declares in the Qur'an: *And (remember, O Messenger,) when your Lord brought forth from the children of Adam, from their loins, their offspring, and made them bear witness against themselves (asking them:) "Am I not your Lord?" They said: "Yes, we do bear witness."* (7:172) When viewed from our perspective and within the framework of time and space, creation follows a descending and ascending line that passes through many stages or realms; exis-

Word has demonstrated convincingly that not only the spirits, but all atoms are the armies of the All-Glorified One, each being a dutiful soldier.

THE SECOND MATTER: An example for the bodies being reanimated: For a celebration in a great city, uncountable lamps may be turned on instantly by flicking a switch in the city's power station. It also would be possible to light an infinite number of lamps throughout the world from a single power station, if such a one existed. If a creation of God, such as electricity, a servant and a candle-holder in this transient realm, can manifest this property on account of its Creator's training and discipline, the Resurrection can surely occur in the twinkling of an eye and within the framework of Divine Wisdom's orderly laws, which are represented and demonstrated by thousands of His light-giving servants, such as electricity.

THE THIRD MATTER: There are thousands of suitable analogies for rebuilding and resurrecting human bodies on the Day of Resurrection. Consider, for example, the way in which trees, which are far more numerous than people, are restored with all their leaves perfectly and almost identically to those of the preceding year within a few days after the beginning of each spring. Consider the way in which the leaves, blossoms and fruits of the trees are re-created, just like those of the preceding spring, with extreme rapidity. Consider the sudden awakening, unfolding and coming to life of countless seeds, kernels and roots, which are the origin of spring growth.

---

tence is within this same line. Just as an article, for instance, has many stages of existence, for example, existing in the mind of the writer, and then as a plan, and then in a written form, so too, every being has a primordial existence in God's Knowledge, then as a general form determined by Destiny, and then in the stages of its material existence. Since our consciousness comes not from our corporeal being, but rather from our spiritual existence, it is completely possible that God may have spoken to us before He sent us, or may speak after He has sent us, to the world, through our spirit or our nature. He has entrusted this covenant to our consciences, which form our conscious nature.

It is also said in the Qur'an: *How can you disbelieve in God, seeing that you were dead, and He gave you life? Then He causes you to die. Then He will bring you to life again; and then you will be returned to Him* (2:28). The expression *You were dead*, implies that each member of humankind has some sort of existence in the world of atoms or particles. It has already been determined in God's Knowledge which atoms in the worlds of elements, plants, and animals will constitute the body of which person. So there is no room for chance or coincidences in the motion of the atoms that constitute human bodies.

The expression also suggests that since death follows life, those atoms are themselves devoid of what we recognize as life, which is a direct gift from God, pointing to Him clearly. (Tr.)

Consider the way in which trees, resembling standing skeletons, suddenly begin to show signs of "resurrection after death" at a single command. Consider the amazing reanimation of countless small creatures, especially the resurrection of different species of fly—particularly of those which, continuously cleaning their faces, eyes, and wings, remind us of our ritual ablution and cleanliness, and caress our faces—during a few days despite being far more numerous than all humans.

This world is the realm of Wisdom; the Hereafter is the abode of Power. Thus, in accordance with the requirements of Divine Names such as the All-Wise, the All-Arranging, the All-Disposing, and the All-Nurturing, creation in the world is gradual and extends over a certain period of time. This is required by God's Wisdom as the Lord. But given that Power and Mercy are more evident than Wisdom in the Hereafter, creation in that realm is instantaneous and free from anything that is related to matter, space, time, or duration. In order to show that what takes a day or a year to do here will be accomplished within an instant in the Hereafter, the Qur'an decrees: *The matter of the Hour is but the twinkling of an eye, even quicker* (16:77). If you seek firmer confirmation that the Resurrection will come just as surely as the next spring, study The Tenth and The Twenty-ninth Words.

Another matter of the Resurrection is the destruction of this world. If a meteorite or asteroid were to collide with this planet on God's command, our dwelling place would be destroyed instantly, in the same way that a palace which took ten years to build can be destroyed in a minute.

The concise explanation above concerning the four matters related to the Resurrection is sufficient for the time being, now we can return to our main subject.

* * *

Is it at all possible that the Qur'an of miraculous exposition, the eloquent interpreter of all the elevated truths of the universe, the miraculous tongue of all the Perfections of the Creator of the universe and wonderful collection of all His purposes, should not be the Word of that Creator? God forbid, to the number of the mysteries of its verses!

Also, is it at all possible that the All-Wise Maker should cause His living, conscious creatures to communicate with one another in their myriad tongues, and that He should hear and know their voices and what they say, responding to them clearly with His acts and bounties, yet Himself not speak or be unable to speak? Is such a thing conceivable? Since it is clear that He speaks and that the chief addressee of His speech, and the one who comprehends it the best, is humankind, then most certainly, all the holy Scriptures, and most importantly the Qur'an, are His words.

Also, in order to make Himself known, loved, and praised, and by satisfying living beings with His multitude of favors, to make their gratitude a response to the bountiful activities and manifestations of His Lordship, the All-Wise Maker has made the universe, with all its realms and elements, a dutiful servant, a dwelling-place, a place of exhibition and a banquet for His living beings. Again, His will to multiply thousands of living creatures is such that He makes the leaves of those trees that do not bear fruit, such as the poplar and the elm, serve as the womb, cradle, and food-store for regiments of numerous kinds of living creatures, which perform their remembrance and glorifications in the air. Is it at all possible that the One Who has done all of this should leave those adorned heavens and light-diffusing stars empty, purposeless, and without an owner, life, spirit or inhabitants? In other words, is it conceivable that He would leave them without angels and spirit beings? God forbid, to the number of those angels and spirit beings!

Also, the All-Wise Maker and Director establishes and inscribes the origins and ends of the commonest plant or the smallest tree, as well as its entire life in its seeds and fruits in perfect order with the Pen of His Destiny. He also establishes and inscribes with perfect order and differentiation the origins and outcomes of the vast spring, as though it were a single tree. He shows that He never remains indifferent to even the most apparently insignificant thing. Is it then at all possible that the One Who does all this should not record the actions and deeds of humanity, which, given that humanity is the most distinguished fruit of creation and the vicegerent on the earth, are of great importance? Is it at all possible that He would not include the acts and deeds of humankind, who has the role of supervision over all kinds of other creatures, in the sphere of Destiny or His Determining? Is it at all conceivable that He would remain unconcerned with what human beings do on earth? God forbid, to the number of the deeds of all human beings, which will be weighed on the scales of the Hereafter.

In short, together with all its truths, the universe declares:

I believe in God, His angels, His Books, His Messengers, the Last Day, and in Divine Destiny—I believe that whatever there is of good or evil exists by God Almighty's leave and creation, and that the resurrection after death is true. I bear witness that there is no deity but God, and I bear witness that Muhammad is His Messenger, may God bestow blessings on him, and on his Family and Companions, granting them peace. Amin.

A SUPPLICATION CONCERNING DIVINE UNITY

What follows is a supplication which has reached us from Imam 'Ali, may God be pleased with him. Making some additions to it, we offer it in his elevated tongue and in ours on his behalf to the Court of the Unique, Single One of Unity.

SUPPLICATION

O God! In the heavens there are no revolving bodies,
no planets, no stars…
In the atmosphere there are no clouds, no glorifying
bolts of thunder and lightning…
On the earth there is no abundance of plants and trees,
no floods of water, no animals, no wonderful creatures…
In the seas there is not a drop of water, nor a fish,
nor any strange creature…
On the mountains there are no stones, no plants,
no treasure troves of minerals…
On the trees there are no leaves, no adorned blossoms, no fruits…
In the bodies of living things there are no processes,
no organs, no well-ordered systems…
In human hearts there are no thoughts, no inspirations,
no illumined beliefs…
but all are witnesses of the absolute necessity of Your Existence,
and proofs of Your Unity, and are subjugated to Your Dominion.

By that Power with Which You have subjugated the heavens and the earth, subjugate my carnal soul and my aspiration to me; subjugate the hearts of Your servants to the *Risale-i Nur* and the hearts of all creatures and spirit beings, be they elevated or lowly, to the service of the Qur'an and belief, O All-Hearing, O All-Near, O Answerer of prayers!

And all praise and gratitude are for God, the Lord of the worlds.

All-Glorified are You ! We have no knowledge save what You have taught us. Surely You are the All-Knowing, the All-Wise.

The Third Ray

The Third Ray

The Treatise of Supplication

Introduction

HIS TREATISE PROVES DECISIVELY THE MOST IMPORTANT OF THE fundamentals of belief, such as the necessary Existence of God, His Unity and Oneness, the magnificence of His Lordship, the immensity of His Power, the comprehensiveness of His Mercy, the universality of His Sovereignty, the all-inclusiveness of His Knowledge and the all-encompassing nature of His Wisdom. Its indications of the Resurrection, especially those emphasized at the end, are also powerful.

Each of the introductory passages of this proof of belief arrives at eight conclusions, together with the evidences used to prove them.

In the Name of God, the All-Merciful, the All-Compassionate.

> Surely in the creation of the heavens and the earth, and the alternation of night and day (with their periods of shortening and lengthening); and in the vessels which sail the seas and bring people profit; and the water which God sends down from the sky, therewith reviving the earth after its death and dispersing therein all kinds of living creatures; and in His disposal of the winds and the subjugation of the clouds between the earth and the sky—surely in all of these there are signs (demonstrating that He is the One God deserving of worship, and the sole Refuge and Helper) for all those people who reason and understand. (2:164)

This treatise of supplication is a form of commentary on the above verse.

O God, O my Lord!

I see through the eye of belief, the instruction and light of the Qur'an, the teachings of God's noblest Messenger, upon him be peace and blessings, and the guidance of the Divine Name the All-Wise that:

There is not a single movement in the heavens but it indicates Your Existence through its orderliness;

There is not a single heavenly body but it indicates or testifies to Your Lordship and Unity by performing its duties in silence and standing without any visible support;

There is not a single star but it demonstrates or bears witness to Your Unity or the magnificence of Your Divinity through its most proportionate structure, its precisely ordered position, its bright countenance, and the stamp of its resemblance to all other stars;

There is not one of the twelve planets but it testifies to Your absolutely necessary Existence and indicates the dominion of Your Divinity through its wise movement, its subjugation to Your law, its orderly duties, and through the satellites which orbit them.

Indeed, just as each of the heavens testifies to Your absolutely necessary Existence, so too, O the Creator of the heavens and earth, all of the heavens, as a totality, clearly bear witness with utter certainty to the absolute necessity of Your Existence. O You Who govern all atoms together with the compounds they form and Who have subjugated all the planets to Your command, making them revolve with their satellites, all of these testify to Your Unity and Oneness so powerfully that the shining proofs to the number of the stars in the heavens confirm their testimony.

With their extraordinarily large bodies, which move at amazing speeds, these unblemished heavens resemble an orderly army or a royal celebration illuminated by numerous electric lamps. They indicate most clearly the magnificence of Your Lordship and the grandeur of Your Power, Which has created all things; they indicate the limitless expanse of Your Dominion, Which dominates the heavens, and of Your Mercy, Which embraces all living creatures. They testify, with utmost certainty, to the all-encompassing nature of Your Knowledge, Which penetrates and orders all of the acts and states of the heavenly creatures, and to the comprehensiveness of Your Wisdom. This testimony and indication are so clear that it is as if the stars were the words of testimony of the heavens and their embodied luminous proofs.

As for the stars, which are like obedient soldiers, orderly ships, extraordinary planes, and astonishing lamps, they exhibit the splendor of the dominion of Your Divinity. As we can see from the sun, which is a soldier in the army of stars, and the duties that it performs with respect to our earth and the other planets under its sway, some of the companion stars of the sun have a relationship with the world of the Hereafter, and may in fact be the suns of the eternal worlds.

O the Necessarily Existent One, O the Single, Unique One!

These wonderful stars, these breathtaking suns and moons have been subjugated, ordered, and entrusted with various duties in Your domain and in Your heavens through Your Command, Power, Rule, and Management. All those celestial bodies glorify the sole Creator, Who has created them, Who administers them, and Who makes them revolve; they magnify Him, and say with the tongue of their disposition, "All-Glorified are You!," and "God is the All-Great." I too declare You to be the All-Holy through their glorifications.

O the All-Powerful One of Majesty, hidden because of the intensity of His manifestation and veiled on account of His Grandeur!

I have understood through the teachings of the Qur'an and the instruction of God's noblest Messenger, upon him be peace and blessings, that:

Just as the heavens with all their stars bear witness to Your Existence and Unity, the atmosphere also testifies to your absolutely necessary Existence and Unity through its clouds, its lightning, its thunder, wind, and rain.

Indeed, it is only by Your Mercy and Wisdom that the lifeless and unconscious clouds send rain, the water of life, to the aid of living creatures, which are in need of it: chance has not the least part in this.

Also, being the brightest and most powerful form of electricity, urging us to benefit from it on account of its illuminating quality, lightning sheds light on Your power in the heavens.

In addition, the thunder, which gives the glad tidings of the coming of rain, makes the vast heavens speak, and the roaring voice of whose glorification resounds in the sky, declares with the tongue of its disposition that

You are the All-Sacred One and testifies to Your being the Lord of the whole creation.

Again, entrusted with many duties, such as bringing living beings their vital sustenance and causing them to respire and refresh themselves, winds transform the atmosphere into a kind of "tablet for effacing and confirming or writing and erasing" on account of certain Divine purposes, thus indicating the activities of Your Power and testifying to Your Existence. Also, through its orderly words of drops milked from clouds and sent to living beings through Your Mercy, rain, which is the embodiment of Your mercy for living beings, bears witness to the comprehensiveness of Your Mercy and Your extensive Affection.

O the Ever-Active One Who controls everything; O the All-Transcending Bestower of abundant bounties!

While the clouds, lightning, thunder, wind, and rain testify individually to the absolute necessity of Your Existence, as a whole, they provide a powerful indication of Your Unity and Oneness through the fact that, despite their differences in nature, they exist and work together in harmony and help each other with their tasks. They also testify to the magnificence of Your Lordship, Which makes the vast atmosphere an exhibition of wonders and frequently fills and empties it; and to the greatness and comprehensiveness of Your Power, Which uses the atmosphere as though it were a tablet of "writing and erasing," and a sponge by means of which You water the garden of the earth. They also testify to the inconceivably vast and all-encompassing nature of Your Mercy and Dominion, Which embrace and maintain all creatures under the veil of the atmosphere.

Also, the employment of the air in so many wise duties and the employment of the clouds and rain for so many benefits which require an all-embracing knowledge, make it quite clear that were it not for an all-embracing Wisdom and an all-encompassing Knowledge, they could not be thus employed.

O He Who does whatever He wills!

Your Power, Which performs actions such as continuously displaying samples of the Resurrection in the atmosphere, and changing summer into winter and vice versa and bringing forth a new world while sending another into the Realm of the Unseen, all within an hour, gives an indication that It will change this world into the Hereafter and demonstrate unending activity therein.

O the All-Powerful One of Majesty!

Air, clouds, rain, lightning, and thunder in the atmosphere are subservient and dutiful in Your domain, through Your Command and by Your Power. These atmospheric creatures, which differ in nature, sanctify their Commander and Sovereign, Who makes them obey immediate commands with rapidity, and they praise Your Mercy.

O the All-Majestic Creator of the heavens and the earth!

Through the instruction of Your wise Qur'an and the teachings of the noblest Messenger, upon him be peace and blessings, I have come to believe in and understand what follows:

In the same way that the heavens, through their stars, and the atmosphere, through its elements, testify to the absolute necessity of Your Existence and Your Oneness, the earth also bears witness to Your Existence and Oneness through all its creatures and circumstances to the number of the existent beings it contains.

There are no transformations on the earth, nor any changes—be they universal or particular—in its plants, trees, and animals, such as the donning of new garments every year, but they bear witness to Your Existence and Oneness.

There is not a single animal but it bears witness to Your Existence and Oneness through the sustenance that is given to it compassionately and in proportion to its needs and weaknesses, and through being wisely equipped with the things that it needs to exist.

Also, there is not a single plant or animal that is resurrected or originated before our eyes every spring but it makes You known through its remarkable art, its fine component parts, its distinguishing features, and the perfect order and proportion in its composition and life.

All these plants and animals that fill the face of the earth as miracles of Your Power are created with perfect differentiation and rich adornment, and with absolutely no faults or flaws, from eggs or seeds that resemble one another and which are made up of almost the same substances. Thus, their testimony to the Existence, Oneness, Wisdom, and boundless Power of their All-Wise Maker is such that this testimony is more powerful and brilliant than the light which bears witness to the existence of the sun.

Also, there is no element in creation, such as air, water, light, fire, or soil but it bears witness to Your Existence and Oneness by performing perfect tasks that require consciousness in spite of their inanimateness, and by bringing perfectly formed fruits and crops of all kinds from the treasury of the Unseen, despite their simplicity and their seemingly random distribution over a vast area.

O the All-Powerful Originator, O the All-Knowing Opener, O the Ever-Acting Creator!

Just as together with all its inhabitants the earth testifies to the absolutely necessary Existence of their Creator, so too, O the Single and Unique One, O the All-Kind and All-Benevolent One, and O the All-Bestowing and All-Providing One, through the stamp on its face and the stamps on the faces of its inhabitants, and through their harmonious co-existence and mutual assistance despite being distributed widely, and through Your Names and Acts Which relate to them as Your being their Lord being the same, the earth clearly testifies to Your Unity and Oneness to the number of the creatures on it.

Also, the fact that the earth is like an army encampment, an exhibition, a place of instructions and drill, and that the hundreds of thousands of plant and animal divisions which form this global army are provided in perfect order with the exact component parts or equipment they need, demonstrates the magnificence of Your Lordship and shows that Your Power commands everything at the same time. Similarly, the fact that innumerable living creatures are compassionately and munificently provided with their sustenance at precisely the right time from simple soil, and that all of them obey the orders of Your Lordship with the utmost subservience, indicates the all-encompassing nature of Your Mercy and Dominion.

Moreover, it is only by virtue of an all-encompassing knowledge and an all-administering wisdom that it is possible for the endless convoys of creatures and all instances of life and death to follow one another on the earth in such perfect order, and for all the plants, trees, and animals to be administered with such perfection and regularity. This obviously indicates the all-encompassing nature of Your Knowledge and Wisdom.

Also, although humanity is entrusted with limitless duties, including the stewardship of all other creatures on earth, and although they are provided with capacities and potentialities so vast that it would take an eternity on earth to fulfill them, the sojourn of the human being on earth is actually a very brief one. One must therefore conclude that the importance given to humanity, the limitless expenditure provided for them, the boundless manifestations of Divine Lordship bestowed on them as the addressee of the All-Glorified One, and the infinite amount of Divine bounties showered upon them—none of these can be intended solely for this brief, fleeting, painful, and calamity-stricken life in this training-ground of the world, this temporary military encampment of the earth, this transient exhibition. Rather, since these things can only be intended for another, eternal life, an everlasting realm of happiness, they indicate, even testify to, the otherworldly bounties in the realm of Hereafter.

O the Creator of all things!

All the creatures of the earth are subservient to and administered by Your Strength, Power, Knowledge, Will, and Wisdom on this earth, which is Your property. And Your Lordship—Your acts of creation, maintenance, provision, nurturing, and administration—which can be observed on the earth, display such vastness and comprehensiveness, and the administration, provision, and nurturing within this Lordship are so perfect and sensitive, and Its actions and operations are replete with such unity, uniformity, and coordination that Your Lordship is clearly universal and indivisible. Also, the earth, together with all its inhabitants and through countless tongues that are more articulate than the speech of humanity, glorifies its Creator and declares Him to be the All-Sacred; through the tongue of His limitless bounties the earth praises and extols its All-Providing One of Majesty.

O the All-Sacred One, Who is hidden because of the intensity of His manifestation and veiled on account of His Grandeur!

With all the earth's glorifications of You and its declarations of You as the All-Sacred, I too declare that You are absolutely exalted above any faults, impotence, or the ascription of partners, and I praise You and offer thanks to You with all their praises.

O the Lord of the land and the sea!

I have understood through the instructions of the Qur'an and the teachings of the noblest Messenger, upon him be peace and blessings, that, just as the earth, the atmosphere, and the heavens bear witness to Your Existence and Oneness, the rivers, springs, and streams also testify clearly to the absolute necessity of Your Existence and Your Oneness.

Indeed, there is not a single creature, indeed, not a single drop of water in the seas, which are in effect our globe's steam boilers and the source of countless marvels, but it makes its Creator known through its existence, orderliness, position, and benefits.

There is not a single one of these amazing creatures, the sustenance of which is provided through simple sand or water, not one of these sea animals, each of which is created in an extremely orderly fashion, not one of the myriad kinds of fish, each laying a million or more eggs, but it indicates its Creator and testifies to its Provider through its creation, its duties, and the way it is administered, provided for, and maintained.

Also, there is not one single precious, ornamented substance or jewel in the sea with distinguishing features but it makes You known through its subtle creation, fascinating composition, and beneficial qualities.

All of these aforementioned creatures testify to You individually. Also, although they exist in extremely great varieties and numbers, and although all are mixed with one another, the facility with which they are brought into being and the stamp of unity displayed by their creation bear witness to Your Unity. Furthermore, the earth remains suspended in space and revolves around the sun at great speed without its lands or seas mixing with one another or its seas invading the lands. Also, all of its minerals and other substances, and all of its terrestrial and marine life are well-formed and extremely varied: created from simple water or soil, all these creatures are administered and nurtured with perfect orderliness. Moreover, despite their extremely abundant existence and the fact that everyday countless numbers of them die, none of their corpses remains on the earth or in the sea for long, with the result that both the face of the earth and the seas are always clean and pure. So, the earth bears witness to Your Existence and to the fact that You are the Necessarily Existent Being to the number of its creatures. In the same way that all these creatures clearly indicate the splendor of Your Lordship and the immensity of Your all-encompassing Power, they also indicate the boundless comprehensiveness of Your Mercy and Dominion, Which embrace everything—from the extremely large stars in the heavens above to the tiny fish at the bottom of the oceans. Also, through their perfect organization and ordered existence, through the benefits they give and the instances of wisdom they display, and through their well-proportioned structure and composition, they indicate Your all-encompassing Knowledge and your all-embracing Wisdom.

You have pools of mercy for the travelers in this guesthouse of the world and You have subjugated these pools for their benefit and for their ship so that they may travel. This indicates that the One Who offers such innumerable gifts from the sea to His guests of one night in a sideway inn—the world—must certainly have eternal oceans of Mercy at His eternal domain of sovereignty, and those here are but their tiny, transient samples. Thus, the way in which the seas skirt the land in such an extraordinary fashion, and the wonderful sustaining and nurturing of the creatures that inhabit their depths all demonstrate self-evidently that they are subservient to Your Command in Your domain through Your Will, Power, and Administration. Through the language of all these facts, they declare You to be their All-Sacred Creator, saying "God is the All-Great."

O the All-Powerful One of Majesty, Who has made mountains as treasure-filled masts for the ship of the earth!

I have understood from the instruction of God's noblest Messenger, upon him be peace and blessings, and from the teachings of the Qur'an that just as the seas recognize You and make You known through their marvels, the mountains also recognize You and make You known through the instances of wisdom in their existence and the benefits they provide. For example, they serve the earth, keeping it solid and unperturbed by the invasion of the seas, and preserving its stability in spite of quakes and the stormy movements within it . They also purify the air of harmful gases, store and preserve water, and function as vast treasure-troves of minerals and metals that are necessary for living beings.

Indeed, there is not a single rock or precious stone in the mountains, there is not a single one of the innumerable kinds of substance that are used as ingredients for medication, there is not a single one of the extremely diverse kinds of minerals or metals that are vital for living beings in general and humankind in particular, there is not a single one from among the countless varieties of plants and trees that adorn the mountains, plains and fields with their flowers, making them prosperous with their fruits—there is not a single one of these but it testifies with utmost clarity to the absolute necessity of the Existence of an infinitely Powerful, Compassionate, and Munificent Maker through their instances of wisdom, their subtle arrangement and composition, their fine creation, their numerous benefits, and the extreme diversity of their tastes and natures, however similar they may appear to be on the surface. Also, in addition to bearing witness to the Maker through their great variety of blossoms and fruits, which show extreme variety despite the fact that they all grow in simple, uniform soil and are nurtured with the same, simple water, trees and flowers also testify to His Unity and Oneness through the similarity of their administration, maintenance, origin, habitat, creation and artistry. They also point to His Unity and Oneness through their abundance and the speed and facility with which they are created, even though each one is a unique work of art and of inestimable value.

Also, the fact that the all of the world's mountains have almost the same composition and that all species of beings are made perfectly, without the slightest flaw, in the same way, in the shortest time imaginable, and without the creation and sustenance of one individual and species being confused with or impeding another—all of this indicates the magnificence of Your Lordship and the immensity of Your Power, for Which nothing is difficult. In addition, the mountains hold many different varieties of plants, trees, and minerals to meet the endless needs, tastes, and appetites of innumerable kinds of living creatures; they also provide the necessary medications for countless kinds of illnesses. All of this indicates the boundless extent of Your Mercy and the infinite vastness of Your Dominion. Although the minerals and the seeds of all these plants and trees lie hidden and intermingled under the ground in darkness, they are grown and prepared with perfect order by virtue of a vast knowledge and an all-encompassing sight. All of these facts indicate the comprehensiveness of Your Knowledge, Which encompasses everything, and the all-embracing nature of Your Wisdom, Which arranges everything perfectly. In addition, through the preparation of medicinal substances and the depositing of minerals and metals in them, mountains obviously indicate the beauties of Your Lordship's compassionate and munificent arrangement and providence and the precautionary subtleties of Your Benevolence.

Again, Your creation of these huge mountains as well-made warehouses of supplies for the future needs of Your guests in this earthly caravanserai and as the perfectly arranged stores of the infinite treasures that are of vital importance for the lives of these guests testify indubitably to the fact that a Maker Who is this munificent and hospitable, this wise and caring, and this powerful and nurturing has most certainly prepared treasures of everlasting bounties for these beloved guests in an eternal world. The stars there will perform the duties of the mountains here in the world.

O the One Who has absolute power over all things!

The mountains are subjugated to the service of humanity in Your domain by Your Power, Knowledge, and Wisdom, as are the creatures that reside in and on them. They glorify and declare to be the All-Sacred their Creator, Who has made them subservient and dutiful in this manner.

O the All-Merciful Creator and All-Compassionate Lord!

I have understood from the instruction of God's noblest Messenger, upon him be peace and blessings, and the teaching of the wise Qur'an that just as the heavens, the earth, the seas, and the mountains, with all their creatures and contents, recognize you and make You known, so do all of the plants and trees on the earth, together with their leaves, flowers, and fruits, also know You and Make You known clearly.

Each leaf of all plants and trees, which commemorates its Maker through its enraptured movements, together with every flower, which describes and defines its Maker through its adornments, and every fruit, which smiles joyously on account of the manifestation of His Mercy, testifies with utmost certainty to the absolute necessity of the Existence of an infinitely Compassionate and Munificent Maker through its perfect and extraordinarily artistic formation, which is utterly impossible to ascribe to chance; it does this also through the perfect balance and proportion in its formation, and the adornment that accompanies that balance and proportion, and through the embroideries that contribute to its adornment, and the many beautiful scents and tastes that are added to its embellishments. As a totality these bear clear witness to the Unity (*Wahidiya*) and Oneness (*Ahadiya*) of the necessarily existent Maker. They do this through their mutual resemblance all over the world and their similarities in their creation, through the relationship between their growth and the way they are provided for, through the interconnectedness of the Divine Names and Acts Which relate to their existence and maintenance, and through the administration and nurturing of the countless individual members of the hundreds of thousands of varieties without flaw or confusion.

In the same way that these testify to the absolute necessity of Your Existence and Your Unity, the perfect and distinctive maintenance of countless members of the hosts of living beings on the earth, formed of hundreds of thousands of "nations," indicates the splendor and uniqueness of Your Lordship and the immensity of Your Power, Which encompasses everything and creates spring as easily as it does a flower. Furthermore, the preparation of countless varieties of food for the innumerable animals and human beings distributed throughout the earth indicates the boundless comprehensiveness of Your Mercy. Moreover, the perfect order in the performance of all these acts of providing, administering, and nurturing, together with the subservience and obedience of everything, down to the tiniest particle or atom, to Your Acts and Commands, provides clear evidence of the all-encompassing nature of Your Dominion. Similarly, the fact that whatever relates to the existence, growth, and nurturing of every leaf, flower, fruit, root, branch or twig is based on certain knowledge and insight, with many wise purposes and benefits in mind, they each point clearly to the all-encompassing nature of Your Knowledge and Wisdom. With innumerable tongues, all of these also praise and extol the beauty of Your infinitely perfect Art and the perfection of Your infinitely beautiful Bountifulness.

In addition, through the hands of the trees and plants in this temporary guesthouse, such invaluable bounties and gifts are offered, such extraordinary expenditure is laid out, and such wonderful munificence is displayed that they clearly indicate, indeed, bear witness to this fact: the Powerful and Munificent All-Compassionate One has prepared, out of His eternal treasure of Mercy, a host of fruit-bearing trees and blossoming plants which are suited to the perpetual Gardens of Paradise, for the servants whom He will favor with eternal life in an everlasting realm. This He does because, in accordance with His will to make Himself known and loved through the bounties He bestows, He does not want His loving friends to complain, saying: "He has given us a taste of them and has now dispatched us to eternal non-existence without being able to enjoy them to the full." Nor does He will to reduce the infinite value of the dominion of His Divinity or cause His loving friends to deny His endless Mercy, thus transforming their love to enmity. All the fruit-bearing trees and blossoming plants in this world are but examples of their eternal counterparts, and are here in this world merely on display for those who would "buy" them for all eternity.

Just as the trees and plants glorify and praise You, and declare You to be the All-Sacred through their words of leaves, flowers, and fruits, each one of these words too proclaims Your absolute sacredness. The glorifications offered by the fruits through the mute eloquence of their disposition—that is, through their attractive shapes, their many different and fascinating colors, their edible parts of infinite variety and their marvelous seeds, and through being offered to the guests of this earthly caravanserai from the hands of the trees or plants—manifest themselves as though spoken words. All of them are subjugated in Your domain through Your Power, Will, Benevolence, Mercy, and Wisdom, and they are perfectly obedient to all of Your commands.

O the All-Wise Maker and All-Compassionate Creator, Who is hidden because of the intensity of His manifestation and veiled on account of His Grandeur!

With the voices of all trees and plants, together with their leaves, flowers, and fruits, and to the number of all of them I praise and exalt You and declare You to be absolutely exalted above and free from defect, impotence, and having partners.

O the All-Powerful Originator, the All-Wise Administrator, the All-Compassionate Nurturer!

I have understood from the instruction of God's noblest Messenger, upon him be peace and blessings, and from the teaching of the wise Qur'an, and I believe that just as plants and trees recognize You and make known Your sacred Attributes and All-Beautiful Names, there too is not a single animal or human but it testifies to the absolute necessity of Your Existence and to Your Attributes. They bear witness through their perfectly and artistically made bodies, equipped as they are with extremely delicate and well-functioning "instruments" that possess the finest order and equilibrium; they give evidence through all of their internal and external organs, which are made to operate with perfect sensitivity and orderliness, and through their members and senses that are arranged in their bodies with perfect balance and for extremely important purposes. For it is absolutely impossible that any random force, unconscious "nature," or blind chance should contribute to an artistry that is so delicate and wise, or to a wisdom that requires such care and consciousness, or to a perfect balance that is so sensitive and purposeful. As for the notion that they form themselves; well, this is a hundred times more impossible and inconceivable. For their self-formation would require each of their particles or atoms to have God-like knowledge and power. Otherwise, how would each one be able to know itself perfectly and bring itself into existence, particularly since it would also have to create all of the other atoms with which it interconnects and has relations, together with all the other elements in the universe which have a part in its existence and operation?

The observable unity in their administration and maintenance as a whole, the perfect similarities among the members of each species, as well as between the species themselves, the stamp of unity that can be observed in their creation and nurturing, and the fact that each of them has eyes, ears, mouths, and so on, and is each directed toward similar goals—all of these and similar other instances of unity bear most decisive witness to Your absolute Unity. And just as all of Your Names are manifested in the universe as a whole, thus indicating Your Unity (*Wahidiya*), they are also manifested in each of the beings in the universe, thus displaying Your Oneness or Uniqueness (*Ahadiya*).

Also, like humankind, hundreds of thousands of animal species that are distributed throughout the world are equipped, trained, and obedient, like a well-organized army, and the commands of Your Lordship operate with perfect order in their kingdom. While this indicates the magnificence of Your Lordship, their extreme value despite their abundance, their perfect composition and organization despite their rapid origination, and the perfect, peerless art they contain despite the facility with which they have been created, all indicate the grandeur of Your Power. From microbes, which exist in all four corners of the globe, to rhinoceroses, and from the tiniest flies to the largest birds, the precision with which they are provided for and nurtured clearly indicates the endless comprehensiveness of Your Mercy. And each of them performs its vital duties without any shortcomings, while the earth, functioning as the parade ground for their mobilization in spring and for their demobilization in fall and winter, indicates the boundlessness of Your Dominion.

Also, every animal is like a sample in miniature of the universe. It is originated through an extremely profound knowledge and fine wisdom, without any confusion in the appointment or placement of any of its atoms, compounds or organs, one within the other, and in their complex relationships with one another. Again, every animal is given a different form and distinguishing features that have no defects, confusions, or faults. As these facts indicate Your all-encompassing Knowledge and Your all-embracing Wisdom to the number of animals in existence, the creation of each one with such artistry and beauty as a miracle of art and a marvel of wisdom also indicates the perfect beauty of Your Lordship's Art, Which you love and will to be displayed. Again, through their delicate nourishment and the gratification of their needs and desires, all of them, and in particular their young, indicate endlessly the sublime beauty of Your Benevolence.

O the All-Merciful, the All-Compassionate, O He Who is absolutely true to His promise, and O the Master of Judgment Day!

I have understood from the instructions of Your noblest Messenger, upon him be peace and blessings, and the teaching of Your wise Qur'an the following:

Since the ultimate result of the universe is life, and the ultimate result of life is the spirit, and since the most elevated among beings with spirit are those with consciousness, and the most comprehensive among those with consciousness is humanity, and since the whole universe serves life, and living beings are sent to the world to serve those among them with spirit, and since beings with spirit are put in the service of humankind, and since human beings have a strong innate love for their Creator, Who both loves and makes Himself loved by them by every means, and since the capacities and immaterial faculties given to humanity are directed primarily toward the eternal life, and their heart and consciousness desire eternity with all their might, and their tongues entreat their Creator with never-ending prayers for everlasting life—since all this is self-evidently true, then it is clear that the One Who loves and is much loved will never distress humankind, whom He has created for eternity, by making them die only to fail to revive them again, which would thus transform their love for Him into eternal enmity. For humanity has been sent to this world to strive for and earn an eternal life of happiness in another, eternal realm. There we will be favored with the eternal manifestations of the Divine Names, Which we mirror in this short and transient life.

Indeed, the faithful friend of the Eternal One will be eternal; the conscious mirror of the Everlasting One must be everlasting.

As can be understood both from authentic Prophetic Traditions and as is required by the truth of Divine Wisdom, Mercy, and Lordship, the spirits of animals will also endure permanently. Moreover, certain members of them, such as the hoopoe which served Prophet Solomon, upon him be peace, and the ant found in the narratives concerning him, as well as the she-camel of Prophet Salih, upon him be peace, and the dog of the People of the Cave will go to the eternal world with their bodies and spirits, while each animal species will continue to exist as a single, representative body for occasional employment.[15]

O the All-Powerful and Self-Subsistent One by Whom all subsist!

All living creatures, all beings with spirit and all beings with consciousness have been made subservient to the commands of Your Lordship and entrusted with duties according to their nature in Your domain through Your Power, Will, Administration, Mercy, and Wisdom. Some of them have been put in the service of humankind—not because of any power or dominance on the part of humanity, but, rather, because of human innate weakness and impotence. By glorifying their Maker and declaring Him to be absolutely exalted above having defects, faults, or partners, and by praising and thanking Him for His bounties, both verbally and through the mute eloquence of their natures and dispositions, each performs its own particular form of worship.

O the All-Sacred One, hidden because of the intensity of His manifestation and veiled on account of His Grandeur!

With the intention of declaring You to be the All-Sacred through the glorifications of all beings who possess spirits, I say: All-Glorified are You, O He Who has made every living thing from water!

---

15 They must be employed by the people of Paradise. For the relevant Prophetic narrations, see, al-Baghawi, *Ma'alimu't-Tenzil*, 3:154; al-Alusi, *Ruhu'l-Ma'ani*, 15:226.

O the Lord of all the worlds! O the Deity of all those who have already come to this world and of all those who are destined to come in the future! O the Lord of the heavens and the globes!

From the instruction of God's noblest Messenger, upon him be peace and blessings, and the teaching of the wise Qur'an, I have come to understand and believe the following:

In the same way that the heavens and the earth, the atmosphere, the land, and sea, the trees, plants, and animals, with all their organs, component parts and atoms, recognize You and testify to Your Existence and Oneness, so too do living beings, which are the essence of the universe, bear witness to the absolute necessity of Your Existence, Your Unity, and Your Oneness. And in the heart of this witnessing stands humanity, the essence of living beings; among humanity are the saints, the purified scholars, and the Prophets, all of whom testify to Your Unity through the observations and unveilings of their intellects and hearts, and through their inspirations and spiritual discoveries. Indeed, their testimony has the certainty of the consensus of hundreds of different groups of scholars with true and expert knowledge, and hundreds of chains of transmitters of knowledge, whose truthfulness and reliability cannot be doubted. Furthermore, they also substantiate the information they provide with their miracles, wonders, and decisive proofs.

Not a single thing occurs to a sound heart but it draws the attention to the One Who inspires it from behind the veil of the Unseen, and testifies to the absolute necessity of His Existence, as well as to His Attributes, Unity, and Oneness. Similarly, there is not a single instance of true inspiration that focuses attention on the One Who inspires but it bears witness in the same way. Also, there is no certain creed that discovers Your sacred Attributes and All-Beautiful Names with a certainty based on experience but it testifies in a similar fashion, nor is there a pure, illuminated heart such as belongs to the Prophets and saints and which observes the lights of the Necessarily Existent One with piercing clarity, but it bears the same witness. And there is not a single enlightened intellect, such as is possessed by the truthful, pure, and saintly scholars, but it confirms with certain knowledge the signs of the necessary Existence and Oneness of the Creator of all things. Indeed, there is no occurrence, no true inspiration, no certain creed, no pure and illuminated heart, no enlightened intellect, in fact, there is nothing but it indicates or testifies to the absolute necessity of Your Existence, Your sacred Attributes, Your Unity, Your Oneness, and Your All-Beautiful Names.

In particular, there is not a single clear miracle of the noblest Messenger, upon him be peace and blessings, who is the leader and essence of all the Prophets, saints, purified scholars, and those who are most advanced in truthfulness, which confirms the glad tidings he brought; there is not a single exalted truth of him which shows his absolute truthfulness; and there is not a single verse in the miraculous Qur'an, the essence of all sacred Scriptures and books of truth, which demonstrates Divine Unity; and there is not a single sacred matter or truth of belief contained in it—there is not a single one of these miracles, truths, verses, or matters but it indicates or bears witness to the absolute necessity of Your Existence, Your sacred Attributes, Your Unity, Your Oneness, and Your All-Beautiful Names.

Also, in the same way that these countless people of truth bear witness to Your Existence and Oneness with their miracles, wonder-working, and rational proofs, they also proclaim and prove with unanimity the magnificence of Your Lordship, Which has perfect knowledge of and control over all things in creation, however large or small—from the universal affairs connected with Your Supreme Throne to the most secret occurrences of the heart and its most hidden desires and prayers: they also proclaim the sublimity of Your Power, Which invents countless things simultaneously and instantly before our eyes, and accomplishes the greatest thing as easily as it does the smallest one, without one impeding the other.

With their miracles and other proofs, all these truthful ones also demonstrate and prove the limitless comprehensiveness of Your Mercy, Which has made this universe a perfect palace for beings which possess spirit, humanity in particular, and Which prepares Paradise and eternal happiness for the jinn and humanity, does not forget even the lowliest being, and gratifies the most powerless heart. These miracles and proofs also demonstrate and prove the infinite vastness of Your Dominion, Which has subjugated all kinds of creatures, from atoms to galaxies, and entrusted them with certain duties, causing them to obey Your Commands. Moreover, these miracles and proofs also testify, as one, to the all-encompassing nature of Your Knowledge, Which has made the universe a cosmic book that is composed of as many volumes as there are particles and compounds in the universe, and Which has recorded all that happens in the lives of all creatures in the Manifest Record and the Manifest Book, which are the registers of the Supreme Preserved Tablet. Your Knowledge has also inscribed completely and without error the contents and programs of all trees in each of their seeds, and the entire life histories of conscious beings in their memories. These miracles and proofs also bear witness, with utmost clarity, to the all-embracing nature of Your Wisdom, Which attaches to each creature numerous instances of wisdom, such as each tree yielding results to the number of its fruits, or placing in each living being as many benefits as it has members or, indeed, compounds and cells, or equipping the human tongue with abilities to the number of tastes it encounters, as well as entrusting it with many duties. Furthermore, these miracles and proofs unanimously bear witness to the fact that Your Names of Majesty and Grace, Whose exemplary manifestations are witnessed throughout the universe, will continue to manifest themselves in the abode of eternity in a more splendid way; that Your gifts and bounties, the compassionate manifestations and samples of which are observed in this fleeting world, will endure in the eternal realm of happiness in a more brilliant fashion; and that those who are fond of them and who discern them in this brief worldly life with pleasure and seek them in love will accompany them through all eternity.

Also, based on the countless proofs of their Prophethood, including their hundreds of evident miracles, and on hundreds of decisive evidences which exist in all the Scriptures You revealed, but primarily in the wise Qur'an, as well as on the promises and threats that You repeat in them frequently; and relying on Your all-sacred Attributes and essential Characteristics such as Power, Mercy, Favoring, Wisdom, Majesty and Grace, Which require Resurrection, and on the dignity of Your Majesty and the dominion of Your Lordship, all the Prophets with luminous spirits, including first and foremost God's noblest Messenger, upon him be peace and blessings, give both jinn and humankind the glad tidings of eternal happiness for the people of guidance, and they warn that Hell awaits the misguided, while themselves being the first to believe in and bear witness to these. And so do all the saints with illuminated hearts, who rely on their spiritual unveilings and visions, and the pure, saintly scholars with enlightened intellects, who are based on their convictions at the degree of certainty of knowledge.

O the All-Powerful and All-Wise! O the All-Merciful and All-Compassionate! O the All-Munificent Who is absolutely true to His promises! O the All-Overwhelming One of Dignity, Grandeur and Majesty!

Failure to bring about the Resurrection would mean contradicting so many truthful friends of Yours, breaking Your vehemently repeated threats and promises, and negating Your sacred Attributes and essential Characteristics, thereby leaving unfulfilled that which is required by the very nature of Your dominion as the Lord; it would mean rejecting and render futile the hopes and prayers for the Hereafter of Your innumerable servants whom You love, and who make themselves loved by You by confirming and obeying You; it would also mean confirming the people of unbelief and misguidance in their rejection of the Resurrection, who through unbelief and disobedience and by contradicting You in Your promises, insult Your Grandeur, attack the dignity of Your Majesty, offend the honor of Your Divinity and disparage your Lordship's compassion. Undoubtedly You are utterly exempt from and infinitely exalted above such a failure! I declare Your infinite Justice, Grace and Mercy to be absolutely free of such unlimited ugliness and unrighteousness. I wish to recite the verse, *All-Glorified is He, and absolutely exalted, immeasurably high above all that they say* (17: 43) as many times as there are particles in my body. Indeed, these numerous truthful Messengers of Yours and heralds of Your dominion are absolutely correct in their testimony to Your eternal treasures of Mercy and Benevolence and the extraordinarily exquisite manifestations of Your All-Beautiful Names in the world of permanence with certainty based on knowledge, and certainty based on vision, and certainty based on experience. They also believe and teach others that the greatest ray of Your Name the Ultimate Truth, Which is the origin, sun, and preserver of all truths, is this greatest truth of the Resurrection.

O the Lord of the Prophets and those most advanced in truthfulness after the Prophets!

All these beloved friends of Yours have been subjugated and dutiful to You in Your domain through Your Command, Power, Will, Administration, Knowledge, and Wisdom. Through their glorification, praise, and declarations of Your Oneness, and through their profession that You are absolutely exalted above having defects, faults, or partners, they have shown this world to be the most expansive house of remembrance and the universe to be the most expansive place of worship.

O my Lord, and the Lord of the heavens and the earth! O my Creator and the Creator of all things!

For the sake of Your Power, Will, Wisdom, Sovereignty, and Mercy, Which subjugate the heavens with their stars, the earth and all that is in it, and all creatures with all their states, make my carnal soul subservient to me and subjugate my desires to me. Subjugate people's hearts to the *Risale-i Nur* purely for the service of the Qur'an and belief. And bestow on me and my brothers and sisters perfect belief and a happy end. Subjugate hearts and intellects to the *Risale-i Nur*, just as You subjugated the sea to Prophet Moses, upon him be peace, the fire to Prophet Abraham, upon him be peace, the mountains and iron to Prophet David, upon him be peace, the jinn and humans to Prophet Solomon, upon him be peace, and the sun and the moon to Prophet Muhammad, upon him be peace and blessings. And preserve me and the students of the *Risale-i Nur* from the evil of the carnal soul and Satan and from the torments of the grave and Hellfire; make us happy in the highest realm of Paradise! Amin! Amin!

> All-Glorified are You! We have no knowledge save what You have taught us. Surely You are the All-Knowing, the All-Wise.
>
> And their invocation will close with "All praise and gratitude are for God, the Lord of the worlds!"
>
> If I have erred by offering this lesson, which I have taken from *al-Jawshanu'l-Kabir* ("The Great Shield"), a supplication of God's Messenger, upon him be peace and blessings, to the Court of my All-Compassionate Lord as a reflective act of worship, O my Lord, I call upon Your Mercy to forgive me for the sake of the Qur'an and *al-Jawshanu'l-Kabir*.
>
> Said Nursi

The
Fourth Ray

The Fourth Ray

God is sufficient for us; how excellent a Guardian He is!

This Ray is derived from the verse, *God is sufficient for us; how excellent a Guardian He is!* (3:173)

Note: Unlike other works, the *Risale-i Nur* develops and unfolds its meanings gradually. The First Aspect in this treatise is particularly subtle and profound, explaining a very valuable truth. Peculiar to myself, in the form of an emotional contemplation, a life-giving treatment based on belief, and a secret discourse in my heart, it proved to be a cure for my various deep-rooted ills. Those who are of the same spiritual mindset will understand it perfectly; those who are not may be unable to experience it in its entirety.

The FirstChapter

In the Name of God, the All-Merciful, the All-Compassionate.

God is sufficient for us; how excellent a Guardian He is!

OWING TO THE FACT THAT THE WORLDLY PEOPLE HAD ISOLATED ME from everything, I was suffering from five kinds of separation.[16] I was also afflicted by five illnesses—arising partly from the sorrows I felt in my old age. Without looking to the consoling and helpful lights of the *Risale-i Nur*, because of heedlessness arising from distress, I turned to my heart and spirit. I saw that as well as infinite impotence and boundless need, I was dominated by an extremely

[16] For these kinds of separation, see: Said Nursi, *The Letters*, (trans.), The Light, 2007, "The Sixth Letter," pp. 35–37. (Tr.)

powerful desire for permanence, an intense attachment to existence, and a great yearning for life. Yet the awesome specter of mortality threatened to extinguish that permanence. In such a mood, I exclaimed like a poet who complains of separation:

My heart desired permanence, but God, the Ultimate Truth,
decreed that my body be mortal;
I am afflicted with an incurable illness; how pitiful it is that even
Luqman is unaware of it!

I bowed my head in despair. Suddenly the verse, *God is sufficient for us; how excellent a Guardian He is!* (3:173), came to my aid, and asked me to read it attentively. So I recited it five hundred times every day. Writing down briefly only nine of its aspects or nine of its numerous invaluable lights which were unfolded before me at the level of "certainty based on vision or observation," I refer readers to the *Risale-i Nur* for the details, which were known at the level of "certainty based on knowledge," not on vision, in the past.[17]

The first luminous aspect of God's Sufficiency

The human being's innate love of permanence and their desire for immortality essentially stem from a manifestation in their being of a Name belonging to the One of Perfection and Majesty, Who is loved naturally because of His absolute Perfection. This manifestation, which is like a reflection or shadow of that Name in human beings, should lead people to direct their desire for immortality toward the Essence, Perfection and Permanence of that Absolutely Perfect One. In my case, however, this love of permanence has lost its way and, owing to heedlessness, has attached itself to the shadow instead. Thus, it had been seeking permanence in this worldly life, which is nothing more than an ephemeral mirror held up to the eternal. Then the Qur'anic statement, *God is sufficient for us*, came and removed the veil. I observed and experienced to the degree of "absolute certainty" that

[17] Muslim scholars have pointed to three levels or degrees of certainty (*yaqin*) based on what is written in the Qur'an: certainty of knowledge, that is, certainty based on or arising from knowledge, certainty of vision—certainty based on vision, and certainty of experience—certainty based on experience. (Tr.)

the true pleasure and happiness of my permanence lay precisely and in more perfect form in the Permanence of the All-Permanent One of Perfection, and in believing and confirming that He is my Lord and Deity. For it is through His Permanence that an undying truth may be realized for me. The consciousness of belief establishes that my essential being is but the shadow of an enduring, eternal Divine Name and therefore lives eternally.

It is also through the consciousness of belief that the Existence of the Absolutely Perfect and Beloved One is known, and the innate, intense love in human beings is satisfied. Also, it is through conscious belief in the Existence and Permanence of the Eternally Enduring One that the perfections of the universe and of humankind are discovered, thus saving the innate infatuation of humanity with perfection from endless pains and allowing them to find true contentment.

Moreover, through the consciousness of belief a connection is formed with the Eternally Enduring One and through belief in that connection a relationship comes into being with all His dominions. And on account of that connection and relationship, which in one sense renders humanity the metaphorical owner of all those infinite dominions, one looks on them with the eye of belief and benefits.

In addition, through the consciousness of belief and that connection and relationship, a kind of bond is formed with all beings. In this way, over and above one's personal existence, through the consciousness of belief and the aforementioned connection, relationship and bond, a boundless existence comes into being which people feel to be their own, thus calming their innate passion for existence.

Furthermore, through that consciousness of belief and that connection and bond, a brotherhood (and sisterhood) is formed with all the people of perfection. Thus, through knowing that on account of the Existence and Permanence of the Eternally Enduring One, those innumerable people of perfection are not lost in eternal non-existence, the permanence of those innumerable loved, appreciated, and admired friends and the perpetuation of their perfections give a pure and most elevated pleasure to those having consciousness of belief.

In addition, through that consciousness of belief and that connection, bond and brotherhood (and sisterhood), I felt an infinite happiness on account of the happiness of my friends—for whose happiness I would gladly sacrifice my life. For a kind-hearted friend will always be happy at the thought of the happiness of their sincere friends. Thus, through the consciousness of belief I understood that through the eternal Existence and Permanence of the All-Permanent One of Perfection, the noblest Messenger, upon him be peace and blessings, and his Family and Companions, together with all the other Prophets, saints and purified scholars—all of whom are my most beloved masters—and all my other innumerable friends had been saved from eternal annihilation and would be favored with everlasting happiness. With great joy I saw that on account of that relationship, bond, brotherhood (and sisterhood) and friendship, their happiness was reflected in me, making me happy as well.

Moreover, through the consciousness of belief, I was saved from the endless sorrows which come from the love that one feels for one's fellow people and the compassion one feels toward relatives, and instead began to experience a boundless spiritual pleasure. For I perceived through the consciousness of belief that my parents, my blood relatives and my spiritual brothers and sisters, for whom I would sacrifice my life with pride, were saved from eternal annihilation and endless pain through the Existence and Permanence of the Truly All-Permanent One, and would be favored with His infinite Mercy. I saw that in place of insignificant and ineffective compassion, which gave me nothing but sorrow and distress, an infinite Mercy was protecting and caring for them. And just as a mother takes pleasure at the ease, comfort and pleasure of her child, I was exhilarated and overjoyed at the salvation and ease under the protection of that Mercy of all those persons for whom I have compassion, and I became profoundly thankful.

Also, through the consciousness of belief, and through the connection it provides with the Almighty, I knew with conviction that the *Risale-i Nur*, which was the duty and product of my life, and the means of my happiness, would be saved from being lost and without benefit; I knew that it would not be annihilated or lose its meaning and that it would remain fruitful and gain permanence. This gave me a deep spiritual pleasure which far outweighed the pleasure I felt regarding my own permanence. For I believed that through the Existence and Permanence of the All-Permanent One of Perfection, the *Risale-i Nur* was not only being inscribed in the hearts and memories of people, but that it was being studied by innumerable sentient creatures and spiritual beings. Furthermore, if God was pleased with it, it was being engraved on the Supreme Preserved Tablet and other "preserved tablets"[18] and adorned with the fruits of reward. I also knew that through its particular connection with and adherence to the Qur'an, and—God willing—its acceptance by the Prophet, upon him be peace and blessings, and through its being favored with God's approval and good pleasure, one moment of Divine appreciation for the *Risale-i Nur* was far more valuable than the appreciation of all the people in the world. I thus came to realize that I am always ready to sacrifice my life for the endurance, statements, and Divine acceptability of each of those treatises, which prove the truths of belief, and I knew that my happiness lies in the fact that they serve the Qur'an. Thus, through the connection with God provided by belief, I understood that through Divine Permanence they might be favored with an appreciation a hundred times greater than the appreciation of the people. From the very bottom of my heart I declared: "*God is sufficient for us, and how excellent a Guardian He is*!"

Moreover, through the consciousness of belief I knew that belief in the Existence and Permanence of the All-Permanent One of Majesty, Who bestows everlasting life, and the results of that belief—such as virtuous deeds—are the everlasting fruits of this fleeting, earthly existence and the means to everlasting life in the next world. Like a seed that breaks through its shell in order to be transformed into a fruit-bearing tree, I convinced my soul to break out of the shell of this apparent worldly permanence in order to yield everlasting fruits. Together with my soul I said: "*God is sufficient for us, and how excellent a Guardian He is*, and His eternal Permanence is sufficient for us!"

In addition, through the consciousness of belief and the relationship with the Almighty which comes from being His servant, I knew with a certainty arising from knowledge that that which lies beyond the veil of the earth is illuminated, that the heavy layer of earth is lifted from the dead, and that the realm under the ground which is entered through the

[18] The Supreme Preserved Tablet, which is in one respect identical to God's eternal Knowledge, is the "Tablet" on which the pre-eternal, primordial existential forms of all beings that will come into existence and the events that will happen in the universe eternally exist. The deeds of all beings are also recorded on it. Other preserved tablets are the real or metaphorical "tablets" on which the deeds of all beings and all events are recorded. Human memories and seeds of trees and plants are examples of these tablets. (Tr.)

door of the grave is not submerged in the darkness of eternal non-existence. With all my strength I cried: "*God is sufficient for us, and how excellent a Guardian He is!*"

Furthermore, I perceived with firm conviction and I knew with certainty based on experience through the consciousness of belief that while my intense, innate desire for immortality indicates the Permanence of the All-Permanent One of Perfection in two ways, as I was veiled by self-adoration, I had lost my true beloved and become so silly that I had begun adoring the shadow or reflection of the beloved. The exceedingly deep and powerful love of immortality which prevailed in my essential being came from a manifestation of one of the absolutely perfect Names of the Absolutely Perfect One, Who is loved and worshipped for Himself and for no other reason, and the Perfection of Whose Essence is absolutely sufficient as the cause of worship. Furthermore, I perceived that by bestowing the above-mentioned enduring fruits—each one of which is worth sacrificing not one worldly or eternal life but thousands—He had made that innate desire even more intense. If I had been able to do so, I would have declared with all the particles of my being: "*God is sufficient for us, and how excellent a Guardian He is!*" I uttered it with precisely that intention.

The consciousness of belief, which seeks eternal life and finds the Permanence of God—some of the fruits of which I have indicated above in the paragraphs beginning with "Moreover... In addition... Also... "—gave me such pleasure and zeal that I uttered with all my spirit and strength and from the depths of my heart and soul: "*God is sufficient for us, and how excellent a Guardian He is!*"

The second luminous aspect of God's Sufficiency

At a time when old age, exile, solitude, and isolation were added to my endless innate impotence, and when "the worldly" were attacking me with their spying and their scheming, I told my heart: "Armies are attacking a single man whose hands are tied, and who is ill and weak. Is there no point of support for me?" I then had recourse to the verse, *God is sufficient for us; how excellent a Guardian He is*, and it informed me of the following:

Through belief you become connected to the Ruler of Absolute Power, Who is such that every spring He equips with perfect order armies of plants and animals on the earth, which comprise hundreds of thousands of different "nations." He also renews the uniforms of the two magnificent armies that are the trees and flying creatures, clothing them afresh. As He changes the outer garments of the hens and peacocks, ever renewing and beautifying them, He also changes the dresses of the mountains and the veils of the plains.

Furthermore, as the All-Merciful One, He places in tiny protective cases the sustenance of all animals and humans in the form of extracts of all kinds of foods, which we call seeds and grains, and which may be likened to meat, sugar and other food extracts recently discovered, but which are a hundred times more perfect. He includes in those extracts the instructions of Destiny or Divine Determination concerning their growth and development into edible foods. The creation of those tiny cases take place with such speed, ease and abundance in the "factory of *Kâf–Nûn*"[19] that the Qur'an states that the Creator merely commands something to exist and it comes into being (i.e., 2:117; 3:47; 6:73). Although all those extracts resemble one another, are of the same matter and would not fill a town, the exceedingly diverse and delicious foods which the All-Munificent Provider cooks from them could fill all the towns on the earth.

Since you have such support through the connection to God enabled by belief, you can rely on infinite strength and power. When I learned this lesson from the verse, I found such a moral strength that I felt my belief was powerful enough to challenge not only my present enemies but the entire world. With all my spirit I proclaimed, "*God is sufficient for us; how excellent a Guardian He is!*"

Seeking a source of help for my infinite poverty and need, once again I had recourse to the verse. It now said this: through the relationship of servanthood and worship you belong to an All-Munificent Master and are recorded in His notebook of provision—a Master Who, every spring and summer, prepares a lavish spread upon the table of the earth and removes it a hundred times over, producing foods from behind the veil of the Unseen, from unexpected places and from beneath the dry earth. It is as though the

[19] The factory of *Kâf–Nûn*" refers to God's command of "*Kun!* (Be!)", which He says to something that He wills to be. The Qur'an declares: *When He wills a thing to be, He but says to it "Be!" and (in the selfsame instant,) it is* (36:82). (Tr.)

years and the days are all containers for the fruits of bounty and foods of mercy that appear in continuous succession. They are exhibitions for the degrees of the bestowal, both universal and particular, of an All-Compassionate Provider. You are the servant of such an absolutely Wealthy One. If you are conscious of your servanthood, your grievous poverty will be transformed into pleasurable appetite. Learning this lesson, I placed my trust in God and proclaimed with my soul: "Surely that is right! *God is sufficient for us; how excellent a Guardian He is!*"

The third luminous aspect of God's Sufficiency

Having found my attachment to the world severed on account of the oppression of exile and illness, the reality of belief brought it home to me that I was destined for perpetual happiness in an eternal world, an everlasting realm. At this point I abandoned those old sighs of regret, which only caused more grief, and became cheerful and happy. However, I also knew that this ideal, this goal of the spirit and ultimate result of human nature could be realized only through the infinite Power of an Absolutely All-Powerful One, Who knows and records the action, inaction, behavior and states, be they in word or deed, of all His creatures, and through His conferring limitless favor and importance on humans, whom He takes as His friends and addressees, and to whom He has given a rank superior to all beings, despite their absolute impotence. Reflecting on these two points—namely, the activity of such a Power and the very real importance of apparently impotent and insignificant human beings—I sought an explanation that would strengthen my belief and satisfy my heart. Again I had recourse to the verse, *God is sufficient for us; how excellent a Guardian He is!* This time it told me to note the Arabic suffix "*-na*," ("*us*") and to be attentive to the beings that join me in saying "*God is sufficient for us*," be it verbally or through the mute eloquence of their disposition.

Immediately I saw that innumerable birds and flies—which are like birds in miniature—and innumerable animals, plants and trees were, like me, reciting the verse *God is sufficient for us; how excellent a Guardian He is!* through the language of their disposition. They remind everyone of the fact that they have such a Guardian with all-majestic Power Who guarantees all essential necessities of their life that every spring in particular, He creates before our very eyes countless species of animals and different varieties of plants and trees in a most balanced and well-ordered fashion, in utmost abundance and on a vast scale, with the greatest ease and the utmost artistry, and in forms which differ one from the other. This He does with no defect, flaw or confusion, producing them from eggs, grains, seeds and drops of fluid that resemble one another and whose component elements are the same. That these beings resemble one another despite the infinite differences between them demonstrates to us His Unity and Oneness, and shows clearly there cannot be any interference or participation in those acts of His Lordship and Creativity by "partners."

Then I noted the "I", that is, my soul, included in the first person plural "us" in the verse *God is sufficient for us*. I saw that among the animate beings, He has created me from a drop of fluid in miraculous fashion. He has opened my ears and positioned my eyes. Also, He has placed in my head a brain, in my breast a heart and in my mouth a tongue; and in each He has created a plethora of tiny weighing scales and measuring instruments with which I am able to weigh, measure and come to understand all of the gifts that He has stored up in the treasuries of Divine Mercy. He has also created in them thousands of instruments to unlock and recognize the treasures of the limitless manifestations of His All-Beautiful Names, and appointed all the smells, tastes and colors as instructions for the assistance of those instruments.

Furthermore, in addition to including with perfect order in this body all those numerous sensitive feelings and senses, and those subtle, non-physical faculties and inner senses, He has created with perfect wisdom all the parts, systems and members of my body necessary for life; this He has done so simply that He might allow me to recognize and experience all the varieties of His bounties, and so that He might allow me to know and experience the myriad of manifestations of His Names. As with the bodies of all believers, He has made this poor, apparently insignificant body of mine into a sort of cosmic calendar or diary; an illuminated, compressed copy of the macrocosm; a miniature sample of the world; a manifest miracle for all His other creatures; a desire-driven seeker of all kinds of Divine bounties and the means of their creation; the pivot upon which the laws and practices of His Lordship are primarily concentrated; an inventory or garden in miniature of the gifts and flowers of His Wisdom and Mercy; and an understanding addressee of His Divine pronouncements. He also has given me existence—the greatest of His bounties—and life, through which my existence may be expanded. For through life, my existence may swell to the outermost reaches of this visible, physical world.

And He has bestowed humanity on me, through which the favor of existence may expand in the physical and spiritual realms, allowing me to benefit—through the senses particular to humankind—from the vast tables of bounties He has prepared. He has also bestowed Islam on me, through which the favor of existence broadens to the extent of the visible world and the World of the Unseen. He has also favored me with true and verifiable belief, through which the favor of existence encompasses both this world and the next. He has favored me with knowledge and love of God that stem from belief, through which He has given me the capacity to stretch out my hands and, through praise and glorification, reach benefits that exist on all levels of creation from the sphere of contingency to the Necessary Realm and the sphere of the Divine Names. In particular, He has also given me knowledge of the Qur'an and the wisdom of belief, through which He has bestowed on me superiority over many creatures.

In short, the nature that He has given me is so comprehensive that it has the capacity to be a perfect mirror to His Oneness and Eternal Besoughtedness, and to respond to His universal, sacred Lordship with extensive worship. Furthermore, as decreed unanimously in all the holy Scriptures and Books that He has sent to humankind by means of His Messengers, and as confirmed with one voice by all the Prophets, saints, and purified scholars, He buys from me my existence, my life and my self—as stated in verses of the Qur'an—which have been given to me in trust. I have understood with a certainty of knowledge and a firm belief that He will save them from being lost and amounting to nothing; indeed, He will preserve them, as He has promised repeatedly and categorically, and He will provide eternal happiness and Paradise as the reward.

Thus, I was taught by the verse *God is sufficient for us; how excellent a Guardian He is!* that I have a Lord of absolute Majesty and Munificence, One Who "opens up" through His Name the All-Opening the forms of hundreds of thousands of varieties of animals and plants from limited, near-identical seeds and drops of fluid with the utmost facility, speed and perfection, and, as we learned earlier, gives humanity this astonishing importance, making them the chief pivot of the works of His Lordship. The verse also taught me that He would bring about the Resurrection, bestow Paradise, and create eternal happiness as easily and certainly as He will create next spring. If I had been able to do so, I would have pronounced through the tongues of all creatures "*God is sufficient for us; how excellent a Guardian He is!*" Instead I utter it with that intention and through my thought and imagination, and I want to repeat it through all eternity.

The fourth luminous aspect of God's Sufficiency

Once, during a period of heedlessness in which I felt overpowered by old age, exile, and illness, I became painfully anxious about my being, for which I felt an attachment so intense that it bordered on infatuation. I was anxious that my being was, together with all other creatures, heading for death and would be stripped of its existence. So once again I had recourse to the same Quranic verse. This time it said, "Take heed of my meaning: look at it through the telescope of belief!"

So I looked and saw with the eye of belief that my minuscule being was the mirror to an unlimited existence; I saw that through infinite expansion it was the means of gaining innumerable existences, and that it was a word of wisdom which would yield fruits of numerous permanent existences more valuable than itself. I came to understand at a degree of certainty arising from knowledge that to live in connection with that unlimited existence, even for an instant, was as valuable as eternal existence. For I understood through the consciousness of belief that my being was a work of art and a manifestation of the Necessarily Existent Being. So, being saved from essentially groundless anxieties of loneliness and from innumerable separations and their pains, I formed relationships and bonds of brotherhood with beings that I love, to the number of the Divine Names Which are the sources of the acts manifested on all creation, and living beings in particular. I knew that there would be a permanent union with all of them after a temporary separation. As everybody knows, those who share the same village, town or country, or serve under the same regiment, commander or master, will feel a close brotherhood or sisterhood and a warm friendship with one another, while those who are deprived of such bonds are in constant darkness and torment. Were the fruits of a tree sentient and conscious, they too would feel that they were the siblings, companions and observers of one another. If the tree ceased to exist, or if they were plucked from it, they would suffer separations to the extent of the number of fruits on the tree.

Thus through belief and the connection that it engenders with the Creator and His creatures, like all believers, my being gains the lights of innumerable existences untroubled by separation. Even if my being departs as others remain behind, it is as happy as if it too had remained. Moreover, as explained in detail in The Twenty-fourth Letter, the existence of every living being, and particularly that of those with spirits, is like a word: it is spoken and written down and then disappears. Yet as it goes, it leaves behind numerous "second degree" existences, such as its meaning, its "ideal" identity and form, and its results. It also leaves behind its rewards—if it has been favored with God's approval and good pleasure—and the truth it has expressed. Only then does it pass beneath the veil.

Similarly, when they are stripped of their external shells, my existence and the existences of all living creatures leave behind their spirits, if they have them; and their meanings, the truths they have expressed, their "ideal" identities, and the worldly results of their personal natures and their fruits pertaining to the Hereafter are also left behind. They also leave their forms and identities in memories and on the "preserved tablets," in films displaying perpetual scenes, and in the exhibitions of the eternal Knowledge of God. They leave the glorifications they have offered through their nature, disposition and lives, which represent them and give them permanence, in the records of their deeds, and they leave in the sphere of the Divine Names their innate responses to the manifestations and inevitable demands of those Names, together with their instances of being mirrors to them. In short, they leave behind numerous immaterial existences like these, more valuable than their external existences and then they depart. This I knew with the degree of "certainty based on knowledge."

Thus, through belief and the consciousness and relationship that result from belief, one may attain the above-mentioned perpetual, immaterial existences. Without belief, one is deprived of all these other existences; indeed, even one's own external existence goes for nothing, as if it had gone into eternal non-existence on one's own account.

I once felt great sorrow at the speedy destruction of spring flowers; I pitied those delicate creatures. But the truth of belief mentioned above shows that these flowers are seeds in the world of meaning. Since each of them becomes like a fruit-bearing tree which produces all the above-mentioned existences apart from the spirit, they yield a hundredfold profit in respect of the lights of existence. Their external existences do not go to non-existence: they are only hidden. Furthermore, they are the renewed forms of the permanent truth of their species. For the beings of this spring, such as leaves, flowers, and fruit, are identical in nature to those of last spring: the difference is only one of physical identity. I realized that even this difference was to allow those words of Wisdom, those phrases of Mercy and those letters of Power to manifest numerous different meanings. Instead of lamenting, I uttered: "What wonders God wills! How great are God's blessings!"

Thus, through the consciousness of belief and the connection that belief creates with the Maker of the heavens and the earth, I perceived to a degree how precious and unique it was to be the work of art of a Craftsman Who adorns the skies with stars and the earth with flowers and other exquisite creatures, displaying a hundred miracles in every one of His artifacts. What pride and honor conscious beings feel when they realize they are the work of such an infinitely wonderful Artist! In particular, the verse taught me that since that infinitely miracle-working Artist had inscribed in the tiny copy of a human being the mighty book of the vast heavens and earth, even making every human being a specially chosen and perfect synopsis of that book, the honor, perfectibility, and value bestowed on human potentiality are great indeed. And it taught me that human beings are favored with this honor and value through belief in God and establishing a relationship with the Creator that results from such belief. With the intention of speaking on their behalf, I uttered with the tongues of all creatures: "*God is sufficient for us; how excellent a Guardian He is!*"

The fifth luminous aspect of God's Sufficiency

At another time when I found myself buffeted by extremely severe circumstances, I focused on my life. I saw that it was passing swiftly, drawing ever closer to the Hereafter: it was gradually ebbing away under harsh conditions. While discussing in the *Risale-i Nur* the Divine Name the All-Living, life is described as having many important tasks, merits, and benefits. I thought sorrowfully that if this were the case, surely life should endure rather than be extinguished so swiftly. Again I had recourse to my teacher, the verse *God is sufficient for us; how excellent a Guardian He is!* This time it said to me, "Consider life from the perspective of the All-Living and the Self-Subsistent, the One by Whom all subsist and Who gives you life!"

Taking the advice of the verse, I saw that if my life pertains to me from one perspective, it pertains to the All-Living and the Self-Subsistent One from a hundred perspectives. And if out of my life's numerous results one looks to me, a thousand look to my Creator. Therefore, one moment of life lived within the bounds of God's good pleasure and approval is enough: a long time is not required. Since this truth and its proofs have been explained in various other parts of the *Risale-i Nur*, it will be summarized here in the form of four "matters."

THE FIRST MATTER: I considered life from the point of view that in its essence, nature, and reality, life relates to the All-Living and the Self-Subsistent One, and I saw that:

- in actual fact, my life was a coffer filled with keys, all designed to open the treasuries of the Divine Names;
- it was a small map of the inscriptions of those Names,
- an index of their manifestations,
- and a sensitive balance and measure with which to recognize and weigh the vast truths of the universe.
- I understood that it was a written word of Wisdom which knows and makes known, and which understands and makes understood, the meaningful and priceless Names of the All-Living and Self-Subsistent One.

When it is seen in this way, life becomes a thousand times more valuable and one hour of it becomes as significant as a whole lifetime. And with regard to its relation to the Eternal One, Who is uncontained by time, it makes no difference whether it is long or short.

THE SECOND MATTER: I considered the essential rights of life and I realized the following:

- My life is a missive of Divine Lordship: it makes itself read by conscious creatures who are my brothers and sisters.
- It is an object of study which makes known its Creator.

- It is also a manifesto that proclaims my Creator's Perfections. Life demands us to be adorned with the priceless gifts and decorations that the Creator has bestowed through it, and to display them consciously and with true belief and gratitude to the Peerless Sovereign in the daily parade of earthly existence.
- Life also demands that we comprehend, observe, proclaim, and bear witness to the praise and glorification offered to the Creator by innumerable living beings.
- Furthermore, life is a means by which the beauties and favors of the All-Living and Self-Subsistent One's Lordship are made known, either verbally or through the mute eloquence of disposition and worship.

Thus I came to realize at the degree of certainty arising from knowledge that elevated rights of life such as these do not require a long time, that they elevate life a thousand-fold, and are a hundred times more valuable than the worldly rights of life. And so I exclaimed: All-Glorified is God! Belief is so valuable and invigorating that it infuses with life everything that it enters! Even a single flame of it removes transience from a fleeting life and bestows on it the gift of eternity.

THE THIRD MATTER: I considered the innate duties of my life and the supra-material benefits of life which relate to my Creator. I saw that life acts as a mirror to its Creator in three ways:

THE FIRST WAY: Through its innate impotence, poverty, and need, my life acts as a mirror to the Power, Strength, Wealth, and Mercy of its Creator. Just as the pleasure of food is experienced in proportion to the degree of hunger, the degrees of light are known through the degrees of darkness, and the degrees of heat are gauged through the degrees of cold, the extent of the Creator's infinite Mercy and Power may be understood from the extent of my absolute impotence and poverty, the way in which He answers my endless needs and wards off innumerable threats to my existence. I also realized the extent of my duties to Him—duties of entreaty, prayer, modesty, humility, and servanthood.

THE SECOND WAY: My life mirrors the universal and all-encompassing Attributes and Essential Qualities or Characteristics of my Creator through its capacities and attributes such as partial knowledge, will, hearing, and sight. Indeed, I came to perceive through my conscious acts such as knowing, hearing, seeing, speaking, and asking that my Creator must have all-encompassing Attributes such as Knowledge, Hearing, Sight, Speech, Will, Power, and Life—but in an absolute and unlimited sense—together with His Essential Qualities such as Wrath and Compassion. I acknowledged and confirmed my belief in this, thus finding another way leading to knowledge of God.

The third way: My life also mirrors the Divine Names, Which are imprinted and made manifest on me in all aspects of my life. As I looked at my life and my physical body, I saw hundreds of kinds of miraculous works, inscriptions, and arts, and could see quite clearly that I was being nurtured with the utmost compassion. From this I understood through the light of belief how extraordinarily generous, merciful, skilful, and gracious was the One Who has created me and given me life; I saw how wonderfully powerful He is and, if one may say so, artistic, watchful, and efficient. I also perceived the innate aims and duties of creation and the results of life such as glorification, sanctification, praise, thanking, exaltation, declaring God's infinite greatness and superiority, and affirming and proclaiming His Unity. Furthermore, I understood to the degree of certainty based on knowledge the reason why life is the most valuable of all of God's creations and why everything is subjugated to it. I also understood the wisdom in everyone's innate passion for life and the fact that belief is the very life of life itself.

The fourth matter: In order to learn where the true pleasure and happiness of my worldly life lie, I deliberated once more upon the verse *God is sufficient for us; how excellent a Guardian He is!*

The purest pleasure and happiness in this worldly life lies in belief—belief that I am the creature, artifact, and bondsman of an All-Compassionate Lord, Who has created me and given me life; belief that I am being nurtured and protected by Him and that at all times I am in absolute need of His favors; belief that He is my Lord and my Deity and that He is most kind and compassionate to me. Belief in these realities gives pleasure and happiness so gratifying, pain-free, and unending that they can hardly be described. Therefore, how appropriate is the praise, *All praise be to God for the favor of belief*! This I understood from the above verse.

And so these four matters, which explain the reality, rights, duties, and pleasure of life, show that the more life relates to the All-Permanent, All-

Living, and Self-Subsistent One and the more belief becomes the spirit and marrow of life, the more perpetual life becomes and the more enduring are the fruit that it yields. Seen this way, life also becomes so elevated that it receives the manifestation of eternity: whether earthly life is long or short is no longer an issue. This much I learned from the verse. And so in the name of all lives and living beings, I proclaimed: *God is sufficient for us; how excellent a Guardian He is!*

The sixth luminous aspect of God's Sufficiency

At a time when old age was reminding me of my own departure from the world amidst the events of the end of time—a reality which suggests the overall destruction of the world and the departure of all beings in general—my innate love of beauty and fondness for perfection were being developed in an amazingly sensitive manner. With extraordinary awareness and sorrow, I saw that transience and decline, which are always destructive, and death, which is a continuous cause of separation, were pounding this beautiful world and these lovely creatures in a terrible manner and destroying their beauty. As my innate love for creation welled up intensely and rebelled against this situation, once again I had recourse to the verse *God is sufficient for us; how excellent a Guardian He is!* to find consolation. It said to me, "Recite me and consider My meaning carefully!"

So I entered the observatory of verse thirty-five of *Suratu'n-Nur* (The Quranic Chapter of Light), which is known as the Verse of Light and begins with *God is the Light of the heavens and the earth*, and looked through the telescope of belief to the most distant levels of the verse, *God is sufficient for us; how excellent a Guardian He is!*, using the microscope of the consciousness of belief to study its most subtle meanings. I saw the following:

Mirrors, pieces of glass, transparent things, and even bubbles, manifest the various hidden beauties of the light of the sun and the seven colors it contains, and through their disappearance, renewal and reappearance, and with different capacities and refractions, they cause the renewal and re-manifestations of these beauties. In the same way, in order to act as mirrors to the sacred Beauty of the All-Gracious, Beautiful One of Majesty, the Eternal Sun, and to the permanent beauties of His All-Beautiful Names, and to cause the constant renewal of their manifestations, these beautiful creatures and most lovely beings arrive and depart in a constant flux. As has been explained in detail in the *Risale-i Nur* with powerful proofs, they demonstrate that the beauties manifested by them are not their own property; rather, they are nothing but signs, indications, gleams and manifestations of an eternal, transcendent, sacred Beauty, Which desires to make Itself manifest. Here, three of these proofs will be summarized.

THE FIRST PROOF: The beauty of a fine piece of embroidery points to the beauty of the act of embroidering; this in turn indicates the beauty of the title of the one who embroiders. The beauty of the title points to the beauty of the attribute of the artist manifested in their art of embroidering. The beauty of that attribute indicates the beauty of the capacity or talent of the artist to embroider. Finally, the beauty of the capacity for embroidery self-evidently points to the artist's own beauty as an embroiderer.

Similarly, the grace and beauty shared by all fine, exquisitely made creatures throughout the universe bears clear testimony to the grace and beauty of the Acts of the All-Majestic Artist. The grace and beauty of these Acts undoubtedly indicate the grace and beauty of the Titles or, more appropriately, the Names Which relate to these Acts. The grace and beauty of these Names indubitably testify to the grace and beauty of the sacred Attributes that are the sources of the Names. The grace and beauty of these Attributes decisively testify to the grace and beauty of the Essential Characteristics or "Capacities" in which these Attributes have originated. And finally, the grace and beauty of the Essential Characteristics or "Capacities" self-evidently testify to the Grace, Beauty and the sacred Perfection of His Essence or Being—the Essence of the One Who is the Author of the Acts, Who is called by the Names, and Who is qualified by the Attributes—and to the holy Beauty of His genuine Truth. This means that the Maker of absolute Grace and Beauty has infinite Grace and Beauty that is befitting His All-Pure and Holy Essence to the degree that one shadow of It has beautified all beings from one end to the other; His transcendent, sacred Beauty is such that a single manifestation of It has made the entire universe beautiful and adorned and has illuminated the entire sphere of contingency with Its rays of grace and beauty.

Just as an embroidered object cannot come into existence without an act, no act can take place without the author of the act. Just as it is impossible for names to exist without the one that is called by them, attributes cannot exist without the one they qualify. Since the existence of a work of art self-evidently indicates the act of making or producing it, and the existence of the act indicates the existence of its author's title or name and attribute that gave rise to the work, it is self-evident that the perfection and beauty of a work indicate the beauty and perfection that are particular to the act which has engendered them. And they, in turn, indicate the beauty that is particular to and fitting for the name of the author of the act; these, in turn, indicate with a certainty of knowledge the beauty and perfection of the essence of the author, which are fitting and appropriate for this essence.

Similarly, it is impossible for the constant activity behind the veil of the works in the universe to be without their Author, or for the names whose manifestations and inscriptions are visible on creatures to be without the One Who is called by them; nor can attributes such as power and will, which are almost observable, be without the One they qualify. Therefore, with their boundless existence, all the works, creatures, and artifacts in the universe clearly indicate the existence of the Acts of their Creator, Maker, and Author; they testify to the existence of His Names, His Attributes, His Essential Characteristics or "Capacities," and to the absolutely necessary Existence of His All-Pure and Holy Essence. Also, all the different varieties of perfection, grace, and beauty that are observed in all these creatures testify to the infinite, unbounded, and transcending beauties and perfections of the Acts, Names, Attributes, Essential Characteristics, and Essence of the All-Majestic Maker—they testify with complete clarity and in a way that is particular to these Acts, Names, Attributes, and Essential Characteristics, and to the All-Holy Essence, and fitting for their sacredness and necessity.

THE SECOND PROOF contains five points:

THE FIRST POINT: Despite the great differences in their paths and methods, the leaders of the people of truth have, on the basis of their illuminations and spiritual unveilings, unanimously believed and concluded that the instances of beauty in all beings are the shadows and gleams of the sacred Grace and Beauty of the Necessarily Existent One, manifested as they are from behind numerous veils.

THE SECOND POINT: All beautiful creatures appear, convoy after convoy, and then disappear, dispatched to extinction. Yet since the elevated and unchanging Beauty Which displays Itself in the mirrors of these creatures continues without cessation to manifest Itself, this most certainly demonstrates that the beauties observed in these mirrors do not belong to the beautiful creatures themselves. Rather, in the same way that the beauty of the sun's rays can be seen in the bubbles floating on a stream, they are the lights which shine from a perpetual Beauty.

THE THIRD POINT: It is clear that illumination comes from something that has light and that existence is given by someone who exists by himself; it is also clear that favor comes from riches, generosity from wealth, and instruction from knowledge. Also, beauty issues forth from one who is beautiful, while grace comes only from one who is gracious. Indeed, it is inconceivable to think it could happen in any other way. Given this reality, we believe that all of the beauties in the universe come from One Who is Beautiful, and that through the tongues of all its creatures, which act as mirrors, this constantly changing and renewed universe indicates and describes His Grace and Beauty.

THE FOURTH POINT: The body is dependent on the spirit and subsists and is animated through it; a word depends on its meaning and is illuminated by it; form is based on substance and acquires value through it. Now this visible, material world is like a body, a word and a form, and it depends on the Divine Names that are behind the veil of the Unseen; it is from the Divine Names that it receives life and beauty. All of the instances of physical beauty originate in the immaterial beauties of the meanings and truths on which they are based. Their truths are illuminated and fed by the Divine Names and are, in a sense, their shadows. This truth has been decisively proved in the *Risale-i Nur*.

This means that all of the different sorts of beauty in the universe are the manifestations, signs, and marks of a faultless, transcendent Beauty, Which is manifested from beyond the veil of the Unseen through the Names. However, the All-Pure and Holy Essence of the Necessarily Existent Being resembles absolutely nothing at all and His Attributes are infinitely superior to the attributes of contingent beings: consequently, His sacred Beauty does not resemble the beauty of creatures or contingent beings, but is infinitely more exalted. Certainly, an everlasting Beauty—a single manifestation of Which is a vast Paradise, together with all its exquisiteness and one hour's vision of Which makes the people of Paradise oblivious to where they are—can neither be finite nor have any like, equal, or peer. Clearly, everything has a beauty particular to itself and in accordance with its nature, and beauty has thousands of varieties, like the differences among species of beings. For example, the beauty perceived by the eye is not the same as the beauty perceived by the ear; an abstract beauty experienced by the mind is different from the beauty of the food tasted by the tongue. Similarly, the beauties perceived and appreciated by the faculties such as the heart and the spirit and by other internal and external senses are all different. For instance, the beauties of belief, truth, light, flowers, spirit, forms, affection, justice, and compassion all differ from each other. In the same way that the beauties of the infinitely beautiful Names of the All-Gracious One of Majesty are different from one another, the beauties shared by beings also differ.

If you would like to observe one manifestation of the beauties of the All-Gracious and Beautiful One's Names in the mirrors of beings, look with the eye of your imagination so encompassing that will enable you to see the face of the earth as though it were a small garden, and be aware that terms such as mercy, compassion, wisdom and justice refer to the Acts, the Names, the Attributes and the Essential Characteristics of God Almighty.

Look at the sustenance of all living creatures, including humanity in particular, which arrives regularly from behind the veil of the Unseen, and see the all-gracious and beautiful countenance of Divine Mercy.

Then look and see how miraculously all infants are provided for; fed as they are by the sources of milk which hang over their heads in the breasts of their mothers, as delightful as the water of *Kawthar*,[20] and see the captivating countenance of the Divine Lordship's Compassion.

Then look and see the matchless, gracious countenance of Divine Wisdom, Which has made the entire universe into a mighty book of wisdom, every letter of which contains a hundred words, every word of which contains a hundred lines, every line of which contains a thousand chapters, and every chapter of which contains thousands of miniature books.

Then see the majestic beauty of a Justice Which holds the whole universe together with all its beings in exact balance, maintaining the equilibrium of all the heavenly bodies, whether large or small, providing symmetry and proportion—the most important elements of beauty. See how that Justice causes everything to be in its optimum state and gives the right to life

[20] *Kawthar* is a pool of Paradise. (Tr.)

to living beings, ensuring that their rights are preserved and their aggressors foiled and punished.

Then look at the inscription of a person's life history in their memory, as tiny as a grain of wheat, and see how the future lives of every plant and tree are encapsulated in its seeds. Look too at the instruments and members necessary for the defense of living beings: the wings of bees, for instance, and their poisonous stings, and the tiny bayonets wielded by thorny plants, the hard shells of seeds, and so on. Look at these and see the subtle, pleasant countenance of the Preservation and Protection of Lordship.

Then look at the countless different foods prepared by Mercy for the guests at the table of the earth of the All-Merciful and All-Compassionate One, Who is absolutely Munificent; and consider their varied tempting aromas and dazzling colors, and their different delicious tastes, as well as the organs and members of all living creatures which facilitate their pleasure and enjoyment. Look at these and see the extraordinarily pleasant countenance and sweet beauty of the Bestowal and Munificence of Lordship.

Then deliberate upon the meaningful forms of all living creatures—human beings in particular—which are opened up from droplets of fluid through the manifestation of the Names the All-Opening and the All-Fashioning; look at the fascinating faces of the flowers of spring as they open up from seeds and tiny nuclei and see the miraculously gracious countenance of Divine Opening and Fashioning.

As these examples show, each of the Divine Names has such a sacred beauty particular to It that a single manifestation of It makes the vast world and the species of beings that comprise innumerable members beautiful. You see the manifestation of the beauty of a Name in a single flower; yet, spring too is a flower, and Paradise is a flower that is yet to be seen. If you can visualize the whole of spring and see Paradise through the eye of belief, then look and understand how majestic that perpetual Beauty is. If you respond to that Beauty with the beauty of belief and the graciousness of worship, you yourself will become a most beautiful creature. But if you respond to it with the infinite ugliness of misguidance and rebellion, not only will you become one of the ugliest creatures on earth, but you will in effect become the object of hatred of all beautiful creatures.

THE FIFTH POINT: It is a fact that every skill tends to display itself, every craft and art tend to be appreciated, every form of perfection tends to show itself, and every beauty tends to reveal itself. Imagine a person who possesses hundreds of extraordinary skills, arts, perfections, and beauties; imagine that that person built a wonderful palace which reveals them all. Whoever sees that miraculous palace immediately considers the skills, beauty, and perfections of its maker and owner. Believing in them and affirming them as though seeing them, observers pronounce: "One who is not beautiful and skilled in every way cannot be the originator of a work so beautiful in every respect. It is as though his beauties and perfections are embodied in this palace."

Similarly, provided that their mind has not rotten and their heart is not corrupted, those who see the beauties of this magnificent palace and exhibition of wonders which we call the universe will certainly understand that this palace is like a mirror, decorated the way it is in order to reveal the beauty and perfection of its Maker. Since there is nothing similar to this palace of the universe, it is clear that its beauties could not have been copied from elsewhere. And so its Maker must possess beauties particular to and befitting Himself and His Names: it is from them that the universe derives its beauty, which is written like a book in order to express them.

The third proof consists of three points:

The First point: This is a truth elaborated with powerful proofs in The Third Station of The Thirty-second Word. Referring detailed discussion of it to that Word, here we will mention it only briefly.

We look at creatures, at animals and plants in particular, and we see that constant acts of decoration, arrangement and beautification, all of which indicate an underlying knowledge, wisdom, intention, and will and are impossible to attribute to mere chance, are ruling over them. We observe in everything an art so delicate, a wisdom so fine, an adornment so elevated, an organization so compassionate, and a situation so agreeable that each is quite clearly intended to focus attention on someone's art and to make it pleasing to and appreciated by those who observe it. From this it becomes self-evident that behind the veil of the Unseen there is such an Artist—One Who wills to make Himself known, appreciated, and praised through the numerous skills and perfections that He displays in each of His works of Art. And in order to please conscious beings and make them indebted, intimate companions of Himself, He bestows on them every sort of delicious bounty from sources which they least expect in a way that is impossible to ascribe to chance.

Also, it is possible to observe a magnanimous treatment and acts of making oneself known, which suggest a deep affection and an elevated sense of compassion; it is possible to see friendly dialogue with the tongue of disposition and a compassionate response to prayers. Clearly, the gift of bestowing bounties and giving pleasure that is observed behind the quality of making oneself known and loved, which is as clear as the sun, arises from a genuine will to be affectionate and compassionate. The existence of such a powerful will to be affectionate and compassionate in One Who is absolutely Self-Sufficient and in need of nothing demonstrates most definitely an infinitely perfect, eternal, peerless, and undying Beauty Whose very nature necessitates Its manifestation and Which therefore wills to be seen and thus displays Itself in mirrors. In order to see and display Itself in various mirrors, this Beauty has taken on the form of compassion and affection and then assumed the attitude of bestowing bounties and munificence in the mirrors of conscious beings; It has then taken the quality of making Itself known and loved and granted the light of adorning creatures and making them beautiful.

THE SECOND POINT: The intense, powerful, genuine and sacred love which exists in humanity, and most particularly, in innumerable distinguished ones among us whose paths are all different, indicates and bears witness to a peerless beauty. Indeed, such a love can only be directed toward such a beauty—rather, it demands this beauty. Moreover, all of the praise and commendations offered by beings verbally or through the tongue of disposition pertain to that eternal Beauty and flow forth toward It. In the view of lovers (of the Divine) like Shams-i Tabrizi,[21] all the feelings and acts of attracting and being attracted and all the captivating truths in the universe are signs of an eternal, attractive truth. And all the ecstatic movements and revolutions which cause the heavenly bodies and all beings to dance and spin like moths and Mevlevi dervishes are loving and dutiful responses to the imperious displays of the sacred beauty of that attractive truth.

---

[21] Shams-i Tabrizi: In Konya, Jalalu'd-Din ar-Rumi became a religious teacher and Sufi at the age of 39, when he met Shamsu'd-Din at-Tabrizi. At-Tabrizi, who was an ecstatic lover of God from Tabriz, Iran, had a profound influence upon Rumi and vivified, like a veritable sun, the growth of his latent spiritual and literary genius. (Tr.)

THE THIRD POINT: As agreed by all veracious scholars, existence is pure good and light, while non-existence is pure evil and darkness. Through meticulous analysis, the leading lights among the people of intellect and the people of the heart have agreed that all instances of good, beauty, and pleasure originate from existence, while all evils, calamities, suffering, and sins are attributable to non-existence.

If you ask: The source of all beauties is existence, but how do you account for the existence of things such as egotism and unbelief?

The answer: Unbelief is non-existence because it is the negation and denial of the truths of belief. As for egotism, since it arises from the wrongful claim to self-ownership and the tendency to assume the imaginary to be real, and since it stems from ignorance of the fact that the essential nature of humanity lies in its being a mirror designed to reflect the Diving Names and Attributes, it is also a form of non-existence which has donned the clothes and coloring of existence. Since the source of all beauty is existence and the source of all evil is non-existence, it is certain that an Eternal Being possessed of Necessary Existence, Which is the firmest and the most elevated and brilliant of all instances of existence, and the one most distant from non-existence, will demand a beauty that is the most powerful, the most elevated, the most radiant, and the most untainted. Indeed, not only will It express such a beauty, but It will actually be that beauty. Just as an encompassing light is necessitated by the sun, so too the Necessarily Existent Being necessitates an eternal beauty; He "radiates" through it.

All praise and gratitude be to God for the gift of belief!

Our Lord, do not take us to task if we forget or make mistakes.

All-Glorified are You! We have no knowledge save what You have taught us. Surely You are the All-Knowing, the All-Wise.

A REMINDER: Since the *Risale-i Nur* belongs to the Qur'an and is a commentary based on proofs proceeding from it, it contains necessary, purposeful, and beneficial repetitions, just as the Qur'an contains meaningful, wise, and necessary repetitions, which are not in the least tiresome. Also, since the *Risale-i Nur* comprises proofs of the truth of Divine Unity, the proclamation of which does not cause weariness, but rather is repeated with pleasure and zeal, the necessary repetitions do not constitute a shortcoming and should not cause tedium.

The Second Chapter

This concerns the various stations or degrees of the meaning of, *God is sufficient for us; how excellent a Guardian He is*! It consists of five points.[22]

THE FIRST POINT

This phrase is a tried and tested remedy for the illnesses which arise from humanity's innate impotence and poverty. Indeed, *God is sufficient for us, how excellent a Guardian He is*[23] is true on account of the following:

He is the One Who is eternally Self-Existent and Who gives existence. Therefore, it does not matter if beings decay and disappear, for the things we love continue to exist through the continued existence of the Necessarily Existent One Who has given them existence.

He is the All-Permanent Maker and Originator, so the decay of creatures should cause no sorrow, for the means by which their Maker is loved—namely His manifestations—are permanent.

He is the All-Permanent Sovereign and Master, so there should be no regrets concerning the decay of His dominions or properties, which, once they have decayed and departed, are continuously renewed.

---

[22] Thirteen years ago, I looked down on the world from the hill of Yuşa, an elevated part of Istanbul. Like everyone, I was captivated by the classes of creatures I could see, one surrounding the other, and by the beauty here. The interest I felt in this was at the degree of intense love. However, I could also see in my mind that all those creatures were moving toward decay and mortality. I then felt a powerful pain of separation, and a darkness arising from endless separations. Suddenly, the verse *God is sufficient for us; how excellent a Guardian He is!* came to my aid with its thirty-three degrees of meaning. I was reciting them in a way to follow and which suggested the possibility of different meanings and realities. Each of the seven blessed phrases that I recite between the evening and late evening or early night Prayers would have been included in *The Gleams*. In the end, only five of them were included: the other two, which are about the ranks or degrees of the meaning of *God is sufficient for us; how excellent a Guardian He is*, and *There is no might and strength save with* God, were left out. They would have been written as The Fifth and Sixth Gleams, but they have been included here in *The Rays*. Since they concern contemplation and remembrance rather than knowledge, they have been written in Arabic.

[23] I once witnessed numerous lights and degrees of meaning in this blessed phrase and it has saved me from many terrible veils of darkness and danger. Referring to these circumstances and the various degrees of meaning in this phrase, I wrote down brief reminders in the form of paragraphs or even words. As a remedy for the very painful and deep ailments that arose from my worries about the decay and death of the vast world and the creatures in it, which fascinated me, I found *God is sufficient for us, how excellent a Guardian He is*! The initial expressions at the beginning of every paragraph indicate this truth.

He is the All-Permanent, All-Knowing Witness, and therefore no grief is felt at the disappearance from this world of the things that we love, for they exist eternally in the Knowledge and Sight of their All-Permanent Witness.

He is the All-Permanent Owner and Originator, and thus there should be no pain felt with regard to the disappearance of things we find beautiful, for the source of their beauty in their Originator's Names endures for all eternity.

He is the All-Permanent Inheritor and Restorer to Life, and so there should be no lamenting at separation from those we love, for the One Who will continue to exist after them and restore them to life is All-Enduring.

He is the All-Permanent All-Beautiful and All-Majestic One, and therefore there should be no distress at the disappearance of beautiful things, for these beautiful things are the mirrors of the All-Beautiful Names, Which endure together with their beauty after the mirrors have disappeared.

He is the All-Permanent All-Worshipped and All-Beloved One, and thus there should be no sorrow for the demise of any created, "metaphorical" beloveds, for the True Beloved is truly Eternal.

He is the All-Permanent All-Merciful and All-Compassionate, All-Loving, and All-Pitying One, and so there should be no distress at and no importance be given to the decay of the apparent givers of bounties and the affectionate ones, for the One Whose Mercy and Affection encompass all things endures forever.

He is the All-Permanent All-Beautiful, All-Gracious and All-Kind One, and thus the decay of gracious and affectionate beings should not cause sorrow or grief, for the One Who substitutes for of all of them, and a single manifestation of Whom, even if they work all together, they cannot substitute, is forever Eternal.

His eternal Permanence, with all the sacred Attributes that are mentioned, is substitute enough for every sort of transient, ephemeral beloved in this world. *God is sufficient for us, and how excellent a Guardian He is!* Truly, in place of the permanence of the world and whatever is in it, the eternal Permanence of their Master, Maker, and Originator is sufficient.

THE SECOND POINT

Sufficient[24] for permanence is that God is He Who is my All-Permanent Deity, my All-Permanent Creator, my All-Permanent Inventor, my All-Permanent Originator, my All-Permanent Master, my All-Permanent Witness, the All-Permanent Object of my worship, and the All-Permanent One Who will restore me to life after my death. Therefore:

There is no harm in the decay of my being and I should feel no sorrow or regret at its passing, for my Maker endures eternally, and His Making and Creating through His Names are permanent. Whatever attribute or characteristic I have in my person is but one of the rays of one of His eternal Names, and so the decay and death of this characteristic does not herald its eternal extinction, for it exists permanently in its Creator's Knowledge and is witnessed eternally within His Sight.

Likewise, it is sufficient for me in respect of permanence and the pleasure derived from permanence that I know, am aware, and believe that I have an All-Permanent Deity and it is the rays of one of His permanent Names which shine in the mirror of my nature. The reality of my nature consists in nothing but a shadow of this Name, and it is on account of Its manifestation in the mirror of my being that my being has a value and is worthy of love. Also, it is due to the permanence of what is manifested in it that my being has many varieties of permanence.

---

24 In the same way that I saw the manifestations of the enduring Names of the All-Permanent One of Majesty behind the ephemerality and decay of the world and of external existence, and was thus absolutely consoled, I also considered my own self. Since the various levels of my inner existence, my personal characteristics and the realities of my personal life, of which I am enamored, are going toward decay and death, I realized that I had been seeking permanence in those transient things under the influence of the innate human desire for immortality. I came to see that I was a place where my Creator's eternally enduring Names were manifested. I observed in the decay of every characteristic of mine a permanent manifestation of the Name Which it had been embodied with. I came to understand, to the point of certainty, that the innate love of permanence in human nature has its source in the love of God. But humans search for their beloved in the wrong way. Instead of searching for and loving the One Who has manifested Himself in the mirror, as they should, they love the mirror itself or the apparent forms of the reflection in the mirror. In this way they come to adore their own selves instead of adoring Him: instead of "He!", the only word on their lips is "I!" They are only able to realize their mistake when decay sets in. The heart and the nature of humankind is a conscious mirror. A human being feels consciously or is aware innately of what is manifested in them, and loves this eternally.

THE THIRD POINT[25]

God is sufficient for us, and how excellent a Guardian He is! For He is the Necessarily Existent One; these flowing beings are but the results of the renewal of the manifestations of His Existence and His giving of existence to others. Endless lights of existence are gained through Him and through being connected to Him and having knowledge of Him: without Him, there is nothing but the endless veils of darkness of non-existence and the limitless pains of separation.

These flowing, transitory beings are but mere mirrors, and with the changing of their relative or nominal determinations they are renewed in six aspects in their transience, decay, and permanence:

The first: The permanence of their beautiful meanings and their "ideal" identities in the World of representations or "ideal" forms.[26]

The second: The permanence of their forms in the "ideal" tablets in the World of representations or "ideal" forms.

The third: The permanence of their results which pertain to the Hereafter.

The fourth: The permanence of their glorifications of the Lord, represented and recorded on their behalf, which is a sort of existence for them.

The fifth: Their permanence in perpetual scenes and in the exhibitions pertaining to Knowledge.

---

[25] I had been reflecting on the degrees of meaning of a very important reality—one which has uncovered the mystery behind the continuous activity that underpins the unending cycles of life and death, which is the most all-consuming dilemma in the universe. It has been explained in The Twenty-fourth Letter. This Point shows the fact that decay and death are the titles of other different kinds of existence, and yield the fruits of numerous instances of existence. It shows that anything which decays or dies leaves behind many instances of existence in its place. So, things which are transient and perishable will continue to exist in many respects. A seed rots and dies under the soil but leaves in its place a shoot to grow into a plant or tree which will yield a hundred fruits containing seeds. It is because of this that it is not proper to fear death or feel regrets at decay.

[26] The World of representations or "ideal" forms is the realm where things exist with their immaterial representations or reflections. Like a building, which has levels or degrees of existence, for example, the building in the mind of its architect, and the building on the plans, and its final, physical existence, things have degrees or levels of existence: they have pure existence in God's Knowledge, and existence as a project of Destiny or Divine Determining, and existence in the form of "ideas" or immaterial representations, and their corporeal existence. (Tr.)

The sixth: The permanence of their spirits, if they possess one.[27]

For the various duties that these beings perform and the states they assume in their death, transience, decay, and annihilation, and in their coming into existence and disappearing are required by the Divine Names. It is because of these duties that beings are like a flood that flows with the greatest speed on the waves of life and death, of existence and non-existence. It is also on account of these duties that there is perpetual activity and continuous creation in the universe. We must all, therefore, declare that: *God is sufficient for us, and how excellent a Guardian He is!* That is, with regard to existence, it is sufficient for me that I am the work of the Necessarily Existent Being: to be favored with this illuminated existence for a passing instant is preferable to millions of years of apparent, fruitless existence. By virtue of connection to God through belief, a minute of this existence is equal to thousands of years without the connection of belief; the existence of that single minute is more complete and extensive than those thousands of years.

Similarly, it is sufficient for me for existence and the value of existence that I am the art of the One Whose Grandeur is in the heavens and Whose signs are on the earth, the One Who has created the heavens and earth in six "days."

It is sufficient for me for existence and its perfection that I am the artifact of the One Who has adorned and lit up the heavens with lamps and decorated the earth with flowers.

It is sufficient for me for pride and honor that I am the creature, bondsman and servant of the One in relation to Whose Perfection and Beauty the universe with all its perfections and beauties is merely a dim

[27] The permanence of the spirit has been convincingly explained in The Twenty-ninth Word. The laws determining their reality and nature and the principles of their composition, have the same meaning for beings that have no spirits as the spirit does for those beings who are endowed with spirit. These laws and principles are permanent. For example, a fig tree decays and dies, but its "spirit," which consists in the laws of its formation, organization and growth that issue from the Realm of Divine Commands, continues to exist in its seeds. This "spirit" does not die, and the forms are renewed exactly in accordance with it, which is how the nature of the tree continues to exist. For its nature is a shadow of one of the eternal Beautiful Names of God, gaining permanence through a ray of that eternally permanent Name, with its identity continuing to exist in numerous "ideal" tablets that belong to the World of representations or "ideal" forms. Therefore, non-existence (in the form of decay and death) is nothing more than the title of the transition of a decaying instance of existence to numerous instances of permanent existence.

shadow, and which is composed of the signs of His Perfection and the indications of His Beauty.

Sufficient for me for all things is He Who stores up in tiny containers between the *kaf* and the *nun*[28] uncountable bounties, and Who, through His Power, deposits tons of bounties in a single handful of these subtle containers, called seeds and grains.

Sufficient for me in place of everything beautiful and beneficial is the All-Gracious, All-Beautiful and All-Compassionate One. For all these beautiful creatures are but transient mirrors for the renewal of the lights of His Grace and Beauty in the course of the seasons, the centuries, and the ages. And all these recurring bounties and successive fruits of spring and summer are but the ever-renewed manifestations of His continuous Act of favoring, in certain degrees, during the lives of creatures and over the course of days and years.

It is sufficient for me for my life and its true nature that I am a map, a summary, a balance, and a measure of the manifestations of the Names of the Creator of life and death.

It is sufficient for me for my life and its functions that as my life is the result of the manifestations of the Essential Characteristics of my Originator and His All-Beautiful Names, I am a word inscribed with the Pen of Power, indicating and making understood the Names of the Absolutely Powerful One, the All-Living and Self-Subsistent.

It is sufficient for me for life and its rights that since the dress of my existence, the gown of my inborn nature, and the necklace of my life are decorated with the gifts of His Mercy, I display and proclaim the manifestations of the Names of my Creator among my brother (or sister) creatures and exhibit them in the sight of the Creator of the universe.

It is sufficient for me for the rights of my life that I understand, observe, and bear witness to all forms of worship living creatures offer to the Bestower of life.

It is sufficient for me for the rights of my life that I have been adorned with the embossed jewels of the bounties of the eternal Sovereign, presenting them to His gaze with the consciousness that comes from belief.

---

28 *Kaf* and *nun* are the letters *k* and *n* of the Arabic imperative *kun* (Be!), which signifies the Divine order "Be!" uttered by God when He wills to bring something into existence. (Tr.)

It is sufficient for me for life and its pleasures that I possess knowledge, conviction, awareness and belief of my being His servant, His artifact, and His creature; it is sufficient that I know I am needy and wanting before Him, and that He is my All-Compassionate, All-Munificent, and All-Gracious Creator, Who bestows on me freely and nurtures me in a manner befitting His Wisdom and Mercy.

It is sufficient for me for life and its value that through my absolute impotence, poverty, and weakness I am a measure of the degrees of the manifestation of the Power of the absolutely Powerful One, the Mercy of the absolutely Compassionate One, and the Strength of the Possessor of absolute strength. Through my limited, particular attributes of knowledge, will and power, I am also a mirror through which the all-encompassing Attributes of my Creator are understood. For instance, I am able to understand His all-encompassing Knowledge through the measure of my limited, particular knowledge.

It is sufficient for me for perfection that I know that my Deity is Absolutely Perfect, and that whatever perfections exist in the universe are signs of His Perfection and indications of It. Also sufficient for me for perfection is my belief in God, for belief is the source of all of humankind's perfections.

And it is sufficient for me, for all my countless different needs, the satisfaction of which is sought through the tongues of my various members and faculties, that my Deity, my Lord, my Creator and Fashioner, possessed as He is of All-Beautiful Names, feeds me and gives me drink, nurtures, and raises me, and speaks to me—exalted is His Majesty and all-inclusive are His favors.

THE FOURTH POINT

Sufficient for me, for all my desires and demands, is He Who has opened up my form and that of all my fellow living creatures from a fluid through His subtle Art, all-penetrating Power, subtle Wisdom, and His subtle Lordship.

Sufficient for me, for all my purposes, is He Who has made me, opening up my ears and eyes, including my tongue and my heart in my body, and placing in them and in my other faculties countless precise scales that weigh up the contents of the varieties of the treasuries of His Mercy. He has also placed in my tongue, my heart, and my nature innumerable sensitive instruments to understand the varieties of the treasures of His Names.

Sufficient for me is He Who has included, through the majesty of His Deity, the graciousness of His Mercy, the grandeur of His Lordship, the munificence of His Kindness, the supremacy of His Power, and the subtlety of His Wisdom, all of these members and organs, limbs and systems, senses and feelings, faculties and spiritual powers in my insignificant, lowly person and in my weak and wanting being in order to make me perceive all the varieties of His bounties and taste and to help me experience most of the manifestations of His Names.

THE FIFTH POINT

I, together with everyone else, should, with pride and thanks, declare verbally and in the tongue of my disposition:

Sufficient for me is the One Who has created me and taken me out of the darkness of non-existence, bestowing on me the light of existence;

Sufficient for me is the One Who has made me a living being, bestowing on me the gift of life, which gives all things to those who possess it and allows them to stretch out their hands to all things;

Sufficient for me is the One Who has made me human, bestowing on me the favor that is humanity, which makes one the microcosm, greater in meaning than the macrocosm;

Sufficient for me is the One Who has made me a believer, bestowing on me the gift of belief, which makes this world and the Hereafter like two tables laden with bounties, and which offers them to the believer with the hand of belief;

Sufficient for me is the One Who has made me a member of the Community of His Beloved, Muhammad, upon him be peace and blessings, bestowing on me love for God and God's love for me, both of which are found in belief and are the highest degrees of human perfection. And through this love, which originates in belief, He has expanded the area of munificence for believers so that they are able to benefit from the infinite contents of the spheres of contingency and necessity;

Sufficient for me is the One Who, by not making me an inanimate object, an animal, or one who has been left in misguidance, has made me superior to the majority of creatures in respect of nature, species, religion, and belief: all praise is for Him and all thanks are due to Him;

Sufficient for me is the One Who, as described in the *hadith qudsi*: "Neither the earth nor the heavens can contain Me, but the heart of my believing servant can contain Me;"[29] has bestowed on me a gift which the universe cannot contain. For, in the same way that the essential nature of humanity is a comprehensive mirror held up to all of the Divine Names Which are manifested in the entire universe, He has made me a comprehensive mirror for the manifestations of His Names;

Sufficient for me is He Who, in order to preserve it and later return it to me, has bought from me the property that He has entrusted to me and promises to give me Paradise in return. All praise and thanks are due to Him, to the number of the atoms of my being multiplied by the number of the atoms in existence;

Sufficient for me is my Lord: exalted is His Majesty!
And Muhammad, the Light, may God's blessings be upon him!
There is no deity but God!
Sufficient for me is my Lord: exalted is His Majesty!
My heart's innermost life is the remembrance of God
And the remembrance of Ahmad, may God's blessings be upon him!
There is no deity but God!

[29] Ahmad ibn Hanbal, *al-Musnad*, "az-Zuhd" 81; ad-Daylami, *al-Musnad*, 3:174.

The Sixth Ray

The Sixth Ray

Concerning the recitations during the seated sections of the Prayer

This consists of only two points.

In the Name of God, the All-Merciful, the All-Compassionate.

HIS RAY CONSISTS OF THE ANSWERS TO TWO QUESTIONS THAT WERE asked concerning the recitation during the seated section (*tashahhud*) of the canonical Prayer, which begins, "All worship (performed by all living creatures through their lives) is God's, and so is all worship (particular to and performed by all the origins of beings such as seeds and eggs), and worship (particular to and performed by all the living beings with spirits), and worship (performed by perfected members of humanity and the angels near-stationed to God)." Postponing an explanation of the other truths of the *tashahhud* to another time, here we will examine only two points out of hundreds.

The first question

The blessed phrases of the *tashahhud* were in fact a conversation between God Almighty and His Messenger on the night of the Messenger's Ascension (*al-Mi'raj*).[30] What, then, is the reason for their inclusion in the canonical Prayer?

---

[30] *al-Mi'rāj*: The Ascension. The miraculous journeying of Prophet Muhammad, upon him be peace and blessings, through the realms of existence beyond the limit of forms. (Tr.)

THE ANSWER: The five daily Prayers are a sort of "ascension" for every believer who performs them. Therefore, the words to be uttered in the *tashahhud* must be those spoken during the supreme Ascension of Muhammad, upon him be peace and blessings. Reciting them allows us to bring to mind this sacred conversation between God and His Messenger. Through this remembrance or recollection, the meanings of those blessed words gain universality and, as such, are no longer restricted to the intellectual or spiritual level of a believer. Their sacred, comprehensive meanings may thus be conceived, and through this conception their value and light are enhanced and expanded.

For example, in order to greet Almighty God on that blessed night, the noblest Messenger, upon him be peace and blessings, said: *at-Tahiyyatu li'llah*. This means: "O my Lord! All the glorifications made by living beings, and all the gifts they present to their Maker, through their lives, are Yours alone. By visualizing them and through my belief, I too offer them to You."

With the word *at-tahiyyat*, God's noblest Messenger, upon him be peace and blessings, was referring to all the worship that living creatures perform through their lives; he then offered this to God. Similarly, by the word *al-mubarakat*, which is the summation of *at-tahiyyat*, he meant the blessedness, abundance and worship of the creatures, and in particular those of seeds, grains, and eggs, which are the means of blessings and abundance and which cause one to exclaim: "How great are God's blessings!" And through the word *as-salawat* he visualized all the particular forms of worship performed by beings endowed with a spirit and who are the summation of living beings, and offered them to the Divine Court with that comprehensive meaning. Finally, through the word *at-tayyibat*, he meant the luminous, elevated worship of perfected human beings and the angels closest in proximity to God, who are the summaries of the beings endowed with spirit; he offered this to the One he worshipped.

On that night, God Almighty said: "Peace be upon you, O (most illustrious) Prophet!" This was an indirect command and an indication that in the future, hundreds of millions of people would say at least ten times a day: "Peace be upon you, O (most illustrious) Prophet!" This Divine greeting gave these words of salutation an extensive light and a most elevated meaning.

The noblest Messenger, upon him be peace and blessings, responded to this greeting by saying: "Peace be upon us and upon all righteous servants of God!" This meant that the Messenger was hopefully and imploringly asking his Creator that in the future his vast Community and its righteous members would be favored with Islam in a way to represent Divine peace and blessings, and that those in his Community would greet one another with the words: "Peace be upon you!" "And upon you be peace!," which is a universal mark of Islam among the believers.

The Archangel Gabriel, upon him be peace, who was party to the conversation, at God's command said on that night: "I bear witness that there is no deity but God and I bear witness that Muhammad is God's Messenger." This gave the glad tidings that all of the Community of Muhammad, upon him be peace and blessings, would testify in the same way until the Last Day.

Through recalling this sacred conversation during the seated sections of every canonical Prayer, the meanings of its words become filled with light and gain comprehensiveness.

A strange state of mind that helped me with the unfolding of the above truth

Once, trapped in a dark state of heedlessness on a dark night of exile, this vast universe appeared to my imagination as a lifeless, spiritless, empty, desolate and dreadful corpse. The past, too, I imagined to be utterly lifeless, empty and full of terror, while boundless space and limitless time assumed the form of a dark wilderness.

In order to be saved from this state of mind, I took refuge in the canonical Prayer. When, during the seated part of the Prayer, I uttered *at-tahiyyat*, the universe suddenly sprang into life: at once it became animated, assuming a living, luminous form. It became a brilliant mirror held up to the All-Living, Self-Subsistent One. I came to know and saw with the certainty of knowledge and experience that the universe, with all of its living parts, was continuously offering various forms of worship and the gifts of their lives to the All-Living, Self-Subsistent One.

Then, when I said "Peace be upon you, O (most illustrious) Prophet!," that limitless, empty time was transformed under the leadership of God's noblest Messenger, upon him be peace and blessings, from a desolate wilderness into a friendly place of recreation filled with living spirits.

The second question

The phrase uttered at the end of the *tashahhud*, "O God! Bestow blessings and peace on our master Muhammad and on the Family of our master Muhammad, as You bestowed blessings on Abraham and on the Family of Abraham," appears to be not in compliance with the rules of comparisons, for Prophet Muhammad, upon him be peace and blessings, was greater than Prophet Abraham, upon him be peace, and was favored with greater mercy. What is the reason for this type of benediction and why is it recited during the *tashahhud* in particular? Also, why has this phrase been repeated in every Prayer since time immemorial, given that if what is sought has already been promised by God, surely, to say it once is enough? To cite another example, although God Almighty has promised in the Qur'an that *Your Lord may well raise you to a glorious, praised station* (17:79), in the supplication that is uttered after the call to the canonical Prayer and the announcement of the start of Prayers, we recite ".... and raise him to the glorious, praised station that You have promised him." The whole community of Muhammad prays that this promise may be fulfilled. Why is this?

THE ANSWER: This question actually contains three questions, and has three aspects.

THE FIRST ASPECT: It is true that Prophet Abraham, upon him be peace, was not at the same degree as Prophet Muhammad, upon him be peace and blessings, but his descendants were Prophets, while the descendants of Prophet Muhammad, upon him be peace and blessings, were saints. Saints cannot reach the level of Prophets. What follows is proof that this prayer for Muhammad's Family has been accepted in a remarkable fashion:

Among hundreds of millions of Muslims, the saints who have descended from only two persons, namely Hasan and Husayn,[31] from among the Family of Muhammad, may God be pleased with them, have in most cases been intellectual or spiritual guides and leaders on the paths of truth and various spiritual orders. This shows that they have been favored with what is stated in the *hadith*: "The scholars of my Community are like the Proph-

---

31 Hasan and Husayn, may God be pleased with them, are the grandsons of God's Messenger, upon him be peace and blessings, through his beloved daughter Fatima and his cousin 'Ali, may God be pleased with them. (Tr.)

ets of the Children of Israel."[32] Those like Ja'far as-Sadiq[33], Ghawthu'l-A'zam 'Abdu'l-Qadir al-Jilani[34] and Shah Naqshband,[35] may God be pleased with them, have guided the greater part of the Community of Muhammad to the way of truth—the truth of Islam; they are the fruits of the acceptance of this prayer for the Family of Muhammad, upon him be peace and blessings.

THE SECOND ASPECT: As for the reason why this sort of benediction is uttered during the canonical Prayer in particular, I would say this: by reciting it, we remember that we follow the same path as the mighty caravan of the Prophets and saints, who are the most luminous, perfect, and righteous among the most renowned of humankind, have opened and followed; it reminds us that we have joined that mighty congregation, whose way has never been confused and the truth of whose path has been confirmed with proofs that are backed by the consensus of the truest, most knowledgeable members of the human race, and that we are accompanying it on the Straight Path. By recalling this, we are saved from satanic doubts and evil delusions.

The members of this caravan are the beloved servants and friends of the Owner of this universe, while its opponents are His enemies and thus objects of rejection. Evidence for this is that from the time of Adam, upon him be peace, this caravan has been confirmed and supported by help that has arrived from the Unseen, while its opponents have been visited by heavenly calamities. While its opponents, such as the people of Noah, the 'Ad and the Thamud, the Pharaoh and Nimrod[36], have all been struck with blows from

---

[32] al-Munawi, *Faydu'l-Qadir*, 4:384.

[33] Ja'far as-Sadiq (d., 765) was the great grand-son of Imam Husayn, son of 'Ali, the fourth Caliph. He was a distinguished scholar in religious sciences who was also known for his piety and righteousness. The Twelve-Imam Shi'ites ("Twelvers") regard him as their sixth *imam*. (Tr.)

[34] 'Abdu'l-Qadir al-Jilani (d., 1166): One of the most celebrated Sufi masters. A student of jurisprudence and Hadith, he became known as *Qutb* ("the Spiritual Pole") of his age and *al-Gwahsu'l-'A'zam* ("the Greatest Means of Divine Help"). Among his well-known books are *Kitabu'l-Ghunyah, Futuhu'l-Ghayb*, and *al-Fathu'r-Rabbani*. (Tr.)

[35] Muhammad Bahau'd-din Shah an-Naqshband (d. 1389): One of the most prominent Islamic spiritual masters and founder of the Sufi Naqshbandiyyah order. Among his books are *Risalatu'l-Warida, Al-Awradu'l-Baha'iyya, Hayatnama*, and *Tanbihu'l-Ghafilin*. (Tr.)

[36] Nimrod was the Chaldaean king who ruled over Mesopotamia during the time of Prophet Abraham, upon him be peace. A fly which entered through his nose caused his tragic death. (Tr.)

the Unseen, which suggests Divine wrath and punishment, the sacred heroes of the mighty caravan, such as Prophet Noah, Prophet Abraham and Prophet Moses, upon them be peace, and Prophet Muhammad, upon him be peace and blessings, have been favored with miracles and Divine gifts from the Unseen in a most extraordinary manner. Just as a single blow demonstrates anger and a single gift indicates love, the fact that thousands of blows have rained down upon the opponents while thousands of favors and instances of assistance have reached the caravan proves beyond doubt that the caravan represents the truth and has been following the Straight Path. The part of the final verse of the *Fatiha* (the Opening Chapter of the Qur'an), *The path of those whom You have favored (with guidance)* refers to the caravan, while the part, *Not of those who have incurred Your wrath, nor of those who are astray* concerns their opponents. The meaning we have explained here is thus made clear in this final verse of the Opening Chapter of the Qur'an.

THE THIRD ASPECT: The reason why something which has already been promised is asked for repeatedly is this: "the Glorious, Praised Station" is the ultimate end of the blessing which is asked for from God. It is a branch of a supreme truth that contains elevated and significant truths like thousands of glorious, praised stations. It is a fruit of the most important result of the creation of the universe. To ask for the ultimate end, the branch and fruit, through prayer is to ask for the realization of that general, supreme truth, to ask for the arrival or realization of the eternal realm, which is the greatest branch of the tree of creation, to ask for the realization of the Resurrection and the opening up of the realm of eternal happiness; these are the greatest results of the universe. By asking for these, one takes part in the worship and prayers of all humankind, which are the most important causes of the existence of Paradise or the realm of eternal happiness. It is indeed not much that countless people pray for an aim that is so indescribably supreme. Furthermore, favoring Prophet Muhammad, upon him be peace and blessings, with such a glorious, highly-praised station indicates his supreme intercession for all his Community in the other, eternal realm. He is deeply concerned with the happiness of all his Community. It is therefore pure wisdom that Prophet Muhammad seeks endless benedictions and prayers for mercy from all of his Community.

> All-Glorified are You! We have no knowledge save what You have taught us. Surely You are the All-Knowing, the All-Wise.

The
Seventh Ray

The Seventh Ray

The Supreme Sign

An important reminder

NOT EVERYONE MAY BE ABLE TO UNDERSTAND ALL THE MATTERS discussed in this significant treatise, but nobody will remain without his or her own share. It is not possible for one who enters a huge orchard to reach and pick up all the fruit therein, but the amount that falls within their grasp will be enough for them. After all, the garden does not exist for that person alone: those who have arms long enough to reach can also have a share of the fruit.

The following five factors make this treatise somewhat difficult to understand:

THE FIRST: I have written down my own observations according to my own understanding and, in the first instance, for myself. I have not written them according to the understanding and perspectives of others, as is the case with other works.

THE SECOND: Since Divine Unity is explicated in the most comprehensive form as based on the manifestation of God's Greatest Name or the relevant Names of God in their most comprehensive manifestation, and since the matters discussed are extremely broad, intensely profound, and sometimes rather long, not everyone will be able to comprehend them all at once.

THE THIRD: Since each matter comprises a great and extensive truth, a single sentence will sometimes extend over an entire page or two, in order not to fragment the truth in question into parts. Similarly, a single proof may sometimes require many preliminaries or premises.

THE FOURTH: Since most of the matters explained here have numerous proofs, the discussion sometimes becomes prolonged, with as many as ten or twenty proofs being grouped together as a single proof. Given that this is the case, limited capacities may not be able to understand the whole of it.

THE FIFTH: The lights of this treatise came to me as a blessing of Ramadan. However, since it was written hastily at a time when I was distracted in a number of respects and when my body was racked by several illnesses, I had to be content with a first draft alone. Moreover, a number of Arabic parts were included. For example, The First Station, which was written entirely in Arabic, was later removed and made into a separate treatise.

Despite the defects and difficulties arising from these five factors, this treatise is important. And it is because of its importance that it has been named "The Supreme Sign" and "The Staff of Moses." This treatise of the Supreme Sign is a true exposition of a supreme verse, namely 17:44: *The seven heavens and the earth, and whoever is therein, glorify Him. There is nothing but it glorifies Him with His praise.*

This treatise, which constitutes The Seventh Ray, consists of an Introduction and two Stations. The Introduction explains four important matters; The First Station is the Arabic part of the exposition of the supreme verse in question, while The Second Station consists of the translation or meaning of that exposition, together with the accompanying proofs.

The Introduction has become longer than it should be due to the ample explanations it contains. However, there may be a need for it to be thus, and some may even regard it as being too short, despite its length.
Said Nursi

Introduction

In the Name of God, the All-Merciful, the All-Compassionate.

> I have not created the jinn and humankind but to (know and) worship Me (exclusively). (51:56)

According to this mighty verse, humankind has been created and sent to this world in order to recognize the Creator of the universe, and to believe in and worship Him. Thus, the primordial duty of humankind is to know God and believe in Him, and to confirm His Existence and Unity with perfect certainty.

Since humanity has an innate desire to live eternally, and since they cherish limitless aspirations and suffer endless pains, anything or any other attainment other than belief in and knowledge of God, which are key to the eternal happiness in the eternal life, is lowly for humanity. Indeed, many of the things other than belief in and knowledge of God may be said to be have no value.

Referring this truth to other parts of the *Risale-i Nur*, where it has been discussed convincingly, here we will discuss two modern obstacles which prevent humanity from attaining certainty of belief or harm it. Each of the obstacles contains two matters.

THE FIRST OBSTACLE AND HOW TO OVERCOME IT

This consists of two matters.

THE FIRST MATTER: As explained in detail in The Thirteenth Gleam, negation or denial in matters of general concern and acceptance has no value in the face of the establishment and demonstration of the truth. For example, if two common persons see the crescent at the beginning of the holy month of Ramadan and testify to it, and thousands of nobles and scholars deny it, saying: "We have not seen it," this negation has neither value nor power. For in the matter of the establishment and demonstration of the truth, each person strengthens and supports the other, thus providing a consensus. However, whether one person denies something or a thousand people deny it, the value—or, rather, lack of value—of that denial is the same. Each person who denies is isolated. For the one who establishes and demonstrates something is referring to that which actually exists and is judging the matter as it is. Thus, in the example above, if one says, "The moon is in the sky," and another confirms this, the two of them unite and are strengthened.

The one who negates or denies, however, does not refer to something that actually exists, and it is a well-known principle that "The denial of something which is not possible to specify in a particular place or position cannot be established." For example, if I affirm the existence of something and you deny it, I can easily establish its existence by merely producing an example of it. But in order to establish the non-existence of the same thing, you will have to scour the entire world in order to deny it, even going so far as to examine the past thoroughly. Only when you have done this can you say: "It does not exist and has never existed."

Since those who negate and deny do not regard the actual reality, but judge rather according to their own perspective or their arbitrary opinion or knowledge, they can in no way strengthen or support each other. For the veils and causes which prevent seeing and knowing are various. Anyone can say, "I do not see it; therefore, in my opinion and belief, it does not exist." But no one can say, "It does not exist in actuality." If someone makes such a claim—particularly in matters of belief that pertain to the whole universe—it will be a lie as vast as the world itself and anyone who makes that claim will never be able to confirm it or have it confirmed by others.

In short: In the case of affirmation or establishment, the result is one and every instance of affirmation supports and is supported by all other instances. But a denial or negation is based on personal, arbitrary opinions or perspectives and is not supported by other denials. Since everyone who denies says, "In my view or opinion," or "according to my belief," the results multiply but do not corroborate each other.

It is because of this reality that the number of those who oppose belief is of no significance: the fact that they exist in their multitudes should not cause any doubts or hesitation in the certainty of believers. Nevertheless, in this age, the negations and denials of some European philosophers have caused doubt in a number of their unfortunate imitators, thus damaging their certainty of belief and destroying their eternal happiness. They assume that death, which comes upon tens of thousands of people each day, is to be seen not as a discharge from worldly duties but as eternal annihilation. By acting as a constant reminder to those deniers of their eternal annihilation, the grave, whose open door can never be closed, poisons their lives with the bitterest of sorrows. Understand from this how great a blessing belief is, and why it is the very essence of life.

THE SECOND MATTER: In a controversial matter concerning a particular branch of art or science, those who are not specialists in it have no authority, however great, knowledgeable or skillful they may be in other branches; nor can their judgments be accepted as decisive or form part of the learned consensus.

For example, the view of a great engineer cannot have as much weight as that of the lowliest physician in the diagnosis and treatment of a disease. In particular, the words of denial of a philosopher who is absorbed in material matters and whose reason is restricted to what he sees with his eyes, and who has therefore become insensitive to the light (of truth) and gradually more and more distant from spiritual issues—his pronouncements on spiritual matters are worthless and should be given no consideration whatsoever.

In view of this reality, with regard to sacred matters and spiritual issues concerning Divine Unity, on which there is total agreement among hundreds of thousands of the people of truth, such as Sheikh al-Jilani, may his mystery be sanctified, who spent ninety years advancing on the spiritual path and was able to observe God's Supreme Throne while still on the earth, and who discovered the truths of belief at the degree of certainty of knowledge or observation or even experience, what value can the words of philosophers have, whose thoughts are scattered and lost among numerous concerns that focus solely on the material world? Are their denials not as weak as the buzzing of a mosquito compared to the roar of thunder?

In essence, unbelief that opposes and struggles against the truths of Islam is denial, ignorance, and negation. Even though it may appear to be an affirmation of some sort, it is in reality a negation and thus devoid of any established facts. However, belief is knowledge and is based on established, observable facts: it is an affirmation and an objective judgment. Any aspect of belief which negates its opposites is either a description of a positive truth or a screen upon which that truth is manifested. Even if, despite the extreme difficulties involved, the unbelievers who struggle against belief attempt to affirm their negative beliefs or negation and rejection of belief in the form of the acceptance and affirmation of non-being (the non-existence of God or afterlife or angels or Prophethood and Revelation, for example), then their unbelief can be regarded as nothing more than a form of mistaken knowledge or erroneous judgment. But, non-acceptance and non-affirmation, both of which can be assented to easily and without thinking, are absolute ignorance and a display of a complete lack of judgment.

In short: unbelief is of two kinds:

THE FIRST has no concern with the truths of Islam. It is a personal, erroneous conviction, a false belief, a mistaken acceptance and an unjust judgment. This kind of unbelief is not included in our discussion. It is not relevant to our discourse here and we have no concern with it.

The second kind opposes the truths of belief and fights against them. This kind of unbelief is itself of two kinds:

The first is non-acceptance. It consists simply of not affirming the truths of belief. It is a kind of ignorance—a sort of "non-judgment"—and as such is something which people fall into easily. This particular sub-branch of unbelief does not concern us here either.

The second sort is the acceptance of non-being. To accept non-being means to confirm the non-existence of the Divine Being or another object of belief. This sort of unbelief is a judgment and a conviction, and involves taking up opposition to belief. Those who take up such opposition are obliged to affirm their unbelief or denial.

As for this sort of denial or negation, again there are two types:

The first type is to deny the truth of any cardinal belief with respect to a particular matter, place, position, or time. This type of denial can be taken into consideration, and it is therefore outside of our discussion.

The second type consists of negating and denying the sacred, basic, and universal truths or matters of belief which concern both this world and the Hereafter, and all times and places. This kind of negation or denial can in no way be substantiated, as we have shown in The First Matter, for there must be a vision that is able to encompass and observe the whole universe, the Hereafter, and all of the past thoroughly.

The Second Obstacle and How to Overcome It

Minds that are absorbed in negligence, sin, and materiality become restricted and narrowed with regard to issues such as Divine Supremacy, Grandeur, and Infinity, and are unable to comprehend extensive or substantive matters. Because of this, they deviate toward denial and negation, puffed up by arrogance on account of the knowledge they believe they possess. Since such people cannot encompass the extremely vast, profound, and comprehensive matters of belief within their spiritually desiccated and narrowed minds or their corrupt and spiritually dead hearts, they throw themselves into unbelief and misguidance and they drown.

If they were able to look at the essence of their unbelief and the true nature of their misguidance, they would see how manifestly absurd and impossible their denial is in comparison with the reasonableness and sublimity of belief. The *Risale-i Nur* has shown this truth convincingly through its explication of hundreds of comparisons. For example, one who is unable to accept vast truths of belief, such as the absolutely necessary Existence, Pre-eternity, and all-encompassing Attributes of God Almighty simply on account of their sheer grandeur and sublimity, may form a creed of unbelief either by attributing the necessary Existence, Attributes, and Pre-eternity of God to uncountable material beings or atoms or nature or certain concepts such as chance, or like the foolish Sophists, they may even renounce reason by denying and negating both their own existence and that of the universe.

Thus, all of the truths of belief and Islam, issuing from and based on Divine Grandeur and Sublimity, secure their own freedom and that of their essential results from the enormous absurdities, the terrifying superstitions, and the dark ignorance of unbelief that confront them, establishing them in sound hearts and minds through utmost assent and submission.

God's Grandeur and Sublimity are constantly proclaimed in most of the public symbols or rites of Islam such as the call to Prayer and the Prayers themselves through the phrases like *God is the All-Great, God is the All-Great.* Also, it is declared in a *hadith qudsi* (sacred Tradition) that "Sublimity is My robe and Grandeur is My cloak." In addition, in his invocations, for example, in the eighty-sixth part of *al-Jawshanu'l-Kabir*, Prophet Muhammad, upon him be peace and blessings, pronounces God's Grandeur and Sublimity in such an elevated way that it reveals the profundity of his knowledge of God as follows:

O You other than Whose dominion there is no dominion;
O You Whose praise and laudation His servants are unable to fulfill;
O You Whose Majesty His creatures are unable to describe;
O You Whose Essence lies beyond the reach of minds;
O You Whose Perfection visions are unable to comprehend;
O You Whose Attributes intellects are unable to grasp;
O You Whose Grandeur minds are unable to perceive;
O You Whose Qualities of laudation humans are unable to describe;
O You Whose Decree His servants are unable to avert;
O You Whose evidences and signs are manifest in everything
—All-Glorified are You; there is no deity but You—
We seek refuge in You, We seek refuge in You, deliver us from the Fire!

All of these show that Grandeur and Sublimity constitute a necessary veil (before God Almighty and His acts).

The Supreme Sign

This consists of the observations (in nineteen steps) of a traveler who questions the universe concerning their Creator.

In the Name of God, the All-Merciful, the All-Compassionate.

> The seven heavens and the earth, and whoever is therein, glorify Him. There is nothing but it glorifies Him with His praise (proclaiming that He alone is God, without peer or partner, and all praise belongs to Him exclusively), but you cannot comprehend their glorification. Surely He is All-Clement, All-Forgiving. (17:44)

As well as explaining the sublime verse above, this Second Station elucidates a brief meaning of the First Station, which is in Arabic and has been left out, and the proofs and arguments it contains.

THE FIRST STEP

In order to make the Creator of the universe known, many Qur'anic verses, like the one given here, mention first the heavens, which are a brilliant page manifesting God's Unity and which all people watch at all times with wonder and joy. Since this is the case, we too should begin in the same way.

Indeed, every guest who comes to the guesthouse or the abode of this world opens their eyes and sees that this exquisite guesthouse is a place of the most generous of banquets, an extremely artistically-built exhibition, a most magnificent military camp and training ground, a most amazing, inspiring, and enthusing place of recreation and observation, and a most meaningful and wise place of instruction. Such a person asks themselves who is the owner of this exquisite guesthouse, the author of this supreme book, the sovereign of this splendid realm. The first thing that they catch sight of is the beautiful face of the heavens, inscribed as they are with the gilt lettering of light. It calls out to this person, saying, "Look at me, and I will guide you to whom you seek."

They then look and see the manifestation of a supreme lordship—mastership and administration—which holds aloft, without any supporting pillars, hundreds of thousands of heavenly bodies, some of which are a thousand times heavier than the earth and which move many times faster than a cannon-ball. It causes these bodies to move together in harmony and at an extraordinarily great speed without colliding. It also causes innumerable lamps to give constant light without the use of any oil; it controls and manages these great masses without any disturbance or disorder; it makes huge bodies like the sun and the moon work at their respective tasks without allowing any rebellion; it operates within infinite space—the measure of which cannot be calculated or expressed with figures—all at the same time, with the same strength, in the same established fashion and manner, without the least fault. It makes all those bodies with their massive, aggressive powers obey its law unconditionally and absolutely, without allowing any aggression; it keeps the face of the heavens constantly clean and shining without allowing any refuse to remain behind to sully it; it causes those bodies to maneuver like a disciplined army, and by making the earth revolve, it shows to the audience of creation many other real or imagined forms of that magnificent maneuver, every night and every year, like the scenes on a movie screen. This supreme mastership and administration manifests subjugation, management, direction, ordering, cleansing, and employment. This is a sublime and comprehensive truth, and with this sublimity and comprehensiveness this truth bears witness to the absolutely necessary Existence and Unity of the Creator of the heavens and testifies openly to the fact that His Existence is clearer than the existence of the heavens. Hence, in The First Step of The First Station, which was written in Arabic and not included in this Ray, it was proclaimed as follows:

> There is no deity but God, the Necessarily Existent One, Whose necessary Existence in His Unity is demonstrated clearly by the heavens with whatever there is in them. This is testified to by the sublimely comprehensive, vast and perfect reality of subjugation, management, direction, ordering, cleansing, and employment, all of which are clearly observable.

THE SECOND STEP

Then the atmosphere, which is a place of wonders, begins to proclaim thunderously to that traveler who has arrived in the world as a guest, "Look at me! You can discover and know through me the One Whom you are seeking, the One Who has sent you to the world!" The traveler looks at the apparently sour, but compassionate face of the atmosphere, and listens to its roaring messages, awesome, yet laden with glad tidings. The traveler comes to observe the following:

The clouds, suspended between the sky and the earth, water the garden of the world in a most wise and merciful fashion, bringing the water of life to the inhabitants of the earth, modifying the natural heat of life, and running to provide aid wherever it is needed. Having fulfilled these and other duties, like a well-organized army that reveals or conceals itself instantaneously according to the commands given to it, the vast clouds, filling the atmosphere, suddenly hide themselves, retiring to rest with their constituent parts so that no trace can be seen. Then, when they receive the command: "March forth to pour down rain!" the clouds come together in an hour, or in a few minutes, filling the atmosphere and standing as though in readiness for further orders from their commander.

Next the traveler looks at the winds and sees that the air is employed wisely and generously in so many tasks that it is as if each of the unconscious atoms of the inanimate air were able to hear and understand the orders coming from the Sovereign of the universe. Without neglecting a single one of them, it carries out its Master's orders in a perfectly methodical fashion, through the Power of the Sovereign. That is, it gives breath to all beings on the earth, conveys to all living creatures the heat, light, and electricity they need, and transmits sound, as well as aiding in the pollination of plants. It is employed by an unseen Hand in these universal tasks in an extremely conscious, knowledgeable, and life-sustaining manner.

The traveler then looks at the rain and sees that in these delicate, shining, and sweet drops that have been sent from a hidden treasury of Mercy there are so many merciful gifts and tasks that it is as if mercy itself were embodied in rain and flowing forth from the Divine treasury in the form of drops. It is for this reason that rain is called "mercy."

Then the traveler looks at the lightning and listens to the thunder and sees that both of these, too, are employed in the most amazing and wonderful tasks.

Taking their eyes off these, the traveler then turns to their reason and says to themselves: "This inanimate, lifeless cloud that resembles carded cotton certainly has no knowledge of us, and it does not come to our aid on its own because it has no consciousness so that it may take pity on us. Nor can it appear and disappear without an external command. Rather, it must act in accordance with the commands of a most Powerful and Compassionate Commander. It disappears without leaving a trace and then suddenly emerges again to embark on its task. By the Decree and Power of a most active and transcendent, a most magnificent and self-manifesting Sovereign, from time to time it fills and empties the atmosphere. It turns the sky into a tablet upon which things are written and erased, inscribing with wisdom and effacing by halting for a while, thus displaying an example of the Resurrection. By the order of a most generous and bountiful, a most munificent and attentive Ruler and Director, it mounts the wind and is laden with the treasuries of rain as heavy as mountains, hastening to the aid of places in need. It is as if it were weeping with pity over those places, spraying gardens with water, causing them to smile with flowers, cooling the heat of the sun and cleansing the face of the earth."

The curious traveler then tells their reason: "These hundreds of thousands of wise, merciful, and ingenious tasks, and these acts of generosity and helpfulness which seem to occur by means of this lifeless, unconscious, unstable, stormy, unsettled, and inconstant air, which cannot possess a conscious aim, prove beyond all doubt that the wind, this assiduous servant, never acts of its own volition; rather, it merely carries out the command of a most powerful and knowing, a most wise and munificent Commander. It is as though each of its atoms were aware of every task and, like a soldier who understands and heeds every order of his commander, were able to hear and obey every Divine command that courses through the air. It serves the breathing and survival of all animals, facilitates the pollination and growth of all plants, and provides all of the substances vital for their existence. It also serves the movement and direction of the clouds, the driving forward of sailing ships and the transmittance of sounds uttered or sent particularly by means of wireless, telephone, telegraph, and radio. In addition to serving in these and other universal functions, and despite being a composition of two simple materials—nitrogen and oxygen—and resembling one another, the particles of air are employed in hundreds of thousands of different tasks with a perfect order by a Hand of wisdom.

> Surely in the creation of the heavens and the earth, and the alternation of night and day (with their periods shortening and lengthen-

> ing), and the vessels that sail the sea for profit to people, and the water that God sends down from the sky, therewith reviving the earth after its death and dispersing therein all kinds of living creatures, and His disposal of the winds, and the subservient clouds, resting between the sky and the earth—surely there are signs (demonstrating that He is the One God deserving worship, and the sole Refuge and Helper) for a people who reason and understand (2:164).

As stated in the above verse, the traveler concludes that the one who disposes of the winds and employs them in innumerable tasks of sustaining, maintaining, and nurturing; who subjugates the clouds so that they may be used in uncountable errands of mercy and who generates and employs the air in the fashion mentioned above—that such a being can be none other than the All-Majestic and All-Munificent Lord, One Who is Necessarily Existent, Who is All-Knowing and in possession of absolute Power over all things.

The traveler then looks at the rain and sees that it has as many merciful uses, benefits, and instances of wisdom as the number of drops contained in it. Moreover, these lovely, delicate, and blessed drops, as well as the drops of hail and snowflakes, are created so beautifully and with such order and are dispatched with such balance and regularity that not even those stormy winds which cause large objects to collide can destroy this order: the drops do not collide with one another or combine in such a way as to form harmful masses of water. This simple substance, water, which is composed of two simple, inanimate and unconscious elements—hydrogen and oxygen—is employed in hundreds of thousands of wise, purposeful tasks and arts, particularly in animate beings. This means that rain, which is the very embodiment of mercy, can be manufactured only in the unseen treasury of mercy of the One Who is All-Merciful. And through its descent it expounds in physical terms the verse: *He it is Who sends down the rain, useful in all ways, to rescue (them) after they have lost all hope, and spreads out His mercy far and wide (to every being). He it is Who is the Guardian, and the All-Praiseworthy* (42:28).

The traveler then listens to the thunder attentively and looks again at the lightning. He perceives that in addition to interpreting in physical terms the verses: *The thunder glorifies Him with His praise* (13:13), and *The flash of the lightning almost takes away the sight* (24:43), these two awe-inspiring atmospheric events also announce the coming of rain, thus giving glad tidings to those in need of it. And in causing the atmosphere to speak suddenly with an extraordinary uproar, in filling the dark atmosphere with the marvelous light and fire of lightning, and in setting alight the clouds that resemble mountains of cotton or spouts from which hail or snow or rain pours, these and other wondrous and wise phenomena strike blows on the heads of the negligent people who "look down and cannot see them." They warn, saying: "Lift up your heads and look at the wonderful acts of an Ever-Active and Powerful Being Who wills to make Himself known. Just as you are not left to your own devices, so too these phenomena are not random events left to chance. Each of them is employed in many wise tasks; each is employed by an All-Wise Director."

Thus, the curious traveler hears the loud and manifest testimony of a truth which is composed of the subjugation of the clouds, the disposal of the winds, the descent of the rain and the direction of atmospheric events, and says: "I believe in God." That which was pronounced in The Second Step of The First Station expresses the above-mentioned observations of the traveler concerning the atmosphere:

> There is no deity but God, the Necessarily Existent One, Whose Necessary Existence is demonstrated clearly by the atmosphere with whatever there is in it. This is testified to by the sublimely comprehensive, vast and perfect reality of subjugation, disposal, and causing to descend, and management or direction, all of which are clearly observable.

THE THIRD STEP

And then the earth addresses that reflective traveler, who has now been accustomed to their journey of reflection, in the tongue of its disposition: "Why are you wandering through space, through the heavens? Come, I will make known to you the One Whom you are seeking. Look at the tasks I carry out and read my pages!"

The traveler looks and sees that, like an ecstatic Mevlevi dervish, the earth, having two movements that are the means for the occurrence of days, seasons, and years, is drawing a circle around the Place of Supreme Gathering. They see that it is a magnificent, subjugated vessel which holds within itself hundreds of thousands of species of living creatures together with all the food and equipment needed by them, a vessel that is traveling around the sun in the ocean of space with perfect balance and order.

The traveler then looks at the pages or sheets of the earth and sees that each page of every chapter proclaims the existence of the Lord of the earth in thousands of its "verses." Having no time to read the entire work, they look at the page which describes the creation and administration of living creatures in spring, and observe the following:

The forms of the numberless members of hundreds of thousands of species are opened up from a simple material with the most extraordinary orderliness and precision; they are then nurtured and raised in a most merciful fashion. Subsequently, the seeds of some of these members are, in a most miraculous fashion, given wings and caused to fly, thus allowing them to be scattered over the earth. All these numberless members of hundreds of thousands of species are directed with the utmost efficiency and fed and nurtured with the greatest affection. Their countless, diverse, and delicious nourishment is provided and made to reach them in the most compassionate manner from nothing more than dry clay, drops of water, and seeds and roots that resemble bones, differing little one from the other. In the same way that cargo is loaded onto a goods wagon, hundreds of thousands of different kinds of food and equipment are loaded on every spring from an unseen treasury and are dispatched with perfect orderliness to living creatures. In particular, the sending of canned milk in these food packages, brought to the mouths of infants in the form of the sweet milk that springs forth from the affectionate breasts of their mothers, demonstrates such affection, compassion, and wisdom that it can clearly be seen to be the gift and most affectionate and attentive manifestation of the Mercy of an All-Merciful One.

In short: By displaying hundreds of thousands of examples of the Resurrection and Supreme Gathering, this living page of spring interprets in brilliant fashion the verse, *Look, then, at the imprints of God's Mercy—how He revives the dead earth after its death: certainly then it is He Who will revive the dead (in a similar way). He has full power over everything* (30:50). Similarly, this verse expresses in a miraculous fashion the meanings of that page. The traveler thus understands that with all its pages the earth proclaims "*There is no deity but He,*" in a fashion and with a strength that is proportionate to its size.

Through the brief testimony of one of the twenty aspects of a single page out of more than the twenty big pages of the earth, in The Third Step of The First Station, the observations the traveler made in the other pages of the earth were expressed as follows:

> There is no deity but God, the Necessarily Existent One, Whose Necessary Existence in His Unity is demonstrated clearly by the earth with whatever there is in and upon it. This is testified to by the sublimely comprehensive, vast and perfect reality of subjugation, management, raising, opening up, the distribution of seeds, preservation, administration, and the provision of all living creatures, and the all-encompassing and all-inclusive mercifulness and compassion, all of which are clearly observable.

The Fourth Step

Then, as that reflective traveler reads each page of the earth, their belief, which is the key to true happiness, begins to gain strength; their knowledge of God, the key to spiritual progress, increases, and the truth of belief in God, the source and foundation of all perfection, develops in them one degree more, bestowing upon them many spiritual pleasures and further arousing their curiosity and eagerness. Having listened to the perfect and convincing lessons taught to them by the heavens, the atmosphere, and the earth, the traveler asks: "Is there more?" At which point they hear the loud, rapturous invocations of God made by the seas and the great rivers which flow into them; they listen awhile to these mournful and pleasant sounds. Both verbally and with mute eloquence they are saying: "Look at us and read us too!" And so the traveler looks, and this is what they see:

Although the seas, which are constantly surging with life, and which have an innate tendency toward pouring forth and flooding the land, and are made to move together with the earth, which revolves around the sun so speedily that it in one year it covers a distance that a person could walk in twenty-five thousand years, they neither disperse nor overflow, never encroaching on the land at whose edge their waters lap. This means that they are made to move and are held in place by the command and power of a most powerful and sublime being.

Looking into the depths of the sea, the traveler sees that in addition to the extremely beautiful, well-adorned, and proportioned jewels, thousands of kinds of animals are provided for, maintained, brought to life and caused to die in a perfectly balanced and orderly fashion. They also see that these creatures are provided for from nothing more than mere sand and water, but in such a perfect way that beyond doubt they establish the Existence of an All-Powerful One of Majesty, an All-Compassionate One of Grace.

The traveler then looks at the rivers and sees that the benefits they supply, the tasks they carry out, and the waters which both flow in and out of them display such wisdom and mercy that they prove quite clearly that all rivers, springs and streams flow forth from the treasury of mercy of an All-Merciful One of Majesty and Munificence. They are fed, preserved and dispensed in such an extraordinary fashion that it has been reported from the Prophet, upon him be peace and blessings: "Four rivers originate from Paradise."[37] That is, since the reality of their flowing transcends apparent causes, they issue forth from the treasury of an immaterial heavenly source, from the superabundance of an unseen and inexhaustible wellspring.

The blessed Nile, for example, (the longest river of the world,) that turns the sandy land of Egypt into a paradise, originates from the Mountains of the Moon (or some highlands or hills or lakes) in central Africa and flows without exhaustion, as though it were a small sea. If the water it carries in six months were gathered together in the form of an iceberg, it would be larger than the mountains (or highlands or lakes) that act as its source. Yet the source of the river in those mountains does not equal even a sixth of their mass. As for the water which feeds the river, and the rain that enters its reservoir, they amount to very little in such a hot region and are quickly swallowed up by the thirsty soil; as a result they are incapable of maintaining the balance between the amount of the water being added to and flowing away from the river. Thus the Prophetic Tradition which says that the blessed Nile originates, in an extraordinary fashion, from an unseen heavenly source is extremely meaningful and expresses a beautiful reality.

Thus, the traveler sees a thousandth part of the ocean-like truths and testimonies contained in the oceans and rivers. All of these truths pronounce unanimously and with a power that is proportionate to the size of the seas, "*There is no deity but He*," while the seas produce as many witnesses for this testimony as all the creatures that inhabit them. This much the traveler perceives.

Intending and expressing the testimony of the seas and the rivers, it was in The Fourth Step of The First Station:

---

[37] *al-Bukhari*, "Bad'u'l-Khalq" 6; *Muslim*, "Iman" 264.

> There is no deity but God, the Necessarily Existent One, Whose Necessary Existence in His Unity is demonstrated clearly by all the seas and rivers with whatever there is in them. This is testified to by the sublimely comprehensive, vast and perfect reality of subjugation, preservation, storing, and management, all of which are clearly observable.

THE FIFTH STEP

Then the mountains and the plains summon that traveler on their journey of reflection, saying: "Read our pages too!" Looking, the traveler sees:

The universal tasks carried out by the mountains, along with the purposes they serve, are so great and full of wisdom that they astonish the mind. For instance, the mountains burst forth from the earth's crust by the command of their Lord and thereby calm down the unrest, anger and fury that arise from commotions within the bowels of the earth. Yet while the earth is delivered from the harmful tremors and upheavals within it and is allowed to breath through the bursting forth of these mountains, it does not disturb the rest or comfort of its inhabitants as it carries out its duty of rotation. Just as masts are placed on ships to protect them against turbulence and maintain their balance, according to the Qur'an of miraculous exposition, the mountains are like masts that have been planted on the deck of the vessel that is the earth:

> And the mountains as masts, (78:7)

> And the earth—We have spread it out, and set therein firm mountains, (15:19; 50:7)

> And the mountains He has set firm. (79:32)

Furthermore, prepared and stored up in the mountains are countless things that are needed by living beings, such as springs, waters, minerals and medicinal substances; these are stored up and preserved there in such a wise, skilful, generous and careful fashion that they can only be the storehouses and servants of one of infinite power and wisdom. This much the traveler deduces, and comparing with these two the other duties and instances of wisdom that are inherent in the mountains and plains, they can see the testimony they give and the Divine Unity they pronounce, saying, "*There is no deity but He*," through the general instances of wisdom hidden in them and, in particular, in regard to the things providentially stored up in them. And seeing that their pronouncement is as powerful and firm as the mountains and as vast and expansive as the plains themselves, the traveler too declares: "I believe in God."

As an expression of this meaning, it was said in the Fifth Step of the First Station:

> There is no deity but God, the Necessarily Existent One, Whose Necessary Existence is demonstrated clearly by all the mountains and plains, with whatever there is in or on them. This is testified to by sublimely comprehensive, vast and perfect reality of storing up and management, by the dissemination of seeds, the preservation and precautionary measures that are particular to Divine Lordship, all of which are clearly observable.

THE SIXTH STEP

Then as that traveler is journeying in their mind through the mountains and plains, the gateway to the world of trees and plants is opened to them. They are invited to enter with the words: "Come, travel through our world and read our inscriptions." Entering there, the traveler sees that they have formed a magnificent and well-adorned assembly that proclaims God's Unity and a circle that mentions Him by His Names and offers thanks to Him. The traveler can understand from the very appearance of all the trees and plants that, with all their species they unanimously proclaim: "*There is no deity but God.*" For they notice three great, universal realities which indicate and prove the fact that in the tongue of their well-proportioned and eloquent leaves, with the phrases of their richly-adorned and fluent flowers, and the words of their well-ordered and articulate fruits, all fruit-bearing trees and plants glorify God and testify to His Unity, saying "*There is no deity but He.*"

THE FIRST REALITY: Each of the plants and trees gives the clear impression that they have been provided with a deliberate purpose and are intentionally maintained. This fact is also observed in the totality of the trees and plants with the brilliance of sunlight.

THE SECOND REALITY: In the countless varieties and species a wise and purposeful distinguishing and differentiation, and a willful and compassionate fashioning, equipping and adorning, none of which is in any way attributable to chance, can be seen as clearly as daylight: they reveal quite clearly the fact that they are the works and embroideries of an All-Wise Maker.

THE THIRD REALITY: Each of the members of these hundreds of thousands of species of plants and trees is given a separate, distinct form with the most perfect order, balance, proportion and beauty, with vitality and wise purposefulness, and without the least error, from simple and solid seeds and grains that are identical or nearly identical to one another. This is a reality more brilliant than the sun and there are as many witnesses that prove this truth as there are flowers, fruits and leaves that appear in spring. The traveler perceives this and says: "All praise be to God for the blessing of belief."

As an expression of these realities and the testimonies given to them it was said in The Sixth Step of The First Station:

> There is no deity but God, the Necessarily Existent One, Whose Necessary Existence in His Unity is demonstrated clearly by all species of trees and plants, which glorify God and speak with the words of their well-proportioned, eloquent leaves, their fluent, richly-adorned flowers and their well-ordered, articulate fruits. This is testified to by the sublimely comprehensive, vast and perfect reality of purposeful and compassionate provision, bestowal and favoring, and of willful and wise distinguishing, adorning and fashioning, all of which are clearly observable. It is also clearly indicated by the fact that each of these trees and plants is given a well-proportioned, decorated, distinctive, separate form from similar or near-identical seeds and grains, all of which are finite and limited.

THE SEVENTH STEP

Then, as that curious traveler, whose journey of reflection becomes more pleasurable with every step, returns from the garden of spring with a bouquet of knowledge of God and belief, itself like a spring, the gateway to the realm of earth's animals and birds open before their truth-perceiving mind and intellect, which has by this time acquired knowledge of God to a certain degree. With hundreds of thousands of different voices and various tongues, they summon the traveler inside. Entering, they see that all the species, groups and nations of the animals and birds of the earth are pronouncing: "*There is no deity but He,*" both verbally and in the language of mute eloquence of their disposition, turning the earth into a vast assembly for the proclamation of God's Unity and the mentioning of Him by His Names. The traveler sees that they are describing their Maker and praising Him as if each is an ode dedicated to Him as the Lord, a word which glorifies Him or a letter that indicates His mercy. It is as if the senses, powers, members and instruments of these animals and birds are graceful, rhythmical, well-proportioned words, or perfect and orderly expressions. The traveler observes three great and comprehensive realities which indicate decisively that they offer thanks to their Creator and Provider and testify to His Unity.

The first reality: Animals and birds are brought into existence from nothing with wisdom, they are created and fashioned with complete artistry and perfect knowledge and given life in a way that displays in twenty aspects the manifestation of knowledge, wisdom and will—all of this, which occurs in such a way that it cannot be attributed to chance, testifies to the Necessary Existence, the Seven Essential Attributes, and the Unity of the All-Living, Self-Subsistent One—a testimony that is based on as many proofs as there are living beings.

The second reality: In the distinction of facial features which exists among these infinite beings, in their adorned forms, and in their perfectly calculated numbers and well-ordered fashioning, there appears a truth so magnificent and powerful that it is absolutely impossible and inconceivable for anyone other than the One Who has absolute Power and Knowledge to be able to achieve such a comprehensive act, an act that displays thousands of wonders and instances of wisdom in every respect.

The third reality: Each of the hundreds of thousands of species of these innumerable animals and birds is given in the most orderly and proportionate fashion and without the least error, a distinctive face and form—a miracle of wisdom—that emerges from eggs and drops of fluid called sperm, which are identical to or closely resemble one another. This is so brilliant a reality that it is illuminated by as many different proofs as there are animals and birds in existence.

Through the consensus of these three realities, all the species of animals testify together that "*There is no deity but He.*" It is as if the whole earth, like a vast human being, were saying "*There is no deity but He*," in a manner commensurate with its vastness, and conveying its testimony to the inhabitants of the heavens. The traveler sees this and understands it perfectly. As an expression of these realities, it was said in The Seventh Step of The First Station:

> There is no deity but God, the Necessarily Existent One, Whose Necessary Existence in His Unity is demonstrated clearly by all the species of the earth's animals and birds, which praise God and bear witness to Him with the measured, well-proportioned and fluent words of their senses, powers, and faculties, and with the perfect and eloquent words of their members, limbs, and organs. This is testified to by the sublimely comprehensive, vast and perfect reality of purposeful inventing, making, and originating, by the reality of purposeful distinguishing and adorning, and by the reality of wise determining, identifying, and fashioning, all of which are clearly observable. It is also decisively indicated by the fact that each of these animals and birds is given a well-ordered, different, and distinctive form that emerges from similar or seemingly-identical eggs and drops of fluid, all of which are finite and limited.

THE EIGHTH STEP

Afterwards, the reflective traveler wishes to enter the world of humanity in order to advance further in the infinite ranks and unlimited degrees of pleasure and the lights of knowledge of God. And thus, humankind, headed by the Prophets, invites the traveler inside. Entering there, and looking first into the vast mansion that is the past, the traveler sees that all of the Prophets, upon them be peace, who are the most luminous and perfect of all people, proclaim in unison: "*There is no deity but He.*" With the power of their innumerable brilliant and confirmed miracles, they are affirming and pronouncing God's Unity, and in order to raise humanity from the rank of animals to that of angels, they are instructing people in belief in God and summoning them to it. Kneeling down in that school of light, the traveler also pays heed to the lesson and observes the following:

All of these teachers, the most exalted and renowned of all celebrated human beings, have in their hands numerous miracles that have been bestowed on them by the Creator of the universe as a sign that confirms their mission. In addition, a large group of people, a whole community, has confirmed their claims and reached belief through their instruction. The traveler sees how powerful, decisive, and definitive a truth it is that was agreed on unanimously and confirmed by these more than one hundred thousand serious and veracious individuals. The traveler also understands that by denying a truth attested to and affirmed by so many absolutely truthful instructors, the people of misguidance are committing a most grievous error—nay, a crime—and are thus deserving of a most painful everlasting punishment. The traveler perceives, in contrast, how truly righteous are those who confirm the message of the Prophets and come to belief, and thus a further degree of the sanctity of belief becomes apparent to the traveler.

Apart from the innumerable miracles worked by the Prophets, upon them be peace, as a sign of God's actual confirmation of them and their mission; apart from the heavenly blows dealt to their opponents, which demonstrate the truthfulness of the Prophets; apart from their individual perfections and veracious teachings, which indicate their truthfulness and righteousness; apart from the strength of their faith, their supreme seriousness, and self-sacrifices, which demonstrate their honesty; apart from the sacred Books and Scrolls they hold in their hands, and apart from their countless pupils who have attained truth, perfection, and light by following them, thus proving the truthfulness of their paths—apart from all of these realities, the unanimous agreement of the Prophets, who are the most earnest conveyors of God's Messages, and their followers on all true, positive matters, and their concord, mutual support, and affinity in establishing and proving the same all constitute a proof so powerful that no power in the world is able to confront it, and no doubt or hesitation can be cast. The traveler comes to understand that belief in all the Prophets, upon them be peace, as one of the pillars of belief, is another source of power, and they derive great benefit of belief from the lessons that they taught.

In expression of the lessons learned by this traveler, in The Eighth Step of The First Station it was said:

> There is no deity but God, Whose Necessary Existence in His Unity is demonstrated clearly by the consensus of all the Prophets with the power of the manifest miracles which confirm (their missions and Messages) and are confirmed (by innumerable people and unanimously accepted reports).

THE NINTH STEP

While the questing traveler, who has derived an elevated taste of truth from the power of belief, is coming from the assembly of the Prophets, upon them be peace, they are invited to step into the schoolroom of the profound, veracious and purified scholars who confirm the claims of the Prophets, upon them be peace, with the most decisive and powerful proofs which reach the degree of certainty based on knowledge. Entering here, the traveler sees that with their profound studies and investigations, thousands of geniuses and hundreds of thousands of veracious and exalted scholars are first and foremost proving the necessity of God's Existence and His Unity, together with all other articles of belief, which are absolutely true. And they are doing this in a manner which leaves absolutely no room for doubt. Indeed, the fact that they unanimously agree on the principles and pillars of belief, despite the fact that they differ in their capacities and outlook, each of them leaning on their own firm and certain proof, constitutes in itself evidence so strong that it cannot be doubted. Or, rather, we can see that it can be doubted only if the doubter possesses more intelligence and perspicacity than all of these scholars combined, and only if they are able to counter their arguments with a single proof that is more compelling than all those of the scholars put together. Otherwise, the deniers can oppose them only in order to display their ignorance—their utter ignorance—and their obstinacy and biased inattention with respect to negative matters that admit neither denial nor affirmation. One with a biased inattention or who closes their eyes turns day into night only for themselves.

The traveler realizes that the lights which these respected and profound scholars disseminate from this magnificent and vast school have been illuminating half of the world for more than a thousand years. The traveler finds in these lights such moral and spiritual power that if all the people of denial were to come together against them, they would neither be able to confuse or shake the traveler.

In a brief reference to the lesson the traveler has learned in this school, in The Ninth Step of The First Station it was said:

> There is no deity but God, Whose Necessary Existence in His Unity is demonstrated clearly by the agreement of all the pure, saintly and veracious scholars with the power of their brilliant, certain and unanimous proofs.

The Tenth Step

As the reflective traveler, who eagerly desires to see the lights and pleasures in the strengthening and development of belief and in the progression from the degree of certainty that arises from knowledge to certainty that comes from vision or observation, is leaving the school of religious sciences, they receive another invitation. This time, it comes from the thousands, indeed, millions of spiritual guides who are working for the truth and have attained the rank of certainty of vision or observation along the highway of Muhammad and in the shade of his Ascension, upon him be peace and blessings. They invite the traveler into a vast, light-diffusing school of spiritual training, a place of the remembrance of God, which has been formed from the merging of countless small schools of spiritual illumination.

Entering here, the traveler sees that these spiritual guides, who are the masters of extraordinary deeds and adept at unveiling the Divine truths and spiritual mysteries, are proclaiming in unison "*There is no deity but He*" on the basis of their unveilings, visions, and wonder-working, and to the entire universe they announce the necessary Existence and Unity of the Lord. The traveler sees here how clear and self-evident this truth is, a truth upon which all of these sacred genius and luminous savants have achieved total consensus, even though they follow numerous different spiritual paths. The traveler sees how, in the same way that the sun radiates seven colors in its light and is known through them, these luminous individuals are, in their knowledge of God, holding fast to an array of colors emitted by the Sun of Eternity, as great in number as the All-Beautiful Names of God Himself. The traveler sees that the supreme consensus formed through the unanimity of the Prophets, the agreement of the purified and veracious scholars and the accord of the saints is more brilliant than the daylight which makes known the existence of the sun.

In a brief reference to the rays of light received by the traveler from the school of spiritual training, in The Tenth Step of The First Station it was said:

> There is no deity but God, Whose Necessary Existence in His Unity is demonstrated clearly by the agreement of the saints with their manifest, verified, and confirmed spiritual discoveries and extraordinary deeds or achievements.

THE ELEVENTH STEP

The traveler is now aware that the greatest and most important of all human perfections, indeed the very origin and foundation of all such perfections, is the love of God that arises from belief in God and knowledge of Him. With this in mind, the traveler wishes with all their strength and faculties to advance still further in strengthening their belief and in the development of their knowledge. And thus the traveler raises their head and, gazing at the heavens, addresses their own reasoning mind as follows:

"Because the most valuable thing in the universe is life and all things in the universe are subservient to life, and because the most valuable beings among all living beings are those which are endowed with spirit, and because the most valuable among beings endowed with spirit are those who are conscious, and because each century and each year the earth is emptied and refilled in order to increase without cessation the number of living beings due to their value—because of all this, one must undoubtedly conclude that these splendid and ornate heavens must also have living, conscious inhabitants that are peculiar to them. Experiences relating to seeing and speaking with the angels—such as the appearance of Archangel Gabriel, upon him be peace, in the form of a human being in the presence of Prophet Muhammad, upon him be peace and blessings, in full view of the Companions—have been transmitted and related from the most ancient times through reliable channels of transmission. Given that this is so, if only I could talk to the inhabitants of the heavens and learn their views on this matter. For their words concerning the Creator of the universe are of utmost importance."

As the traveler is thinking thus, he suddenly hears a heavenly voice: "If you wish to meet us and hear our words, then know that we before all others have believed in the truths of belief that we conveyed to the Prophets, and first and foremost to Prophet Muhammad, upon him be peace and blessings, who brought the Qur'an of miraculous exposition.

"Furthermore, all of the pure spirits from among us who have appeared before human beings have, unanimously and without exception, borne witness to the necessary Existence and sacred Attributes of the Creator of the universe, and proclaimed this with one accord. The concord and mutual correspondence of these uncountable proclamations is a guide for you that is as bright as the sun." As a result, the traveler's light of belief grows more radiant and ascends from the earth to the heavens.

In a brief reference to the lesson the traveler has learned from the angels, it was said in The Eleventh Step of The First Station:

> There is no deity but God, Whose Necessary Existence in His Unity is demonstrated clearly by the agreement of the angels who appear to human beings in human form and who speak to the spiritually distinguished ones among humankind with their mutually corresponding and conforming messages.

THE TWELFTH AND THIRTEENTH STEPS

Then the extremely inquisitive and ardent traveler, who has already learned from the tongues and dispositions of various species and nations that belong to the visible realm, expresses the desire to travel through the realm of the Unseen and the Intermediate Realm in further pursuit of the truth. And so there opens before them a door that leads to the world of upright and enlightened intellects and of sound and illuminated hearts, which are like the seeds of humankind, the fruit of the universe, and which can expand to embrace virtually the whole of the universe, despite their small size. The traveler looks and sees that these intellects and hearts form a link between the Unseen and visible realms, and that the contacts and exchanges between these two realms which relate to humankind occur at this point. Addressing their reason and heart, the traveler says: "Come, the path leading to the truth through the gate of these counterparts of yours is shorter. We should benefit from studying the qualities, natures, and colors that belief has given them, in a manner different from that which we have employed in learning through the tongues which pertain to previous paths."

Beginning this study, the traveler sees that the belief and firm conviction concerning Divine Unity which all upright and enlightened intellects possess and display throughout their lives is, despite their varying capacities and their different and sometimes opposing methods and outlooks, in complete accordance; the traveler sees that their constant and ever-confident certainty and assurance are as one. This means that they are holding fast to a single, unchanging truth: their roots have penetrated deeply into this truth and cannot be pulled out. As a result, their agreement concerning belief and the necessary Existence and Unity of God is like a luminous, unbreakable chain, a brightly lit window that opens onto the truth.

The traveler also sees that the rapturous spiritual discoveries and visions of all these sound and illuminated hearts concerning the pillars of belief are, despite their different spiritual paths, in correspondence with one another, and that they are in absolute agreement on Divine Unity. All of these illuminated hearts, each of which is an embodiment of truth, a small throne of knowledge of God and a comprehensive mirror that is held up to the Eternally Besought One, are like windows that open onto the sun of the truth. Taken together, they are a supreme mirror, like an ocean that reflects the sun. Their agreement and unanimity concerning the necessary Existence and Unity of God is an unfailing and most perfect guide, a most elevated master. For it is in no way possible or conceivable that any false assumption or erroneous belief should be able to delude or deceive so many sharp, truth-seeing eyes at the same time. Not even the foolish sophists, who denied the existence of the universe, could agree with the corrupt and dissipated intellect that deemed such a thing possible. Understanding all of this, our traveler says with their heart and intellect: "I have come to believe in God."

In a brief reference to the knowledge of belief which the traveler has learned from upright intellects and illuminated hearts, in The Twelfth and Thirteenth Steps of The First Station it was said:

> There is no deity but God, the Necessarily Existent, Whose Necessary Existence in His Unity is demonstrated clearly by the unanimous agreement of all upright, enlightened intellects, with their congruent creeds, their convictions and corresponding certainties, despite their differences in capacity and outlook. His Necessary Existence in His Unity is also demonstrated by the agreement of all sound, illuminated hearts, with their mutually supporting discoveries and their congruent observations and visions, despite their varying paths and methods.

THE FOURTEENTH AND FIFTEENTH STEPS

Then that traveler, who is journeying with their mind and heart, begins to look at the Realm of the Unseen more closely. Knocking inquisitively on the door of that world in order to learn its message, they think to himself: "It is obvious that behind the veil of the Unseen is One Who wills to make Himself known through all these innumerable, finely adorned artifacts in the visible world; He wills to make Himself loved through these countless, sweet, and adorned bounties, and to make His hidden Perfections known through these uncountable, miraculous, and skilful works of Art. It is clear that there is One Who reveals His will to make Himself known and loved, and to make His hidden Perfections known, in a manner more manifest than speech. Given this, just as He reveals His will through acts and deeds, it is clear that He must also make Himself known and loved through speech. Thus, we must know Him from His manifestations with regard to the World of the Unseen." Thinking this, the traveler enters that world with their heart and sees the following with the eye of their intellect:

The truth of the Revelations prevails at all times throughout the World of the Unseen as the most powerful means of manifestation. A testimony to God's Existence and Unity that is much more powerful than that of the universe and its contents proceeds from the One All-Knowing of the Unseen through the truths of Revelation and inspiration. He does not restrict the recognition and affirmation of Himself, His Existence, and Unity to the testimony of His creatures alone. Rather, He speaks with a pre-eternal Speech which befits His own Being. The Speech of the One Who is Omnipresent everywhere with His Knowledge and Power is also infinite, and just as the meaning of His Speech makes Him known, His discourse also makes Himself known together with His Attributes.

The truth of Revelation has been established and made clear to a self-evident degree through the consensus of more than one hundred thousand Prophets, may peace be upon them, and through the fact that all the instructions and proclamations of these Prophets are based on Divine Revelation; it has also been made clear through the evidence and miracles contained in the sacred Books and heavenly Scrolls, which are the fruits of Revelation and guides for all human beings, the overwhelming majority of whom have confirmed the truths therein. Realizing this, the traveler understands further that the truth of Revelation sets forth the following five sacred realities.

THE FIRST REALITY: Revelation is a form of Divine kindness or condescension and is described as "God's lowering His speech to the level of human capacity so that they can understand it." God enables all of His conscious creatures to speak and understands their speeches, so it is a requirement of His being the Lord of all creation that He participates in them with His own speech.

THE SECOND REALITY: The One Who, in order to make Himself known, has created a universe filled with miraculous, invaluable artifacts that cause countless tongues to speak of His Perfections, will, self-evidently, make Himself known with His own words also.

THE THIRD REALITY: It is a characteristic of His being the Creator that God responds with His speech, as He does with His deeds, to the supplications and thanks that are offered by the most select, the neediest, the most delicate and the most ardent of His beings—those who are truly human.

THE FOURTH REALITY: The attribute of speech, which is an essential requirement of knowledge and life and a luminous manifestation of both, will by necessity be found in a comprehensive and eternal form in the Being Who has comprehensive Knowledge and eternal Life.

THE FIFTH REALITY: It is a consequence of Divinity that the Being Who endows His most loved and lovable, His most anxious and indigent creatures—those who are most in need of a point of reliance and who are most desirous of finding their Owner and Master—with innate impotence and yearning, poverty and need, worries about the future, and love and adoration—it is a consequence of His Divinity that He should communicate His own Existence to them by way of His speech. Thus, the universal, heavenly Revelations, which involve the realities of God's lowering His speech to the level of human understanding, His will as the Lord to make Himself known, and His merciful response, majestic conversation, and self-communication as the Eternally Besought One, bear unanimous witness to the Existence and Unity of the Necessarily Existent One. This testimony is a proof that is more powerful than the testimony of the rays of sunlight to the existence of the sun. This is what the traveler has come to understand.

The traveler then considers the gift of inspiration and sees that true inspiration resembles the Revelation in one respect and is a form of the Lord's discourse. However, Revelation and inspiration differ in two respects:

THE FIRST DIFFERENCE: Revelation, which is much more exalted than inspiration, is generally conveyed by angels, whereas inspiration generally comes directly.

For example, a king has two ways to speak and communicate his orders. The first is that, in the name of the glory of his kingdom and his sovereignty over the whole country, he sends a lieutenant to a governor. Sometimes, in order to demonstrate the magnificence of his sovereignty and the importance of his imperial order, he may hold a meeting with his lieutenant, and then the decree is conveyed to the governor. The second is that he speaks on his private phone, not with the title of monarch or in the name of kingship, but in his own person, to a trusted servant or some ordinary subject with whom he has a special relationship or a particular business.

Similarly, the Pre-Eternal Sovereign may either, with the Name, the Lord of all the worlds and with the Title, the Creator of the universe, speak through Revelation or the comprehensive inspiration that has the function of Revelation, or He may speak in a private fashion, as the Lord and Creator of every and each living being, from behind a veil and in accordance with the capacities of the addressee.

THE SECOND DIFFERENCE: Revelation is clear, pure and reserved for the most elect. Inspiration, however, is not as clear as Revelation; colors may intervene in it and it is more general. There are numerous different kinds of inspiration, such as that which comes to angels, that which occurs to human beings, and that which is vouchsafed to animals; inspiration thus forms a field for the multiplication of God's words to the extent of the drops in the oceans. The traveler understands that the multiplication of God's words is a kind of commentary on the verse: *Say: "If all the sea were ink to write my Lord's words, the sea would indeed be exhausted before my Lord's words would be exhausted, even if We were to bring the like of it in addition to it."* (18:109)

Then the traveler looks at nature, wisdom, testimony, and the result of inspiration and sees that they comprise the following four lights:

THE FIRST LIGHT: This emerges because God is the All-Loving and the All-Merciful and thus He makes Himself loved through word, presence, and conversation just as He makes Himself loved by His creatures through His deeds.

THE SECOND LIGHT: This is a consequence of God's being the All-Compassionate; in the same way that He answers His servants' prayers in the form of deeds, He also answers them in words, from behind veils.

THE THIRD LIGHT: God's Lordship demands that just as He responds in deed to the pleas and cries for help of those creatures of His who have been afflicted with grievous tribulations and hardships, He also comes to their aid with words of inspiration, which are like a form of His speech.

THE FOURTH LIGHT: Just as God makes His existence, presence, and protection perceptible through His deeds to those among His conscious creatures who are poor, weak, and most in need of finding their Master, Protector, Guardian, and Preserver, it is also a consequence of His being the All-

Affectionate Deity and the All-Compassionate Lord that He should also communicate His presence and existence by speech, through the filter of true inspiration—a mode of His discourse as the Lord—to individuals in a manner befitting them and their capacities, through the "telephone" of their hearts. This the traveler has come to understand.

The traveler then looks at the testimony of inspiration and sees that, for example, if the sun possessed consciousness and life, with the seven colors in its light being its seven attributes— like the seven positive or affirmative Attributes of God—then it would also possess a kind of speech through the rays and manifestations of its light. As it has reflections and images in all transparent things, it would speak to all mirrors, shining objects, fragments of glass, bubbles and droplets of water in accordance with the capacity of each. It would respond to the needs of everything in which it is reflected and all of these would testify to the existence of the sun. Furthermore, none of its acts would form obstacles to other acts, and addressing one object would not prevent it from addressing all other objects simultaneously. Similarly, the Speech of the Sun of Eternity, the eternal All-Majestic Sovereign, the All-Glorious, All-Gracious Creator of all things, Which is universal and all-encompassing, like His Knowledge and Power, manifests Itself according to the capacity of each thing or being. Its response to one request does not form an obstacle to Its response to all other requests, nor does any task It performs prevent Its fulfillment of other tasks. No matter how many beings It addresses, It never becomes confused. The traveler comes to understand, to the degree of certainty based on knowledge and vision, that all these manifestations, conversations, and inspirations—separately and together—bear unanimous witness to the Omnipresence and necessary Existence of that Sun of Eternity and to His Unity and Oneness.

In a brief reference to the lesson the inquisitive traveler has received regarding knowledge of God from the World of the Unseen, it was said in The Fourteenth and Fifteenth Steps of The First Station:

> There is no deity but God, the Necessarily Existent One, the Single and the All-Unique, Whose Necessary Existence in His Unity is demonstrated clearly by the consensus of all true Revelations that involve God's lowering His Speech to the level of human understanding, His glorious discourses, His self-communication as the Lord, His responses to the pleas of His servants as the All-Merciful, and His in-

> dications of His Existence to His creatures as the Eternally Besought One. His necessary Existence in His Unity is also demonstrated by the unanimous agreement of all veracious inspirations that involve instances of God's making Himself loved, His responses to the prayers of His creatures as the All-Merciful, His responses to the appeals of His servants for help as their Lord, and His intimations of His Existence and Omnipresence to His creatures as the All-Glorified.

THE SIXTEENTH STEP

The traveler then addresses their own intellect, saying: "Since I am seeking the Creator and Owner of this universe by means of these creatures, I should first visit the most renowned of His creatures—one who, as confirmed even by his enemies, is the most perfect of them, and the most accomplished commander, the most celebrated ruler, the most exalted orator and possessor of the most brilliant intellect. I should visit the person who has illuminated the past fourteen centuries with his virtues and with the Qur'an: Muhammad the Arabian, upon him be peace and blessings. We should go together to the Age of Happiness in order to ask him about that which I seek." And so the traveler enters that age together with their intellect and sees that, thanks to Muhammad, upon him be peace and blessings, this was an age of true happiness; this man had transformed a most primitive and illiterate people into the masters and teachers of the world and he had done this in a very short time by means of the light he brought.

The traveler says to their intellect: "First of all, we must know as a certainty the value of this extraordinary being, the veracity of his words and the truthfulness of his messages. Then we should ask him about our Creator." And so the traveler begins to investigate. Here we will refer briefly to nine of the countless universal and conclusive proofs that the traveler finds. They are as follows:

FIRST: This person, upon him be peace and blessings, possessed all possible laudable virtues and excellent characteristics; this was affirmed even by his enemies. In addition, it has been reported through reliable channels of transmission that hundreds of miracles were performed by his hands, such as the splitting of the moon with a mere gesture, or causing many soldiers to flee by tossing a handful of soil at them—miracles which are referred to in the verses, *And the moon split* (54:1), and *It was not you who threw when you threw, but God threw* (8:17). He also famously quenched an entire army's thirst with water that flowed forth in abundance from his fingers. In fact, more than three hundred of these miracles have been set forth with decisive proofs in The Nineteenth Letter, known as *Miracles of Prophet Muhammad*. Readers wishing to learn about the Prophet's other miracles should refer to that treatise. And so the traveler concludes: "One who in addition to his most noble characteristics and perfections performs such clear miracles must be the most truthful in speech. How could he ever lower himself to lies and trickery, which are the vices of vile people?"

SECOND: Prophet Muhammad, upon him be peace and blessings, holds in his hand the Decree of the universe's Owner, namely the mighty, glorious Qur'an, which has been accepted and confirmed in every century by hundreds of millions of people. The fact that the Qur'an is the word of the Creator of the universe and is miraculous in at least forty aspects has been explained with convincing proofs in The Twenty-fifth Word, known as *Miraculousness of the Qur'an*. Readers interested in learning more about those aspects should refer to that treatise. Understanding this, the traveler says: "The translator, expounder and conveyor of such a Decree of pure truth could not lie, for that would violate the Decree and betray its Owner."

THIRD: Consider the following:

- Prophet Muhammad, upon him be peace and blessings, appeared with a Sacred Law, a Religion, a code of worship, a mode of prayer, a message and a way of belief the like of which has never existed. And without him, none of these could ever have come to pass. The peerless Law brought by that unlettered Prophet has ruled over one-fifth of humankind for fourteen centuries in a just and precise manner.
- Islam, which originated in and is represented by the Prophet's deeds, sayings, states, and example, is also without peer. Regardless of time or place, it has served hundreds of millions of people as a guide and competent authority in their lives. It has taught and trained their minds, illuminated and purified their hearts, trained and refined their souls, and perfected their spirits.
- Prophet Muhammad, upon him be peace and blessings, is the best example of the mode of worship that is prescribed by Islam; he is the most God-conscious and God-revering person of all. He worshipped

with the utmost care and attention, down to even the minutest details, during times of great peril and throughout a life of constant struggle and activity. He imitated no one in his worship, and perfectly combined the alpha and omega of spiritual evolution.

- His prayers and his knowledge of God are similarly unparalleled: with *al-Jawshanu'l-Kabir* alone, which is just one of his thousands of prayers and supplications, he describes his Lord with such a degree of knowledge that no saint or gnostic has ever been able to achieve a similar degree, despite their having been able to build upon the achievements of their predecessors. Even a cursory study of just one of the ninety-nine parts of *al-Jawshanu'l-Kabir* will show that there can never be another one even remotely like it.
- While conveying his message and calling his people to the truth, the Prophet, upon him be peace and blessings, displayed such steadfastness and courage that he never faltered or hesitated. And this was despite the hostilities of the surrounding powers and religions, as well as those of his own people and tribe, including even his uncle. He successfully challenged the whole world, thereby making Islam superior to all other religions and systems. This proves that no other person can equal him in his preaching to humankind or his calling them to the message of truth.
- His belief was so extraordinarily strong and assured, so miraculously developed and ingrained in his heart, and so elevated and world-enlightening that none of the ideas, beliefs, philosophies or spiritual teachings prevalent at the time could engender any doubt within him. Despite the opposition and hostility of his enemies, they were unable to shake him or make him unsure of his cause. Moreover, the saints of all ages, first and foremost his Companions, who have advanced in spirituality and through the various degrees of belief, have always benefited from his faith, which they admit to be of the highest degree. This proves that his belief is also without peer.

The traveler who seeks God thus understands and, with his intellect, concludes that lying and deception can have had no place in the traits of one who brought such a unique law and peerless Religion, who displayed such a wonderful form of worship and extraordinary excellence in prayer, whose preaching was admired the world over, and whose belief was at a degree of miraculous perfection.

FOURTH: Just as the consensus of the Prophets forms very strong proof of God's Existence and Oneness, it also represents a sound testimony to that exalted person's truthfulness and Messengership. For history confirms that he possesses to the utmost degree all of the sacred attributes, miracles and duties that indicate a Prophet's mission and veracity. Just as the previous Prophets predicted his coming by giving glad tidings of him in the Torah, the Gospels, the Psalms, and other Scriptures—more than twenty of the clearest of these joyous predictions have been set forth in The Nineteenth Letter—they also confirmed him with their own missions and miracles, attesting to the truthfulness of this person, who is the most perfect in carrying out the mission and tasks of Prophethood, in effect putting their signature to his claims. The traveler perceives that all of the previous Prophets bore witness to this person's truthfulness through the unanimity of their actions, just as they testified to God's Oneness through verbal consensus.

FIFTH: Having attained truth, perfection, the rank of working wonders, insight into the reality of things, and spiritual discovery and vision by following that person's deeds and principles, thousands of saints bear witness unanimously to God's Oneness and to the truthfulness and Messengership of that person, who is their master. The fact that through the light of their sainthood the saints witness some of the truths he proclaimed concerning the World of the Unseen, and through the light of belief they believe in and confirm all of these at the degrees of certainty of knowledge or certainty of vision or certainty of experience, demonstrates in a manner more brilliant than the sun the extent of the truthfulness and rectitude of that person, who is their master.

SIXTH: Millions of exacting, meticulous, purified, and truthful scholars and sages, all of whom have reached the highest station of learning through the teaching contained in the sacred truths that have been brought by that unlettered person, through the sublime sciences which he introduced, and through the knowledge of God which he discovered—all prove and affirm with unanimity not only God's Oneness, which is the foundation of Prophet Muhammad's mission, but also the truthfulness of that supreme master and the veracity of his words. This is proof of his Messengership and truthfulness that is as clear as daylight.

SEVENTH: After the Prophets, the Family and Companions of Prophet Muhammad, upon him be peace and blessings, are the most elevated in insight, discernment, and perfection; they are the most renowned, respected, pious, and keen-sighted members of humankind. Having thoroughly scrutinized all of the Prophet's thoughts and his hidden and apparent states and conditions, they have concluded unanimously that he was the noblest and most truthful and honest person in the world. The traveler understands that such an unshakable affirmation of him from such extraordinary people proves the truth of his cause, just as daylight proves the existence of the sun.

EIGHTH: This universe indicates the Maker, Author, Inscriber and Designer Who determined and fashioned it and Who controls and administers it like a palace, a book, and an exhibition of marvels. Given this, there should therefore exist an exalted herald, a truthful revealer, an exacting master, and a veracious teacher who knows and makes known the Divine purpose behind the creation of the universe, who teaches others about the Divine wisdom that underpins the universe's purposeful motions and transformations, who declares its inherent value and the perfections of the creatures in it, and who expounds the meanings of this great cosmic book. The traveler comes to realize that the one carrying out such duties most perfectly is the most truthful in his cause, serving as the most trusted and exalted officer of the Creator of the universe.

NINTH: Behind the veil of creation is One Who, through these purposeful and skilled works, wills that His perfect skills and artistry be displayed. Behind that veil there is One who wills to make Himself known and loved through the countless adorned creatures that He brings into being, and to evoke praise and thanksgiving in return for His boundless precious bounties, encouraging worship with gratitude and appreciation for His Lordship by means of His affectionate and protective sustaining of life, as well as by satisfying the most delicate tastes and appetites that His creatures possess. He also wills to demonstrate His Divinity through His wise and awe-inspiring creativity and through the magnificent, majestic, and purposeful activity that is displayed, for example, during the changes of seasons and the alternation of day and night—all of this so that humankind may come to believe in, submit to, and obey Him in His Divinity. Furthermore, He wills the manifestation of His Justice, Rightfulness, and Uprightness by protecting virtue and the virtuous while destroying evil and those who perpetrate it, and by annihilating liars and oppressors with heavenly blows.

Thus, the most beloved creation and the most devoted servant in the sight of that Unseen Being will certainly be the one who serves the above-mentioned Divine purposes to the highest degree. This will be one who discloses the mystery and talisman of the creation of the universe, who always acts in the name of His Creator, and who asks Him alone for help and success, and receives both. This is Prophet Muhammad al-Qurayshi, upon him be peace and blessings.

The traveler addresses their reason or intellect, saying: "Since these nine truths testify to the truthfulness of that person, he must undoubtedly be the source of humanity's honor and the pride of the world. Therefore he is worthy of being called 'the Pride of the World' and 'the Glory of Humankind.' Moreover, the Qur'an, that miraculous Word and Decree of the All-Merciful which this person held in his hand has drawn half of the old world into its magnificent spiritual domain. Together with the Messenger's personal perfections and elevated virtues, it shows that he is the most important being in the world, and accordingly that his words about our Creator are the most important."

Come now and see! Based on the strength of his hundreds of miracles and thousands of sublime, established truths contained in Islam, his sole aim was to prove and bear witness to the Necessarily Existent Being's Existence and Oneness, and to proclaim Him with all His Attributes and Names. He is the "spiritual sun" that enlightens the universe, our Creator's most brilliant proof and the "Beloved of God." Each of the following forms of great, truthful, and unshakable consensus affirms and corroborates the witness that he bears:

First: The unanimous confirmation of the illustrious community known and celebrated as Muhammad's Family and descendants, among whom are thousands of spiritual poles and supreme saints who have such keen spiritual insight that they can even penetrate into the Unseen. Imam 'Ali, for instance, said: "Were the veil to be lifted from the Unseen, my certainty would not increase."[38] And then there is 'Abdul-Qadir al-Jilani, who

[38] as-Subki, *Tabaqatu'sh-Shafi'iyatu'l-Kubra*, 6:61.

observed God's Supreme Throne and the Archangel Israfil's awesome form while still on this earth.[39]

Second: The unanimous confirmation of the Companions, which was based on a belief so strong that they were prepared to sacrifice their lives and properties, their parents and their tribes for its sake. Although brought up among a primitive people and in a climate of ignorance devoid of any positive notions about social life or administration, devoid of a guiding Scripture and immersed into the darkness of the uncivilized era when there were no Prophets, these people began to follow in Muhammad's footsteps and soon became the masters, guides, and just rulers of the most civilized and socio-politically advanced peoples and states of their time.

Third: The unanimous confirmation, which is based on certainty of knowledge, of innumerable exacting and profound scholars among his Community. Each century has seen thousands of people like these who have become extraordinarily advanced in every branch of science and art.

Thus, this person's testimony to God's Existence and Unity is so universal and unshakable that even if all beings hostile to it were to unite, they would still be unable to challenge it. Such is the conclusion reached by the traveler. In reference to the lesson which the traveler learned in that school of light while visiting the Age of Happiness in their mind, it was said in The Sixteenth Step of The First Station:

> There is no deity but God, the Necessarily Existent One, the Single and Unique, Whose necessary Existence in His Unity is demonstrated clearly by the Pride of the World and the Glory of the children of Adam, through the majesty of the Qur'an's sovereignty, the splendor of Islam's inclusiveness, the multiplicity of his perfections, and the sublimity of his moral qualities, as confirmed even by his enemies. Again, he bears witness through the strength of hundreds of miracles that prove his truthfulness and which have been firmly established, and through the strength of thousands of evident and decisive truths contained in his Religion, as affirmed by the consensus of his illustrious, light-diffusing Family and descendants, the agreement of his Companions with penetrating sight and prudence, and the concord of the scholars of his Community with their enlightening proofs and insight.

---

[39] Diyau'd-Din al-Gumushhanawi, *al-Majmu'atu'l-Ahzab*, 561.

THE SEVENTEENTH STEP

The tireless and insatiable traveler, who realizes the aim and essence of life in this world to be belief, addresses their own heart and says: "Let us have recourse to the book known as the Qur'an of miraculous exposition, which is said to be the Word of the Being Whom we are seeking: let us examine 'the most famous, most brilliant and wisest book' in the world, one which issues a challenge in every age to whoever refuses to submit to it. Let us see what it says. But first, we must establish that this book is from our Creator." Saying this, they begin to investigate.

Since the traveler lives in the present age, they first look at the *Risale-i Nur*, which comprises gleams from the miraculousness of the Qur'an, and they see that its one hundred and thirty parts consist of the subtle meanings, lights and well-founded explanations of certain verses from that Criterion between truth and falsehood—the Qur'an. They understand from its content and forceful diffusion and defense of the Qur'anic truths in this age of obstinacy and unbelief that the Qur'an, its master, source, authority, and sun, is a revealed book. Among the hundreds of proofs for the Divine authorship of the Qur'an in the different parts of the *Risale-i Nur*, The Twenty-fifth Word, which is a single proof of the Qur'an, and the end of The Nineteenth Letter establish forty aspects of the Qur'an's miraculousness in such a way that whoever sees them will not only raise any criticism or objection but will also have to appreciate their arguments highly. Therefore, leaving the establishment of the Qur'an as God's Word and the explanation of its various aspects of miraculousness to the *Risale-i Nur*, the traveler notices a few points that briefly demonstrate the Qur'an's greatness.

FIRST POINT: Just as the Qur'an, with all its aspects of miraculousness and truths that show its veracity is a miracle of Prophet Muhammad, upon him be peace and blessings, Prophet Muhammad himself, with all his miracles, proofs of Prophethood and perfections of knowledge is a miracle of the Qur'an and a decisive proof that it is the Word of God.

SECOND POINT: As well as bringing about a substantial, happy, and enlightening transformation in human social life, the Qur'an has brought about a revolution in the souls, hearts, spirits, and intellects of people, and in their individual, social, and political lives. Furthermore, it has perpetuated this revolution in such a way that at every moment over the past fourteen centuries it has been read with the utmost respect by more than a hundred million people, training and refining their souls and purifying their hearts. For spirits it has been a means of development and advancement; for intellects, a guidance and light; and for life, it has been life itself and felicity. Such a book is without doubt unparalleled in every respect: it is a wonder, a marvel and a miracle.

THIRD POINT: From the age of its revelation down to the present day, the Qur'an has demonstrated such eloquence that it caused the value attached to the "Seven Hanging Poems"—poems which were recognized as the best, written in gold and hung on the walls of the Ka'ba during the Age of Ignorance—to decrease to such a low level that when taking down her father's ode from the Ka'ba, the daughter of (the famous poet) Labid said:[40] "Compared with the verses of the Qur'an, this no longer has any worth."

A Bedouin poet once heard the recitation of the verse which means: *Proclaim what you are commanded to convey openly and in an emphatic manner* (15:94) and immediately prostrated. When they asked him: "Have you become a Muslim?" he replied: "No! I was merely prostrating before the eloquence of this verse!"[41]

Also, thousands of scholars, authors and geniuses of the science of eloquence and rhetoric, such as 'Abdu'l-Qahir al-Jurjani,[42] Sakkaki[43] and Zamakhshari,[44] have unanimously concluded that the eloquence of the Qur'an is beyond human capacity and cannot be replicated by any created being.

---

40 Labid was one of the leading poets of the Age of Ignorance—the age before the advent of the Prophet, upon him be peace and blessings. He lived long enough to witness the Prophethood of Muhammad, upon him be peace and blessings, and accepted Islam. (Tr.)

41 as-Suyuti, *al-Itqan*, 2:149.

42 'Abdu'l-Qahir al-Jurjani (1010–1079) was one of the most leading scholars of the language of literature of Arabic. He was known as the master of eloquence. *Asraru'l-Balagha* ("Mysteries of Eloquence") and *Dalailu'l-I'jaz* ("Evidences of Inimitability") are his most famous books. (Tr.)

43 Abu Ya'qub Yusuf ibn Abu Bakr al-Sakkaki (?–1229) was one of the leading scholars of the Arabic language and rhetoric. *Miftahul-'Ulum* ("Key to Sciences") and *al-Miftah fi'n-Nahw wa't-Tasrif wa'l-Bayan* ("A Key to Grammar, Inflection, and Syntax and Style") are among his most well-known works. (Tr.)

44 Abu'l-Qasim Jarullah Mahmud ibn 'Umar az-Zamakhshari (1075–1144) was a *Mu'tazili* scholar of Islam, one among the most well-known interpreters of the Qur'an. He lived in Kwarazm. His interpretation of the Qur'an called *al-Kashshaf* was famous for its deep linguistic analysis of the verses. (Tr.)

Moreover, from the outset, the Qur'an has also challenged all arrogant and egoistic poets and rhetoricians by saying, in a manner that will bring down their arrogance: "(If you do not believe that I am the Word of God, then) either produce a single *sura* like mine or accept perdition and humiliation in this world and the Hereafter." Despite this challenge, the obstinate rhetoricians of that age abandoned the shorter route of attempting to produce a single *sura* like the Qur'an and instead chose the longer route of (fighting against it and) casting their persons and property into danger. This proves that the shorter route cannot be taken.

Millions of Arabic books are in circulation, written since that time either by friends of the Qur'an in order to imitate it or by its enemies in order to confront and criticize it; such books have been improved over time with developments in science and thought. However, to this day not one of them has been able to attain the level of the Qur'an. Should even a common human being listen to them, he would be sure to say: "The Qur'an does not resemble these other books and is in a different class entirely. It must be either below them or above them." And since no-one in the world—not even an unbeliever or a fool—can say that it is below them, one must therefore conclude that in eloquence it is higher than all of them.

A man once read the verse which means, *Whatever is in the heavens and on the earth glorifies God* (57:1). He said: "I cannot see any miraculous eloquence in this verse." He was told: "Go back to that age in your mind and listen to the verse as it was recited there." Imagining himself to be there, he saw that all the beings in the world were perceived as lifeless and without either consciousness or purpose, living in an unstable, transient world, surrounded by empty, infinite and unbounded space, and floundering in confusion and darkness. Suddenly he heard the above verse proclaimed by the voice of the Qur'an. At once the verse removed the veil from the face of the universe and illuminated it. This pre-eternal Speech, this eternal Decree, gave instruction to all conscious beings, drawn up in the ranks of succeeding centuries, in such a fashion that the universe became like a vast mosque. The whole of creation, and in particular the heavens and the earth, were engaged in vital remembrance of God and proclamation of His Glory, fulfilling this function with joy and contentment. All of this the traveler has observed. Thus, by tasting one degree of the eloquence of the Qur'an and comparing the other verses to it, the traveler can understand one of the many thousands of wise reasons why the eloquence of the Qur'an has conquered half of the earth and a fifth of humanity; they see how it has increased its majestic dominion, without let or hindrance, and with utmost respect throughout the fourteen centuries since its advent.

FOURTH POINT: While repetition of even the most pleasant thing eventually leads to disgust, the sweetness of the Qur'an is such that however many times it is recited, it causes neither tiredness nor repulsion. Indeed, it has become axiomatic that for those whose hearts are not corrupted and whose taste has not been spoilt, repeated recitation of the Qur'an leads not to weariness but, rather, to an increase in its sweetness and appeal. Also, the Qur'an demonstrates such freshness, youth, and originality that even though it has lived for fourteen centuries and been available to everyone, its vitality is such that one would think it has only just been revealed. Every century has seen the Qur'an enjoy a new youth, as though it were addressing that century in particular. Similarly, even though scholars in every branch of learning keep the Qur'an at their side constantly in order to benefit from it and follow its method of exposition, they see that the Qur'an continues to maintain the originality of its style and manner of explanation.

FIFTH POINT: One wing of the Qur'an is in the past and one is in the future. Its root and one wing are the unanimously confirmed truths of the former Prophets, who affirm it with the tongue of unanimity and whom it in turn affirms and corroborates. Similarly, all saints and purified scholars—the other wing—those fruits of the Qur'an who have received life from it, have shown through their vital spiritual progress that their blessed "Tree" is the living and most radiant means to truth, and beneficial in every respect. All the true spiritual paths or ways of sainthood and Islamic sciences, which have all grown under the protection of the Qur'an's second wing, unanimously testify that the Qur'an is truth itself and a collection of truths that is unequaled in comprehensiveness.

SIXTH POINT: The Qur'an is luminous in each of its following six aspects or sides, all of which indicate its truthfulness and veracity:

- Beneath it lie the pillars of argument and proof;
- above it shine the gleams of the stamp of miraculousness or inimitability;
- before it stand the gifts of happiness in both worlds as its goal;

- behind it are the truths of the heavenly Revelation as its point of support;
- to its right is the well-documented and substantiated confirmation of innumerable sound and upright minds;
- and to its left one can see the true satisfaction, sincere attraction, and submission of sound hearts and pure consciences.

These six, taken together, prove that the Qur'an is an extraordinary, firm, and unassailable heavenly citadel that stands on the earth. From these six aspects it is clear that the Qur'an is pure truth, that it is not human words, and that it contains no errors at all.

Also:

- The Controller and Director of the universe, Who has made it His practice to always exhibit beauty in the universe, to protect goodness and truth, and to eliminate imposters and liars, has confirmed and set His seal on the Qur'an by giving it the most acceptable, highest, and most dominant place of respect and success in the world.
- The person who represented and communicated Islam and interpreted and explained the Qur'an throughout his life, upon him be peace and blessings, believed in it much more powerfully than anybody else and held it in greater respect.
- He assumed a different state when it was revealed.
- His own words (*hadiths*) did not resemble the Qur'an and could never be on the same level.
- Despite being illiterate, with the Qur'an as his basis, he was able to describe with complete confidence many past and future events and numerous cosmic phenomena from behind the veil of the Unseen.
- As the supreme translator of the Qur'an, in whose behavior no trickery or shortcoming had ever been witnessed, even by the sharpest eyes, he believed in and affirmed every pronouncement of the Qur'an with all his might, allowing nothing to shake him in his conviction.

All of these six facts serve to confirm beyond doubt that the Qur'an is the Divinely-revealed Word of his All-Compassionate Creator.

Furthermore:

- More than a fifth of humanity has devoted themselves to the Qur'an with piety and rapture, paying heed to it eagerly in their desire to know the truth. According to the testimony provided by many indications, events, and spiritual unveilings, the jinn, the angels, and the spirit beings gather around it in truth-adoring fashion, like moths, whenever it is recited. This too serves to confirm that the Qur'an enjoys universal acceptance and occupies the highest position.
- In addition, each of the different classes of humankind, from the simplest and lowly to the cleverest and learned, is able to take its full share of the Qur'an's instruction and understand its most profound truths (each according to their capacity).
- Moreover, all of the celebrated scholars in all branches of the religious sciences, in particular the great interpreters of the Supreme Shari'a, together with the brilliant and exacting scholars of theology and the basic principles of the Religion are able to exact all the answers needed for their various disciplines from the Qur'an. All of these facts confirm that the Qur'an is a source of truth and a mine of reality.
- Also, although the disbelieving ones among the Arab authors and poets, the most advanced in literature and eloquence, felt the greatest need to dispute the Qur'an, they were never able to match it in eloquence by producing the like of even a single *sura*, despite the fact that eloquence is only one of the seven most prominent aspects of the Qur'an's miraculousness. Up until today, not even renowned rhetoricians or linguistic experts who have contested the Qur'an in order to make a name for themselves have been able to oppose even a single aspect of its miraculousness, and as a result have been forced to remain in impotent silence. This is further confirmation that the Qur'an is a miracle and completely beyond human capacity.
- The value, superiority, and eloquence of speech are based on the answers given to the questions posed with regard to it: "Who does it come from, for who is it intended, and what is its purpose?" In respect to these points, the Qur'an has no like, and none can approach it. For the Qur'an is a speech and address by the Lord and

Creator of all the worlds; it is His conversation with us that is in no way derivative or artificial. It is addressed to the one who was sent in the name of all humanity, indeed of all beings, the most famous and renowned of humankind; it is addressed to the one whose belief had such a strength and breadth that it gave impetus to mighty Islam and raised its owner to the station of "The nearness (with God) of the distance between two bow strings, or even nearer,"[45] returning him as the addressee of the Eternally Besought One. It describes and explains matters concerning happiness in this world and the next, the results of the creation of the universe, and the purposes of the Lord within it. It expounds also the belief of its first and primary addressee—Prophet Muhammad—which is the highest and most extensive belief, encompassing all the truths of Islam. It reveals and shows every facet of the enormous universe like a map, a clock, or a house, describing it in a manner which befits the Craftsman Who made it. To produce the like of this Qur'an of miraculous exposition is therefore not possible, nor can its degree of miraculousness be attained.

- Also, thousands of meticulous, learned scholars of high intelligence have written commentaries that expound upon the Qur'an, some of which consist of as many as seventy volumes, proving with clear evidence and argument its innumerable qualities, characteristics, mysteries, subtleties, and elevated meanings, showing numerous indications concerning every sort of hidden or unseen matter. The one hundred and thirty parts of the *Risale-i Nur*, in particular, each proves with decisive arguments one quality or subtle point of the Qur'an. Each part of it—such as The Twenty-fifth Word on the miraculousness of the Qur'an; The Second Station of The Twentieth Word, which deduces many things from the Qur'an concerning the wonders of civilization such as the railway and the

---

[45] This is the meaning of verses 53:9–10: *Then, he drew near and came close, so he was (so near that there was left only the distance between) the strings of two bows (put adjacent to each other), or even nearer (than that)*. During God's Messenger's Ascension, God manifested His nearness to him and attracted him toward Him, and the Messenger, upon him be peace and blessings, ascended toward Him, high enough to "meet with" Him. This meeting, which signifies the Messenger's unparalleled nearness to God, is expressed in verse 9 as the "(nearness of the distance between) the two bow strings (put adjacent to each other)." (Tr.)

> airplane; The First Ray, called *Signs of the Qur'an*, which explain some verses' allusions to electricity; the eight short treatises known as *The Eight Signs*, which show how well-ordered, full of meaning, and mysterious the words of the Qur'an actually are; the small treatise ("The Seventh Gleam" in *The Gleams*) which proves five aspects of the miraculousness of the verses at the end of *Suratu'l-Fath* (*sura* 48) from the perspective of their giving news of the Unseen—in short, each part of the *Risale-i Nur* shows one truth or one light of the Qur'an. All of this serves to confirm the fact that the Qur'an has no like: it is a miracle and a wonder; it is the tongue of the World of the Unseen in this visible earthly realm, and it is the Word of One Who is the All-Knowing of the Unseen.

It is on account of these qualities and characteristics of the Qur'an that we have indicated above, in eighteen points contained in the successive three groups, that its sublime, luminous sovereignty and its sacred, mighty rule have been able to continue with perfect splendor, illuminating the faces of the centuries and the visage of the earth for (more than) thirteen centuries. It is also on account of these qualities of the Qur'an that each of its letters has the sacred distinction of yielding at least ten rewards, ten merits, and ten eternal fruits; indeed, the letters of certain verses and *suras* yield a hundred or a thousand fruits, or even more, while at certain blessed times the light, reward, and value of each letter multiplies a hundredfold. Our traveler, journeying through the world, understands this and says in their heart: "The Qur'an, which is thus miraculous in every respect, through the consensus of its *suras*, the agreement of its verses, the accord of its lights and mysteries, and the concurrence of its fruits and works, testifies with its proofs to the Existence, Unity, Attributes, and Names of a Single Necessarily Existent One, and its testimony has caused to issue forth the permanent testimony of all believers."

Thus, in a brief reference to the instruction in belief and Divine Unity that the traveler received from the Qur'an, it was said in The Seventeenth Step of The First Station:

> There is no deity but God, the Necessarily Existent, the One and Unique, Whose necessary Existence in His Unity is demonstrated clearly by the Qur'an of miraculous exposition, the Book accepted and desired by all species of angels, humanity and jinn; the verses of

which are read each minute of the year, with the utmost reverence, by hundreds of millions of people and whose sacred sovereignty is permanent over all regions of the earth and the universe and the face of time; its spiritual and luminous authority has run over half the earth and a fifth of humanity for fourteen centuries with the utmost splendor. This is also testified to and evidenced by the unanimity of its sacred and heavenly *suras*, the agreement of its luminous Divine verses, the congruence of its mysteries and lights, and the correspondence of its fruits and effects, by witnessing and clear vision.

THE EIGHTEENTH STEP

The traveler who is journeying through life now knows that belief is the most precious capital a human being can have, for it bestows on indigent humanity not some transient field or dwelling, but a huge universe, an eternal property that is as vast as the world. Belief also bestows ephemeral humankind with all that they need for eternal life; it delivers from eternal annihilation a wretched one who is waiting as though on a gallows for the arrival of fate, opening to humanity an eternal treasury of everlasting happiness. The traveler then says to themselves: "Onward! In order to gain a further degree from among the infinite degrees of belief, let us consider the totality of the universe and listen to what it says. We should perfect and illuminate the lessons we have received from its components and parts."

Looking through the broad and comprehensive telescope they have taken from the Qur'an, the traveler sees that the universe is so meaningful and well-ordered that it appears as an embodied book, a created Qur'an, of the All-Glorified Lord, a finely adorned palace of the Eternally Besought One and an orderly city of the All-Merciful. Through their constant, meaningful effacement and reaffirmation, and through their wise changes, alterations, and transformations, all of the *suras*, verses and words of that book of the universe—even its very letters, lines, pages, chapters, and divisions—describe the Existence and Presence of One Who has absolute power over and knowledge of all things as the Author of the book—a Perfect and All-Majestic Inscriber Who sees all things in all things and knows the relationship of all things with all things.

Similarly, with all its numerous divisions, species, and particles, with all its inhabitants and contents, with all that enters it and leaves it, and with all the providential changes, transformations, and wise processes of renewal and refreshment that occur in it, the universe also proclaims the Existence and Unity of an All-Exalted Craftsman, a peerless Maker Who acts with limitless power and infinite wisdom. The testimony of the following two mighty realities, as immense as the universe itself, affirms this supreme witness of the universe.

THE FIRST REALITY: This is the reality of "coming into existence within time and space" and "contingency," which has been established with countless proofs by gifted scholars of the principles of the Religion and the science of theology, as well as by the sages of Islam. According to these illustrious people, since change and alteration are observed in the world and in all things, the world must be ephemeral and created within time: it cannot be uncreated and pre-eternal. If it has been created, then there must be a Maker Who has created it. And if it is equally possible for something to come into existence or not and if there is no necessary or imperative cause for it to come into existence or not—a cause which essentially originates in itself, then that thing cannot be necessary or imperative and eternal in the past. It has also been proven with decisive arguments that it is not possible for things to create each other one after the other until eternity in the past; in other words, things cannot go back to eternity in cycles with the former having created the latter. Hence, the existence of a Necessary Existent One becomes necessary—One Whose like cannot exist, Whose similitude is impossible, and all other than Whom is contingent and created by Him.

The reality of "bringing or coming into existence within time and space" has permeated the whole of the universe. Many instances of this are visible to the eye, while the rest can be seen by the intellect. For in front of our eyes a whole world dies every fall; together with it perish hundreds of thousands of different kinds of plants and small animals, each member of each species being like a small universe in itself. It is, however, so orderly a death that all things leave behind in their places seeds and eggs—tiny miracles of Mercy and Wisdom, of Power and Knowledge—so that in spring they will be the means of a new resurrection and rebirth. They hand to the seeds and eggs the books of their deeds and the plans and records of the duties they have carried out, entrusting them to the Wisdom and Protection of the All-Majestic Preserver, and only then do they die.

In spring, the dead trees, roots, and some among the animals come to life again exactly as they were, thus providing hundreds of thousands of examples, specimens, and proofs of the supreme Resurrection. In the place of some others, plants and animals that closely resemble them are brought into being and life, thus publishing the pages of the beings of the preceding spring, together with their deeds and functions, just like an advertisement. Thus, they demonstrate one meaning of the verse, *And when the scrolls (of the deeds of every person) are laid open* (81:10). And then, each fall, a whole world dies, and each spring a fresh world comes into being.

This death and rebirth proceeds in such an orderly fashion, and the death and rebirth of so many species occur within them in such a methodical and regular fashion, that it is as if the world were a guesthouse where animate beings reside for a time, where traveling worlds and migrant realms come, fulfill their duties, and then go on their way. And so, apparent to all intellects, with the clarity of the sun, is the necessary Existence, the boundless Power and the infinite Wisdom of an All-Majestic Being Who creates and brings into existence in this world numerous animate realms and dutiful universes with perfect wisdom, knowledge, harmony, balance, order, and regularity, and Who then employs them for purposes of training, sustaining, raising, and maintaining—all for the sake of Divine aims and Merciful goals, with absolute power and compassion. We leave to the *Risale-i Nur* and books of theology the further discussion of matters related to the bringing and coming into existence within time and space.

As for contingency, it too prevails over and surrounds the entire universe. For we see that all things—be they universal or particular, large or small, from the highest firmament down to the ground, from the atom to the planet—have been brought into existence with a particular essence, a specific form, a distinct identity, particular attributes, wise qualities, and beneficial components. Now,

- to bestow on that particular essence and nature its characteristics from amongst infinite possibilities;
- to clothe it in its specific, distinctive, and appropriate form from among possibilities and probabilities as numerous as the forms that may be conceived;
- to distinguish that being with the identity suited to it from among the possibilities as numerous as the members of the species;

- to give it unique, suitable, and beneficial attributes while it is formless and hesitant amidst innumerable possibilities and probabilities that are as numerous as the varieties of the attributes and their degrees;
- and to bestow wise qualities and beneficial organs upon that formless creature, perplexed and aimless as it is amidst innumerable possibilities and probabilities resulting from the infinite number of conceivable paths and modalities—all of these are indications and proofs of the necessary Existence, the infinite Power, and the unlimited Wisdom of the Necessarily Existent Being: they confirm that it is He Who assigns, chooses, specifies, distinguishes, and creates the specific concrete forms and shapes, attributes and situations of all these contingent beings, whether they be universals or particulars. They indicate, too, that no object or matter is hidden from Him, that nothing is difficult for Him, and that the greatest task is as easy for Him as the smallest; they show that He can create a spring as easily as a tree and a tree as easily as a seed. All this, then, pertains to the reality of contingency, and forms one wing of the supreme witnessing borne by the universe.

Since this testimony of the universe, with its two wings and two realities under discussion has been established and explained in various parts of the *Risale-i Nur*, in particular in The Twenty-second and Thirty-second Words, as well as in The Twentieth and Thirty-third Letters, we refer our readers to these treatises and cut short here what has been an extremely long exposition.

THE SECOND REALITY: This reality proceeds from the entire scheme of the universe, which is also the second wing of its great and universal testimony. It is as follows:

There is a reality of cooperation or mutual assistance that can be observed among beings who are trying to maintain their existence—and, if they are animate, their life—and to fulfill their duties in the midst of the constant agitation stirred up by various revolutions and transformations, an endeavor that lies far beyond their capacities.

We see that the elements hasten to aid living being: clouds, in particular, come to the aid of the plant kingdom, while the plant kingdom hastens to help the animal kingdom, and the animal kingdom rushes to help the world of humans. Milk gushes forth from breasts, like the fountain of Paradise, to provide for the young; living beings are given their sustenance and other necessities of life from unexpected places in a manner that is completely beyond their capacity; particles of food hasten to sustain and repair the cells of the body, and so on. These and many other similar examples of the reality of cooperation under the absolute control, direction, and employment of the All-Merciful Lord demonstrate the universal and compassionate Lordship of the Master of all worlds, Who runs the universe like a palace.

Indeed, objects which are solid, inanimate, and unfeeling, but which nonetheless help one another in a tender and conscious fashion, are undoubtedly caused to rush to each other's assistance by the Power, Mercy, and Command of an infinitely Compassionate and Wise Lord of Majesty.

The universal cooperation prevalent throughout the universe; the all-inclusive balance and all-embracing preservation which prevail with the utmost order in all things, from the planets to the members, limbs and bodily particles of animate beings; the adornment whose pen glides over the entire universe, from the gilded face of the heavens and the ornate face of the earth to the delicate faces of flowers; the ordering and organizing that prevail over all things, from the Milky Way to the vegetables and fruits, such as corn and pomegranates; and the assigning of duties to all things, from the sun, the moon, the elements and the clouds, right down to honey-bees—all of these vast realities offer a testimony in proportion to their vastness, and their testimony forms the second wing of the testimony offered by the universe. Since the *Risale-i Nur* has explained this elsewhere, we will be content here with this brief indication.

In a brief reference to the lesson of faith which the traveler through the world learned from the universe, it was said in The Eighteenth Step of The First Station:

> There is no deity but God, the Necessarily Existent, the like of Whom can in no way exist, and all other than Whom are contingent; the Single, the Unique, Whose necessary Existence in His Unity is demonstrated clearly by the universe—that huge book clothed in a corporeal form, the supreme Qur'an incarnate, the ornate and orderly palace, the magnificent and well-arranged city—with all of its *suras*, verses, words, letters, chapters, parts, pages and lines, and with the agreement of its basic divisions, species, parts and particles, its inhabitants and contents, and what enters it and what leaves it. This is tes-

> tified to by the sublimely comprehensive, vast and perfect reality of bringing or coming into existence within time and space, by change and contingency, and by the agreement of all scholars in the science of theology. It is a testimony which also comprises the reality of the changing of its form and contents with wisdom and regularity and the renewal of its letters and words with order and harmony. It is also a testimony offered by the greatness and all-inclusiveness of the reality of cooperation, mutual response, solidarity, interconnectedness, measure, balance, and preservation—all of which are clearly observable in all of the beings which exist within it.

THE NINETEENTH STEP

The inquisitive and yearning traveler, who has by this stage reached the throne of truth by having advanced through the above-mentioned eighteen ranks, and who has risen from the rank of knowing the Creator of the world indirectly to the station of addressing Him directly, addresses their own spirit as follows: "At the beginning of the *Fatiha* (the Opening Chapter of the Qur'an) we praise God indirectly, (saying: "All praise and gratitude are for God."). However, when we reach the word *iyyaka* ("You alone"), we enter His Presence and address Him directly. Taking our cue from this, we should abandon this indirect search and address the One Whom we are seeking, questioning Him directly about Himself. After all, if one wishes to know about the sun, which shows all things, one should ask the sun itself."

That which shows all things shows itself even more clearly. Just as we perceive the sun through its rays, we can also try to know our Creator through His All-Beautiful Names and Sacred Attributes, in accordance with the extent of our capacities. We will set forth here, with brevity and concision, two of the countless paths which lead to this goal; we will explain two of the innumerable stages of these two paths and two of the numerous realities of these two stages.

THE FIRST REALITY: We are able to observe quite clearly the comprehensive, constant, orderly, and awesome reality of an all-prevailing activity which directs, changes, and renews all things and beings in the heavens and on the earth. Within the reality of that comprehensively wise activity one is able to perceive immediately the truth of the manifestation of Lordship. In turn, within the truth of that comprehensively merciful manifestation of Lordship, one is able to recognize the truth of the demonstration of Divinity.

From behind the veil of this constant, imperious, and wise activity, the Acts of an All-Powerful and All-Knowing Doer can be discerned so clearly that it is as though one is witnessing them directly. And from behind the veil of these nurturing, directing and administering acts of Lordship, the Divine Names Which are manifested in all things can be perceived most clearly. Then from behind the veil of the All-Beautiful Names, Which manifest themselves with majesty and grace, the existence and operation of the seven sacred Attributes can be deduced at the degree of certainty of knowledge, or rather, the degree of certainty of vision or observation, or even certainty of experience. And as is evidenced by the whole of creation, through the endless manifestations of these seven Attributes, that is, Life, Knowledge, Power, Will, Hearing, Seeing, and Speech, the Existence of the Necessarily Existent One described by these Attributes, that Single One of Unity known by these Names, that All-Independent, Eternally Besought One, becomes known self-evidently, necessarily, with the eye of faith in the heart, as though He were being seen more clearly and brilliantly than the sun.

For a beautiful and meaningful book and a well-built house presuppose the acts of writing and building respectively; the acts of writing beautifully and building well self-evidently presuppose the titles of writer and builder; the titles of writer and builder obviously imply the arts and attributes of writing and building; and these arts and attributes necessitate clearly one who is qualified by these names and attributes, and who is an artist, a craftsman and an agent. For, just as it is impossible for there to be a deed without a doer, or a name without one designated by the name, it is also impossible for there to be an attribute without one qualified by the attribute, or for there to be a craft without a craftsman.

On the basis, then, of this reality and principle, the universe and all that it contains resembles a collection of countless meaningful books and letters written by the Pen of Divine Destiny and countless buildings and palaces constructed with the tools of Divine Power. All of these, individually in thousands of ways and together in innumerable ways, provide infinite testimonies to the limitless deeds of Lordship and Mercifulness. Together with these deeds, one thousand and one All-Beautiful Names, Which are the origins of these deeds, and the seven Attributes of Majesty, Which are the source of the Names, testify, through their endless manifestations, and in endless and infinite ways, to the necessary Existence and

Unity of an All-Majestic Being Who is the source of these seven sacred, all-embracing Attributes and is qualified by them. And so too, all the instances of beauty, grace, value, and perfection that are found in those beings testify as one to the sacred beauties and perfections of the acts of Lordship; they testify to the Divine Names and Attributes of the Eternally Besought and the Essential Characteristics of the All-Glorified, which are fitting and worthy of them. And together with all these Names, Attributes, and Characteristics, they bear witness to the sacred Beauty and Perfection of the All-Pure and Sacred Divine Essence.

Thus, the truth of Lordship that manifests itself within the reality of all activity reveals itself in qualities and acts such as creating, inventing, making, and originating with knowledge and wisdom; it shows itself in determining, fashioning, directing, and administering with order and balance; it manifests itself in transforming, changing, causing to descend, and perfecting with purpose and will; it makes itself known through feeding, nurturing, and the bestowal of bounties and gifts with tenderness and mercy. And the reality of the self-demonstration of Divinity found and perceived within the reality of the manifestation of Lordship makes itself known and recognized through the compassionate and munificent manifestations of the All-Beautiful Names and through the Majestic and Graceful manifestations of the seven established, positive or affirmative Attributes: Life, Knowledge, Power, Will, Hearing, Seeing or Sight, and Speech.

Just as the Attribute of Speech makes the All-Sacred Divine Essence known through Revelation and inspiration, the Attribute of Power makes Him known through Its skilled works and effects, which are Its embodied words. Presenting the entire universe in the form of a book of embodied criteria that distinguish truth from falsehood, the Power describes and makes known an All-Powerful One of Majesty.

As for the Attribute of Knowledge, through all of the innumerable wise, well-ordered, and balanced artifacts, and through all of the countless beings that are administered, directed, adorned, and made distinct through knowledge, It makes known a single, All-Knowing and All-Sacred Divine Essence.

As for the Attribute of Life, It is established both by Its own proofs and by all the works that proclaim God's Power; It is made known by all the well-ordered, wise, balanced and adorned forms and states that indicate

God's Knowledge, as well as by all proofs provided by the other Attributes. Thus Life, which together with all Its proofs shows as witnesses all living beings, which act as Its mirrors, makes known an All-Living and Self-Subsistent Being. Life also makes the universe into a supreme mirror which is composed of countless smaller ones—a mirror that is continuously changed and renewed in order to display an ever-changing array of fresh and varied manifestations and designs. Similarly, each of the Attributes of Sight and Hearing and Will and Speech reveals and makes known the All-Sacred Divine Essence in the same way that the universe does.

Moreover, just as the Attributes demonstrate the Existence of the All-Majestic Divine Essence, they also indicate in evident fashion the existence and reality of Life and the fact that the Divine Essence is eternally living. For knowing is a sign of life; hearing is an indication of being alive; seeing belongs only to the living; and willing is possible only through life. Purposeful power is found only in living beings, while speech is a faculty of those who are endowed with life and knowledge. It follows from all these realities that the Divine Attribute of Life has proofs seven times as great as the universe, and proofs that proclaim both Its own existence and the existence of the One Whom It qualifies. It is because of this that Life is the foundation and source of all other Attributes: it is the origin and axis of God's Greatest Name. Since the *Risale-i Nur* has established this primary truth with powerful proofs and, to a certain extent, clarified it, we will content ourselves now with a drop from this ocean.

THE SECOND REALITY: This is the Divine discourse which stems from the Divine Attribute of Speech.

As stated in the verse: *If all the sea were ink to write my Lord's words, the sea would indeed be exhausted before my Lord's words would be exhausted, even if We were to bring the like of it in addition to it* (18:109), Divine Speech is infinite. The most manifest sign demonstrating the existence of a being is its speech. Thus, this reality constitutes an infinite testimony to the Existence and Unity of the Eternal Speaker. As has been expounded in the Fourteenth and Fifteenth Steps of this treatise, Revelation and inspiration are two powerful proofs of this reality; the divinely-revealed Books are, as mentioned in The Tenth Step, an expansive proof, and as indicated in The Seventeenth Step, the Qur'an of miraculous exposition is a most brilliant and comprehensive proof. So, referring the explanation of this reality to those

Steps, and being content with the lights and mysteries of the mighty verse: *God (Himself) testifies that there surely is no deity but He, and so do the angels and those endowed with knowledge, being firm in upholding truth and uprightness: (these all testify that) There is no deity but He, the All-Glorious with irresistible might, the All-Wise* (3:18), which proclaims this reality in a miraculous fashion and adds its own testimony to all of the preceding ones, our traveler goes no further.

In reference to the brief meaning of the lesson that the traveler has learned at this sacred station, it was said in The Nineteenth Step of The First Station:

> There is no deity but God, the Necessarily Existent One, the Single, the Unique, Who possesses the All-Beautiful Names and the all-exalted Attributes, and to Whom applies the most sublime description. His necessary Existence in His Unity is demonstrated clearly by all His sacred and all-encompassing Attributes and all of His All-Beautiful Names, Which manifest themselves constantly, and the manifestations of Which are demonstrated by the concurrence of His Essential Characteristics and operative Acts. This is testified to by the sublime reality of the self-revelation of Divinity in the manifestation of Lordship, Which reveals Itself in constant, all-permeating activity through the acts of inventing, creating, making, and originating through Will and Power, through the acts of determining, fashioning, administering and directing through Choice and Wisdom, and through the acts of expending, ordering, preserving, managing and providing through Determining and Mercy—all with complete order, harmony, and balance. It is also testified to by the sublime and all-inclusive truth of the mysteries of the verse: *God (Himself) testifies that there surely is no deity but He, and so do the angels and those who possess knowledge, being firm in upholding truth and uprightness: (these all testify that) There is no deity but He, the All-Glorious with irresistible might, the All-Wise* (3:18).

NOTE

Each of the truths that have been demonstrated in the Nineteen Steps of The First Chapter of The Second Station above not only bear witness to God's Necessary Existence through their actual existence, but also testify to the Divine Unity and Oneness through their comprehensiveness. However, as they primarily establish Divine Existence most clearly and explicitly, they have been regarded as proofs of the necessity of God's Existence.

As for The Second Chapter of The Second Station, since the truths to be set forth primarily and clearly establish and prove Divine Unity, proving Divine Existence secondarily, they are considered to be proofs of Divine Unity. In reality, the proofs set forth in both chapters prove both the Existence and Unity of God. However, in order to indicate their difference, it has repeatedly been said in The First Chapter: "This is testified to by the sublimely comprehensive reality (or truth)…," while in the Second Chapter it will be said: "This is observed in the sublimely comprehensive reality (or truth)...," in reference to the evident visibility of Divine Unity.

I intended to explain the steps of The Second Chapter in the same way that I did in the First, but because of various obstacles I am compelled to keep things concise. The reader may refer to other parts of the *Risale-i Nur* for their explanation.

The Second Chapter: Proofs for Divine Unity

The traveler who was sent to the world in order to attain faith, and who has made an intellectual journey through the whole universe, asking all things concerning their Creator and seeking their Lord in every place, has finally found their Deity with the certainty of experience, particularly with regard to His Necessary Existence, and now says to their intellect: "Come, we will set out on a new journey in order to see the proofs of the Unity of our Necessarily Existent Creator."

THE FIRST STAGE

And so they set out together. At the first stage, they see that four sacred realities or truths prevailing over the whole universe necessitate self-evidently the Unity of God.

THE FIRST TRUTH: *Absolute Divinity*

Every division of humankind is engaged in or manifests a mode of worship through its "natural" life: the services dictated by the creation and vital functions of other living beings, as well as inanimate creation, are in effect a form of worship particular to them; each of the material and spiritual bounties and favors is a means inciting beings to worship and praise the One Who is uniquely worthy of worship and praise. Indeed, all the manifestations from the Unseen and spiritual emanations and radiations such as Revelations and inspirations proclaim unanimously the certain fact that there is a Deity Who is worshipped and worthy of worship. All of this proves self-evidently the certain fact that there is an absolute Deity prevailing over the whole universe. And this Deity can in no way accept partnership. This is because those who respond to this Deity or the fact that He is being worshipped and is worthy of worship with thanks and praise are the conscious fruits on the further parts of the tree of the universe. If others were able to gratify and place under their obligation those conscious beings in such a way as to cause them to abandon their true Object of Worship, Who may be swiftly forgotten because of His invisibility, this would be in such utter contradiction to the very nature of Divinity and Its sacred purposes that it could in no way be countenanced. It is for this reason that the Qur'an so repeatedly and vehemently refutes polytheism and threatens the polytheists with Hellfire.

The Second Truth: Absolute Lordship

It is observed throughout the universe, particularly in the lives of living beings that a wise and compassionate hidden hand operates for their provision and administration everywhere in the same fashion, yet usually in an unexpected form. This is most certainly a reflection of absolute Lordship and a decisive proof for Its actual existence.

Since an absolute Lordship exists, It certainly cannot accept any partnership. For since the most important aims and purposes of Lordship—such as the manifestation of Its beauty, the proclamation of Its perfection, the exhibition of Its precious arts and the display of Its unknown skills—are combined and concentrated in particulars and living beings, any participation of another "lordship"—even in the most particular of things and the smallest of living beings—would frustrate the attainment of those purposes and destroy those aims.

Also, since any participation of another "lordship" would avert the faces of conscious beings from those purposes and the One Who has willed them, and turn those faces toward means and causes, it would be totally opposed and hostile to the very nature or essence of Lordship: given this, absolute Lordship cannot in any way permit it. It is because of this fundamental truth that with all its frequent proclamations of God's sanctity, and of His absolute freedom from having any defects and partners, the Qur'an guides people constantly to God's absolute Unity with all its chapters, verses and letters.

THE THIRD TRUTH: Perfections

Just as all of the exalted instances of wisdom in the universe, and all of its wonderful beauties, just laws and wise purposes indicate most evidently the existence of perfections related to the existence of the universe, they also testify most clearly to the Perfections of the Creator Who has originated the universe and Who directs it miraculously and beautifully in every way, and to those of humanity, which is the conscious mirror of the Creator.

Since the existence of perfections is a reality; and since the Creator, Who has created the universe perfectly and endowed it with perfections, possesses essential perfections Himself; and since humankind has been endowed with perfections or distinctions as the most valued of God's creations, the most important fruit of the universe and the species of being chosen to settle on the earth in order to cultivate, develop and administer it according to God's laws, then indubitably the participation of another "lord" and "deity" in the creation and life of the universe and humanity is absolutely impossible and false. For the existence of such a "partner" would turn the universe, which is endowed with perfections and instances of wisdom, into a vain plaything of chance revolving pointlessly toward utter destruction: it would be reduced to a realm of amusement for nature, a cruel slaughterhouse for living beings and an awful house of sorrows for the conscious; it would reduce humanity, whose (relative) perfections are visible in their works, to the level of the most wretched, distressed and degraded of animals; and it would cast an impenetrable veil over the infinite sacred Perfections of the Creator that are reflected in the mirror of all beings, thus nullifying the result of His Activity and denying His Creativity.

Since it has been proven convincingly in The First Station of The Second Ray that associating partners with God is in direct contradiction to the existence of Divine, human and creational perfections, we refer our readers to that section and cut short the argument here.

THE FOURTH TRUTH: Sovereignty

Whoever looks at the universe with due attention will see it in the form of a most prosperous and active country, or a city governed most wisely and ruled most firmly; they will find therein all things and all species engaged obediently in a particular duty.

According to the military metaphor contained in the verse, *God's are the hosts of the heavens and earth* (48:4, 7), all of the Divine hosts from the armies of atoms, the brigades of the vegetable kingdom and the battalions of the animal kingdom to the armies of the stars live in utmost obedience to the prevailing commands, imperative orders and royal edicts of creation and life. This indicates self-evidently the existence of an absolute Sovereignty and a universal, all-encompassing Authority.

Since there is the truth of absolute Sovereignty, there can be no truth in associating partners with God. For as it is declared decisively in the verse, *Had there been in the heavens and the earth any deities other than* God, *both (of those realms) would certainly have fallen into ruin* (21:22), if numerous hands intervene in the same task, they cause chaos. If there are two kings in one country, or even two headsmen in one village, order will be destroyed and government would be reduced to chaos. However, there prevails everywhere such an order, be it in the wing of the fly or in the lamps of the heavens, in the cells of the body or in the constellations of the heavens, that it is impossible for there to be any partners with God.

Furthermore, sovereignty is a station of majesty and honor: to admit a rival would damage the majesty and honor of sovereignty. The fact that a human sovereign, who needs the help of many people on account of his impotence, is ready to murder his brothers and offspring for the sake of retaining his minor, apparent and temporary sovereignty shows that sovereignty rejects rivalry and partnership. If one who is so weak acts in such a way for the sake of a sovereignty that is so insignificant, then it is in no way possible that the absolutely All-Powerful One, Who is the Master of the whole creation, should allow one other than Himself to have a share in His sacred Sovereignty, the means to His real and universal Lordship and Divinity.

Since this truth has been explained with powerful proofs in The Second Station of The Second Ray and many other places in the *Risale-i Nur*, we refer our readers to those sections.

Having observed these four truths, our traveler came to know Divine Unity to the level of certainty of vision, and their belief grew more radiant as a result. With all their might they say, "There is no deity but God, the One, Who has no partner." In a brief reference to the lesson they learned from this stage, it was said in The Second Chapter of The First Station:

> There is no deity but God, the One, the Unique, Whose Unity and necessary Existence are demonstrated clearly through the observation of the sublime truth of the self-revelation of the absolute Divinity, as well as through the observation of the sublimely comprehensive truth of the manifestation of the absolute Lordship, Which demands Unity; and the observation of the sublimely comprehensive truth of perfections, which arise from Unity; and the observation of the sublimely comprehensive truth of the absolute Sovereignty, Which prevents and contradicts any partnership.

The Second Stage

Then that restless traveler says to their heart: "The fact that the people of belief, and particularly those following a spiritual path, proclaim repeatedly, *There is no deity but He*, thus recalling and declaring God's Unity, is an indication that belief in and affirmation of God's Unity has many degrees. Such belief and affirmation is also a most important, enjoyable and exalted sacred duty—an act of worship that is required by creation. Come, then, and in order to discover a further degree, let us open the door of another mansion in this abode of instruction. For the true affirmation of God's Unity that we seek is not merely some mental construct or conception: it is, rather, an affirmation or confirmation—called knowledge—which is based on proof, and is thus different from, and far more valuable than, that which the science of logic calls conception."

The true affirmation of God's Unity is a judgment, a conclusion, a confirmation and an acceptance which is such that one who has attained it can find their Lord by means of everything in the universe: someone who attains this level will see in all things a path leading to their Creator, and nothing will be able to prevent their seeing Him present everywhere. For otherwise it would always be necessary to tear down the veil of the universe in order to find the Lord.

"Onward, then," says the traveler to themselves and knocks on the door of God's Grandeur and Sublimity. And so they enter the mansion of

God's deeds and workings, the world of creation and origination, where they see that five comprehensive truths prevailing over the entire universe, offering self-evident proof of the Divine Unity.

THE FIRST TRUTH: Grandeur and Sublimity

Since this truth was explained with adequate proofs in The Second Station of The Second Ray and various other places in the *Risale-i Nur*, we will keep our discussion here brief:

The Being Who creates and then administers simultaneously and in the same single fashion the stars that are thousands of light years distant from each other; Who creates at the same single moment and in the same single form the countless members of the same species of flower, distributed over all four corners of the earth; Who, as though willing to provide on the face of the earth hundreds of thousands of examples of the supreme Resurrection every spring, and to prove before our eyes an extremely remarkable past, unseen event, namely the creation of the heavens and the earth in six "days," as indicated in the verse, *He it is Who has created the heavens and the earth in six days* (57:4), brings into existence and adorns hundreds of thousands of different plant and animal species in five or six weeks, and manages, nurtures and distinguishes between them with the utmost order and harmony, and without any confusion, defect or error, even though they are all mingled with one another; the Being Who, as stated explicitly in the verse, *He makes the night pass into the day, and He makes the day pass into the night* (57:6), causes the earth to revolve, and produces and alternates the pages of the day and night, on which He inscribes daily events—this same Being knows and administers through His Will, all at the same time, the most secret and hidden thoughts which occur to our hearts. Since each of the acts mentioned is in reality a single, uniform act, it follows necessarily that their One and All-Powerful Possessor of Majesty has such Grandeur and Sublimity that nowhere, in nothing, in no way, does It allow the slightest possibility for there to be any partners with Him.

Since One of such Grandeur and sublimity of Power exists, and since that Grandeur is infinitely perfect and comprehensive, it is certainly in no way possible that they should allow any intervention or participation from another. For this would mean imputing impotence to that Power, fault to that Grandeur, defect to that Perfection, restriction to that Comprehensiveness and a limit to that Infinitude. No sound intellect could regard this to be possible.

Since it offends God's Grandeur and the dignity of His Majesty and Sublimity, the association of partners with God is deemed such a crime that the miraculous Qur'an asserts most earnestly that *Assuredly, God does not forgive that partners be associated with Him; less than that, He forgives to whomever He wills* (4:48).

THE SECOND TRUTH

This is the absoluteness, comprehensiveness and manifestation in infinite form of the acts of the Lord observed at work in the universe.

It is only God Almighty's Wisdom and Will that limit and restrict those acts, together with the inherent capacities of the objects and places in which those acts are manifested. Random chance, unconscious nature, blind force, inanimate causality and the elements that are scattered in every direction without restriction and mixed with everything—none of these can play any role in the most balanced, wise, purposeful, insightful, life-giving, orderly and firm acts of the Creator. Rather, they are used by the Command, Will and Power of the All-Majestic Maker as an apparent veil over His Power.

We will set forth three meaningful examples of this which one reads in *Suratu'n-Nahl*:

The first:

> And your Lord inspired the (female) bee: "Take for yourself dwelling-places in the mountains, and in the trees, and in what they (human beings) may build and weave." (16:68)

With regard to its creation and duties, the honeybee is such a miracle of Divine Power that a whole chapter of the Qur'an —*Suratu'n-Nahl* (*Sura* 16)—has been named after it. For the complete program for the fulfillment of its important duty has been inscribed in the minute head of that little honey-machine; the sweetest of foods has been placed in its tiny stomach; and it has been given a sting capable of killing certain beings without causing damage to it. Now, since all of this is accomplished with the utmost care and knowledge, with extraordinary wisdom and purpose, and with perfect orderliness, precision and balance, is it at all possible for deaf, unconscious, disorderly and discordant nature and chance to interfere or participate in any of it?

The comprehensiveness of this Divine craft, this act of Lordship, which is miraculous in the three respects mentioned—its appearance or presence in the countless bees scattered throughout the earth, with the same wisdom, the same care, the same balance, at the same time and in the same fashion—is a self-evident proof of God's Unity.

The second verse:

> And surely in the cattle there is a lesson for you: We give you from that which is within their bodies, from between the waste and blood, milk that is pure and palatable to those who drink. (2:66)

This verse is a proclamation full of wisdom and lessons. For God Almighty produces in the midst of blood and waste a substance that is the exact opposite of them—pure, tasty, nutritious white milk—but which is polluted by neither. This He places in the breasts—those milk-producing factories—of female mammals, and inspires in their hearts a self-sacrificing tenderness that is sweeter and more valuable than the milk itself. All of this requires such a degree of mercy, wisdom, knowledge, power, will and care that it cannot in any way be the work of turbulent chance, randomly mingled elements and blind forces.

The comprehensive manifestation and working of such a wise and miraculous art of Lordship throughout the earth and in the hearts and breasts of innumerable mothers of hundreds of thousands of species, in the same instant, in the same fashion, and with the same wisdom and the same care—all of this demonstrates most clearly the Unity of God.

The third verse:

> And there are (among the produce that God brings forth as nourishment for you on the revived earth) the fruits of the date-palm, and grapes: you derive from them intoxicants and good, wholesome nourishment. Surely in this there is a sign for people who reason and understand. (2:67)

This verse draws one's attention to the date and the grape, saying: "For those possessed of intellect there is a great proof of Divine Unity in these two fruits." For the date and the grape are sources of nourishment and sustenance, yielding fruit both fresh and dry, and giving rise to the most delicious forms of food. Yet the trees that bear them stand in waterless sand and dry soil! Each of them is like a factory which produces sugar and syrup; as such they are miracles of Power and wonders of Wisdom—works of art created with such a sensitive balance and perfect order, and with such wisdom and care that anyone with an iota of intellect would have to admit that "The one who has made them in this fashion can only be the One Who has created the universe."

For in front of our eyes each vine branch the thickness of a finger holds as many as twenty bunches of grapes, and in each bunch there are about one hundred of tiny pumps containing sugary syrup. Dressing each grape in a delicate, thin and subtly colored protective coat; placing in its soft heart seeds with their hard shells, which are like its memory, its program of formation and action and its life-history; manufacturing in its stomach a sweet like the halva of Paradise and a honey like the water of the fountain of Paradise; and creating an infinite number of such fruits over the face of the entire earth, with the same care and wisdom and wonderful art, and at the same time and in the same fashion—all of this demonstrates self-evidently that the one who fulfils these tasks can be none other than the Creator of the whole universe, and that this act, requiring as it does infinite power and wisdom, can be by His doing alone.

The blind, disorderly, unconscious, aimless, anarchic and pervasive forces of nature and causality cannot play any real role in the engendering of this most skilful art, this most sensitive balance and this most wise manifestation of order and equilibrium. Such forces are merely employed through the command of Lordship as means—apparent causes which veil the Hand of the Divine Power so that those who cannot understand the real nature and wisdom of certain seemingly unpalatable events and effects should not blame God Almighty.

Just like the three meaningful facts proving Divine Unity that are contained in the three verses above, the countless manifestations and operations of the infinite acts of Lordship testify unanimously to the Oneness of a Unique One of Unity, the All-Majestic One.

THE THIRD TRUTH

This is the creation of beings, particularly plants and animals, with absolute speed and in absolute abundance, and yet with absolute orderliness; it concerns the creation of all things with absolute ease and yet at the same time with extreme skill, talent, accuracy, precision and order; it concerns the bestowing of existence on all beings with great value and distinction, despite the extreme abundance and intermingling of all created entities.

To produce beings in absolute abundance and with extreme rapidity, and yet most skillfully and artistically; and with incredible facility and yet with the utmost care and order; and to produce them with extreme value and distinction despite abundance and intermingling, without any form of confusion or deficiency—this can only be through the Power of a Unique One for Whom nothing is ever difficult. For that Power the creation of stars is as easy as the creation of atoms, the creation of a whole species is no more taxing than the creation of a single member of that species, the bringing into being of a tremendous and comprehensive universal is the same as the bringing into being of the most minor of particulars. For It the revival of the whole earth is no more onerous than the revival of a single tree, the creation and nurturing of a single tree is no more difficult than the creation of a seed the size of a fingernail. All of these deeds He performs before our eyes.

And so by discovering this significant mystery of this rank of the manifestation of Divine Unity, this third truth or the word of Divine Unity—namely the fact that for Divine Power the greatest universal is like the smallest particular and the most abundant is no different from the least; by discerning this talisman or riddle beyond the reach of the intellect, this most significant foundation of Islam, this most profound source of faith, this greatest basis of belief in the Divine Unity—by doing this, the talisman of the Qur'an is solved and the most secret riddle of the creation of the universe—a riddle which human philosophy is unable to comprehend—becomes known. Thanks and praise one hundred thousand times the letters of the *Risale-i Nur* be to my All-Compassionate Creator that the *Risale-i Nur* has solved this amazing talisman. Especially toward the end of The Twentieth Letter, where "He is the All-Powerful over everything" is discussed; in the discussion entitled "The One Who will bring about the Resurrection is able to do so" in The Twenty-ninth Word; and in the section devoted to the explanation of the degrees in understanding Divine Power entitled "The ranks of *God is the All-Great*" in The Twenty-ninth Gleam, it has been explained clearly. Referring readers who desire a more elaborate explanation to those parts of the *Risale-i Nur*, it was my intention here to set out briefly the foundations and proofs that solve this talisman and to elucidate thirteen mysteries in thirteen steps. However, while I have been able to discuss the first two mysteries, two powerful obstacles—one material, the other immaterial—have caused me to abandon the rest.

The first mystery: If something originates in an essence and is therefore essential in itself, its opposite cannot have access to the essence in which that thing originate: to do so would mean the union of two opposite essences in the same single essence, which is inconceivable. Given this, since Divine Power originates in the Divine Essence Itself and is essential to Him, for sure, impotence—the opposite of that Power—cannot in any way gain access to that All-Powerful Essence.

Furthermore, the existence of degrees in a thing is because of the intervention in it of its opposite. For example, strong and weak degrees of light result from the intervention of darkness; high and low degrees of heat come from the intervention of coldness; and greater and lesser amounts of strength are due to the intervention and opposition of resistance. It is therefore impossible that degrees should exist in the Divine Power, Which is essential, or in one respect identical, to the Divine Being. He creates all things as if they were but a single thing. And since degrees do not exist in the Power essential to the Divine Being, and since weakness or deficiency cannot have access to It, no impediment can in any way obstruct It; nor can the creation of anything cause It difficulty. Since, then, nothing is difficult for Divine Power, He creates the supreme Resurrection as easily as spring; He creates spring with the same ease as a single tree; and He creates a single tree with the same facility as a single flower. Similarly, He creates a flower as artistically as a tree; a tree as miraculously as a spring; and a spring as comprehensively and extraordinarily as a resurrection. All of this He accomplishes before our eyes.

It has been proven in the *Risale-i Nur* with many decisive and strong arguments that were it not for Divine Unity, the creation of a flower would be as difficult as a tree or even more difficult, and the creation of a tree would be as hard as a spring or even harder. Furthermore, they would also lose their value and their artistic quality. A living being that now takes a minute to produce would be produced with great difficulty in a year; in reality, of course, we know that it would and could never be produced.

It is because of this truth that these fruits, flowers, trees and animals, all of which are of the highest value despite their abundance and multiplicity, and which are of the highest artistry despite the swiftness and ease of their creation, appear in an absolutely orderly fashion and set out to fulfill their tasks. When they fulfill their duty of proclaiming God's Glory completely, they depart, leaving behind their seeds in their stead.

The second mystery: Just as, on account of its light, the transparency of the objects on which it shines, the manifestation of its essential power and the obedience of the whole universe to the same laws, a single sun is reflected in a single mirror with its light, so too, through Divine command and on account of the extensive activity of its unrestricted power, it is also able to reflect with its light and heat quite easily in innumerable mirrors, shining objects and droplets. The many and the few are the same before it: there is no difference between them with regard to the sun's reflection in them.

Similarly, just as a single word can enter the ear of one person without difficulty, thanks to the infinite comprehensiveness of boundless Creativity, it may, by Divine permission, enter a million ears with the same ease: a single listener and a thousand listeners are equal. Also, thanks to the infinite comprehensiveness of Divine Activity embodied in the manifestation of mercy, a single eye or a single luminous being such as Archangel Gabriel may, through Divine Power, look at, enter, or be present in thousands of places at the same time, as easily as they look at, enter or are present in a single place: there is no difference between the many and the few.

Similarly, since the eternal Power of God's Essence is the most subtle and purest of lights—the light of all lights—and since the natures, essences and inner dimensions of all things are luminous and lustrous like mirrors; and since all things, from the atom, the plant, and the living creature to the moon, the sun and the stars, are wholly obedient and submissive to the command of that Power of the Divine Essence, it is clear that He creates countless things as easily as a single thing, and is omnipresent beside each of them. No task prevents Him from doing another. Great or small, many or few, particular or universal—all are the same for that Power: nothing is difficult for It.

As discussed in The Tenth and Twenty-ninth Words, through the connections or universal realities of orderliness, balance, obedience to command and confirming to or following the order, a child is able to steer a great ship as big as a hundred houses as easily as he moves his toy with his little fingers. Also, just as a commander sends a single private into battle with the order of "March!", he is also able to send a whole obedient army into the fray with the same single order.

Let us also suppose that two mountains are weighed on a large and extremely sensitive scale. Just as a single walnut placed on one of the pans of the scale in which two eggs are being weighed can cause that pan to drop and the other to rise, so too, through a law of wisdom, can the same walnut produce the same result with the scale upon which the mountains are being weighed: it would cause one pan with its mountain to rise and the other to fall.

So, since there is also inherent in God's absolute, infinite, luminous, essential and perpetual Power an infinite Wisdom, Which is the origin, source and basis of all order, balance and harmony in creation, and an infinitely sensitive Divine Justice; and since all things, be they universal or particular, great or small, are subservient to the command of that Power and submissive to Its operations—it follows that through the order based on wisdom, He causes the stars to revolve and to move as easily as He directs and moves the atoms. Just as in spring He brings to life a single fly easily with a single command, so too, through the wisdom and balance inherent in His Power, He restores to life with the same ease and the same command the whole fly species, as well as all of the innumerable plants and animals, and then sends them forth onto the plain of life.

In the same way that He swiftly revives a tree in spring and endows its seemingly dead trunk and branches with vitality through His wise, just and absolute Power, He also restores to life in spring the corpse of the vast earth as easily as He revives a tree, thus bringing about hundreds of thousands of different examples of the Resurrection. Just as He restores the earth to life with a single creational command, as stated in the verse *It is but one single blast, and see, they will all have been (raised and) arraigned together before Us (for judgment)* (36:53), all humankind and jinn will be brought forth in His Presence on the plain of the Supreme Resurrection with but a single command. Again, as declared in the verse ... *the matter of the Hour (of Doom) is (in relation with the Divine Power) but the twinkling of an eye, or even quicker* (16:77), destroying the world and bringing about the Resurrection will take no longer than the blink of an eye, or even less. Also, the verse *Your creation and your resurrection are but as (the creation and resurrection) of a single soul* (31:28), shows that the creation and resurrection of all humankind are as easy for His Power as the creation and resurrection of a single soul. The three verses mentioned above declare that God will bring all humankind and jinn, all animals, spirit beings and angels to the field of the Supreme Gathering and place them before the Supreme Balance with a single command and with the same ease. One task will not impinge on the fulfillment of another.

(The remaining mysteries, from the third to the thirteenth, have had to be postponed to another time.)

The Fourth Truth

The existence of all beings and their appearance in the field of existence; their living together and their being either the miniature or magnified versions of each other; the fact that some of them form or represent wholes and universals while others are their parts or individual members; the fact that they resemble each other in bearing the stamp of creation and the impression of artistry, together with many other commonalities and points of unity such as their mutual cooperation with respect to their essential duties as creatures of God—all of these point self-evidently to Unity of the Creator and make it clear that the universe is an indivisible whole under the control and direction of the same single Lord.

For example, each spring He creates, directs and provides for the innumerable members of hundreds of thousands of different species of plants and animals, all together and intermingled, simultaneously and in the same fashion, without any error or mistake, and with the utmost wisdom and perfection of artistry. Similarly, He creates all the different species of birds—from tiny flies, which are like birds in miniature, to eagles, which are the most majestic of birds—and equips them with the means of flight and subsistence. Furthermore, in addition to populating the skies with numerous species of birds, He imprints on their countenances a miraculous stamp of artistry, on their bodies an administrative seal of wisdom, and in their nature the evidence of particular attention, provision and nurturing. Also, with absolute wisdom and mercy He causes particles of food to hasten to the assistance of the cells of the body, plants to come to the assistance of animals, animals to rush to the aid of humans, and all mothers to attend swiftly to the needs of their powerless infants. Moreover, He works on and uses all things, be they particular or universal, from the Milky Way, the solar system and the elements of the earth to the veil which covers the pupil of the eye, the petals of the rose, the husk of the corn, and the seeds of the melon, like a series of intersecting circles, with the same orderliness, perfection of artistry, the same act and perfect wisdom. The fact that He does all of this establishes the following with self-evident certainty:

- He who does these deeds is One and Unique, having His stamp on all things.
- In the same way that He is not in any one place, He is present in all places.
- Like the sun, all things are distant from Him, but He is close to all things.
- Just as objects such as the Milky Way and the solar system are not difficult for Him, so are the red and white corpuscles of the blood and the thoughts that occur to the heart not secret from Him, nor are they beyond the reach of His absolute control and direction.
- However great a being may be, its creation is as easy for Him as the smallest thing, for He creates with consummate ease a fly on the model of an eagle, a seed with the nature of a tree, a tree in the form of a garden, a garden with the artistry of a spring, and a spring on the scale of a resurrection.
- And He grants us the things most valuable in art most economically. The price that He asks of us is merely that we say "In the Name of God" and "All praise and gratitude are for God." That is to say, the acceptable price for all those numerous precious bounties is to say when we begin to use or consume them "In the Name of God, the All-Merciful, the All-Compassionate," and, once we have taken benefit from them, to utter the words "All praise and gratitude are for God."

Since this fourth truth is also explained elsewhere in the *Risale-i Nur*, we content ourselves here with this brief indication.

THE FIFTH TRUTH

This is what our traveler perceives at the second mansion or stage: There is a most perfect order in the universe as a whole and in its primary divisions, its subsidiary parts and in all the individual beings contained in it. The substances and duty-bound things (such as air, fire, water and soil) that are the means for the administration and maintenance of that vast realm, and which are related to its general scheme, all display uniformity in every corner of this realm. Also, the Divine Names and Acts that are at work in that magnificent city, that vast exhibition hall, both individually and together encompass and prevail most—and in some cases, all—things, despite their existing one within the other and each having the same nature wherever they operate and prevail. Furthermore, the elements and species that are the means for the construction, population and administration of that well-adorned palace are diffused over the whole face of the earth all together and individually, despite their existing one within the other and each having the same nature wherever they are. All of this demands, proves and affirms, necessarily and self-evidently, the following:

- The Maker and Administrator of this universe, the Sovereign and Nurturer of this realm, the Owner and Builder of this palace is One, Sole, Unique.
- He has neither like nor equal, neither minister nor aide. He has neither partner nor opposite; neither inability nor deficiency.

Indeed, order is in itself a perfect expression of unity; it demands a single orderer. It leaves no place for the intervention of others, which would give rise to dispute and dissension.

Since there is a wise and precise order in all things, whether universal or particular, from the totality of the universe and the daily and annual rotation of the earth down to the countenance of humans, the complex of senses in their head, and the circulation of red and white corpuscles in their blood, it is clear that nothing or no-one other than the Absolutely Powerful and Absolutely Wise One can stretch out its hand with the intention of creation and direction toward anything; nor can it interfere or intervene in its creation in any way. On the contrary, all things are passive recipients which manifest the Acts of an Absolute Agent or the ground where He operates.

Also, since pursuing certain purposes and ordering things with a view to providing certain benefits can be possible only through knowledge and wisdom, and can be performed only with will and choice, it is clear that this general order, which is based on and directed to certain instances of wisdom, and this infinitely varied and beneficial ordering of creatures before our very eyes demonstrate and testify self-evidently that the Creator and Director of all beings is One, an Agent Who does whatever He wills and however He wills it. Everything comes into existence through His Power, assumes a particular state through His Will, and takes on a particular and most accurate form through His Choice.

Also, since the heat-giving lamp of this guesthouse—the world—is one; its candle which serves as the basis for the division and measuring of time (in lunar calendar) is one; its merciful sponge is one; its fiery cook is one; its beverage that is the source of life is one; its preserving field is one[46]—because of all of these instances of oneness, it is obvious that this unity attests to the fact that the Maker and Owner of this guesthouse is also One. It demonstrates clearly that He is extremely generous and hospitable, employing those high-ranking and great officials to serve the living guests of His guesthouse.

Also, the same Names such as the All-Wise, the All-Compassionate, the All-Giving One of forms, the All-Directing, the All-Reviving, and the All-Nurturing; the same Characteristics such as Wisdom, Mercy and Grace; and the same Acts such as Formation, Direction, Disposition and Nurturing—all of these are at work throughout the universe, individually and together, one within the other and prevailing everywhere in the utmost degree. They complete and perfect the imprints of one another in such a way that it is as if they were being united one with the other: it is as if Power becomes identical with Wisdom and Mercy, and Wisdom becomes identical with Grace and Life. As soon as the activity of the Name the All-Giving One of life appears in a thing, the activity of numerous other Names such as the Creator, the All-Giving One of form and the All-Providing also appear at the same instant, in the same thing and in the same system. This testifies self-evidently that the One known by these Names and the Doer of the comprehensive Acts Which appear everywhere in the same fashion is One, Single and Unique. We believe this and confirm it wholeheartedly!

---

46 The heat-giving lamp of this guesthouse that is the world is the sun; its candle which serves as the basis for the division and measuring of time is the moon; its merciful sponge is the cloud; its fiery cook is also the sun; its beverage that is the source of life is water; its preserving field is soil. (Tr.)

Also, since the elements that constitute the substance and material of creation encompass the whole earth, and since all of the species of creation—that bear various stamps indicating Unity—are scattered throughout the earth, this also proves self-evidently that those elements together with their contents, and those species, together with their separate members, are the property of a Single Being. They are the artifacts and servants of One so Powerful and Unique that He employs those vast and pervasive elements as absolutely obedient servants and deploys those species scattered throughout the earth as well-disciplined soldiers. Since this truth also has been established and explained in certain other parts of the *Risale-i Nur*, we content ourselves here with this brief indication.

Summing up their observations and expressing their feelings with a joy arising from the effulgence of faith and the pleasure of Divine Unity that they derived from these five realities, our traveler said to their heart:

Look at the colorful page of the book of the universe,
and see what the golden Pen of the Power has inscribed upon it!
No point has been left dark for those
who can see with the eyes of their hearts.
It is as if God has inscribed His signs with light.

Know too that:

The sheets of the book of the universe are of infinite kinds;
The lines of the events of time are works without number.
Written in the printing house of the Preserved Tablet of Truth,
Each creature in the universe is a meaningful, embodied word.

Listen also to this:

While all things proclaim, "There is no deity but God," they also proclaim in unison, "O the Ultimate Truth!" and say with one voice, "O the All-Living One!" In everything there is a sign which demonstrates that He is One.

All this they say to their heart, and together with their heart, their soul also affirms the truth of their words, uttering, "Yes, indeed!"

In a brief reference to the five realities of Divine Unity which the guest in this world, the traveler through the universe, observed at the second mansion or the second stage of their journey, it was said in The Second Chapter of The First Station:

> There is no deity but God, the One, the Unique, Whose Unity and necessary Existence are demonstrated clearly through the observation of the truth of Grandeur and Sublimity in the perfection and comprehensiveness of each; through the observation of the truth of the appearance of Divine Acts in absolute fashion, in infinitude, without any limitation except that of God's Will and Wisdom; through the observation of the truth of the creation of beings in absolute multiplicity with absolute swiftness, the creation of creatures with absolute facility and absolute accuracy, and the origination of things in absolute abundance with utter perfection of artistry and value; through the observation of the truth of the existence of beings as universals and wholes, interconnected and interrelated; through the observation of the truth of the universal order, which contradicts absolutely any notion of partnership with God; and through the observation of the truth of the unity of the sources of the gratification of the needs of the universe, which attests most clearly to the Unity of its Maker and the union of the Names and the Acts with their all-encompassing operation, and of the elements and the species which cover the face of the earth.

THE THIRD STAGE

Then as our observer is traveling through the different ages, they enter the school of the famed Renewer of the Second Millennium, Imam ar-Rabbani Ahmad al-Faruqi[47], and attend a most important lesson. The words of the Imam were as follows:

> The most important result (or fruit) of all spiritual journeying is to attain complete perception of the truths of belief.

He also said:

> The complete perception of a single truth of belief is preferable to a thousand wonders and spiritual pleasures.[48]

---

47 Imam Rabbani, Ahmad Faruqi al-Sarhandi (d., 1624): The "reviver of the second millennium." Born in Sarhand (India) and well-versed in Islamic sciences, he removed many corrupt elements from Sufism. He taught Shah Alamgir or Awrangzeb (d., 1707), who had a committee of scholars prepare the most comprehensive compendium of Hanafi Law. His work, *al-Maktubat* ("The Letters") are very famous and widely known throughout the Muslim World. (Tr.)

48 Imam ar-Rabbani, *al-Maktubat* ("The Letters"), Letter no. 210. (Tr.)

The Imam added:

> In former times, great saints predicted that someone would arise from among the scholars of the science of theology. They predicted that he would prove all the truths of belief and Islam with rational proofs and the utmost clarity. I hope that I may be that man.

With that hope in mind, he taught that belief and the affirmation of Divine Unity were the foundation, substance, light and life of all human perfection. Furthermore, he taught that the *hadith* "An hour's reflection is better than a year's (supererogatory) worship,"[49] concerns reflection on the truths of belief, and that silent invocation and remembrance of God is preferred in the Naqshbandi Sufi Order because it is a form of this most excellent reflection.

The traveler listens intently to all of the Imam's teaching. Then they turned to their soul and address it as follows: "It is thus that this heroic Imam speaks. Increasing the strength of one's belief by as much as an atom is worth more than a ton of gnosis or other forms of perfection; it is sweeter than the honey of a hundred spiritual pleasures. Also, the doubts and objections of Western philosophers which have accumulated for a thousand years against Islamic belief and the Qur'an are at present finding a way to attack the believers. They wish to shake the pillars of belief, which are the key, the source and the foundation of eternal happiness, of everlasting life and of eternal Paradise. We should therefore strengthen our belief by basing it on investigation and experience rather than on mere imitation.

So come on, let us advance! In order to bring the twenty-nine ranks of faith that we have found, each as powerful as a mountain, up to the blessed number of thirty-three, the number of the glorifications that follow each of the canonical or prescribed Prayers, and in order to reach a third mansion or stage in this realm of instruction, let us knock on the door of the maintenance of the living world by the Lord and open it with the key of *In the Name of God, the All-Merciful, the All-Compassionate*." So saying, they knock imploringly on the gate of this third mansion, which is an assembly of wonders and an exhibition of marvels. They open it with the key of "In the Name of God, the All-Opening," and thus gain entrance to the third

---

49 al-Qurtubi, *al-Jami' li-Ahkami'l-Qur'an*, 4:314.

mansion. There they see that four great and comprehensive truths were illuminating that mansion and demonstrating the truth of Divine Unity as brightly as the sun.

THE FIRST TRUTH: the truth of Opening up

That is, innumerable varied and distinct forms everywhere are opened up simultaneously from a single simple substance by a single Act, through the manifestation of the Name the All-Opening. Through the manifestation of this Name, God's Power of origination has opened up in the garden of the universe innumerable orderly forms like flowers, bestowing a distinct identity on each of them. Similarly, in even more miraculous fashion, He has given each of the hundreds of thousands of living species in the garden of the earth its particular form, which is symmetrical, adorned and full of artistry and wisdom.

As indicated in the verses,

> He creates you in the wombs of your mothers, one act and phase of creation after another, in three veils of darkness. This is God, your true Lord (Who creates and sustains you): To Him belongs the sovereignty. There is no deity but He. How, then, are you turned away (to misleading ways)? (39:6)

> Surely God—nothing whatever on the earth and in the heaven is hidden from Him. It is He Who fashions you in the wombs as He wills. There is no deity but He, the All-Glorious with irresistible might, the All-Wise. (3:5–6)

the most powerful proof of Divine Unity and the most remarkable miracle of Divine Power is God's opening up of forms. For this reason, the truth of the opening up of forms is established and expounded repeatedly in different ways in various parts of the *Risale-i Nur*, particularly in The Sixth and Seventh Steps of The First Chapter of The Second Station of this treatise. Referring the reader to those sections, we say here only this:

As demonstrated by extensive research undertaken by scholars of botany and zoology, the opening up of forms is so comprehensive and artistic an act that none other than a Single, Unique and Absolutely Powerful One, able to see and do all things in all things, could achieve it. For this act of opening up of forms entails infinite wisdom, attention and comprehensiveness that could exist only in an infinite Power Which is present at all times and in all places. This Power, in turn, can be found only in the Unique Being Who administers the whole universe.

As is shown in the above-mentioned verses, God's Attribute of Opening, expressed in the measured, distinct and orderly opening and creation of the forms of people within three veils of darkness in their mother's wombs, without any error, confusion, or mistake is a most powerful proof of God's Unity. Similarly, the opening up of the forms of all human beings, animals, and plants all over the earth with the same Power, the same Wisdom and the same Artistry offers a most powerful proof of God's Oneness, allowing no room for any partnership with God. Just as the nineteen truths presented in The First Chapter in the form of nineteen steps bear witness to the necessary Existence of God and attest to the Existence of the Creator through their own existence, they also bear witness to His Unity through their comprehensiveness.

Our traveler then witnesses the second truth in the third mansion:

THE SECOND TRUTH: the truth of Mercifulness

We see with our own eyes that there is One Who has covered the face of the earth with thousands of gifts of Mercy, turning it into a veritable feasting-place. He has laid it out as a table where hundreds of thousands of different delicious foods of Mercifulness are arranged. He has also made the inside of the earth a storehouse containing thousands of precious bounties of Compassion and Wisdom. Furthermore, He sends us the earth, with its annual revolution, like a commercial ship or train laden with hundreds of thousands of the finest vital human necessities that issue from the World of the Unseen. He also sends us the season of spring like a wagon carrying food and clothing for us. He nurtures us with utmost compassion. And in order for us to profit from these gifts and bounties, He has endowed us with hundreds or thousands of appetites, needs, feelings, sensations and senses.

As was explained in The Fourth Ray concerning the verse on God's All-Sufficiency:

- He has given us a stomach that is created in such a way that we are able to derive pleasure from infinite varieties of food which pass through it.

- He has granted us a life that is structured in such a way that, through its senses, we are able to derive benefit from His innumerable bounties in the vast corporeal world, which resembles a banqueting table.
- He has bestowed on us the gift of humanity, which is such that through instruments like the intellect and the heart we may take pleasure in the boundless gifts which come from both the Unseen and visible worlds.
- He has conveyed to us Islam as a way of life, which is such that it enables us to derive light from the unrestricted treasuries of the Unseen and visible worlds.
- He has guided us to a faith which is such that we are able to be illumined by and get benefit from the innumerable lights and gifts of this world and the Hereafter.

This universe is like a palace that has been furnished and adorned by Divine Mercy with innumerable antiques and valuable artifacts. The keys to open all of the chests and chambers in that palace have been placed in the hands of humanity, who has also been endowed with all of the needs and senses that they require to make use of them. Thus this Mercy Which embraces this world and the Hereafter with all they contain must without doubt be a particular manifestation of God's Oneness within the overall manifestation of His Unity.

Just as the light of the sun is a parable of God's Unity (*Wahidiya*)—His all-encompassing or overall manifestation of His Names—with respect to the fact that it comprehends all things that face it, the fact that every bright and transparent object which, in accordance with its capacity, receives an image of the sun or a reflection of it with its heat and light and the seven colors in its light is a parable of God's Oneness (*Ahadiya*)—the particular manifestation of His Names in a particular thing or being. Hence, whoever sees its all-comprehending light will conclude that the sun of this earth is one. On seeing a reflection of the sun with its heat and light in all bright objects, and even in drops of water, they will say that a single sun is present with its attributes close to all things: it is at the mirror-like heart of all things.

Similarly, the fact that the extensive Mercy of the All-Merciful One of Beauty and Grace encompasses all things like a light demonstrates the Unity of that All-Merciful; it shows that He in no way could have any "partner." Also, the fact that under the veil of that all-embracing Mercy the lights of most of the Names of the All-Merciful and a sort of manifestation of His Divine Essence are present in all things—humankind especially—and the fact that this gives each individual a comprehensive nature arising from life which causes it to have relations with the whole universe proves the Oneness of the All-Merciful: it demonstrates beyond all doubt that He is present with all things and does all things in all things.

Just as the All-Merciful shows the splendor of His Majesty in the whole of the universe and all over the earth through the unity and comprehensiveness of His Mercy, through the manifestation of His Oneness He also assembles in every member of every living species, and particularly that of every human individual, samples of all His bounties. These He arranges in the form of the tools and instruments of that living member, making the whole universe into a particular home for them, thus proclaiming the special tenderness of His Grace and Beauty and announcing that all the varieties of His bounty are concentrated in every member of humankind.

For example, a melon exists in a concentrated form in its seed; from this we can understand that the One Who makes the seed must necessarily be the One Who makes the melon. Then, with the special balance of His Knowledge and the particular law of His Wisdom, He draws the seed out from it and clothes it with a body. Nothing or no-one other than the One and Unique Master Craftsman Who makes the melon is able to make its seed. Similarly, since through the manifestation of Mercifulness the universe is like a tree or a garden, the earth is like a fruit or a melon, and every living being—a human being in particular—is like a seed, it follows that the Creator and Lord of the smallest living being must be the Creator not only of the whole earth but also the entire universe.

In short: just as the making and unfolding of the proportionate and orderly forms of all beings through the truth of the all-encompassing Divine Opening proves without doubt the truth of Divine Unity, the same is proven by the truth of all-embracing Mercifulness. For It nurtures all living beings that come into existence and enter the life of this world, particularly the newborn, with the utmost order and regularity, causing all that they require to reach them, without ignoring or forgetting any of them. The fact that Mercy reaches all individuals everywhere at the same instant demonstrates both Divine

Unity and Divine Oneness along with Unity. Since the dimensions of the truth of Mercifulness have been expounded in other sections of the *Risale-i Nur* where the Names the All-Wise and the All-Compassionate are discussed, we will restrict ourselves here to this brief indication.

THE THIRD TRUTH: *The truth of Disposing and Administering*

Which our traveler observes in the third mansion or stage is the *truth of Disposing* and *Administering*.

This is the truth or reality of the disposal and administration, with complete order and balance, of all things, from the awesome and swiftly moving celestial bodies to the needy, weak creatures of the earth. For they are caused to help each other and are administered in cooperation with each other: all of the measures needed for their care are taken, and as they are taken, the vast world is made into a perfect state, a magnificent city, a magnificently adorned palace. Leaving aside the vast spheres of this imperious and merciful administration, we will, by means of a comparison, present a brief picture of a single page or stage of it which manifests itself on the face of the earth in spring. Readers desiring a more detailed explanation may refer to other sections of the *Risale-i Nur* such as The Tenth Word.

Let us suppose that some great world conqueror assembles an army from hundreds of thousands of different tribes and nations, and supplies the clothes and weapons, the instructions and salaries of every member of each tribe and nation, separately and variously, without any defect and flaw and without error or mistake, all at the proper time without any delay or confusion, with the utmost order and in the most perfect manner imaginable. Now, no cause or agent other than the extraordinary power of that great commander could stretch out a hand to play a part in that vast, complex, subtle, balanced, multidimensional and just administration. Were it to stretch out a hand, it would destroy the order and cause confusion.

Similarly, we see with our own eyes that an Unseen Hand creates and administers every spring a magnificent army composed of hundreds of thousands of different species. In fall —a sample of the Last Hour—this Hand discharges the great majority of those hundreds of thousands of species of plants and animals from their duties in the form of death. In spring—a sample of the Supreme Resurrection and assembly of all beings on the Day of Judgment —It raises hundreds of thousands of examples of the Supreme Resurrection in a few short weeks with the utmost order and discipline. After displaying four minor examples of the Resurrection on a tree—that is, restoring the tree itself to life and creating the exact likenesses of its former leaves, flowers and fruits—It gives each of the tribes and species of that army of glory, which comprises hundreds of thousands of different species, its appropriate provision, its multifarious defensive weapons and distinctive garments, its instructions and discharges, and all of its extremely varied tools and instruments, with the utmost order, without error or flaw, without confusion or omission, from unexpected sources and at the most appropriate time. It thus proves Its Unity, as demonstrated by the all-embracing manifestations of Its Attributes and Titles; It's Oneness, as displayed by the particular manifestations of His Attributes and Titles on particular things; and Its All-Independent Uniqueness, Its infinite Power and Its limitless Mercy within the perfection of Lordship, Sovereignty and Wisdom, writing with the Pen of Divine Destiny this proclamation of absolute Unity on the page of every spring on the tablet of the earth.

After reading only a single page of this proclamation in spring, our traveler says to themselves:

> That All-Compelling One of absolute Power, that All-Overwhelming One of Majesty, Who brings about in each spring thousands of resurrections more amazing that the Supreme Resurrection, has promised and assured all of His Prophets thousands of times that He will bring about the Supreme Resurrection. He also has set forth thousands of indications of its reality in the Qur'an and proclaimed it explicitly in thousands of its verses. And so the punishment of Hell is pure justice for those who commit the error of denying the Resurrection, for such denial would be to contradict the numerous promises and to deny the Power of that of that All-Compelling One of absolute Power, that All-Overwhelming One of Majesty.

When the traveler has said this, their soul has echoed their sentiments by saying: "I too believe!"

The fourth truth: *The truth of Compassionateness and Providing*

Which constitutes the thirty-third step, that the traveler has observed in the third mansion or stage is *the truth of Compassionateness and Providing.*

We can see with our own eyes that all living beings on earth, in the skies and in the seas, particularly those endowed with spirit, and among them especially the impotent, the weak and the young, are given all of their necessary sustenance, be it material or immaterial, in the most solicitous manner, at the most appropriate time, in the most orderly fashion, and without any omission or confusion, by an Unseen Hand. Some kinds of sustenance are derived from dry soil, some from dry, bone-like pieces of wood, while vast amounts of other kinds of sustenance come from a single seed. The most delicate of all of them is that which comes from between blood and waste matter.

The verse, *Surely God—it is He Who is the All-Providing, Lord of all might, and the All-Forceful* (51:58), restricts to God only the bestowal of provision, while the verse, *No living creature is there moving on the earth but its provision depends on God, and He knows its every lodging and disposition (every stage of its life), and the duration of its stay, and the moment of its transition therefrom. All is in a Manifest Book* (11:6), declares that the Lord has undertaken to give all humankind and animals the sustenance that is essential for their lives. Similarly, the verse, *How many a living creature there is that does not carry its own provision (in store), but God provides for them, and indeed for you. He is the All-Hearing, the All-Knowing* (29:60), establishes the fact that it is God Who guarantees and provides for all impotent, weak and wretched creatures that are unable to work to secure their sustenance, producing it from unexpected places—indeed from the Unseen or even out of nothing. For example, insects on the ocean bed and their young are provided for virtually out of nothing; all the young are provided for from unexpected sources, while all animals receive their sustenance every spring as if from the Unseen. The above verse establishes and proclaims even to those who ascribe everything to material causes or nature that it is He Who bestows provision from behind the veil of causality. In addition, numerous other Qur'anic verses and cosmic evidences demonstrate beyond doubt that it is through the Compassionateness of a single All-Providing One of Majesty that all animate beings are nurtured.

Indeed, since the trees, which need a certain form of sustenance, have neither power nor will, and therefore remain in their places in complete reliance on God, their provision comes hastening to them. The sustenance of the powerless young flows to their mouths from amazing small pumps, ceasing only when they acquire a little power and will. The sustenance of human infants in particular comes to them aided by the affection and tenderness of their mothers. These various instances show that lawful sustenance is not proportionate to will and power; rather it comes in relation to weakness and impotence, which stimulate trust in God.

Will, power and cleverness, which lead to greed and are a source of loss in most cases, often drive certain learned or literary people toward a form of beggary, while the trusting weakness of many ignorant, crude and common people may lead them to plenty. It is because of this that "How many are the learned whose path has led nowhere; how many are the ignorant who are knee-deep in riches." has become a proverb. This shows that a person is not led to lawful provision on account of power and will; rather, lawful provision is given to those whose labor and striving is deemed acceptable by the Giver of Mercy: it is granted by a Compassion that takes pity on their neediness.

Now provision is of two kinds:

The first kind is true provision, which is absolutely essential for life: this is guaranteed by the Lord. It is indeed so regular and well-ordered that the part of this basic provision stored in the body in the form of fat and other things, for example, is enough to ensure survival for at least twenty days, even if nothing is eaten. Those who appear to die of hunger before the twenty or thirty days are over or before the basic provision stored up in their body is consumed, die in reality not from a lack of provision but rather from a disease that results from bad or disrupted habits.

The second kind is the provision which is not really vital, but which has become necessary over time on account of habit, wastefulness and misuse. This kind of provision is not under the guarantee of the Lord but depends rather on His Generosity: sometimes He may give it, sometimes He may not.

With respect to this second form of provision, happy are they who regard the lawful acquisition of livelihood and the virtues of frugality and contentment—themselves sources of happiness and pleasure—as a form of worship and active prayer for sustenance. They accept what God grants to them gratefully and appreciatively, and spend their life in happiness.

On the contrary, wretched are those who abandon lawful acquisition of livelihood on account of their wastefulness and greed—sources of wretchedness, loss and distress—and instead knock on every door, spending their life in indolence, oppression and complaint, to the extent that they are ready to destroy their own lives.

In the same way that a stomach demands sustenance, the five senses of humans and their other faculties such as the heart, the spirit, the intellect, and the power of imagination also request, and receive with gratitude, their sustenance from the All-Compassionate Provider. The sustenance of each is granted to them separately and in an appropriate form from the treasury of Mercy, giving them pleasure and filling them with joy. Indeed, in order to grant them sustenance more generously, the All-Compassionate Provider has created each of these senses and faculties in the form of a key to His treasury of Mercy. For example, the eye is a key to the treasure chest which contains such precious jewels as beauty and loveliness on the face of the universe. Similarly, each of the other faculties and senses is a key to a different world, allowing humans to benefit from them through faith.

We now turn to our main discussion:

In the same way that the All-Powerful and All-Wise Creator of the universe has fashioned life to be a comprehensive summary or extract of the universe, concentrating all of His purposes and the manifestations of His Names therein, He has also made provision a comprehensive locus of His Acts within the world of life. Having created living beings with appetites and the taste for provision, He causes them to respond to His Lordship and His will to be loved by them with a permanent and universal sense of gratitude, thankfulness and worship, which constitute a most significant purpose and instance of wisdom of His for the creation of the universe.

For example, one of the Divine Acts demanded by the wisdom of His Lordship is the creation of beings appropriate to every part of His domains and His populating the universe with them: the celestial realm He fills with angels and similar supra-material beings; the Realm of the Unseen He populates with spirits; and the material world—in particular the atmosphere and the earth—He fills with numerous kinds of living beings, from the birds in the air to the flies and beasts of the field, from the fish in the seas to human beings on land. By endowing these living beings with an innate need for sustenance, He impels them to strive for their provision by making it pleasurable for them, and thus saves them from indolence and lethargy. Had it not been for such significant instances of wisdom, He would have made their essential provision hasten to animals without any effort on their part, just as He makes the provision of trees hasten to them.

Were we able to see the whole surface of the earth simultaneously in order to be able to perceive the gracious manifestations of the Names the All-Compassionate and the All-Providing and how they bear witness to Divine Unity, we would see what exquisite grace and sweet beauty are contained in the affectionate manifestation of the All-Compassionate Provider. For example, we would see how, at the end of winter when their provisions are almost exhausted, He sends to whole caravans of animals an abundance of varied and most delicious foods from His unseen treasury of Mercy: this sustenance, which is succor from the Unseen and a gift of His Compassion, comes to them by means of the hands of plants, the crowns of trees and the breasts of mothers. Were we able to see all of this, we would realize the following:

The One Who makes a single apple and provides a human being with it munificently can only be the One Who makes one season follow another and causes night to follow day; it can only be the One Who causes the cargo ship that is the earth to revolve, bringing the products of each season to His needy guests. For since the stamp of Creation, the seal of Wisdom, the signet of His Eternal Besoughtedness and the imprint of Mercy on the face of the apple can also be found on all apples and all other fruits, plants and animals, the true Owner and Maker of the apple must certainly be the All-Majestic Master and All-Gracious Creator of all the inhabitants of the earth, who are the peers, fellows and siblings of the apple. The Creator of that single apple must also be the Creator of the vast earth that is the garden where the apple is grown, of the tree that is the factory where it is manufactured, of the seasons that are the workshop where it is produced, and of the seasons of spring and summer that are its place of maturing. In short, every fruit is a seal of Divine Unity that makes known the Author and Maker of its tree, of the earth which is its garden, and of the book of the universe: it demonstrates His Unity and shows that this garden or book is a Divine decree to which the seal of Unity to the number of fruits is affixed.

Being a manifestation of the Names the All-Compassionate and the All-Wise, the *Risale-i Nur* has expounded numerous mysteries of the truth of Compassionateness in many of its parts. Readers who wish for a more elaborate discussion of these truths may refer to those parts, while we content ourselves here with this brief indication.

And so our observant traveler now says: "All praise be to God, for I have seen and heard thirty-three truths which bear witness to the necessary Existence and Unity of my Creator and Master, the One Whom I was seeking and enquiring after everywhere. Each of the truths is as strong as a mountain and as bright as the sun, leaving no point in darkness. Each of them, by being an established fact, bears decisive witness to His Existence, and with its comprehensiveness proves His Unity in manifest fashion. While also proving all the pillars of faith, the totality of these truths causes our belief to develop from the imitative to the investigative; it then allows us to verify our belief, and advance from certainty arising from knowledge to certainty arising from vision or observation, and therefrom to certainty based on experience. All praise and gratitude be to God, for this is nothing but a pure gift from my Lord!"

> All praise and gratitude are for God, Who has guided us to this. If God had not guided us, we would certainly not have found the right way. The Messengers of our Lord did indeed come with the truth. (7:43)

In a very brief reference to the lights of belief the inquisitive traveler derived from the four tremendous truths they observed at the third mansion or stage, it was said in The Second Chapter of The First Station concerning these truths:

> There is no deity but God, the One, the Unique, Whose Unity and necessary Existence are demonstrated clearly through the observation of the sublimely comprehensive truth of Opening, which, as testified by botany and zoology, is manifested in the unfolding of hundreds of thousands of species of living beings, perfect and without any defect; through the observation of the sublimely comprehensive truth of Mercifulness, all-embracing and absolutely orderly, without any deficiency, as can be clearly seen; through the observation of the sublimity of the truth of Administering, Which encompasses all living beings in an absolutely orderly fashion, without error or defect; and through the observation of the sublimely comprehensive truth of Compassionateness and Providing, Which embrace all consumers of sustenance at every time of need, without any mistake or forgetfulness. All-Exalted is the Majesty of their All-Merciful, All-Compassionate, All-Kind and Caring, and All-Bounteous and Favoring Provider. Universal are His gifts, all-embracing is His Favoring, and there is no deity but He.

All-Glorified are You! We have no knowledge save what You have taught us. Surely You are the All-Knowing, the All-Wise.

O Lord, for the sake of In the Name of God, the All-Merciful, the All-Compassionate, O God, O the All-Merciful, O the All-Compassionate, bestow peace and blessings upon our master Muhammad, his Family and all his Companions, to the number of all the letters in the *Risale-i Nur*, multiplied by all the seconds of the minutes of all of our lives in this world and the Hereafter, multiplied by the number of particles in my body throughout the course of my life. Forgive me and those who help me in sincerity with the copying and writing of the *Risale-i Nur*, for the sake of every peace and blessing, and forgive our parents, our masters, our teachers, our sisters, our brothers and the loyal students of the *Risale-i Nur*, particularly those who write and copy this treatise. Forgive us by Your Mercy, O Most Merciful of the Merciful, Amin. *The conclusion of their prayer is, "All praise and gratitude are for God, the Lord of all the worlds!"*

NOTE: Since the other parts of the *Risale-i Nur* were not available in the place where the above treatise was written, certain important matters included in *The Words* and *The Gleams* have been repeated in it. This has been done in the hope that each of these matters may strengthen the cause of the whole *Risale-i Nur* for its pupils in this area.

Said Nursi

* * *

On the purpose of the Risale-i Nur

I recently listened to a substantial discussion regarding the purpose of the *Risale-i Nur*. What follows is a summary of that discussion:

Someone said: "The *Risale-i Nur* is forever setting forth new treatises and proofs for the sake of belief and the Divine Unity. While even one hundredth part of its contents is enough to silence the most obstinate denier, what is the reason for the fervent increase in its publication?"

The following answer was given: "The *Risale-i Nur* is not repairing some minor damage done to some small house; it is repairing the incalculable damage that has been inflicted on the all-embracing citadel which contains Islam, the bricks of which are the size of mountains. It is not striving to reform a single heart or an individual conscience; rather, with the wonderful medicines of the miraculous Qur'an and true belief, it endeavors to heal the public heart, severely wounded as it has been by the weapons and instruments of corruption for over a thousand years. It is also striving to cure the public conscience, which is becoming corroded by the continuous attacks on the foundations, values and public symbols or marks of Islam, which are a refuge for the mass of believers and a point of support and reference for them.

"Certainly, to address and cure such terrible damage, destruction and wounding, incredibly strong proofs and arguments at the level of certainty based on experience, and numerous tried and tested medicines are necessary. The *Risale-i Nur*, which issues from the miraculousness and miraculous meanings of the Qur'an, performs this function, and is also the means by which one is able to progress through the infinite degrees of belief."

I listened to this long discussion intently and, when it was over, offered endless thanks to my Lord. I curtail the matter here.

Said Nursi

The Ninth Ray

The Ninth Ray

A powerful proof for the Resurrection

This Ray is the first part of a significant addendum to The Tenth Word.

In the Name of God, the All-Merciful, the All-Compassionate.

So glorify God when you enter the evening and when you enter the morning—and (proclaim that) all praise and gratitude in the heavens and on the earth are for Him—and in the afternoon, and when you enter the noon time. He brings forth the living out of the dead, and brings the dead out of the living, and revives the earth after its death. It is in this way that you will be brought forth from the dead. And among His signs is that He created you from earth; then, you have grown into a human population scattered widely. And among His signs is that He has created for you, from your selves, mates, that you may incline towards them and find rest in them, and He has engendered love and tenderness between you. Surely in this are signs for people who reflect. And among His signs are the creation of the heavens and the earth, and the diversity of your languages and colors. Surely in this are signs indeed for people who know. And among His signs is your sleeping at night and in the day, and your seeking (livelihoods) out of His bounty. Surely in this are signs for people who pay heed. And among His signs is His displaying before you the lightning, giving rise to both fear and hopeful expectation, and that He sends down water from the sky, and revives with it the earth after its death. Surely in this are signs for people who reason and understand. And among His signs is that the heaven and the earth stand firm by His Command. In the end, when He calls you forth from the earth, then

> (at once) you will come forth. To Him belongs all that is in the heavens and on the earth. All are obedient to Him in humble service. He it is Who originates creation in the first instance and then reproduces it, and will bring it back: and that is easier for Him. Whatever attribute of sublimity there is in the heavens and the earth, it is His in the highest degree, and He is the All-Glorious with irresistible might, the All-Wise. (30:17–27)

NE MOST SIGNIFICANT ARGUMENT INCLUDED IN THESE SUBLIME heavenly verses, which point to one pole of belief, in these exalted sacred proofs that establish the Resurrection's reality, will be explained in this Ray. It is a subtle Divine favor that at the end of *Muhakemat* ("The Reasonings"), which he wrote thirty years ago as an introduction to the Qur'anic commentary, the Old or Former Said wrote, "A Second Summation of Two Other General Proofs: This explains the two verses of the Qur'an which indicates the Resurrection. *In the Name of God, the All-Merciful, the All-Compassionate*"... and then put down his pen, unable to continue. Praise and thanks to my All-Compassionate Creator to the number of the signs and proofs of the bodily Resurrection, He has enabled me to resume that task.

Nine or ten years ago, God granted me The Tenth and Twenty-ninth Words, two works containing numerous strong proofs and interpretations of the Divine Decree—*Look upon the imprints of God's Mercy, how He revives the earth after its death. Certainly it is He Who will revive the dead (in a similar way), and He has full power over everything* (30:50). The Tenth and Twenty-ninth Words silenced those who denied the Resurrection. Now, a decade or so later, He has granted to me the interpretation of the supreme verses quoted above, unassailable fortresses of belief in the Resurrection. It consists of some parts, the first of which, (which we will discuss here,) is in the form of an introduction.

Part One: Introduction

> This Introduction consists of two points that briefly expound one of the many spiritual benefits of belief in the Resurrection and one of its vital comprehensive results. They also show how that belief is essential for human life, particularly social life, and summarize one of its many comprehensive proofs. Also included is an explanation of how evident and indubitable a matter is belief in the Resurrection.

The First Point

We will relate only four of the many arguments for belief in the Hereafter as the very basis and bedrock of human social and individual life, and as the foundation of all happiness and achievement.

The First Argument: Children make up a third of humanity. They cannot endure death, which must seem to them an awful tragedy, unless it be tempered by the idea of Paradise, which gives spiritual strength to their weak and fragile spirits. It gives them the hope to live joyfully, despite the vulnerability of their nature. Keeping Paradise in mind, they may say: "My little sister has died and become a bird in Paradise. She is flying there and enjoying a better life than us." If they could not do this, their awareness of the deaths of those around them would overwhelm them: it would crush their powers of resistance and inner strength, causing their eyes and all inner faculties, heart, mind and spirit to weep, and transforming them into the most wretched and distraught of creatures.

The Second Argument: The elderly make up another one-third of humanity. They can endure the grave, which is never far from them, only by believing in the afterlife; this consoles them to some extent in the face of what they see as the inevitable extinction of their lives, to which they are so attached, and the fact that their precious and lovable worlds have come to an end. Only the hope of eternal life allows them to counter the pain and despair which the anticipation of death and separation give rise to in their child-like, fragile temperament and spirit. Without such a hope, our venerable elders who are so worthy of compassion, those aged parents of ours who need a serene and steady heart, would become so distraught and distressed in heart and spirit that their world would seem to be a dark prison and their lives a ghastly torment.

The Third Argument: Young people are the mainspring and foundation of social life. Only the thought of Hell enables them to control the stormy energy of their feelings and passions, their tempestuous, evil-commanding souls, from destructiveness and oppression, and divert them into serving the collective interest of society. Without this fear, and drunk on the energy of youth, they would follow the principle of "Might is right" and give free rein to their passions and caprices. This would turn the world into a hell for the weak and powerless; it would lower human life to the level of beasts.

THE FOURTH ARGUMENT: The family is the most important core of our worldly life; it is our most fundamental resource, and the paradise, home and citadel of our worldly happiness. Each person's home is his or her own miniature world. The vitality and happiness of our homes and families depend upon sincere and devoted respect, true kindness and self-denying compassion. All of this, in turn, depends upon eternal friendship and companionship; it depends on an immortal bond, as well as the belief that feelings and relations between parents and children, brothers and sisters, and husbands and wives will be everlasting.

For example, a man can say: "My wife will be my eternal companion in an eternal world. Even if she is now old and not as physically beautiful as before, her eternal beauty will show itself in the Hereafter. For the sake of that companionship in eternity, I will make every sacrifice and show her as much compassion as I can in this world." Thus he can regard his aged wife with love, care and compassion as though she were a beautiful *houri*. A relationship that ends in permanent separation after a few hours of physical proximity can only be slight, transient and insecure: it would produce only a superficial love and respect based on physical attraction and sexual desire. Eventually, other interests and powerful emotions would arise and, defeating that respect and concern, turn a worldly paradise into hell on earth.

One of the numerous benefits in the Resurrection and afterlife therefore relates to human social life. If many other related aspects and benefits are deduced by analogy with these four, it will be clear that the realization of the truth of the Resurrection and its occurrence are as certain as our own existence and our universal needs. It will be even more evident than the argument that the stomach's need for sustenance testifies to the existence of food. Were it not for the Resurrection and afterlife, then the lofty status of being human—a status so significant, exalted and vital within creation—would be reduced to that of a carcass fed upon by microbes. Let those concerned with humanity's orderly life, morals and society focus on this matter. If the Resurrection is denied, with what will they fill the resulting void and cure humanity's deep wounds?

THE SECOND POINT

Among innumerable proofs of the truth of the Resurrection, we set out succinctly the support offered by the other pillars of belief. It is as follows:

- All miracles which affirm the Messengership of Muhammad, upon him be peace and blessings, all proofs of his Prophethood, and all evidence of his truthfulness establish and bear witness to the realization of the truth of the Resurrection. For after the Unity of God Almighty, all the claims which that exalted person set forth during his life focused on the Resurrection.
- Also, all the miracles and proofs of all other Prophets that attest to their Prophethood and urge humanity to attest to the same bear witness to this same truth.
- In addition, all the signs and proofs which establish the Divine-authorship of all the Divine Scriptures and therefore make completely clear the testimony to the Messengers, bear witness to this truth also.
- All miracles and proofs which establish the reality and truth of the Qur'an also establish and prove the realization of the truth of the Resurrection. For about a third of the Qur'an deals with the Hereafter: most of its short *suras* begin with powerful verses evoking it, and its truth is expressed explicitly or implicitly in hundreds of verses. For example:

> When the sun is folded up. (81:1)
>
> O humankind, keep from disobedience to your Lord in piety, the violent convulsion of the Last Hour is an awesome thing. (22:1)
>
> When the earth quakes with a violent quaking destined for it. (99:1)
>
> When the heaven is cleft open. (82:1)
>
> When the heaven is split asunder. (84:1)
>
> What are they asking each other about? (78:1)
>
> Has the account of the overwhelming event come to you? (88:1)

Just as the initial verses of about twenty *suras* state that the truth of the Resurrection is a most important and essential reality of creation, many other verses affirm and provide other evidences of the same truth. Given that the truth of the Resurrection has been established in a manner as clear as the light of day by numerous arguments and proofs of the Qur'an—a Book every verse of which has yielded innumerable fruits in both the religious and the natural sciences—would denial of this truth not be similar to denial of the existence of the sun itself? Would such a thing not be absurd?

A sovereign sometimes sends his army into battle merely to prove the truth of one of his statements. Is it then conceivable that the truth of that most solemn and glorious sovereign's innumerable words, promises and threats stand contradicted? Is it possible that they should be false? A single indication from that glorious sovereign—namely the Qur'an—is enough to prove the truth of the Resurrection, particularly given that it has ruled over and educated countless spirits, intellects, hearts and souls in perfect truth and righteousness for more than thirteen centuries. Having demonstrated this truth with thousands of explicit proofs, what else can we say except that those who continue to deny this truth are deserving of punishment in Hellfire? Would that not be pure justice?

Furthermore, all Divine Scriptures and sacred Books other than the Qur'an, each of which was addressed to a specific age and time, accept the truth of the Resurrection—a truth which the Qur'an, addressing all times, explains and establishes in detail and with explicit arguments. Even their brief and sometimes allusive explanations affirm it so powerfully that they constitute an irrefragable endorsement of what the Qur'an teaches.

We offer here an argument drawn from The Treatise of Supplication, The Third Ray. This argument, which includes the testimony of belief in the Last Day by the other pillars of belief—in particular, belief in God's Messengers and Books—is forceful and may suffice to end all doubt. In this supplication, we say:

> O my All-Compassionate Lord! Through the teaching of the noblest Messenger and the instruction of the wise Qur'an I have understood that all Divine Books and Prophets—primarily the Qur'an and Your noble Messenger—assert and testify that all Your Names of Majesty and Grace, Whose exemplary manifestations are witnessed throughout the universe, will continue to manifest themselves in the abode of eternity in a more brilliant way; that Your bounties and blessings, the merciful manifestations and samples of which are observed in this fleeting world, will endure in the eternal realm of happiness in a more brilliant fashion; and that those who are fond of them and who dis-

cern them in this brief worldly life with pleasure and seek them in love will accompany them through all eternity.

Also, based on the countless proofs of their Prophethood, including their hundreds of evident miracles, and on hundreds of decisive evidences which exist in all the Scriptures You revealed, but primarily in the wise Qur'an, as well as on the promises and threats that You repeat in them frequently; and relying on Your all-sacred Attributes and essential Characteristics such as Power, Mercy, Favoring, Wisdom, Majesty and Grace, Which require Resurrection, and on the dignity of Your Majesty and the dominion of Your Lordship; all the Prophets with luminous spirits, including first and foremost God's noblest Messenger, upon him be peace and blessings, and all the saints with illuminated hearts and the pure, saintly scholars with enlightened intellects, who rely on their spiritual unveilings and observations, along with their convictions at the degree of certainty of knowledge and certainty of vision or observation—all of these prominent members of humanity give both jinn and humankind the glad tidings of eternal happiness for the people of guidance, and they warn that Hell awaits the misguided, while themselves being the first to believe in and bear witness to this happiness and Hell.

O the All-Powerful and All-Wise! O the All-Merciful and All-Compassionate! O the All-Munificent Who is absolutely true to His promises! O the All-Overwhelming One of Dignity, Grandeur and Majesty!

Failure to bring about the Resurrection would mean contradicting so many truthful friends of Yours, breaking Your vehemently repeated threats and promises, and negating Your sacred Attributes and essential Characteristics, thereby leaving unfulfilled that which is required by the very nature of your dominion as the Lord; it would mean rejecting and render futile the hopes and prayers for the Hereafter of Your innumerable servants whom You love, and who make themselves loved by You by confirming and obeying You; it would also mean confirming the people of unbelief and misguidance in their rejection of the Resurrection, who through unbelief and disobedience and by contradicting You in Your promises, insult Your Grandeur, attack the dignity of Your Majesty, offend the honor of Your Divinity and disparage your Lordship's Compassion. Undoubtedly You are utterly exempt from and infinitely exalted above such a failure! I declare Your infinite Justice, Grace, and Mercy to be absolutely above such limitless ugliness and unrighteousness. We believe with all our heart that all of the Prophets—those more than one hundred thousand truthful messengers of Yours and heralds of Your dominion—and saintly, purified scholars and saints are absolutely correct in their testimony to Your eternal treasures of Mercy and Benevolence and the

> extraordinarily exquisite manifestations of Your All-Beautiful Names in the world of permanence with certainty based on knowledge, and certainty based on vision, and certainty based on experience. What they have indicated is true and conforms with reality. They also believe and teach other servants of Yours that the greatest ray of Your Name the Ultimate Truth, Which is the origin, sun and preserver of all truths, is this greatest truth of Resurrection.
>
> O Lord! For the sake of what they teach and in veneration of it, bestow on us and all students of the *Risale-i Nur* perfect belief and a happy end to our earthly lives. And allow us to receive their intercession. Amin!

All arguments and evidences which establish the veracity of the Qur'an and all other Divine Books, as well as the miracles and proofs establishing the Prophethood of Muhammad, the beloved of God, upon him be peace and blessings, and of all other Prophets also point to the truth and reality of the Hereafter; indeed, after the Unity of God, the reality of the Hereafter is the teaching which they emphasized the most. Similarly, most arguments and evidences for the Necessarily Existent Being's Existence and Unity also affirm the existence and appearance of the Abode of Happiness—that Realm of Eternity where God's Lordship and Divinity will be manifested most fully. For the Existence of the Necessarily Existent One, as well as most of His Names, and all His Attributes and His essential Characteristics such as Lordship, Divinity, Grace, Wisdom, and Justice necessitate most certainly the existence of an eternal realm—the Hereafter—and the resurrection of the dead for the meting out of just punishment and reward.

Since an All-Eternal God exists, most certainly there is a Hereafter, the everlasting pivot of His Divine Sovereignty. Since we see that a most magnificent, wise, caring, purposeful and absolute Lordship exists throughout the entire universe, there must certainly be an eternal realm of happiness to which admission is granted, so that the majesty of that Lordship is not extinguished, His Wisdom is rendered futile, and His Caring is not destroyed by betrayal and oppression.

Since these infinite visible bounties, blessings, kindnesses and instances of generosity and mercy show to hearts and minds that are not dead the fact that an All-Merciful and All-Compassionate Being exists beyond the veil of the Unseen, there must of necessity be an eternal life in an eternal world, for it is the existence of such a world which can show that His Divine bounties are not for nothing, that His Act of bestowing is not in truth an act of deceit, that His Favoring His servants is not something deserving only of enmity, that His Mercy is not in reality a torment, and that His generosity is not in actual fact an act of betrayal. In addition, eternity and everlastingness will allow all bounties and blessings to assume their true and perfect forms.

Also, each spring on the narrow page of the earth, a Pen of Power tirelessly inscribes before our eyes innumerable books one within the other without the slightest error. The Owner of that Pen has promised repeatedly: "I will write a beautiful, imperishable book in a place far more spacious than this and 'more easily' than this cramped and intermixed book of spring, which is written on such a narrow page, and I will allow you to read it." He mentions this book in all of His decrees. Given this, its draft has been written already, and it will be set down in writing with all its additions and footnotes on the Day of Resurrection. And all the records of people's deeds will be included in it.

Also, the earth has a special importance. For on account of the multiplicity of its inhabitants and the fact that it is the abode, origin, workshop, and place of display and resurrection of countless constantly changing species of living beings and beings with spirits, it is the very heart, center and core of the universe; indeed, it is the very reason for the creation of the universe. Despite its small size, the heavenly Decrees hold it equal to the vast heavens, describing God as the Lord of the heavens *and* the earth. And there is humanity, which dominates the earth. We have dominion over most of its creatures; we subordinate and gather around ourselves almost all animate beings, and order, display and ornament most of the creation according to our needs and desires. We catalogue and classify all things in their wonderful variety, each species in its own place, and in such a way that all people and jinn, all dwellers of the heavens and the universe, gaze upon it with appreciation; even the Lord of the universe bestows His appreciative glance upon it. We have thus a very high value and importance, and through our arts and sciences we show that we are the reason for the creation of the universe and its most important and valuable fruit. We have been chosen and appointed to administer the earth and develop it according to our Creator's laws. Since we demonstrate and arrange most excellently the miraculous works of our Maker in this world, we are given a respite here despite our rebellion and unbelief, and our punishment is postponed.

On account of the services we perform, we are granted a temporary stay and are favored with success.

However, despite being endowed with such qualities, we are in reality extremely weak and impotent when it comes to fulfilling the demands of our nature and disposition: we have innumerable needs and are subject to innumerable pains. And yet a most powerful, wise and caring Ruler provides for us in a way altogether beyond our power and will. He makes the planet a storehouse stocked with every kind of mineral and food we need and with all the merchandise we desire. Thus does the Ruler nurture and take care of us and grant our wishes.

The Lord Who does all this loves us and makes Himself our beloved. He is eternal and has eternal worlds. He does all things with justice and wisdom. But the magnificence of this All-Eternal Ruler's Sovereignty and the eternality of His Rule cannot be encompassed within the transient life of this fleeting, temporary world. Furthermore, many of the enormous injustices which humanity commits, and which are hostile and contrary to the wise order, just balance and harmonious beauty of the universe, go unpunished in this world, as does much of the rebellion, betrayal, denial and unbelief of countless people with respect to their Benefactor and Provider. The cruel and the treacherous appear to live charmed lives, while the oppressed and downcast live in wretchedness. But the absolute justice, traces of which can be seen throughout the universe, is by its very nature totally at odds with the notion that the cruel and the treacherous—who die just like the oppressed and the desperate—should never be resurrected to account for their crimes at a supreme tribunal.

Since the Owner of the universe has chosen the earth out of the universe and humankind out of the earth, giving both a high rank and significance. Out of humankind, He has chosen the Prophets, saints, and pure, saintly scholars—true human beings who conform to His purposes as the Lord of creation and make themselves loved by Him through belief and submission. He has taken them as friends and addressees, ennobling them with miracles and Divine support, while punishing their opponents with wrathful blows from above. And out of these lovable and most valued friends He has chosen their leader and source of pride, Prophet Muhammad, upon him be peace and blessings. For long centuries He has illumined with his light the half of the globe and one-fifth of humanity. As though the universe were created solely for his sake, all of its exalted purposes become manifest through him, his Religion, and the Qur'an revealed through him. Although he was deserving of an infinite reward for the inestimable value of the services he rendered—services that would take ordinary people thousands of years to perform—he was granted a brief life of no more than sixty-three years spent in hardship and struggle. Is it then at all likely that he should not be resurrected, together with all his peers—the other Prophets—and Companions? Or that he should not, even now, be alive in the spirit? Or that they should die and disappear into eternal extinction? The entire universe and the truth on which it is based demand his being again, demand his life from the Owner of all that is.

Thirty-three powerful arguments in The Supreme Sign, The Seventh Ray, have established that the universe is the handiwork and property of a Single Being. They have also demonstrated self-evidently His Unity and Oneness, Which give rise to all His Perfections. Through His Unity and Oneness all beings become His duty-bound soldiers and absolutely obedient officials. And by means of the Hereafter, His Perfections remain ever free of defect; thanks to the existence of the world to come, His Absolute Justice will never become reduced to absolute treachery, His universal Wisdom to foolish pointlessness, or His all-inclusive Mercy to frivolous tormenting. Thanks to the Hereafter, His all-dignified Power is saved from being reduced to impotence.

Without doubt, and as is necessitated by the universal truths discussed—the truths from among the many which arise from the cardinal truth of God's Existence and Unity—the Resurrection will occur. The dead will be resurrected and gathered together on the Place of the Supreme Gathering, and the realm of reward and punishment will open its gates. All this will occur so that the real significance and centrality of the earth, and the true significance and value of humanity may be truly realized. It will occur so that the Justice, Wisdom, Mercy and Sovereignty of the All-Wise Ruler, Who is the Creator and Lord of us and our planet, will be established wholly and eternally. It will occur so that all true friends and ardent lovers of the All-Permanent Lord may be delivered from eternal annihilation, and that the nearest and dearest of them, upon him be peace and blessings, may be rewarded for the sacred services with which he graced the world. And the All-Eternal Sovereign's Perfections will show themselves to be without defect, His Power will show Itself to be without incompetence, His Wisdom without foolishness and His Justice without oppression.

In sum, the Hereafter exists because God exists.

The three pillars of faith mentioned above—belief in the Existence and Unity of God, belief in Prophethood and belief in the Qur'an and other Divinely-revealed Scriptures—bear witness to the truth and reality of the Resurrection. Similarly, the remaining two pillars of faith—belief in angels and belief in Divine Decree and Destiny—also require the Resurrection and bear witness to the reality of that eternal realm. We will elucidate as follows:

All proofs which establish the existence of the angels and their duties of worship, as well as numberless human observations of them and conversations held with them, also attest to the existence of the world of spirits, the World of the Unseen, the Hereafter, the world of permanence and the abode of happiness and Hell, which in the future will be peopled by human beings and jinn. For the angels are able to see and enter these worlds by Divine leave. All the angels who are close to the Divine Throne and who communicate with humanity, such as Gabriel, are unanimous in reporting their existence and their travels in these abodes. Even if we ourselves have never been to America, for example, the reports of travelers returning from there leave us in no doubt as to its existence. Similarly, the reports given by angels, which have the authority of numerous undisputed narrations, should leave us in no doubt as to the existence of the eternal realm of the Hereafter and of Heaven and Hell.

All arguments contained in the Twenty-sixth Word (on Divine Decree and Destiny) which establish the pillar of faith also attest to the Resurrection, to the revealing in the world to come of all our recorded deeds in this world, and of their being weighed in a Supreme Balance. For the apparent order, regularity and balance in the universe provide an indication of the fact that the lives of all things were pre-recorded and lived out according to that eternal program. Also, the life history of every animate being is inscribed in its memory or its seed, and other tablet-like forms; the deeds of every being endowed with spirit, especially human beings, are recorded on preserved tablets. Such an all-embracing determining, such wise and purposive ordaining, such detailed and precise recording and inscribing exist only to enable the meting out of permanent reward or punishment at the

Supreme Tribunal on the Day of Judgment. Were this not the case, such comprehensive, meticulous recording and registering would have no purpose or meaning; it would be contrary to sense and reality. Moreover, if there were no Resurrection, all of the carefully established meanings inscribed by the Pen of Divine Destiny in the book of the universe would be annihilated. This would be tantamount to denying the existence of the universe itself.

In short, then, the five pillars or articles of faith and their proofs bear witness to and necessitate the Resurrection: they require that the Realm of the Hereafter appear and open its gates. It is because, in keeping with its vastness and sublimity, the truth of Resurrection has such firm and tremendous supports that approximately a third of the miraculous Qur'an is devoted to it. The Qur'an makes it—next to belief in God—the bedrock of all of its truths and constructs everything on its basis.

The Tenth Ray

This comprises descriptions of the contents of treatises that have been written following The Fifteenth Gleam in *The Gleams*. It was written by certain leading students of the *Risale-i Nur*. Since it was published as a separate book, it is not included here.

The Eleventh Ray

The Eleventh Ray

A treatise on the fruits of belief

This is the response of the *Risale-i Nur* to heresy and absolute unbelief. It is our true defense in this incarceration of ours, for it is this and this alone which occupies us here. This treatise is a fruit and souvenir from Denizli Prison, and the product of two Fridays.

Said Nursi

In the Name of God, the All-Merciful, the All-Compassionate.

So he remained in prison for some years more (12:42).

ACCORDING TO THE MEANING OF THIS VERSE, PROPHET JOSEPH, upon him be peace, is the patron-saint or guide of prisoners: prison may be seen to be a kind of "School of Joseph." Since this is the second time that students of the *Risale-i Nur* have been sent to prison, it is necessary to study and teach in this school a number of matters connected with imprisonment, which are explained by the *Risale-i Nur*. In the hope that we may benefit from them thoroughly, we will explain five or six of those matters in brief.

The First Matter

As expounded in the Fourth Word, every day our Creator bestows on us twenty-four hours of life as a kind of capital with which to obtain that which is necessary for our lives in both this world and the next. If we spend twenty-three of these hours on this extremely fleeting worldly life and fail to spend the remaining one hour—which is sufficient for the five obligatory canonical Prayers—on the very lengthy life of the Hereafter, it is clear that we will have committed an error of the greatest magnitude. One can hardly imagine what a great loss this would be or the extent of the distress that our mind and spirit would be made to feel as a result of our shortsighted behavior. Not only would our future actions be ruined by our distress, we would also be unable to reform our conduct on account of the despair that would overwhelm us.

However, if we spend that one hour on the five obligatory Prayers, the profit to be had is inestimable. For each hour of this calamitous term of imprisonment will at times be equal to a whole day's worship, while the single hour devoted to the canonical Prayers will be transformed into many permanent hours. In addition, the despair and distress we feel in our hearts and spirits will begin to fade, and one hour's Prayer will serve as atonement for the errors that led to imprisonment in the first place, thus allowing them to be forgiven. Furthermore, it will also help us to receive training and improvement, which is the purpose of imprisonment. How beneficial this is and how pleasing a consolation it is for us and our companions in hardship!

As was written in The Fourth Word, let us suppose that a person gives five or ten liras out of his twenty-four to a lottery in which a thousand people are taking part in order to win the thousand-lira prize, but fails to give a single lira to buy a ticket for an everlasting treasury of jewels. See how he rushes to the former, even though the possibility of his winning the thousand liras in that worldly lottery is no more than one in a thousand. And see how he flees from the latter, even though according to the reports given by a hundred and twenty-four thousand Prophets, and the confirmation provided by countless numbers of truthful informers from among the saints and purified saintly scholars, the chances of a true believer winning that 'lottery', the prize of which is everlasting felicity in the Hereafter, is nine hundred and ninety-nine out of a thousand. Now think how irrational this is, to rush towards the former but to flee from the latter!

Prison governors and wardens, and indeed the country's administrators and guardians of public order, should be pleased with this lesson that is provided by the *Risale-i Nur*, for it has been witnessed and experienced on numerous occasions that the management and disciplining of a thousand religious people who constantly have in mind the prison of Hell is far easier than that of ten people who have no belief at all, who do not perform the obligatory Prayers, who care only about worldly imprisonment, who have no consideration for what is licit or illicit, and who have become habituated to living undisciplined lives.

A Summary of the Second Matter

As explained in the treatise entitled *Gençlik Rehberi* ("A Guide for Youth") in the *Risale-i Nur*, death is as inevitable as night following day, or winter following fall. Just as this prison is a temporary guesthouse for those who enter and leave it one after the other, the earth too is a like a caravanserai on a long road; here caravans, rushing to get to their destination, stay overnight before moving on. Surely death, which has emptied all of the cities of the earth into the bowels of the earth a hundred times over, places demands on us far greater than those demanded by life. The *Risale-i Nur* has explained this awesome truth, a brief summary of which follows:

Since death cannot be eliminated and since the door of the grave cannot be closed, we must look for a way that can save us from being condemned by the executioner of death to the solitary confinement of the grave and eternal perdition in the world to come; surely this should be humankind's greatest concern and surely it is in our best interest to investigate this possibility? There is such a way—a way shown by *Risale-i Nur* and inspired by the teachings of the Qur'an. What follows is a brief summary:

Death is either eternal execution—a gallows on which a person and their friends and relatives will be hanged—or it is a kind of entrance ticket to another, permanent realm, a palace of happiness prepared for those who possess belief. As for the grave, it is either a dark, bottomless pit of solitary confinement or a door which opens outward from the prison of this world onto a permanent, illuminated garden and place of feasting. This truth has been expounded in the *Gençlik Rehberi* as follows:

For example: many gallows have been set up in this prison yard, and immediately beyond the wall a huge lottery office has been opened; everyone in the world has purchased a ticket. There is no doubt whatsoever that the five hundred people in this prison are certain to be called one by one, without exception, to that yard: there is no hope of escape. One can hear the announcements being made: "Come and receive your document of execution and mount the gallows!" or "Take in your hand the decree condemning you to eternal solitary confinement and enter through that door!" or "Congratulations! Yours is the winning ticket that is worth millions. Come and take it!" We see with our own eyes that people are mounting the gallows, one after the other. Yet, while some mount the gallows only to be hanged, we learn from the reports of the earnest officials who are working in the prison yard that some of the people are using the gallows as one would a ladder, and are scaling the wall to enter the lottery office that lies beyond.

At this juncture, two delegations enter our prison. One delegation brings musical instruments, wine and apparently delicious sweetmeats and pastries, which they endeavor to make us eat. But the sweetmeats are in fact poisonous, for demons in human form have put poison in them.

The second delegation brings papers of education and training, lawful foods and licit drinks. The members of this delegation present these things to us and say with great earnestness:

"The gifts brought by the first delegation are a test; if you accept and consume them, you will be hanged on the gallows over there, like the others that you have seen hanged before them. However, if you accept the gifts that we have brought you at the command of this country's ruler, and if you recite the supplications and prayers written on these papers of education and training, you will be saved from execution. Believe without a shadow of a doubt that each of you will receive the winning lottery ticket worth millions as a royal favor. But if you eat these unlawful, poisonous sweets, it is written in these decrees—decrees with which we all concur—that you will suffer the effects of the poison until the very moment that you are taken to the gallows to be hanged."

As in this comparison, for the people of belief and obedience—provided that they depart in a state of true belief—the ticket for an eternal and inexhaustible treasury will be drawn from the lottery of human fate beyond the gallows at the appointed hour, of which we are always aware. However, for those with no belief in the Hereafter and who persist in vice, unlawful actions, unbelief and sin, there is a hundred per cent probability that they will, unless they repent, be condemned by judicial decree to execution and eternal perdition. For those who believe in the immortality of the human spirit, yet still tread the path of vice and sin there is a ninety-nine per cent probability that they will be condemned to permanent solitary confinement. Certain news of this was given by one hundred and twenty-four thousand Prophets, all of whom were equipped with innumerable miracles as evidence of their truthfulness. The same news has been given by more than one hundred and twenty-four million saints, who discern and affirm through spiritual uncovering the traces and shadows—as though seen on a movie screen—of the news brought by the Prophets. Similarly, thousands of millions of exacting scholars, interpreters of the Islamic law and veracious scholars have, with decisive proofs and powerful arguments, established with rational and logical certainty the information provided by these two eminent groups of people.

Consider, then, the situation of someone who, on the advice of a single individual, abandons the safe path they have been following and opts for a longer and much more dangerous one, ignoring the collective wisdom of the people of truth mentioned earlier—those moons, suns and stars, those sacred leaders of humanity—who have pointed out the straight path which leads directly to eternal felicity.

The situation of such a person is this: having embarked on this journey, the wretch hears someone say that by taking the short path there is a one per-cent chance of danger and the possibility of a month's incarceration at the end of the road. So, on the spurious advice of a single person, our traveler abandons the short path and takes a longer route. They do this because it appears harmless, although in reality there is no benefit in this path. At the same time, innumerable wise and well-informed individuals warn them not to abandon the shorter and easier of the routes—the one which will, with utmost certainty, lead them eventually to Paradise and eternal happiness. However, they chose to ignore their words and opt for the rougher, more troublesome route—the one which, with ninety-nine percent certainty, will lead to incarceration in Hell and everlasting misery. Surely, such a wretch has lost their mind, their heart and their spirit, for only a drunken lunatic would flee from the slight sting of a few mosquitoes on the safe path and rush onto a route along which dragons hide, waiting to attack and tear the poor wretch limb from limb.

Since this is the reality of the situation, we prisoners should accept the gifts of the second, blessed delegation so that we may avenge ourselves completely for the calamity of our incarceration. That is to say, just as the pleasure of a minute's revenge or a few minutes of vice has condemned us to years of incarceration, making our worlds into a prison, in order to take revenge we should transform an hour or two of our prison lives into a day or two of worship. In this way we will be able to transform two or three-year sentences into twenty or thirty years of permanent life thanks to the gifts of that blessed delegation; in this way we will be able to turn prison sentences of twenty or thirty years into a means of forgiveness from millions of years of incarceration in Hell, thus allowing our everlasting lives to smile in retaliation for the weeping that has characterized our transitory worlds. Demonstrating that prison is a place of training and education, we should try to be well-behaved, trustworthy, and useful members of our nation and country. Prison officers, wardens, and administrators should also see that the men whom they considered to be bandits, vagrants, murderers, and men of vice—and thus harmful to the country—are in fact students engaged in study in this most blessed place of education. And they should feel pride and offer thanks to God for this bounty.

The Third Matter

What follows is a summary of an instructive incident that is described in *Gençlik Rehberi*:

I was once sitting by a window in Eskişehir Prison during the National Republic Day. The young girls in the school opposite the prison were playing and cheering in the schoolyard. Suddenly, I saw them fifty years on, their future conditions played out to me like a film on a movie screen. I saw that of those fifty to sixty girl students, forty to fifty had turned to dust in their graves and were suffering. The other ten were unattractive septuagenarians, despised by those from whom they might have expected love, on account of the fact that they had not preserved their chastity when young. Observing this, I wept at their pitiable states. Some of my friends in the prison heard my weeping and asked me what was wrong, but I had to tell them to leave me alone for a while.

You must understand that what I saw was real and not imaginary. Just as summer and fall are followed by winter, the summer of youth and the fall of old age are followed by the winter of the grave and the Intermediate Realm. If there were a device which could show future events in the same way that films can show the events of the past, then those of fifty years ago would be shown in the present, and the people of misguidance and vice would be shown their condition fifty years from now; they would cry out in pain and disgust, bemoaning bitterly their present state of apparent felicity and illicit pleasures.

While preoccupied with these observations in Eskişehir Prison, a sort of collective persona, which encourages vice and misguidance, appeared embodied before me like a devil in human form. It said:

"We want to taste all the pleasures and joys of life, and to make others taste them too; do not interfere with us!"

In response I said:

"Since for the sake of pleasure and enjoyment you do not recall death but, rather, plunge yourself into vice and misguidance, know for a fact that because of your misguidance all the past is dead and non-existent: it is a desolate and most dreadful graveyard, filled with rotted corpses. The pains that arise from those innumerable separations you have suffered and from the deaths of your friends—pains which, since there is no hope of reunion with your loved ones, have had a grievous effect on what remains of your heart and mind—will soon destroy those insignificant drunken pleasures which constitute your present. As for the future, well, because of your lack of belief, that too is nothing more than a dark, dead, and desolate wasteland. And since the unfortunate wretches who are destined to come from there to emerge in this realm of existence and in the present will also be beheaded by the executioner's sword of death and, according to your assumption, thrown into non-existence, on account of your concern and relationship with them which stems from your being a creature with intelligence, grievous worries will rain down continuously on your disbelieving head, devastating beyond recognition your petty, dissolute pleasure.

"If you abandon misguidance and vice and enter the sphere of true belief and righteousness, you will see through the light of faith that the past is neither non-existent nor a graveyard filled with rotted corpses; rather, it is a real, luminous world that has been transformed into the future: it is a waiting-room for the immortal spirits who will enter palaces of happiness in the world to come. Since it is so, it gives no pain; on the contrary, depending on the degree and strength of one's belief, it causes a sort of paradisiacal pleasure in the world. The future, too, when seen through the eye of belief, is not a dark, desolate wasteland, but a ground in whose palaces of eternal happiness banquets and exhibitions of gifts have been set up by an All-Merciful, All-Compassionate One of Majesty and Benevolence—One Who has infinite Mercy and Munificence and Who makes spring and summer into tables laden with bounties. Since the movie screen of belief reveals the future to be like this and since belief also gives the awareness that people are being dispatched there through the door death, everyone can experience some sort of the pleasure pertaining to that permanent realm while still in this world, to the degree and strength of their belief. *In conclusion, true, pain-free pleasure can be found only in belief and is possible only through belief.*

"Since it is related to our discussion, we will explain something which was included in *Gençlik Rehberi* as a postscript, namely a single instance of the thousands of benefits and pleasures that belief produces even in this world. It is as follows:

"Imagine, for example, that your beloved only child is suffering the pangs of death and you are desperately worried about her painful demise. Suddenly, a physician like Khidr or Luqman appears with a wonderful medicine, which he gives to your loved one. Your dear, most adorable child opens her eyes, delivered from death. Can you imagine the joy and relief that you would feel at her recovery and escape from death?

"Like the child in the example, countless people whom you love and for whom you are concerned are, in your view, about to rot away for all eternity in the graveyard of the past. Suddenly, like Luqman the Wise, the truth of belief shines a light from the window of the heart onto the grave, which is thought of as a vast place of eternal annihilation. Thanks to the truth and light of belief, all of the dead spring to life, as though saying, 'We did not die and will not die; we will meet with you again!' What boundless joy and exhilaration you would feel at experiencing this reality! By giving the same boundless joy and exhilaration in this world, belief proves that it is like a seed—a seed which, were it to be embodied, would grow into a private paradise, a veritable *Touba*-tree of eternal felicity."

Persisting in its obduracy, that devil in human form responded thus:

"At least we can pass our lives like animals, immersed in pleasure and enjoyment, indulging ourselves with amusement and dissipation, and casting all thought of these subtle and delicate matters out of our minds!"

My answer was as follows:

"No, you cannot live like an animal, not least because neither past nor future exists for animals. They feel neither sorrow nor regret over the past nor worry or fear with regard to what is yet to come. An animal receives unalloyed pleasure. It lives and sleeps in comfort, offering thanks and praise to its Creator. Even an animal that is about to be slaughtered does not feel anything. It feels pain as the knife cuts its throat, but that pain is momentary and disappears in an instant. This means that keeping the Unseen unknown, without revealing what will happen there, is a great instance of Divine mercy and compassion; it is an even greater blessing for innocent animals. But on account of the fact that human beings are sentient, and because their past and future can be seen to emerge from the Unseen to some extent, what lies beyond the veil of the visible world cannot remain wholly hidden; as a result, O human being, you are unable to live as carefree and unconcerned as animals. Regrets about the past, the pain of separation and worries about the future reduce to ashes your fleeting present pleasures, making them a hundred times less appealing than those enjoyed by the animals. Since this is a fact, either abandon your intellect, turn yourself into an animal, and achieve salvation that way or, alternatively, come to your senses through true belief, pay heed to the Qur'an, and experience pure pleasure also in this transitory world, which is a hundred times greater than that enjoyed by animals."

For a while, these words of mine silenced my adversary. But in his obstinacy he turned to me once more and said: "Well, then, we can at least live like the irreligious people of the West."

I replied:

"In the same way that you cannot live like animals, you cannot live like the irreligious people of the West either. For even if they deny one Prophet, they believe in others. Even if they do not recognize the Prophets, they may believe in God. And even if they do not know God, they may have certain personal characteristics and virtues through which they find fulfillment. But if a Muslim denies the final Prophet, the greatest of God's Messengers, upon him and them be peace and blessings, whose religion and mission are universal, to what can they turn? For they will be unable to accept any other Prophet and will even have to turn their back on God Himself. For their knowledge of God and all the other Prophets has reached them through Prophet Muhammad, upon him be peace and blessings; without him, how can other Prophets have a place in anyone's heart? It is because of this that while many people have, since the earliest times, abandoned other faiths to enter Islam, few, if any, Muslims have become true Jews or Christians. Muslims who abandon Islam tend rather to become completely irreligious: as a rule, their characters are corrupted and they become a danger to the country and nation."

Hearing this argument, the obstinate devil in human garb could find no further straw at which to clutch. Unable to respond, it disappeared and went to Hell.

So, classmates of mine in this School of Joseph! Reality is as I have described it, affirmed by the *Risale-i Nur* which, with its proofs, has worn down the obduracy of many an obstinate soul and caused numerous people to believe over the past twenty years. Since it is thus, we should therefore follow the way of belief and correct conduct—a way which is safe and easy, and which benefits our lives and those of the members of our nation not only in this world but also in the next. Instead of indulging ourselves with pointless and ultimately painful fantasies, we should spend our free time reciting the *suras* of the Qur'an that we have memorized and learn their meaning from friends who can teach them. We should make up for the canonical Prayers we have failed to perform in the past. And, taking advantage of each other's good qualities, we should try to transform this prison into a blessed garden in which the seeds of good character can be nurtured. With righteous deeds such as these, we should do our best so that the prison governor and those concerned may be kindly masters and guides charged with the duty of preparing people for Paradise in the School of Joseph and supervising their training and education, rather than dispensers of torment, like the Angels of Hell, who stand over criminals and murderers.

The Fourth Matter

Again, this matter has been explained in *Gençlik Rehberi*. I was once asked the following question by some brothers who were helping me:

"For fifty days now you have asked nothing at all, nor have you shown any curiosity, about this terrible World War which has thrown the whole world into chaos, even though it is connected closely with the fate of Islam and the Muslim World. However, some of the religious and the learned listen to the radio intently, and some are even distracted from congregational Prayers as a result. Is there some other event more momentous than this war? Or is it in some way harmful to be preoccupied with it?"

My reply was as follows:

"The capital of life is very little and the work to be done very great. Like concentric circles, everyone has certain spheres of concern which exist one within the other: they have the spheres of the heart and the stomach; the spheres of body and home; the spheres of the quarter in which they reside and the town or city in which they live; the sphere of their country, the spheres of the earth and humankind, and the sphere of all living beings and the world as a whole. Each person may have certain duties in each of those spheres, but the most important and permanent duties are those which pertain to the nearest, smallest sphere, while the least important and temporary duties pertain to the furthest, largest one. According to this standard, there may be duties, the importance and sphere of which are inversely proportional to each other. But because of the appeal of the largest sphere, those vital duties that pertain to the smallest sphere tend to be neglected, as people become preoccupied with unnecessary, trivial, and peripheral matters. It destroys the capital of their life for nothing and causes them to waste their precious time on worthless things. For example, someone who follows the events of the war may come to support one side in their heart, and as result may even look favorably on tyranny and become a part of it.

"With regard to the first part of the question, all people—Muslims especially—are faced continuously with events more momentous than this World War, and an issue infinitely more important than that of world dominion. Indeed, if everyone had the wealth of the Germans and the English, plus an iota of sense, they would spend it all on finding a solution to this issue. This issue, about which hundreds of thousands of Prophets, saints, and purified scholars have informed us, relying on the thousands of promises and pledges given by the Owner and Disposer of the universe, is as follows:

"For everyone there exists the possibility of winning, thanks to belief, an eternal property that is as vast as the earth, filled with gardens and palaces. Without belief, however, that property cannot be gained. In this age, many are losing because of the plague of materialism. A certain saintly scholar, who was capable of unveiling certain hidden realities, once observed in one district that out of forty people who lay on their deathbeds, only a few won; the others lost. Can anything, even power and dominion over the whole world, substitute for such a loss?

"We *Risale-i Nur* students know that it would be foolhardy to abandon the duties conducive to felicity in the Hereafter, and to give up on that excellent lawyer who helps ninety-nine percent of the people to win their case, and instead preoccupy ourselves with trivia as though we would remain in this world forever. For this reason, we *Risale-i Nur* students are convinced that if each of us were a hundred times more intelligent than we are now, we would still use our intellectual capital on the same right cause.

"To my new brothers here who share with me the calamity of imprisonment I would say this. You have not yet come to know the *Risale-i Nur* as well as my old brothers, who entered this place with me. Calling on them and thousands of students like them as witnesses, I assure you that the *Risale-i Nur* is the leading 'lawyer' of the age, inspired by the miraculousness of the wise Qur'an and able to help those who study it to win the most important case of their lives. Indeed, over the past twenty years it has helped twenty thousand people to attain true belief—itself a guarantee that their case will be successful. Although for the past eighteen years my enemies and various heretics and materialists have cruelly turned some members of the government against me and the authorities have imprisoned us in order to silence us, something they have tried to do before, they have been able to criticize only two or three of the one hundred and thirty pieces of 'equipment' which make up the steel fortress of the *Risale-i Nur*. In other words, the *Risale-i Nur* is enough for one who wants to engage an advocate to win the case of their life. Also, do not fear, for the *Risale-i Nur* cannot be banned! With two or three exceptions, its most significant treatises are circulating freely among representatives and other leading figures of the government. By God's leave, a time will come when venerated governors and officials will distribute these lights to the prisoners as though they were food and medicine in order to turn the prisons into truly effective houses of reform."

The Fifth Matter

As described in *Gençlik Rehberi*, there is no doubt that a person's youth will one day disappear: just as summer gives up its place to fall and winter, and just as day eventually becomes evening and then night, youth will one day become old age and end in death. All Divinely-revealed Scriptures tell us that if the young spend their youth on righteous deeds, behave chastely and act within the bounds of good conduct, they will eventually gain eternal youth. However, if they waste their youth and spend it on dissipation, they will lose it forever. Just as a murder resulting from a minute's fury brings in its wake millions of minutes of imprisonment, the illicit pleasures of youth will, as every young person may confirm from their own experience, prove to contain more pain than pleasure. As well as the regrets that one feels in this world with the passing of such pleasures and the penalties one often receives here as a result of sin, there is the torment of the grave to consider, as well as the fact that one will have to answer for one's misconduct in the Hereafter.

For example, the temporary pleasure to be found in illicit love is changed into poisonous honey on account of the pangs of jealousy, separation, and not being loved in return. If you want to understand why young people frequently end up in hospital with physical and mental diseases on account of their excesses, or in prison on account of their misconduct, or in bars and dens of vice, you only have to visit those places. And the graveyards are full of those who were destroyed as a result of the distress caused by the inability of young human hearts to find true nourishment through the performance of their proper duties. Visit the hospitals and prisons and listen to the sighs of regret and watch with pity the tears that are shed for a youth that has been frittered away on excess, misconduct, and illicit pleasure.

The Qur'an and all other Divinely-revealed Scriptures and Decrees inform us in many of their verses that if it spent within the bounds of good conduct, youth will be preserved in the Hereafter, where, as a Divine favor, it will become immortal. Since the sphere of the lawful is sufficient for human enjoyment, and since an hour of unlawful pleasure sometimes leads to years of punishment in prison, surely it is vital to spend the sweet bounty of youth correctly and within the bounds of righteous conduct as thanks for that bounty.

The Sixth Matter

The following is a brief indication of one of the thousands of the universal proofs of the pillar of belief in God, many of which, together with explanations, can be found in the *Risale-i Nur*.

In Kastamonu some high-school students asked me: "Tell us about our Creator, for our teachers do not speak of Him." I said to them: "All of the sciences you study speak continuously of God, the Creator, in its own tongue, and makes Him known. Do not listen to your teachers; listen to them.

"For example, a well-equipped, well-designed pharmacy has many medicines and pills, composed of different, precisely-measured components. This indicates, without a doubt, to the existence of an extremely skillful and learned pharmacist. In the same way, the pharmacy of the earth is stocked with countless life-giving cures and medicines. Through the science of medicine, even the blind can know the All-Wise One of Majesty Who is the Pharmacist of the largest pharmacy of the earth.

"Let us use another example. A wonderful factory that produces thousands of different cloths woven from a simple material indicates without a doubt the existence of a manufacturer and a skillful mechanical engineer. Similarly, the factory of the Lord, which we call the earth, has countless parts, and each part possesses hundreds of thousands of machines. Without a doubt, the factory that is the earth makes known, through the science of engineering, the existence of its Manufacturer and Owner.

"Another example is a shop that has a well-organized storage place for numerous varieties of provisions brought there from hundreds of different places. The very existence of the shop indicates in turn the existence of a shop owner who prepares, stores, and distributes those provisions. Now the earth on which we live may be seen as a huge storehouse of mercy or a Divine vessel which traverses a vast orbit each year, housing innumerable species which require different foods: as it passes through the seasons on its journey, it fills spring, which is like a huge wagon, with a great variety of provisions and brings them to all the living creatures whose sustenance was exhausted during the winter. This storage depot, which is the earth, surely indicates, through the science of economics which you are studying, the existence of the Owner, Manager, and Organizer of this depot that is the earth and makes Him loved.

"Or imagine, for example, an army that consists of numerous tribes and nations, each one requiring unique provisions, weapons, uniforms, drills, and demobilization. If its miracle-working commander meets all their needs on his own, without forgetting or confusing any of them, surely the army and its camp will serve as an indication of this commander's existence and make him appreciated. Similarly, every spring a single Commander-in-Chief provides a newly recruited army of countless animal and plant species with uniforms, rations, weapons, training, and demobilizations in a perfect and regular fashion. He forgets nothing and does not become confused. This Divine army of spring indicates, through military science, the existence of that most attentive and sensible Ruler of the earth, its Lord, Administrator and All-Holy Commander, and makes Him loved, praised, glorified, and acclaimed.

"Or imagine a magnificent city illuminated by millions of mobile electric lamps with an inexhaustible fuel and power source. Such a set-up would evidently point to the talent of a wonder-working artisan and extraordinarily skilful electrician who makes the lamps, establishes the power source, and provides the fuel. And it would cause others to admire and congratulate this electrician.

"Now many of the lamps—the planets and the stars—which adorn the roof of the palace that is the world, in the city that is the universe, are a thousand times larger than the earth and move with an amazing speed. Yet despite their rapidity, they move most precisely without colliding with one another; they are not extinguished, nor do they run out of fuel. The science of astronomy, which you study, tells us that our sun, which is like a lamp or a stove in the guesthouse of the All-Merciful, is hundreds of thousands of times larger than the earth and several billion years old. To keep burning each day, it needs as much oil as there are seas on the earth, as much coal as there are mountains, or as many logs and pieces of wood as exist on ten earths.

"It is clear, then, that such lamps indicate with their fingers of light the existence of an infinite Power and Sovereignty Which, in turn, illuminates the sun and other similar stars without oil, wood, or coal, allowing them to travel at great speed without colliding with one another or being extinguished. Thus, the science of electricity and the testimony of those radiant stars indubitably indicate the existence of the Sovereign, Illuminator, Director, and Creator of the greatest light exhibition of the universe, and make Him loved, glorified, and adored.

"Now imagine a marvelous book. Within each line of that book, another, smaller book has been written, and within each word, a whole chapter—a *sura*—has been inscribed with a fine pen. This book is most meaningful and expressive, and all of its topics corroborate each other. Such a book shows as clearly as daylight that it must be the product of a particular artist, who is possessed of extraordinary perfections, arts, and skills. It makes us appreciate the author and call down God's blessings upon him.

"What is true of the book in the example is true of the vast book that is the universe. For example, we see with our own eyes a pen inscribing on the page of the earth hundreds of thousands of plants and animal species, each one of which is like an entire volume in itself. And they are inscribed all together, one within the other, without error or confusion; they are inscribed with such perfection and precision that an ode is compressed in a single word, like a tree, and an entire book is to be found within a point that is a seed. However much vaster and more perfect and meaningful than the book in the example mentioned above is this infinitely meaningful compendium that is the universe, this embodied 'macro-Qur'an,' in every word of which there are numerous instances of wisdom, to that degree—through the natural sciences that you study, it makes known the Inscriber and Author of this book of the universe with His infinite Perfections. Proclaiming "God is the All-Great," it makes Him known; declaring His sacredness with "All-Glorified is God," it describes Him; and praising Him with such expressions as "All praise and gratitude are for God," it makes Him loved.

"Indeed, through its extensive measure, its particular mirror, its far-reaching view, and its searching and instructive perspectives, each of the hundreds of sciences makes the All-Majestic Creator of the universe known with His Names, Attributes and Perfections.

"It is in order to elucidate the evidence explained above, which constitute a most convincing and magnificent proof of Divine Unity, that the miraculous Qur'an frequently describes our Creator in terms such as 'the Lord of the heavens and the earth' and 'the Creator of the heavens and the earth'."

I told the students all of this and they accepted and affirmed it, saying: "Endless thanks be to God, for we have received a true and sacred lesson. May God be pleased with you."

I added as follows:

"A human being is a living machine subject to many sorrows and capable of knowing many pleasures. Although totally impotent, we have infinite physical and spiritual enemies. Although completely destitute, we have infinite internal and external needs, and we suffer continuously from the blows of gradual decay and separation. But if, through belief and worship, we can establish a connection with the All-Majestic Sovereign, we will find a source of support against all of our enemies and a source of help for all of our needs. Everyone takes pride in the honor and rank of those in high places with whom they enjoy a connection. Given this fact, if one establishes a connection through belief with the infinitely Powerful and Compassionate Sovereign; if one enters His service through worship and, by so doing, changes the sentence of execution at the appointed hour of death into a most welcome acquittal and discharge, imagine the pride, joy, and contentment they will feel."

To the calamity-stricken prisoners I repeat what I said to the schoolboys: those who recognize and obey Him are prosperous, even if they are in prison, while those who forget Him are like wretched prisoners even if they live in palaces.

Once a wronged but fortunate man—fortunate on account of his belief and ensuing martyrdom—said to the wretched wrongdoers who were executing him: "I am not being executed; rather, I have been discharged from my duties and am going forward to eternal happiness. However, I can now see that you are condemned to eternal punishment; this suffices as my revenge upon you." And saying "There is no deity but God," he died a happy man.

> All-Glorified are You! We have no knowledge save that which You have taught us. Surely you are the All-Knowing, the All-Wise.

The Seventh Matter

This is the fruit of one Friday in Denizli Prison.

In the Name of God, the All-Merciful, the All-Compassionate.

> The matter of the Hour (of Doom) is (in relation with the Divine Power) but the twinkling of an eye, or even quicker. Surely God has full power over everything (16:77).

> Your creation and your resurrection are but as (the creation and resurrection) of a single soul. (31:28)

> Look, then, at the imprints of God's Mercy—how He revives the dead earth after its death: certainly then it is He Who will revive the dead (in a similar way). He has full power over everything (30:50).

Those inmates of Denizli Prison who were able to have contact with me also read the lesson in The Sixth Matter that I had given to the high school students in Kastamonu—those who had asked me: "Tell us about our Creator." Having acquired a firm belief, they felt a longing for the Hereafter, and said to me: "Teach us about the Hereafter too, so that our evil-commanding souls and the devils of the age do not cause us to deviate from the Straight Path and end up in prison again." And so the request of the *Risale-i Nur* students in the Denizli Prison and the readers of The Sixth Matter has made it necessary to explain in brief the pillar of belief that is the Hereafter. Here I will offer a short summary of the relevant discussions on the Hereafter in the *Risale-i Nur*:

In The Sixth Matter we asked the heavens and the earth about our Creator, and they revealed Him to us as clearly as the sun through the tongue of the sciences. Having come to know our Lord, we will first ask Him about the Hereafter; we will then ask our Prophet, then the Qur'an, then the other Prophets and Scriptures, then the angels and finally the universe itself.

Our first step is to ask God Himself about the Hereafter. He replies through all the Messengers He sent, through the decrees He revealed in the form of Books or Scriptures, and through all of His Names and Attributes: "The Hereafter exists, and I am dispatching you there." The Tenth Word has explained the Hereafter with twelve decisive arguments based on a number of Divine Names. Contenting ourselves with these explanations, we will give only brief indications of them here.

There is no sovereignty that does not reward those who obey it or punish those who rebel against it. Therefore an eternal Sovereignty, Which is at the degree of absolute Lordship, will certainly reward those who adhere to It through belief and submit to Its decrees; similarly It will punish those who deny It through unbelief and rebellion. Reward and punishment will be meted out in a manner befitting God's Mercy and Grace, and His Dignity and Majesty respectively. Thus do the Names the Lord of all worlds, the Sovereign, the Supreme Ruler and the All-Requiting One reply to our question.

What is more, we see a universal Mercy and an all-embracing Compassion and Munificence on the earth as clearly as we see daylight. Every spring, for example, Mercy dresses all the fruit-bearing trees and plants like the *houris* of Paradise and fills their hands with every kind of fruit. And it is as if these trees hold out their fruits to us, saying: "Please help yourselves and eat!" Mercy, Compassion, and Munificence also offer us healing sweet honey to eat from the poisonous bee and dress us in the softest silk by means of a tiny insect without hands. They also deposit for us in a handful of minute seeds numerous kilos of food, making those tiny stores into reserve supplies. Surely such Mercy and Compassion would not annihilate for all eternity those lovable, grateful, worshipping believers whom they nurture so tenderly? Rather, they discharge them from their worldly duties in order to bestow on them still more radiant gifts of Mercy and Compassion. Thus do the Names the All-Compassionate and the All-Munificent answer our question, affirming that Paradise will truly come.

Also, we see clearly that a hand of Wisdom is at work in all creatures on the earth with such skill and that events take place according to standards of Justice with such precision that the human mind cannot conceive of any wisdom or justice superior to them. For example, that eternal Wisdom inscribes in the human memory, a human faculty from among hundreds of faculties and no bigger than the tiniest seed, the entire life-story of a human being, together with the numerous events that fill it, making it in effect a small library. In order to remind human beings continuously of their deeds—deeds which are recorded and will be published openly so that they can be judged in the Place of Resurrection—that Wisdom inserts this small library into the mind, as a note of the record of our deeds. As for perpetual Justice, It endows all creatures with organs and members in an exceedingly balanced and harmonious manner, from the microbe to the rhinoceros, from the fly to the eagle, from the tiniest flowering plant to the countless millions of plants and flowers that make up spring, and makes each one into a wonderful work of art. This It does according to a precise balance and order, with due proportion and exquisite beauty and with no waste at all. It also gives all living creatures their rights of life in perfect measures and makes good things produce good results and evil things evil results. And since the time of Adam, upon him be peace, this Justice has made Itself felt forcefully through the blows It has dealt to rebellious and tyrannical peoples. Certainly, just as the sun is linked inextricably with daylight, eternal Wisdom and everlasting Justice are linked inextricably with the Hereafter and necessitate its existence. It is inconceivable that they would allow the most tyrannical and the most oppressed to be equal in death, without true justice being dispensed; they would never tolerate such iniquity, unfairness, or such a lack of wisdom. Thus do the Names the All-Wise, the

All-Judging, the All-Equitable and the All-Just give a conclusive answer to our question.

Also, whenever living creatures seek their natural needs, which are beyond their power, through the language of their innate capacities and essential neediness, which is itself a kind of supplication, these needs are provided by a most compassionate Hand from the Unseen. Moreover, approximately seventy percent of voluntary verbal supplications offered by human beings, and especially by the Prophets and other most distinguished believers, are accepted in a manner that lies outside the normal course of events. It can thus be understood clearly that behind the veil of the Unseen there is One Who is All-Hearing and All-Answering, Who listens to the sighs of every suffering creature and the prayers of every needy soul. He sees the most insignificant need of the smallest living being and hears its most secret sigh. Having compassion on them, He duly answers them and satisfies them.

There is one from among humankind, the most important of God's creations, who includes in his prayers the universal invocation of all humanity concerning the eternal life, which is connected with all the Divine Names and Attributes and, indeed, the entire universe. This being has the support of all the other Prophets, and the suns, stars and leaders of humankind, who exclaim, "Amin! Amin!" so that his prayer may be accepted. Also, every devout person in his Community of believers invokes God's peace and blessings on him several times a day, and adds an "Amin!" to his prayer. And all the other creatures also take part in his prayer, saying, "O Lord, give him what he asks for; we too ask for what he asks for!" While there are countless reasons why the Resurrection must of necessity come about, it is no exaggeration to say that a single prayer of Prophet Muhammad, upon him be peace and blessings, everlasting life and happiness in the Hereafter is sufficient for the existence of Paradise and the creation of the world to come, which is as easy for Divine Power as the creation of spring. Thus, do the Names the All-Answering, the All-Hearing, and the All-Compassionate provide an answer to our question.

Also, it is as clear as the daylight which indicates the existence of the sun that behind the veil of the visible world is an unseen One Who shows Himself in the control and management of the earth, in the deaths and revivals which take place as the seasons come and go. He administers the mighty earth with the ease and orderliness of a garden or even a tree; He tends to the splendid spring as though it were a single flower, and with the same facility, decoration, and sense of proportion; He displays the countless species of plants and animals as though they were hundreds of thousands of books exhibiting hundreds of thousands of examples of the Resurrection. The Pen of Power Which inscribes these things one within the other, all intermingled yet without the least disorder, confusion, fault, flaw, or error, and with perfect order and purposefulness—this vast, comprehensive Power operates with limitless mercy and infinite wisdom. The One Who possesses that Power has subjugated, decorated, and furnished the vast universe for human beings as though it were a house, and has appointed human beings as ruler of the earth, bestowing on them the "Supreme Trust"[50]—a trust which the mountains, sky and earth would not take on, and from which they shrank in fear. He has favored human beings with the rank of commander over other living beings to a certain degree, and honored them by making them the recipient of the Divine address and conversation, thus conferring on them a supreme status. Moreover, in all the revealed Decrees He has promised humanity eternal happiness and permanence in the Hereafter. From all this it follows that for humankind, whom He has so ennobled and honored, He will certainly open up that realm of happiness, which is as easy for His Power as the creation of spring, thus bringing about the Resurrection and the Last Judgment. So, the Names the All-Reviving, the All-Dealing One of death, the All-Living, the Self-Subsisting, the All-Powerful, and All-Knowing answer our question.

If one considers the Power Which every spring brings back to life the roots of all the trees and plants that have died in winter and creates hundreds of thousands of plants and animals as examples of the Resurrection, and if one visualizes the thousand-year period of each of the communities of Prophets Moses, upon him be peace, and Muhammad, upon him be peace and blessings, it can be seen that the two thousand springs display innumerable examples and proofs of the Resurrection to come. One would have to be completely blind and senseless to imagine that that bodily Resurrection is difficult for such a Power.

50 The Supreme Trust is human selfhood or being human or human nature as the focus of the manifestations of God's Names that are manifested throughout the universe. (Tr.)

Furthermore, a hundred and twenty-four thousand Prophets, the most renowned of all humankind, attested unanimously to the truth of eternal happiness and permanence in the Hereafter; not only did they rely on God Almighty's countless promises in this regard, but they proved it themselves through their own miracles. Also, innumerable saints have testified to the same truth through their illuminations and spiritual unveilings. Since this is so, surely this truth is as clear as the sun, and those who doubt it must be mad.

The opinions and judgments of one or two scholars or scientists concerning their particular field of expertise are sufficient to refute the opposing ideas of a thousand people who lack such expertise, even though they may be masters in their own fields. Similarly, two people who testify to the existence of something are able to defeat a thousand who deny its existence simply by producing an example of that thing. For instance, if two trustworthy people claim that they have seen the crescent moon which heralds, say, the lunar month of Ramadan, on a day when the sighting of the new moon is unlikely, although not impossible, their claim is accepted as veracious even if everyone else denies it. Also, if two people claim that there is a garden on the earth where coconuts resembling cans of milk are grown, their claim will be verified if they bring forth a single coconut or, alternatively, indicate the place where they can be found. Those who deny this claim, however, can prove their point only by searching all four corners of the earth in order to demonstrate that no such coconuts exist anywhere. Thus one who claims that Paradise exists can prove his claim simply by demonstrating a trace, a shadow, or a manifestation of it. Those who deny it, however, can prove their point only by scouring the whole universe and traveling throughout all time, from pre-eternity to post-eternity, in order to demonstrate its non-existence. It is because of this that scholars have agreed on the rule "Provided that they are not inherently inconceivable, denials or negations which are not concerned with a specific matter but which pertain to the whole universe, such as the truths of belief, cannot be proven," and accepted it as a fundamental principle.

Because of this undeniable truth, the opposing opinions of thousands of philosophers should not cast even the slightest doubt or suspicion on even one truthful and trustworthy individual who brings reports concerning matters of belief. You may understand, then, what lunacy it is to fall into doubt concerning the pillars of belief or faith—pillars upon which countless thousands of Prophets, saints, and scholars have agreed—on account of the denial of a handful of philosophers who rely solely on their physical senses and who have grown distant from all matters spiritual.

Also, it is as clear as daylight itself that working in ourselves and all around us there is a comprehensive Mercy, an all-embracing Wisdom, and constant Grace and Favoring. We also observe the traces and manifestations of an awesome sovereignty of Lordship, a precise and elevated Justice and the dignified activity of Majesty. Indeed, Wisdom, Which affixes to a tree as many instances of wisdom as there are fruits and flowers on that tree; Mercy, Which bestows favors and bounties and on every human being to the number of their members, senses, and faculties; and the dignified, gracious Justice, Which protects the rights of the downtrodden and punishes wrongdoers such as the rebellious people of Noah, Hud, Salih, and the Pharaoh, and the verse:

> And among His signs is that the heaven and the earth stand firm (subsisting) by His Command. In the end, when He calls you forth from the earth (with a single, particular summons), then (at once) you will come forth (30:25),

all state the following with consummate succinctness:

Obedient and well-disciplined soldiers in their barracks spring to their feet and rush to their duties as soon as their commander summons them and the bugle has been sounded. Similarly, when the dead of the heavens and the earth, which are like two well-ordered barracks for the obedient soldiers of the Eternal Sovereign, are summoned by the Trumpet of the Archangel Israfil, upon him be peace, they will immediately don the "uniforms" of their bodies and rise up. This is similar and testified to by the fact that those lying dead in the barracks of the earth in winter act in similar fashion every spring with the trumpet-blast of the Angel of Thunder. It is therefore impossible that the sovereignty of Lordship, which can be understood from this mighty event and which is explained in The Tenth Word convincingly, would allow the infinite grace and beauty of Mercy to change into infinitely ugly cruelty by not bringing into existence the abode of the Hereafter, the realm of the Resurrection, or the Supreme Gathering, all of which are most definitely required and necessitated by that Mercy, Wisdom,

Favoring, and Justice. It is utterly impossible for that limitless perfection of Wisdom to be turned into infinitely worthless futility and wastefulness, for that sweet Favoring to change into utterly bitter treachery, for that precisely balanced and equitable Justice to be transformed into the most severe tyranny, for that infinitely majestic and powerful eternal Sovereignty to decline and lose all Its magnificence, and for the perfections of Lordship to be tainted with impotence or defect. Such a thing would be completely unreasonable and inconceivable; it is false, precluded, and completely beyond the bounds of possibility.

Anyone with consciousness would surely understand how cruel it would be if, having been nurtured so tenderly and endowed with faculties such as the intellect and heart, which long for eternal happiness and everlasting life, humanity were to be annihilated completely and consigned to nothingness. How contrary to wisdom it would be if the myriad purposeful faculties and endless capacities of the human mind were to be wasted completely through eternal annihilation; how utterly opposed to the magnificence and perfection of Divine Sovereignty and Lordship would it be if God were to be revealed—God forbid!—as impotent and ignorant due to His failure to carry out His countless promises. Thus do the Names the All-Merciful, the All-Wise, the All-Just, the All-Munificent, and the All-Sovereign answer with the above truths the question we asked our Creator concerning the Hereafter, proving it beyond a shadow of a doubt.

We also see clearly that a vast, all-encompassing Act of Preservation prevails over creation. It records the numerous forms of all things, beings, and events, the duties they perform throughout their lives, and their deeds, which are like the glorification of God in response to the Divine Names manifested in them, on the tablets that belong to the World of representations or "ideal" forms, in their seeds and in their memories, which are tiny samples of the Supreme Preserved Tablet, as well as in the capacious libraries that have been placed in the mind, and in other material and supramaterial mirrors, where they are reflected. It inscribes, records and preserves them, and then, when the time comes It displays before us all these immaterial inscriptions in physical form: every spring, a mighty flower of Divine Power, proclaims to the universe an amazing truth of the Resurrection which is expressed in the verse: *And when the scrolls (of the deeds of every person) are laid open* (81:10), in billions of languages and with the force of millions of examples, proofs, and samples. In this way It offers the most powerful proof that created beings, humans in particular, are not destined for eternal annihilation and non-existence. Rather, they have been created in order to advance continuously toward and through eternity, to gain permanence through perpetual purification and refinement, and to embrace the everlasting duties necessitated by their endless innate capacities.

Every year we observe that the innumerable plants which die in the doomsday of fall, and all of the trees, roots, seeds, and grains which are resurrected in the spring, recite the verse: *And when the scrolls (of the deeds of every person) are laid open*. By carrying out the same duties as it performed in previous years, each interprets one meaning or aspect of this verse in its own language. In this way, they all testify to that vast Act of Preservation. By displaying in everything the four tremendous truths of the verse, *He is the First, the Last, the All-Outward and the All-Inward* (57:3), they inform us of this Preservation and the Resurrection with the ease and certainty of spring.

These four Names manifest themselves and act on all things, be they particular or universal. For example, receiving or being favored with the manifestation of the Name The First, a seed, which is a tiny case containing the precise program of the tree and the faultless systems of its creation and growth, proves indubitably the vastness of Divine Preservation.

Similarly, every fruit, which manifests the Name The Last, is a coffer that contains in its seeds the list of the contents of all the duties the tree has performed, together with the principles of the life of another tree identical to it. So it too testifies completely to the act of Divine Preservation.

The physical form of the tree, on which the Name The All-Outward manifests Itself, is a finely proportioned, skillfully decorated garment, resembling the multi-colored, gilt-embroidered robes of the *houris* of Paradise. As such it visibly demonstrates the tremendous Power, the perfect Wisdom, and the awesome grace and beauty of Mercy which are manifested in the Act of Divine Preservation.

The inner mechanism of the tree, which is favored with the manifestation of the Name The All-Inward, is like a an orderly, miraculous factory, a workshop where innumerable chemical processes take place and which possesses a precisely measured cauldron of food, which leaves none of its branches, fruits, or leaves without nourishment. So flawless is this mechanism that it proves beyond all doubt the perfection of the Power and Justice and the grace and beauty of Mercy and Wisdom that are manifested in the Act of Divine Preservation.

Similarly, with regard to the annual seasons, the earth resembles a tree. Through the manifestation of the Name The First, all the seeds and grains entrusted to Divine Preservation in the season of fall are like tiny collections of the Divine Commands and lists of principles that issue from Divine Determination or Destiny concerning the formation of the tree of the earth which will put forth billions of branches and twigs, flowers and fruits when it is eventually dressed in the garments of spring. These seeds and grains are also lists and tiny records of the tasks and deeds that the tree has performed in the previous summer. This quite clearly demonstrates that they work through the infinite Power, Justice, Wisdom and Mercy of an All-Preserver of Majesty and Munificence.

Then in the season of fall, the tree of the earth deposits in tiny cases all the duties it has performed, all the glorifications it has made in response to the manifestations of the Divine Names, and all the records of its deeds that will be published in the following resurrection of spring: these it submits to the hand of the Wisdom of the All-Preserving One of Majesty, reciting before the whole universe *He is the Last* in countless tongues.

By opening hundreds of thousands of different kinds of blossoms, which demonstrate hundreds of thousands of examples and signs of the Resurrection, and by spreading out innumerable banquet tables of Mercy, Providence, Compassion, and Munificence for living beings, the outer form of the tree offers praise and commendation, reciting *He is the All-Outward* in languages to the number of its fruits, flowers, and foods. And in so doing it demonstrates beyond all doubt the truth of: *When the scrolls (of the deeds of every person) are laid open* (81:10).

As for the inner face of this splendid tree, it is, as mentioned earlier, a kind of kitchen or workshop, operating numerous well-arranged machines and finely balanced factories with perfect order and in a regular fashion; these enable it to produce thousands of kilos of food out of one ounce to offer to the hungry. It works with such precision and balance that it leaves no room for chance. Like certain angels who glorify God with a thousand tongues, the inner face of the tree that is this earth exclaims *He is the All-Inward* in a hundred thousand ways.

In addition to resembling a tree with regard to its annual cycle, which makes the Divine Preservation manifested through those four Names a key to the door of the Resurrection, the earth is also a well-organized tree with regard to its entire worldly life; the fruits of this tree are sent to the market of the Hereafter. It is a place for the manifestation of these four Names which is so vast; it is a road that leads to the Hereafter which is so broad that our minds are incapable of comprehending them. All we can say is this:

The hands of a weekly clock which count the seconds, minutes, hours, and days resemble one another and indicate the nature and function of one another. Therefore, one who sees the movement of the second hand cannot help but admit the movement of the other hands and the other pieces of the clock's mechanism. Similarly, the days which count the seconds of this world, which is a vast clock of the All-Majestic Creator of the heavens and earth, the years which count its minutes, the centuries, which show its hours, and the eras, which make known its days—all of these resemble one another and indicate the nature and functions of one another. Finally, this clock of the earth, which counts the days, years, centuries and eras of the world, informs us with the certainty of night being followed by dawn and winter by spring that the dark winter of this transient world will be followed by the glorious spring of the everlasting realm. And so in this way, the Names the All-Preserving, The First, The Last, The All-Outward, and The All-Inward give truthful answers to the question we put to our Creator concerning the Resurrection.

Also, we see and understand that humanity is:

- the final and most comprehensive fruit of the tree of the universe and, with respect to the Truth of Muhammad, upon him be peace and blessings, its original seed;
- the supreme sign of the cosmic Qur'an and its Verse of Divine Supreme Seat[51], which bears the manifestation of the Greatest Name of God;

---

[51] The Qur'an's Verse of Divine Supreme Seat, to which Said Nursi likens humanity with respect to humanity's place in the universe compared with the place of this verse in the Qur'an, is as follows:

> God, there is no deity but He; the All-Living, the Self-Subsisting (by Whom all subsist). Slumber does not seize Him, nor sleep. His is all that is in the heavens and all that is on the earth. Who is there that will intercede with

- the most honored guest in the palace of the universe and the most active official empowered with stewardship over the other inhabitants of the palace;
- the official responsible for monitoring income and expenditure and for planting and cultivating the gardens in the quarter of the earth in the city of the universe;
- its most vocal and responsible minister, equipped with hundreds of sciences and thousands of arts and skills;
- a kind of inspector, a vicegerent appointed by the Sovereign of all eternity to oversee, under His close scrutiny, the country of the earth in the realm of the universe;
- the race which has been given the authority to control and deploy it, and whose actions, be they particular or universal, are all recorded;
- is the division of living creatures which has agreed to bear the Supreme Trust, from which the heavens, the earth, and the mountains all shrank in fear;
- the kind of being in front of whom lie two roads, one of which leads to utter wretchedness, while the other to utter contentment;
- a universal servant of God charged with most extensive worship;
- the kind of being favored with the manifestation of the Greatest Name of the Sovereign of the universe;
- a comprehensive mirror of all God's Names;
- a special intimate and addressee of God, with the best understanding of His Divine addresses and speech;
- the neediest of all living beings in the universe: a wretched creature who, despite their endless poverty and impotence, has innumerable desires and goals and yet also countless adversaries and things which threaten to harm them;

Him save by His leave? He knows what lies before them and what lies after them (what lies in their future and in their past, what is known to them and what is hidden from them); and they do not comprehend anything of His Knowledge save what He wills. His Seat (of dominion) embraces the heavens and the earth, and the preserving of them does not weary Him; He is the All-Exalted, the Supreme. (2:255)

- the kind of being who is most blessed in potential, yet the most prone to suffering with respect to the pleasures of life, which are made poison by the existence of ghastly pains;
- a most wonderful miracle of the Power of the Eternally Besought One;
- a most amazing product of creation who is both the most in need of everlasting life and the most worthy of receiving it;
- the kind of being who seeks eternal felicity with endless prayers—indeed, were they to be given all of the pleasures of this world, they would not satisfy their desire for everlasting life in the least;
- the kind of being who loves to the degree of adoration the One Who bestows bounties on them and makes Him loved and is loved by Him;
- the kind of being whose faculties, which are as vast as the universe itself, show by their very nature that they have been created to acquire eternity.

In short, humanity is bound to God Almighty's Name the Ultimate Truth through the above universal realities, and their actions are recorded continuously by the All-Preserving, Who sees the most particular need of the tiniest living being, hears its pleading, and responds to it. The deeds of humanity, which are related to the entire universe, have been written down by the noble scribes of that All-Preserving One, and it is humanity who, more than any other creature, receives Its attention. Given this, surely this noblest of beings will be granted a resurrection and a judgment. And at this judgment, in accordance with the Name the Ultimate Truth, humankind will receive reward for their duties or punishment for their crimes; they will be called to account for all their actions, universal or particular, which have been recorded by the Name the All-Preserving. The doors of the banquet halls of everlasting happiness in the eternal realm will be opened, as will the gates of the prison of eternal misery. The "officer" who has stewardship over numerous species of beings in this world, who intervenes in them and sometimes casts them into confusion, will not escape interrogation concerning their actions once they are in the soil; nor will they be allowed to lie down in hiding without ever being roused.

To hear the buzz of the fly and to answer it by giving it its rights of life, but to ignore the invocations for eternity which arise from innumerable human rights and are made through the language of the above truths—invocations which reverberate through the heavens and earth like thunder—would be pure injustice and a transgression of these rights. Similarly, to take into careful account the tiniest of creatures—the wing of a fly, for example—but then to disregard and waste the abilities, hopes, and desires of humankind, which extend to eternity, together with the countless bonds and truths in the universe which nurture these abilities and desires—this would constitute a tyranny and injustice so ugly and despicable that all beings which testify to the Names such as the Ultimate Truth, the All-Preserving, the All-Wise, the All-Gracious and the All-Compassionate would reject it, declaring it utterly impossible. Thus do these Names reply to the question which we asked our Creator about the Resurrection. They say: "Just as we are true and have substantial realities, and the beings that testify to us are also true, so too is the Resurrection true and certain."

I was going to write more, but since the above is enough to show that the truth of the Resurrection is as clear as daylight, I have curtailed the discussion here.

Thus, as also can be understood from the truths explained above, just as through their manifestations and reflections in beings, each of God Almighty's hundred, indeed thousand, Names that relate to and show themselves in the universe prove self-evidently the existence of the One Whom they signify, so too do they demonstrate the Resurrection and the Hereafter, and definitively prove them.

Just as our Lord and Creator gives us sacred, decisive answers to the question we asked Him with regard to the Resurrection through all of His revealed Books and Scriptures and most of His Names, He also causes His angels to answer the same question in their own language:

"There have been hundreds of incidents from the time of Adam that testify indubitably to your meeting both with us and with other spirit beings. There are also other innumerable signs and proofs of both our existence and the existence of those other spirit beings, and of our servanthood and obedience to God. In agreement with each other, we have told your leaders whenever we have met with them that we travel through the halls of the Hereafter and around some of its mansions. We have no doubt that these fine, everlasting halls and well-furnished, decorated palaces and dwellings beyond them have been made ready for important guests who are to be accommodated there. We give you irrefragable news of this." Such is the reply of the angels to our question.

Also, our Creator appointed Prophet Muhammad, upon him be peace and blessings, as the greatest teacher, the best master and the truest guide, one who neither goes nor leads astray, and sent him as His last Messenger. Thus, in order that we may advance in our knowledge of God and our belief in Him, progressing from certainty based on knowledge through certainty arising from vision and on to certainty arising from experience, we should first of all ask this master the same question that we put to our Creator. For, just as that person proved through his numerous miracles that the Qur'an is the true Word of God, the Qur'an, through its forty aspects of miraculousness also proves that he was God's true and rightful Messenger. As the tongue of the visible world, the Prophet declared the truth of the Resurrection throughout his life and was confirmed by all the Prophets and saints; the Qur'an, as the tongue of the Unseen World, also declared the truth of the Last Day and the Hereafter, and was confirmed in its declaration by all other Divinely-revealed Books and Scriptures. Given this, the existence of the Resurrection is proven beyond all reasonable doubt.

Such an awesome matter as the Resurrection, the understanding of which transcends normal reasoning, may be perceived best through the instruction of these two wonderful masters—Prophet Muhammad and the Qur'an—and thereby understood.

The reason the early Prophets did not explain the Resurrection in as detailed a manner as the Qur'an was that theirs were the eras of relative primitivism, or the "childhood" of humanity. There is little point in giving detailed and intricate explanations to those who are undergoing elementary education.

To sum up: since most of the Divine Names require the Resurrection, all the proofs which demonstrate the existence of these Names also demonstrate to some extent the existence and necessity of the Resurrection.

And since the angels inform us that they have seen the spheres and mansions of the eternal realm of the Hereafter, the proofs which establish the existence and worshipfulness of the angels, spirits, and spirit beings also help to establish the truth of the existence of the Hereafter.

And since after Divine Unity, the matter emphasized with the greatest insistence by Prophet Muhammad, upon him be peace and blessings, was the Hereafter, it follows that all of the proofs and miracles which testify to His Prophethood also testify indirectly to the existence of the Hereafter.

And since a quarter of the Qur'an concerns the Resurrection and the Hereafter, with approximately a thousand of its verses offering proofs of the life to come, all of the evidence and arguments which establish the veracity of the Qur'an also indirectly establish the existence of the Hereafter.

Now see how firm and certain this pillar of belief really is!

A Summary of the Eighth Matter

In The Seventh Matter, we were planning to question numerous different beings with regard to the Resurrection. However, since the replies given by our Creator's Names were so powerful and convincing, we contented ourselves with them, seeing no real need to question anyone or anything else. Now, in this Eighth Matter we were planning to elucidate a hundredth of the benefits that belief in the Hereafter has for humanity and their felicity in both this world and the next. However, since the miraculous Qur'an leaves no need for further explanation concerning the benefits of belief in securing happiness in the Hereafter, and since the benefits of belief for humanity in this world have been discussed in detail in the *Risale-i Nur*, readers may refer to the Qur'an and the relevant sections of the *Risale-i Nur*. Here, we will summarize only three or four out of the hundreds of results of belief in the Hereafter concerning human individual and social life.

THE FIRST: Just as a person has relations with their home, they also have relations with the world beyond it. Similarly, just as they have relations with their relatives, they also have relations with the rest of humankind. And just as they desire a kind of temporary permanence in this world, they also yearn passionately for an enduring permanence in the realm of eternity. In the same way that a person strives to meet the need of their stomach for food, they are, by nature, compelled to strive to provide sustenance to the metaphorical stomachs of their mind, heart, spirit and humanity. Their desires and demands are such that nothing but eternity and everlasting felicity can satisfy them. As mentioned in The Tenth Word, when I was young I asked myself: "Do you want to live for a million years as ruler of the world but then be dispatched into eternal non-existence? Or would you prefer to have an ordinary and at times difficult existence, but live forever?" I saw that my imagination always opted for the latter, saying: "I want to live forever, even though it be in Hell!"

Thus, since the pleasures of this world do not satisfy the imaginative faculty, which is a servant of the human essence, it follows that the comprehensive essence of humanity is, by its very nature, attached to eternity. For despite being preoccupied with boundless hopes and desires, humanity has only an insignificant faculty of will as their capital, stricken as they are with absolute poverty. Belief in the Hereafter, then, is such a powerful and sufficient treasury, such a means of happiness and pleasure, such a refuge and source of assistance and benefit, and such a means of consolation in the face of the endless sorrows of this world that if the life of this world had to be sacrificed in order to gain it, it would still be a cheap price to pay.

ITS SECOND FRUIT AND BENEFIT PERTAINING TO HUMAN PERSONAL LIFE: This was explained in The Third Matter, and can be found in *Gençlik Rehberi* as a footnote.

The most constant and over-riding anxiety of humanity is that we will one day enter the grave, as our friends and relations have before us. The wretched human being, who is ready to sacrifice their very soul for a single friend, imagines that the countless millions of human beings who have entered the grave before them have been condemned to eternal annihilation, and this supposition makes them suffer the torments of Hell. Just at this point, belief in the Hereafter appears, opens our eyes and raises the veil. It tells us: "Look!" And looking with belief, we can see that our companions have been saved from eternal annihilation and are awaiting us happily in a light-filled world; realizing this, we receive a spiritual pleasure that is a reflection of the pleasures of Paradise. Contenting ourselves with the explanations of this second fruit in the *Risale-i Nur*, we will curtail the discussion here.

A THIRD BENEFIT: Human beings are superior to other living beings on account of their elevated characteristics, their comprehensive abilities, their universal ability to worship and the extensive spheres of existence which make up their life. However, the virtues which characterize the human being, such as love, zeal, brother and sister-hood and humanity, are acquired in accordance with the extent of this fleeting present time, which is constricted between the past and the future, both of which are dark and non-existent.

For example, a person loves and serves their father, brother or sister, their spouse, nation or country, none of whom they knew before; they will see none of these people once they have departed from this world. Since the fleeting nature of life means that it is highly unlikely that a person would be able to achieve complete loyalty or sincerity in any one relationship, their virtues and excellences are proportionately diminished. Then, just at the point where they fall to a level lower than that of the animals and become more wretched than they already are because they have intellect and reason, belief in the Hereafter comes to this person's assistance. It expands the present, which is as narrow as the grave, to the extent that it encompasses the past and future and manifests a sphere of existence as broad as the world, stretching from pre-eternity to post-eternity. Realizing that relations with one's spouse, parents and siblings will continue for eternity in Paradise, they love, respect, help and have mercy on them while in this world. With this new realization, a person will not exploit such important duties based on the relationships that encompass this broad sphere of life and existence for the sake of the worthless affairs of this world and its petty interests. Being able to achieve earnest loyalty and sincerity, a person's good qualities and attainments begin to develop accordingly, and their humanity becomes exalted. While they cannot match even a sparrow in enjoyment of this life, they can become the noblest and happiest of guests in the universe, superior to all animals, as well as being the best loved and most appreciated servant of the universe's Owner. Since this matter has also been explained in the *Risale-i Nur*, we content ourselves here with this much.

A FOURTH BENEFIT OF BELIEF IN THE HEREAFTER, WHICH RELATES TO HUMAN SOCIAL LIFE: What follows is a summary of this benefit, expounded in the Ninth Ray of the *Risale-i Nur*:

Children, who make up a third of the human race, can live a truly human life and maintain truly human capacities only if they have sincere belief in the Hereafter. Without belief in the Hereafter, they are forced to compensate for the anxiety they feel over their eventual oblivion by filling their worldly life with trivia and meaningless distractions. For the constant deaths around them of children like themselves have such an effect on their sensitive minds and weak hearts, which cherish far-reaching desires, and vulnerable spirits, that it makes life torture for them and their reason a tool of suffering. If, however, they are brought to belief in the Hereafter, the anxieties they once felt at the deaths of their playmates, which they try to escape by immersing themselves in meaningless distractions, will give way to joy and exhilaration as they realize the truth. For supported by belief in the Hereafter they will say: "My sibling or playmate has died and become a bird in Paradise. He (or she) is now flying around and enjoying himself much more than we are. And although my mother has died, she has gone to the realm of Divine mercy. One day I will see her in Paradise, where she will take me into her arms once again." Such a realization will enable these children to live in a state which befits them as human beings.

It is only through believing in the Hereafter that the aged, who constitute another third of humankind, are able to find consolation in the face of what they see as the inevitable extinction of their lives and the fact that they too will soon be consigned to the bowels of the earth and their precious and lovable worlds have come to an end. Without belief in the Hereafter, those compassionate, respected fathers and those tender, self-sacrificing mothers would become so distraught and distressed in heart and spirit that their world would seem to be a prison of despair for them and life a heavy burden of torment. But belief in the Hereafter addresses them, saying: "Do not worry! A radiant, everlasting life awaits you and there you will enjoy eternal youth. You will be reunited in joy with your beloved children and the relatives that you have lost. All your good deeds have been preserved and you will be rewarded for them there." Belief in the Hereafter gives them such solace and joy that were they to experience old age a hundred times over, it would not cause them to despair.

A third of humankind is made up of the youth. With their turbulent passions and emotions and the difficulty they have in controlling their bold intellects if they lose their faith in the Hereafter and do not bring to mind the torments of Hell, the property and honor of the upright members of society, along with the peace and dignity of the weak and the elderly, will be at serious risk. One youth is able to bring down destruction on a happy home for the sake of one minute's pleasure, and the years of imprisonment that follow will turn them into a wild animal. But if belief in the Hereafter comes to their assistance, they quickly come to their senses, thinking: "It is true that the government informers do not see me and I can hide from them, but the angels of the All-Majestic Sovereign, Who has a prison known as Hell, see me and are recording all of my evil deeds. I am not free and left to my own devices: I am a traveler charged with duties. One day I too will be old and weak." Suddenly this person begins to feel sympathy and respect for those they would have assaulted before without thinking twice. Being content with the explanations of this truth which the reader may find in the *Risale-i Nur*, we cut the discussion short here.

Another important section of humankind comprises the sick, the oppressed, the poor, those like us who are disaster-stricken and prisoners languishing in jail, subject to severe punishment. If belief in the Hereafter does not come to their aid, their lives are bound to be filled with torment. For illness reminds them constantly of death; the haughty treachery of the oppressor, in the face of whom they are unable to save their honor, causes them extreme distress; the loss of property or offspring in serious disasters brings untold despair; and the intolerable hardship of having to spend five or ten years in prison causes immeasurable pain and mental suffering. Without belief, all of these calamitous situations turn the world into a terrible prison for those who experience them and life becomes a living hell. But if belief in the Hereafter comes to their aid, they begin to feel relief and, to the degree of their belief, their distress, despair, anxiety and desire for vengeance diminish and, sometimes, even disappear completely.

I can even go so far as to say that if belief in the Hereafter had not come to the aid of myself and some of my brothers in the fearsome calamity that is this wrongful imprisonment, we would not have been able to bear a single day of incarceration: it would have been as unbearable as death and might even have driven us to say goodbye to life altogether. But boundless thanks be to God, for despite suffering the distress of my brothers, whom I love as much as my own life; despite the loss and the weeping over thousands of copies of the *Risale-i Nur* and my precious, gilded books, which I love as much as my eyes; and despite the fact I could not bear the slightest insult or stand to be dominated by others, I swear that the light and strength of belief in the Hereafter gave me the patience, endurance, solace, and steadfastness to cope. Indeed, this has given me enthusiasm to gain a greater reward through bearing the painful exertions of my ordeal, for as I said at the outset of this treatise, I considered myself to be a student in a place of instruction worthy of being called the School of Joseph. Were it not for the occasional pains and illnesses of old age, I would have learned my lessons more diligently and with greater ease of mind. However, we have digressed, and for this I hope I will be forgiven.

Also, everyone's home is a small world for them, perhaps even a small paradise. If belief in the Hereafter does not underpin the happiness of that home, the members of that family will suffer anguish and anxiety in proportion to the compassion, love, and attachment they feel for their family. Their paradise will turn into Hell and they will have no option but to numb their minds with temporary amusements and distractions. Like an ostrich that sticks its heads into the sand thinking they cannot be seen by the hunter, these poor people plunge their heads into heedlessness in the hope that that death, decline, and separation may not find them. They seek a way out of their terrifying predicament by temporarily anesthetizing themselves. The mother, for example, trembles constantly at seeing her children, for whom she would sacrifice her soul, exposed to danger. Children, for their part, feel constant sorrow and fear at being unable to save their father or siblings from calamities that visit families only too often. Thus, in this tumultuous worldly life, the supposedly contented life of the family loses its happiness in many respects, and the kinship and close connections forged in this brief earthly existence do not result in true loyalty, heartfelt sincerity, disinterested service, or real love. Good character declines proportionately and is often lost completely. However, if belief in the Hereafter enters that home, it illuminates it completely: its members develop respect, love, and compassion for each other, not merely for the sake of relationships in this brief worldly life, but for the sake of their continuance in the eternal realm of happiness that is the Hereafter. They respect, love, and show compassion to each other sincerely; they are loyal to one another and ignore each other's faults and their good character increases accordingly. As a result, the happiness of true humanity begins to develop in the home. Since this too is elucidated in the *Risale-i Nur*, we cut the discussion short here.

Also, a town is like a large home for those who live there. If the members of that large family do not have belief in the Hereafter, rather than sincerity, cordiality, virtue, mutual love and assistance, self-sacrifice, and the seeking of Divine pleasure and otherworldly reward—all of which form the basis of good conduct—vices such as self-interest, pretentiousness, hypocrisy, artificiality, bribery, and deception will dominate. Anarchy and savagery will hold sway beneath the façade of superficial order and a nominal humanity, poisoning the life of the town. The children will become idle troublemakers, the youth will plunge themselves into drunkenness, the powerful will embark on oppression, and the elderly will be left to weep.

By analogy, a country is also a home—the home of a national family. If belief in the Hereafter rules in such a home, sincere respect, earnest compassion, selfless love, mutual assistance, honest service, good social relations, unostentatious charity, and many other excellences and virtues will begin to flourish.

Belief in the Hereafter says to the children: "Stop messing around, for there is Paradise to be won!" and teaches them self-control through instruction from the Qur'an.

It says to the youth: "Hell truly exists: give up your heedlessness!" thus bringing them to their senses.

It says to the oppressor: "Severe torment will be your lot if you continue on this path!" and makes them bow to justice.

It says to the elderly: "In the world to come there exists not only perpetual happiness far greater than anything you could experience in this world, but also eternal youth. Try to win them for yourselves!" thus turning their tears into smiles.

Belief in the Hereafter shows its favorable effects in every group, particular or universal, and illuminates them. Let the sociologists and moral philosophers, who are concerned with the social life of humankind, take note of this. If the rest of the thousands of benefits to be had from belief in the Hereafter are compared with the five or six we have indicated briefly, we can understand that it is only belief that is the means of happiness in this world and the next.

* * *

In The Twenty-Eighth Word and other treatises of the *Risale-i Nur*, powerful replies were given in order to silence the insubstantial doubts which exist concerning bodily Resurrection. Readers who desire a more detailed discussion may refer to these writings; here we will content ourselves with the following brief indication:

Just as the most comprehensive mirror of the Divine Names is to be found in corporeality, so the richest and most active centre of the Divine purposes for the creation of the universe is also in corporeality. Likewise, the greatest variety of the multifarious bounties of the Lord lies in corporeality, together with the greatest multiplicity of the seeds of the prayers and thanks offered by many to their Creator through the language of their needs. And the greatest diversity of the seeds of the metaphysical and spirit worlds also lies in corporeality.

Since hundreds of universal truths are centered in corporeality, in order to multiply it and favor it with manifestations of the above truths on the earth, the All-Wise Creator clothes successive caravans of beings in corporeal existence and sends them with awesome speed and activity to that glorious exhibition. Then He dismisses them and sends others in their place, constantly making the factory of the universe operate. Weaving corporeal products, He makes the earth into a seed-bed of the Hereafter and Paradise. In fact, in order to gratify the appetite of the stomach, He listens intently to the supplication for permanence which it makes in the form of hunger and accepts it. In order to respond to this prayer, He prepares innumerable sorts of ingenious foods and precious bounties, all of which produce different pleasures. This demonstrates, beyond a shadow of a doubt, that in the Hereafter the most numerous and diverse pleasures of Paradise will be corporeal, as will the bounties of that eternal abode of happiness to which all human beings aspire.

The All-Powerful and Compassionate, the All-Knowing and Munificent One, accepts the invocation offered by the stomach in the form of hunger and answers it with care and deliberation by providing it with an almost infinite variety of foods. The human is the most important result of the universe and has been appointed as the ruler of the earth: we are the Creator's choice being and adorer. Is it at all possible, then, that the All-Powerful and Compassionate, the All-Knowing and Munificent One, Who accepts the prayer of a stomach and answers it, would not accept the numerous, universal supplications offered by the stomach of all humanity for universal, elevated corporeal pleasures in the eternal realm, which are innately desired and aspired to by humankind? Is it at all possible that He should not answer it with bodily Resurrection, thus gratifying humankind eternally? Would He listen to the buzz of the fly, but not the roar of thunder? Would He be attentive to the needs of a common soldier, but ignore the needs of a whole army? To do so would be infinitely impossible and absurd.

Indeed, as is stated explicitly in the verse: *There will be therein all that souls desire, and eyes delight in* (43:71), the people of Paradise will experience, in a form befitting their state, the corporeal pleasures with which they are most familiar, samples of which they have tasted during their earthly existence. The rewards for the sincere thanks and particular worship offered by each of their members—the tongue, the eye, the ear, and so on—will be given in the form of corporeal pleasures particular to those members. The miraculous Qur'an describes the corporeal pleasures so explicitly that it is impossible not to accept their literal meanings: there is no need to look for metaphorical interpretations.

Thus, the fruits and results of belief in the Hereafter show that just as the existence, nature, and needs of the stomach are decisive proof of the existence of food, the innate need and desire of humankind for eternity, together with the excellences and potentials they possess which demand the consequences and benefits of belief in the Hereafter, provide indubitable proof for the existence of the world to come and of Paradise and its eternal corporeal pleasures. Also, the perfections and meaningful signs which fill the universe, and the existential realities of humanity which are related to these signs, testify absolutely to the certain existence of the realm of the Hereafter, the Resurrection, and the opening up of Paradise and Hell. This fundamental truth has been explained convincingly in several treatises of the *Risale-i Nur*, including in particular The Tenth, Twenty-eighth and Twenty-ninth Words, and The Third and Ninth Rays. For a more detailed discussion, readers are referred to these writings.

The Qur'anic descriptions of Hell are so clear and explicit that they leave no need for further description. Detailed discussions of the subject can be found in the *Risale-i Nur*; here we will clarify in brief just two or three points in order to dispel one or two insignificant doubts.

THE FIRST POINT: The thought of Hell does not diminish the pleasures of the above fruits of belief with the fear it provokes. For infinite Divine Mercy says to the fearful person:

"Come to me! Enter through the door of repentance, so that the existence of Hell will, rather than frighten you, make known in full the pleasures of Paradise and enable you and all creatures whose rights have been violated to avenge, as well as giving you enjoyment. If you have drowned in misguidance, from which you cannot emerge, the existence of Hell is still immeasurably better than eternal annihilation; it is also a kind of compassion for the unbelievers. For humans, and even animals with young, derive pleasure from the pleasure and happiness of their relatives, offspring and friends, and in one respect become happy themselves.

"And so to the disbelieving materialists I would say this: because of your misguidance, you will either fall into eternal non-existence or you will enter Hell. As for non-existence, it is absolute evil, and since it also means the eternal annihilation of you yourself and all those relatives, ancestors and descendants of yours, whom you love and whose happiness also makes you happy, the thought of eternal non-existence pains your heart and spirit more grievously than a thousand Hells. For if there were no Hell, there would be no Paradise. Through your unbelief, everything falls into non-existence. But if you go to Hell and remain within the sphere of existence, your loved ones and relatives will either be happy in Paradise or be favored with compassion in one respect within the sphere of existence. This means that you should defend the notion that Hell exists, for to oppose it is to support non-existence, which in turn is to support the obliteration of the happiness of innumerable relatives and loved ones."

Hell is an awesome, majestic realm which performs the wise and just function of being the place of imprisonment belonging to the Sovereign of Majesty in the sphere of existence, which is pure good. In addition to performing the function of being a prison, Hell has numerous other duties, serving many wise purposes and carrying out many tasks related to the everlasting realm. It is also the awe-inspiring dwelling of many living beings, such as the Angels of Hell.

THE SECOND POINT: The existence and terrible torments of Hell are not contrary to the infinite Mercy, true Justice and balanced Wisdom of God. Rather, Mercy, Justice, and Wisdom demand its existence. For to punish an oppressor who tramples on the rights of a thousand innocents or to kill a savage animal who tears to pieces a hundred cowering animals is not only just, it is a great mercy for the oppressed. To pardon the oppressor and to leave the savage beast free shows a gross lack of pity for hundreds of innocent wretches in return for a single act of misplaced mercy.

Among those who will enter Hell are the absolute unbelievers. They will enter that place on account of the fact that they have transgressed the rights of the Divine Names by denying them, and they have transgressed the rights of all creatures who testify to those Names by denying their testimony and the elevated duties of glorification they perform in the face of the manifestation of the Names in creation. Also, by denying the fact that all creatures are mirrors for the manifestation of Divine Lordship and respond to this Lordship with worship, which is the *raison d'être* of the creation and continued existence of the universe, they transgress the rights of all other creatures even further. Unbelief is therefore such a tremendous crime that it cannot be forgiven; it truly deserves the threat enshrined in the verse: *Assuredly, God does not forgive that partners be associated with Him* (4:48, 116). Not to cast that unbeliever into Hell would be a misplaced act of compassion, and would serve to withhold justice and mercy from those innumerable claimants whose rights have been transgressed. In the same way that these claimants demand the existence of Hell, the Divine dignity of Majesty and the grandeur of His Perfection most certainly demand it.

If a rebellious outlaw who assaults the people affronts the dignity and authority of a town's governor by saying: "You can't put me in prison!", even if there is no prison in the town, the governor will have one built just to imprison that ill-mannered wretch. Similarly, through their unbelief, the absolute unbelievers commit a serious assault on the dignity and authority of God's Majesty; through their denial they affront the grandeur of His Power and through their aggression offends the perfection of His Lordship. However many functions Hell may or may not have, and however many reasons or instances of wisdom there are which necessitate its existence, it is the Dignity and Majesty of God more than anything else which demand the creation of Hell for unbelievers such as those described above.

Moreover, even the essence of unbelief suggests Hell. For example, if the essence of belief were to be embodied, it would, with its pleasures, assume the form of a private paradise and, in so doing, provide a taste of the Paradise yet to come. Similarly, as has been discussed previously and in other parts of the *Risale-i Nur*, the spiritual pains and torments of unbelief, hypocrisy, and apostasy are such that, if they were to be embodied, they would take on the form of a private hell for those fettered by unbelief and would give them a taste of the Hell yet to come. Also, bearing in mind that the little truths in the field of this world will grow into elaborate trees in the Hereafter, this poisonous seed that is unbelief foreshadows the emergence of the tree of *Zaqqum*, saying:

"I am its origin. For the wretched who bear me in their hearts my fruit is a private sample of that bitter tree of *Zaqqum*."

Since unbelief is a violation of so many rights, it is certainly an infinitely evil crime that will deserve infinite punishment. Human justice considers a sentence of fifteen years imprisonment—approximately eight million minutes—to be appropriate for a murder that has been committed in a minute or less; human justice regards such a sentence to be in conformity with the public interest and the good of society as a whole. Therefore, since one instance of absolute unbelief is the equivalent of a thousand murders, to suffer torments for nearly eight billion minutes for one minute's absolute unbelief is in conformity with that law of justice. A person who passes a year of their life in unbelief deserves punishment lasting countless billions of minutes, thus manifesting the meaning of the verse: *They will abide therein for ever* (4:169; 33:65).

The miraculous descriptions of Paradise and Hell in the wise Qur'an and the proofs of their existence contained in the *Risale-i Nur*, which issues from and interprets it, leave no need for further explanations.

Numerous Qur'anic verses such as:

> They (the people of discernment) reflect on the creation of the heavens and the earth (and they pray): "Our Lord, You have not created this (the universe) without meaning and purpose. All-Glorified are You, so save us from the punishment of the Fire!" (3.191)
>
> "Our Lord! Ward off from us the punishment of Hell; its punishment is surely constant anguish: how evil indeed it is as a final station and permanent abode!" (25:65–66).

and the prayers of Prophet Muhammad, upon him be peace and blessings, and all other Prophets and people of truth in order to be saved from the punishment of Hell, saying "Preserve us from Hell-fire! Deliver us from Hell-fire! Save us from Hell-fire!"—it becomes clear from all these that the most important issue for humankind is how they are to be saved from eternal perdition in Hell. Hell is an extremely significant, tremendous and awesome reality—one which some of the people endowed with inner vision and the capacity for spiritual unveiling have been able to gaze upon, or see its manifestations and shadows. And such vision has led all of them to cry out in terror, "Save us from it!"

The confrontation, co-existence, and intermingling of good and evil, pleasure and pain, light and darkness, heat and cold, beauty and ugliness, and guidance and misguidance in the universe are there for an extremely important purpose and are full of wisdom. If there were no evil, the existence of good would be indiscernible. If there were no pain, pleasure would have no meaning. Light without darkness would have no importance and the different degrees of heat are realized only through the existence of cold. Through ugliness, a single truth of beauty becomes a thousand truths, and thousands of varying degrees of beauty come into existence. If there were no Hell, many of the pleasures of Paradise would remain hidden. Extrapolating from these examples we see that in one respect everything becomes known through its opposite; a single truth contained in any one thing produces numerous shoots and becomes numerous truths. Since these intermingled beings flow from this transient abode into the abode of eternal permanence, certainly, just as things such as good, pleasure, light, beauty, and belief flow into Paradise, so harmful matters such as evil, pain, darkness, ugliness, and unbelief pour into Hell. The floods of this continuously agitated universe are emptied into these two lakes. We curtail this discussion here, referring readers to the subtle and meaningful Points and Matters at the end of The Twenty-Ninth Word.

To my fellow students here in this School of Joseph, I would say this: If we take advantage of our worldly imprisonment for the good and, as we are saved from the many sins which are not possible to commit here, repent our former sins and perform our obligatory religious duties, we will be able to make every hour of our prison life into the equivalent of a whole day's worship. If we can do this, our imprisonment will be the best opportunity we have to be saved from that terrible eternal imprisonment; it will be our key to the door of that light-filled Paradise. But if we miss this opportunity, our afterlife will be filled with misery, just as this world is filled with misery, and we will receive the chastisement indicated in the verse: *He (thereby) incurs loss of both this world and the Hereafter* (22:11).

THE CONNECTION OF "GOD IS THE ALL-GREAT" WITH THE RESURRECTION

It was during the Feast of the Sacrifice that this part was being written. On these blessed days of Sacrifice, three hundred million (now over a billion) people declare in one voice: "*God is the All-Great! God is the All-*

Great! God is the All-Great!" It is as if the earth would have its fellow planets in the skies hear the sacred words *God is the All-Great!* Also, on the hill of 'Arafat, tens of thousands (now millions) of pilgrims declare in unison *God is the All-Great!* This is the same declaration made by God's Messenger and his Companions fourteen hundred years ago, and is a response in the form of extensive, universal worship to the universal manifestation of Divine Lordship through God's sublime titles *the Lord of the earth* and *the Lord of the heavens*. I was able to imagine all of this and become convinced of it.

Then I wondered whether this sacred phrase has any connection with the question of the Resurrection we have been discussing. It suddenly occurred to me that together with this sacred phrase, similar other phrases and symbols of the Islamic faith such as *There is no deity but God; All praise and gratitude are for God!* and *All-Glorified is God!*, which are referred to as "enduring good works," recall this in both a particular and universal fashion and imply its realization.

For example, the phrase *God is the All-Great!* means in one respect that God's Power and Knowledge are greater than everything: nothing at all can escape His Knowledge or the control and authority of His Power. They are infinitely greater than the things we fear most. This means that they have the absolute ability to accomplish things that are much greater than bringing about the Resurrection, saving us from non-existence, and granting eternal happiness. They are able to do things that we may see as strange, unbelievable, or even unimaginable. For this reason, as is stated explicitly in the verse: *Your creation and your resurrection are but as (the creation and resurrection) of a single soul* (31:28), the resurrection of humankind and their being gathered together in the Place of Resurrection are as easy for that Power as the creation of a single soul. It is in connection with this truth that, when faced by serious disasters or attempting important undertakings, all Muslims say: "*God is the All-Great! God is the All-Great!*" making it a source of consolation, power, and support for themselves.

As was explained in The Ninth Word, the phrases *God is the All-Great!*, *All-Glorified is God!* and *All praise and gratitude are for God!* form the seeds and summaries of the canonical Prayers—the zenith of all worship—and in order to emphasize the meaning of these Prayers and compensate for any defects in them, they are included in recitations both during and after the Prayers. They also point to three supreme truths and provide powerful answers to the questions which arise in our mind from the amazement, pleasure, and awe we feel at the strange, exquisite, and extraordinary things that we see in the universe—things that fill us with wonder and lead us to offer thanks on account of their awe and grandeur. Furthermore, as mentioned at the end of The Sixteenth Word, a private soldier may enter the king's presence in the company of a field marshal at a festival and come to know him directly; at other times, however, he knows him only through the person of his immediate commander. Similarly, like the saints to a certain extent, a person performing the *Hajj* begins to know God through His titles *the Lord of the earth* and *the Lord of all worlds*. As the levels of the manifestations of Divine Grandeur unfold in a person's heart, by repeating the phrase *God is the All-Great!* they answer all of the astounding questions that overwhelm the spirit. Moreover, as was explained at the end of The Thirteenth Gleam, the phrase *God is the All-Great*! provides the most effective replies to the most cunning intrigues of Satan, cutting them off at the root; similarly it also gives a most succinct but powerful answer to the question we posed concerning the Hereafter.

The phrase *All praise and gratitude are for God* also suggests and demands the Resurrection. It says to us: "Without the Hereafter, I would be virtually meaningless. For what I mean with this phrase is this: to God are due all the praise and thanks offered from pre-eternity to post-eternity, regardless of who has offered them and to whom they have been offered. It is only the promise of eternal happiness—the supreme bounty—that actually makes bounties bountiful and saves all conscious creatures from the permanent calamity of non-existence. It is only in eternal happiness that my existence can find true meaning."

Every believer's recitation of *All praise and gratitude are for God*!, uttered at least a hundred and fifty times a day after the canonical Prayers, is not only an act of worship in itself, but it is also the expression of praise and thanks that extends from pre-eternity to post-eternity: this can only be the advance price and immediate fee for Paradise and eternal felicity. The praise and thanks offered through them cannot be restricted to the fleeting bounties of this world, which is marred by the pains of transience; people see these quite rightly as means to the attainment of eternal bounties.

As for the sacred phrase, *All-Glorified is God!*, which declares that God is exalted above having partners, faults, defects, injustice, impotence, mercilessness, need, or deception—indeed, any negative attributes that are opposed to His absolute Perfection, Grace, Beauty, and Majesty—it also points to the eternal happiness of the Hereafter and its Paradise, which are the means to the splendor and glory of His Grace, Beauty, and Majesty, and the perfection of His Sovereignty. For, as has been explained previously, if there were no eternal happiness, His Sovereignty and His Perfection, His Majesty, Grace, Beauty, and Mercy would be sullied by fault and defect.

Like these three sacred phrases, *In the Name of God*; *There is no deity but God* and other similar utterances are all seeds of the pillars of faith: they are extracts of both the pillars of belief and the truths of the Qur'an. In addition to their being the seeds of the five daily Prayers, the three phrases mentioned above are also the seeds of the Qur'an, sparkling like brilliant gems at the beginning of a number of radiant *suras*. They are also the true sources and foundations of the *Risale-i Nur*, many parts of which began to form in my mind while reciting these phrases after the canonical Prayers; they are the seeds of its truths. Also, from the perspective of the worship of Prophet Muhammad, upon him be peace and blessings, and of the sainthood included in his Messengership, these phrases are the regular recitations of the "Muhammadan Way." As such, they are repeated by hundreds of millions of believers after each of the five daily Prayers, as though they were forming a vast circle of remembrance. Their prayer beads in their hands, they declare *All-Glorified is God!* thirty-three times, *All praise and gratitude are for God!* thirty-three times, and *God is the All-Great!* thirty-three times.

Now you must surely understood how worthy and full of reward such recitations are, and how, as explained above, they are the extracts and seeds of the Qur'an, of belief, and of the canonical Prayers.

Just as the first matter discussed at the beginning of this treatise provided an agreeable lesson regarding the five daily canonical Prayers, this last matter has also turned out to be an important lesson regarding the regular recitations following the Prayers.

> All praise be to God for His favors!
>
> All-Glorified are You! We have no knowledge save what You have taught us; surely You are the All-Knowing, the All-Wise.

The Ninth Matter

In the Name of God, the All-Merciful, the All-Compassionate.

> The Messenger believes in what has been sent down to him from his Lord, and so do the believers; each one believes in God, and His angels, and His Books, and His Messengers: "We make no distinction between any of His Messengers (in believing in them)." (....To the end of the verse) (2:285)

An awesome question and a state of mind that arises from the unfolding of a vast Divine favor have led me to explain a lengthy, universal point concerning this comprehensive, elevated, and sublime verse.

It was asked: While belief in God and the Hereafter must, like the sun, remove all darkness of unbelief, why is it that if one denies one of the truths of belief, they are deemed to be an unbeliever? Why, if they do not accept that particular truth, are they considered not to be a Muslim? Moreover, why is it that a person who denies one of the pillars and truths of belief is deemed an apostate, one who has fallen into absolute unbelief and who has left the community of Islam? Surely their belief in the other pillars must save them from absolute unbelief?

The answer: Belief is a single, united truth composed of six pillars: it cannot be divided up. It is something universal that cannot be separated into parts: it is an indivisible whole. For each of the pillars of belief proves and establishes the other pillars with the proofs that prove and establish it. They are all supremely powerful proofs of one another. Since this is so, one invalid notion that cannot shake all of the pillars together with all their proofs cannot in reality invalidate a single one of those pillars or even a single truth; it cannot deny them. One can only shut their eyes purposefully under the veil of only non-acceptance—not utter rejection—and commit a kind of unbelief that stems from sheer obstinacy. However, they would fall into absolute unbelief by degrees: as a result, their humanity would be destroyed and both their body and spirit would be dispatched to Hell. So in this context, with God's grace, we will explain this supreme matter in Six Points in the form of brief summaries and conclusions.

The first point: Belief in God establishes, with its own proofs, all of the other pillars and belief in the Hereafter, as has been clearly shown in The Seventh Matter of Fruits of Belief. We clearly see that a pre-eternal and everlasting sovereignty of Lordship, an eternal Divine rule, governs the boundless universe and all it contains as though it were a palace, a city, or a country. This Sovereignty makes the globe of the earth revolve in a balanced and orderly fashion, changing it with innumerable instances of wisdom, and equips and directs atoms, planets, flies, and stars all together as though each were a well-disciplined, well-organized army; It continuously drills them and impels them to act, travel, and carry out various duties by His Command and Will as though they were engaged in sublime maneuvers or a worshipful parade. Is it then possible at all that this eternal, perpetual, enduring Sovereignty would not have an eternal locus or everlasting place of manifestation, namely the Hereafter? God forbid! This means the Sovereignty of God Almighty's Lordship and—as described in The Seventh Matter—most of His Names and the proofs of His absolutely necessary Existence all require the Hereafter and testify to it. So see and understand what a powerful support this pillar of belief has and believe in it as though you could see it!

Also, just as belief in God is not possible without belief in the Hereafter, it is neither possible without belief in His Messengers and Books. For in order to manifest His Divinity and to show that He has the exclusive right to be worshipped, God, the All-Worshipped One, has created the universe as an embodied book which demonstrates that its Creator is the Eternally Besought One. Every page of this book is in itself a smaller book full of meanings, and every line a page filled with wisdom. This book is like such an embodied Qur'an that it is filled with endless creational "verses" and words, with points and letters, each of which is a miracle. It is like a magnificent mosque of Mercy, the interior of which is decorated with innumerable inscriptions and adornments, and in every corner of which are species of beings each preoccupied with the worship dictated by its nature and the Divine purposes of its existence. Is it then at all possible that God, the All-Worshipped One, should create the universe in this way and not send masters to teach the meanings of this vast book? Is it at all likely that He should fail to task commentators with the interpretation of the verses of that vast "Qur'an," which shows that it is the work of the Eternally Besought One? Is it at all possible that He should not appoint imams to lead all those who are worshipping in numerous ways in this huge mosque, or that He should not give Decrees—the Divine Scriptures or Books—to those masters, commentators, and leaders of worship? God forbid, a hundred thousand times!

Also, in order to display to conscious beings the beauty of His Mercy, the excellence of His Compassion and the perfection of His Lordship so that He may encourage them to praise and thank Him, the All-Compassionate and All-Munificent Maker has created the universe as a banqueting hall, an exhibition centre, and a place of excursion, in which are arranged infinite varieties of delicious bounties and priceless, wonderful arts. So, is it at all possible that He would not speak to these conscious beings at the banquet or fail to inform them through His Messengers of their duties of thanks for the favors He has given them, and their duties of worship in response to the manifestations of His Mercy and His making Himself loved? God forbid, a thousand times over!

Also, the Maker loves His Art and wants it to be loved. As is indicated, for example, by His taking into account the thousand pleasures to be had by the human mouth, He wants His Artistry to be met with appreciation and approval. And so He has adorned the universe with priceless arts and displayed throughout the universe the traces of His transcendent Beauty in such a way that it becomes clear that He wills to make Himself both known and loved. Is it possible, then, that such a Maker would not speak to humanity, the commander of living beings in the universe, through some of the most eminent people whom He has sent as Messengers? Is it at all likely that His fine arts should remain unappreciated and the extraordinary beauty of His Names unvalued? Is it all likely that there should be no response to those Acts of His Which are designed to make Him known and loved? God forbid, a hundred thousand times!

Also, through His infinite bounties and gifts, which indicate purpose, choice, and will, the All-Knowing Speaker answers clearly and at exactly the right time all of the supplications made by living beings for their natural needs, together with all the requests they make through the tongues of their innate disposition. Is it possible, then, that He should speak to the most insignificant living creature and address their most trivial needs, yet fail or refuse to speak to the spiritual leaders of humankind, the choicest of His creations, the one who has stewardship over creation and enjoys the position given to them of commander over most creatures on earth? Given that He speaks to all other living beings, should He not speak to humans and send them His Decrees— the Divine Scriptures or Books? God forbid that this should be so!

Thus, with its certainty and its innumerable proofs, belief in God proves and establishes belief in the Prophets and the sacred Books or Scriptures.

In response to the One Who makes Himself known and loved through all His artifacts, and Who wills and orders that He be thanked, Prophet Muhammad, upon him be peace and blessings, knew Him and made Him known, loved Him and made Him loved, thanked Him and inspired others to thank Him too; he did all of these in the most perfect way through the truth of the Qur'an, which causes the universe to resonate. Also, with his declarations of "All-Glorified is God!" "All praise and gratitude are for God!" and "God is the All-Great!" Prophet Muhammad caused the earth to ring out, echoing through the heavens and bringing the land and sea to heights of ecstasy. Furthermore, for fourteen centuries Prophet Muhammad has led half of the globe or a fourth of humankind, responding to all the manifestations of the Creator's Lordship with extensive, universal worship, and to His Divine purposes by announcing and teaching the messages of the Qur'an to the universe and through the centuries. Thus Prophet Muhammad, upon him be peace and blessings, demonstrated the honor, value, and duties of humankind and was himself confirmed by the Creator through his countless miracles. Is it at all then possible that Prophet Muhammad, who is so worthy in God's sight, should not have been the choicest of God's creatures, the most excellent of envoys, and the greatest Messenger? God forbid! A hundred thousand times, God forbid!

Thus with all its proofs, the truth of "I bear witness that there is no deity but God" proves and establishes the truth of "I bear witness that Muhammad is the Messenger of God."

Also, is it at all possible that the Maker of the universe should cause creatures to speak to one another in myriad tongues, that He should understand and hear their speech, but that He Himself should remain silent? God forbid!

Also, is it at all reasonable that He should not proclaim His purposes and instances of wisdom in the universe through some kind of decree? Is it at all possible that He would not send a book like the Qur'an, which solves the riddle of the universe and provides true answers to the three awesome questions asked by all souls, namely: "Where do creatures come from?",

"Where are they going?", and "Why do they follow on, convoy after convoy, stopping for a while and then pass on?" God forbid!

The miraculous Qur'an has illuminated fourteen centuries of human history. It circulates every hour through hundreds of millions of respectful tongues and is inscribed with its sacredness in the hearts of the millions of those who commit it to memory. Through its laws it governs a considerable part of humankind, educating, purifying, and instructing their souls, spirits, hearts, and minds. As demonstrated in certain parts of the *Risale-i Nur*, the Qur'an has forty aspects of miraculousness. It is explained in The Nineteenth Letter that through each of these aspects the Qur'an addresses a different class or level of humankind. Moreover, Prophet Muhammad, upon him be peace and blessings, who is himself a miracle of the Qur'an, proves decisively through his numerous miracles that the Qur'an is the Word of God. Is it then at all possible that this miraculous Qur'an should not be the Word and Decree of the Eternal Speaker and the All-Permanent Maker? God forbid! A hundred thousand times, God forbid!

That is to say, with all its proofs, belief in God proves and establishes that the Qur'an is the Word of God.

Also, is it all possible that the All-Majestic Ruler, Who continuously fills and empties the earth with living beings and populates this world of ours with conscious creatures in order to make Himself known, worshipped, and glorified—it is possible that He should leave the heavens and stars empty and vacant, without creating inhabitants appropriate to them and settling them in these lofty palaces; is it possible that in His most extensive lands He should leave the sovereignty of His Lordship without servants, majesty, officials, envoys, lieutenants, supervisors, spectators, worshippers, or subjects? God forbid! To the numbers of the angels, God forbid!

Also, the All-Wise Ruler, the All-Knowing, and the All-Compassionate One, has written the universe in the form of a book; He inscribes the entire life-stories of trees and the life-duties of grasses and plants in their seeds. He has the lives of conscious beings recorded precisely in their memories, which are as tiny as mustard seeds; He preserves with innumerable photographs all the actions and events which occur in all His dominions and in all the spheres of His Sovereignty. He creates mighty Paradise and Hell, the Supreme Bridge, and the Supreme Scales of Justice in order to allow for the manifestation and realization of absolute justice, wisdom, and mercy, which are among the most significant foundations of His Lordship. Is it at all possible that the One Who does all this should not have all the acts of humankind relating to the universe recorded? Is it possible that He would not have their deeds recorded so that they may be rewarded or punished, nor write their good and bad deeds on the tablets of Divine Destiny? God forbid! To the number of letters inscribed on the Supreme Tablet of Divine Determining or Destiny, God forbid!

Thus the truth of belief in God proves and establishes the truth of both belief in the angels and belief in Divine Determining or Destiny. The pillars of belief prove and establish each other as clearly as the sun shows the daylight and daylight shows the sun.

THE SECOND POINT: All the claims made by the Divinely-revealed Books and the Prophets—the Qur'an and Prophet Muhammad, upon him be peace and blessings, in particular—are established on five or six basic points, which they have continuously striven to teach and prove. All the proofs and evidences which testify to their Prophethood and veracity are concerned with these fundamentals and corroborate their truthfulness. These fundamentals are belief in God, belief in the Hereafter, and belief in the other pillars of faith.

That is to say, it is not possible to separate the six pillars of belief. Each one proves the rest and they all require and necessitate each other. The six form a whole that it is absolutely indivisible. Consider a mighty tree—like the *Touba* tree of Paradise—whose roots are in the heavens. Each branch, fruit, and leaf of that mighty tree relies on its universal, inexhaustible life. A person unable to deny that powerful life, which is as clear as the sun, cannot deny the life of a single one of the leaves that are attached to it. If one does deny it, the tree will refute them to the number of its branches, fruits, and leaves, and that person will be silenced. Belief, with its six pillars, is similar to this.

At the beginning of this Matter, I intended to expound the six pillars of belief in thirty-six points, each pillar in a point with six sub-sections. I also intended to give a detailed reply to the awesome question at the beginning, but certain unforeseen circumstances have intervened. However, I think that the first point provides a sufficient basis, leaving no need for further explanation, particularly for those of keen intellect.

It must by now be fully understood that if a Muslim denies one of the pillars of belief, they will fall into absolute unbelief. Unlike other religions, Islam elucidates its pillars of belief with incomparable comprehensiveness, and the pillars of belief are inextricably bound together. A Muslim who does not recognize Prophet Muhammad, upon him be peace and blessings, and does not confirm him will also fail to recognize God with His Attributes and will not know the Hereafter. A Muslim's belief is based on powerful and unshakeable proofs which are so innumerable that there is no excuse for denial: these proofs quite simply compel human reason to accept them.

THE THIRD POINT: I once said "All praise and gratitude are for God!," and searched for a Divine gift that would be equal to its infinitely broad meaning. Suddenly the following sentence occurred to me:

"All thanks be to God for the gift of belief in God, for His necessary Existence, His Unity, and for His Attributes and Names, to the number of the manifestations of His Names from pre-eternity to post-eternity."

I looked and saw that it was completely appropriate.

The Tenth Matter: The Flower of Emirdağ[52]

The following is a persuasive response to objections that have been raised about the apparent repetitions in the Qur'an.

My dear, faithful brothers (and sisters)!

Confused and ill-expressed though it may be on account of my distressing situation, the following is a reflection on one aspect of the Qur'an's miraculousness. While I find it difficult to articulate, since it concerns the Qur'an, it will be instructive and lead to reflection. It may be likened to the wrapper on a bright, invaluable gem. So consider the gem being offered, rather than its shabby covering. I wrote this with some speed and concision during a few days in Ramadan while I was malnourished and ill, so please forgive any shortcomings it may have.

My dear, faithful brothers (and sisters)!

The Qur'an issues, first of all, from the greatest and most comprehensive rank of the Eternal Speaker's universal Lordship. It is addressed, first of all, to the comprehensive rank of the one who received it in the name of humankind, indeed of the entire universe. Its purpose is to guide humanity

52 A district of Afyon province (western Turkey) where Said Nursi lived for some time. (Tr.)

from the time of its revelation until the end of time. It therefore contains entirely meaningful and comprehensive explanations concerning the Lordship of the Creator of the universe, Who is the Lord of this world and the Hereafter, the earth and the heavens and eternity, and clarifications of the Divine laws which pertain to the administration of all creatures. It is because of these and similar other attributes of the Qur'an that this Divine discourse is so comprehensive and elevated, and therefore so inclusive and miraculous—so much so that even its most apparent, literal meanings which target the simple minds of ordinary people, who make up the largest group of the addressees of the Qur'an, is enough to satisfy those among the people who have attained the highest and most sophisticated levels of understanding. Even its narratives are not a collection of historical stories that were revealed to teach only the people of a certain age, but it addresses and is revealed to every age and all levels of understanding and learning as a collection of universal principles. For example, while describing the punishments meted out to the people of Pharaoh or of 'Ad and Thamud for their sins, and with its severe threats against wrongdoers, it warns all tyrants and criminals, including those of our own time, of the consequences of their tyranny and wrongdoing. By mentioning the final triumphs of Prophets such as Abraham and Moses, upon them be peace, it consoles wronged believers of all eras.

The Qur'an of miraculous expression revives the past, which, for those mired in heedlessness and misguidance, is a lonely and frightful realm, a dark and ruined cemetery. It transforms the past centuries and epochs into living pages of instruction, into a wondrous, animated realm under the direct control of the Lord—a realm that has significant connections with us. By transporting us back to those times or displaying them to us like the scenes on a cinema screen, the Qur'an teaches us, in its own inimitable and most elevated and miraculous style. In the same manner, it shows the true nature of the universe. The misguided see it as an unending, lifeless, lonely, and frightening place, replete with decay and separation, while the Qur'an shows it to be a book of the Eternally Besought One, a city of the All-Merciful and a place where the Lord's works of Art are exhibited. In it, lifeless objects become animate beings performing their particular duties and helping one another within a perfect system of communication.

This most glorious Qur'an, which enlightens and instructs angels, jinn, and humanity in Divine Wisdom in the most pleasing manner, has sacred distinctions which are such that a single letter of it sometimes brings ten merits, sometimes a hundred and sometimes a thousand or, indeed, thousands. If all the jinn and human beings pooled their talents, they would not be able to produce anything to rival or equal the Qur'an in any way. It speaks to all people and the whole universe in the most appropriate way; it is inscribed continuously and with great facility on the minds of millions of people; however frequently it is recited, it never bores or tires its listeners; despite its similar sentences and phrases which may confuse some, children are able to commit it to memory with ease; it gives pleasure and tranquility to the sick and the dying, for whom listening to even a few human words causes great discomfort. The Qur'an causes its students to attain felicity in both this world and the next.

Observing the unlettered nature of the one who conveyed it, and without any hint of pretentiousness or ostentation, the Qur'an preserves its stylistic fluency and purity while never ignoring the level of understanding of the common masses. At the same time it instructs people in the extraordinary miracles of Divine Power and meaningful instances of Divine Wisdom which underpin all events that occur in the heavens and the earth, thereby displaying a fine aspect of miraculousness within the grace of its status as a book of guidance.

The Qur'an demonstrates that it is a book of prayer and invocation, a call to eternal salvation, and a declaration of God's Unity, all of which require reiteration. Consequently it repeats this or that sentence or story, giving numerous meanings to many different groups or categories of addressees, and informs its readers that its Author treats with compassion even the slightest and apparently most insignificant things and events, including them in the sphere of His Will and Control. By paying attention to even the most particular or apparently trivial events involving the Companions of the Prophet in the establishment of Islam and the legislation of its laws, it presents universal principles and suggests that those events function as though they were seeds, destined to produce numerous important fruits in the establishment of Islam with its Law. In this way, it demonstrates another aspect of its miraculousness.

When needs are expressed repeatedly, answers must accordingly be repeated. Therefore, the Qur'an answers many questions which were asked repeatedly during the twenty-three years of its revelation and seeks to satisfy all levels of understanding and learning. To prove that all things, from minute particles to vast stars, are controlled by a Single One and that He will destroy the universe in order to bestow on it a new form on Doomsday, replacing it with the extraordinary realm of the Hereafter; to establish a mighty and all-comprehensive revolution in minds that will, for the sake of the purposes and results of the creation of the universe, demonstrate the Divine rage and wrath in the face of the human injustice and wrongdoing which fill the universe, the earth and the heavens with rage, the Qur'an repeats certain verses and phrases that are the conclusions of innumerable proofs and which are as weighty as thousands of conclusions. In such cases, repetition is an extremely powerful aspect of Qur'anic miraculousness, an extremely elevated example of its eloquence and the beauty of its language that is in conformity with the requirements of the subject matter.

For example, as is explained in The Fourteenth Gleam and The First Word of the *Risale-i Nur*, the phrase *In the Name of God, the All-Merciful, the All-Compassionate*, which appears a total of 114 times in the Qur'an—at the beginning of every *sura* apart from *at-Tawba* and once in the middle of the *sura* entitled *an-Naml*—is a truth that links the earth to God's Supreme Throne as well as to all the spheres of the universe, thus illuminating the universe. As everybody is in constant need of this, it is worth repeating millions of times. We need it not only every day, in the same way that we need bread, but at every moment, in the same way that we need oxygen and light.

Another example is *Your Lord is He Who is the All-Glorious and All-Mighty, the All-Compassionate*, which has the strength of thousands of truths and is repeated eight times in *Suratu'sh-Shu'ara*. It tells of the Prophets' final triumph and salvation and the ruin of their rebellious peoples. If, for the sake of the purposes or results of the universe's creation, in the name of God's universal Lordship, and to teach people that the Lord's Glory and Dignity require the wrongdoers' ruin and His Compassion demands the Prophets' triumph and salvation, this sentence were to be repeated thousands of times, there would still be a need for it. Thus it is a concise and miraculous aspect of the Qur'an's eloquence.

Also, the verses: *Which of the favors of your Lord will you two deny?* (55:13) and *Woe on that day to the deniers* (77:15), which are repeated several times in their respective *suras*, are threats repeated in front of jinn and humanity throughout the ages, and across the heavens and the earth, concerning the ingratitude, unbelief, and wrongdoing of all those whose unrighteousness provokes the fury of the heavens and the earth, ruin the results of the universe's creation, and show contempt and denial in the face of the Divine Sovereign's Majesty. They also denounce the violation of the rights of all creatures. Since they constitute a universal teaching which has the strength of a thousand truths, even if these two verses were repeated thousands of times, it would still not be enough. Therefore this repetition represents a majestic example of conciseness and the miraculousness of eloquence in grace and beauty.

Also, the invocation of the Prophet known as *al-Jawshanu'l-Kabir* (The Great Shield), inspired by the Qur'an, consists of a hundred sections, each of which ends with the words: *All-Glorified are You! There is no deity but You. Mercy! Mercy! Deliver us from the Fire!* These sentences contain affirmation of God's Unity, which is the greatest truth in the universe. This affirmation is the greatest of the mighty duties of all created beings toward their Lord, namely glorification, praise, and declaring Him to be All-Holy and free from all defect, exalted above what polytheists attribute to Him. It is also a supplication for humanity to be saved from eternal punishment, which should be our most immediate concern and is the expected result of our servanthood to God and our helplessness before Him. And so, even if we were to repeat these phrases thousands of times over, it would still not be enough.

Thus, the Qur'an includes reiterations on account of such substantial principles. As required by the occasion and the demands of literary eloquence, and to facilitate understanding, it sometimes expresses the truth of Divine Unity twenty times in one page, be it explicitly or implicitly. Yet, it never bores its listener; rather, it enforces the meaning and gives its reader encouragement.

The *suras* revealed in Makka and Madina differ from one another in eloquence and miraculousness, and in degrees of elaboration and conciseness. The Makkans were mainly Qurayshi polytheists and unlettered tribesmen. Given this, the Qur'an uses forceful, eloquent, and concise language with an elevated style, repeating certain points to better establish its truths.

In the Makkan *suras*, the pillars of belief and the categories and degrees of Divine Unity's manifestations are expressed repeatedly in a forceful, emphatic, concise, and most miraculous language. They prove the beginning and end of the world, the Existence of God and the coming of the Hereafter with powerful proofs and are expressed not only on a single page, or in one verse, sentence, or word, but sometimes even in a single letter, through such subtle changes in word order, through the use or non-use of definite articles or the inclusion or omission of certain words, phrases, and sentences that masters of the art of literary eloquence have been amazed. The sublime eloquence and conciseness of the Makkan chapters have been discussed in *Isharatu'l-I'jaz* and The Twenty-Fifth Word, which explain forty aspects of the Qur'an's miraculous inimitability.

The *suras* revealed in Madina, during the second phase of the Prophet's mission, are in the main addressed to believers, Jews, and Christians. As required by the rules of eloquence and the practical need for guidance, rather than the pillars and principles of belief, they focus more on explaining the laws and commands of the Shari'a in a simple, clear, and detailed language. However, in the unique, peerless style that is particular to the Qur'an, the explanations are usually concluded with an elevated, powerful sentence or phrase related to belief, Divine Unity, or the Hereafter, thus securing obedience to them by relating them to belief in God and the Last Day. By doing so, the Qur'an also uses certain particular events as a basis upon which the universality of the Shari'a's laws is established.

For an understanding of the elevated aspect of eloquence and the subtleties to be found in the phrases that come at the end of certain verses, such as *God has full power over everything*; *God has full knowledge of all things*; *He is the All-Glorious and All-Mighty, the All-Wise*; *He is the All-Glorious and All-Mighty, the All-Compassionate*, the reader may refer to The Second Ray of The Second Light in The Twenty-Fifth Word.

While explaining Islam's secondary principles and social laws, the Qur'an draws its audience's attention suddenly to elevated, universal truths, leading them from the lesson of the Shari'a to the lesson of Divine Unity, and changes from a plain style to an elevated one. In so doing it demonstrates its aim of guidance on every occasion and shows itself to be a book of law and wisdom, a book of creeds, belief, reflection, invocation, prayer, and the call to the Divine Message. Thus, the Qur'an's Madinan chapters display a most miraculous eloquence and purity of language which is different from the styles evident in the Makkan chapters.

For example, by modifying *Lord* with *your* or *my* or *his* or *her* (your, my, his, her Lord) or *the worlds* (the Lord of the worlds), the Qur'an declares, respectively, God's Oneness in His particular relationship with a person as his or her Lord (*Ahadiya*) or His Unity in His universal relationship with the whole of creation (*Wahidiya*). In using *my Lord* or *your Lord*, it introduces God from the perspective of His special attentiveness and compassion, while in using *the Lord of the worlds*, it introduces Him with all His Majesty, expressing the latter (*Wahidiya*) within the former (*Ahadiya*). Sometimes when the Qur'an sees and fixes an atom in the pupil of the eye, it uses the same "hammer" to fix the sun in the sky and make it an eye of the heavens.

For example, in the expressions: *He has created the heavens and the earth* (57:4), and *He makes the night pass into the day and He makes the day pass into the night* (57:6), the Qur'an considers the understanding of common people, including those who are unlettered among them. However, it concludes the verses with: *He has full knowledge of whatever lies in the bosoms* (57:6); this means: "Together with the magnificent creation and administration of the earth and the heavens, He also has full knowledge of whatever occurs in people's hearts." Thus, the simple style of speech that is aimed at ordinary people is manifested here as an elevated and appealing address for the guidance of all.

QUESTION: Sometimes an important truth may remain hidden to superficial views. Also, the reason for ending the narration of an ordinary event with a universal principle or an aspect of Divine Unity cannot always be readily discerned. Some may consider this Qur'anic style defective. For example, after narrating how Prophet Joseph, upon him be peace, managed to detain his brother (12:69–76), the Qur'an mentions an exalted principle: *Above every owner of knowledge there is (always) one more knowledgeable.* From the perspective of the rules of eloquence, this seems unrelated to the actual context. What is the reason for this?

THE ANSWER: The Qur'an is a book of belief, reflection, and invocation, as well as a book of law, wisdom, and guidance; it therefore contains numerous "books." For this reason, in many pages and passages of long and medium-length *suras*, each of which is a small Qur'an, many teachings and aims are pursued. For example, in order to express the all-comprehensive and magnificent manifestations of Divine Lordship, since it is a kind of copy or reflection of the great book of the universe, the Qur'an gives instructions on every occasion that concerns knowledge of God, aspects of Divine Unity, and the truths of belief. Whenever a suitable occasion arises, no matter how insignificant it seems, the Qur'an expounds different teachings, thus using that occasion to present new instructions or to reveal certain universal rules or principles. This corresponds perfectly to the discussion and adds to the Qur'an's eloquence.

Question: Be it implicitly or explicitly, the Qur'an dwells much on Divine Unity, the Hereafter, and God's judgment of humanity. Why is this so?

The Answer: The Qur'an was revealed to teach humanity about the Existence of God, Divine Unity, and the absolute control that He exercises over the universe and the changes, upheavals, and revolutions which take place in it; it was revealed to dispel all doubts concerning these truths and to break the obstinacy of those who continue to desist from confirming them. It was also revealed to instruct humanity, who has accepted to bear the Supreme Trust as vicegerent of the earth, which they are to rule and develop in accordance with Divine laws, in the mightiest and most important aspects of humanity's duties concerning eternal happiness or perdition. In order to have humanity confirm the instructions of the Qur'an and assent to the most essential matters concerning them, even if the Qur'an were to focus attention on these matters a million times, this would not be a waste of time or words; they would be read and studied over and over again without causing the least boredom.

For example, we read in *Suratu'l-Buruj*:

> Those who believe and do good, righteous deeds, for them there are Gardens through which rivers flow. That is the great triumph. (85:11)

This verse teaches us that death, which stands ever present before us, is something that saves us, our world, and our loved ones from eternal annihilation, for it leads us to a magnificent, everlasting life. Even if this verse were repeated billions of times, and if as much importance were attached to it as is attached to the whole of existence, it would still not be excessive enough to devalue or detract from its meaning. In teaching countless, invaluable matters of this sort and in trying to prove and make people aware of the awesome revolutions that continuously change and renew the universe, the Qur'an draws attention to these matters repeatedly, either in an explicit manner or through allusions. Since they are bounties like light, air, food, and medicine—things which we always need and which require constant renewal and refreshment—the fact that they are repeated so often in the Qur'an is an instance of Divine grace.

Also, consider the following:

The Qur'an reiterates severely, angrily, and emphatically such threatening verses as:

> For the wrongdoers there is a painful punishment (14:22); and

> As for those who disbelieve, for them is the fire of Hell (35:36).

As discussed in detail in the *Risale-i Nur*, humanity's unbelief is such a heinous violation of the rights of the universe and most of its creatures that it angers the earth and infuriates the elements. It is for this reason that they smite unbelievers with floods and similar disasters.

As is stated explicitly in

> When they are cast into it, they will hear its raucous breath (by which they are sucked in) as it boils up, almost bursting with fury... (67:7–8)

Hell is so furious with the unbelievers that it is described as if it were nearly bursting with rage. If, not from the perspective of the physical insignificance of humanity but of the enormity of the unbeliever's wrongdoing and the awesomeness of unbelief as a heinous crime and boundless aggression, and in order to show the importance of His subjects' rights as well as the ugliness in the unbelief and iniquity of unbelievers, the Sovereign of the universe were to describe and denounce such crimes a billion times, it would still not count as a defect. Countless people have read these words every day for fourteen centuries with the utmost eagerness and without the slightest feeling of boredom or weariness.

Every day, for each person a world disappears and the door of a new world is opened. Thus by repeating *There is no deity but God* a thousand times out of need and with the desire to illuminate each of our transient worlds, we make each repetition a lamp for every changing scene. In the same way, one of the reasons the Qur'an repeats the Eternal Sovereign's threats and punishments so often is to seek to break humanity's obduracy and free them from their rebellious carnal soul. It thus seeks to prevent them from darkening the changing scenes and the freshly-recruited worlds, from disfiguring their images which are reflected in the mirror of their lives, and from turning against them those fleeting scenes that will testify for them in the Hereafter. For this reason, even Satan does not consider the severe and forceful repetition of threats in the Qur'an as being out of place. These threats demonstrate that the torments of Hell are pure justice for those who do not heed them.

Another example is the repetition of the stories of the Prophets, particularly that of Moses, upon him be peace.

Such stories contain many instances of wisdom and benefit. The Qur'an shows the Prophethood of all previous Prophets as an evidence of Muhammad's Messengership, upon him be peace and blessings. This means that from the point of view of truth, no-one can deny Muhammad's Messengership unless one denies all the other Prophets. Also, since not everyone can recite the entire Qur'an every time they open it, it includes these stories, together with the essentials of belief, in almost all the long and medium-length *suras*, thus making each *sura* like a miniature Qur'an. This is done because it is demanded by the principles of literary eloquence and also because the Qur'an wishes to show that Prophet Muhammad, upon him be peace and blessings, is the most important of people and the noblest phenomenon in the universe.

The ritual declaration of belief in Islam—the *Kalimatu't-Tawhid*—is *There is no deity but God and Muhammad is God's Messenger*. The Qur'an accords the highest status to the person of Muhammad and since part of this declaration—*Muhammad is God's Messenger*—points to four of the six pillars of belief, it is often considered equal to the first part, namely *There is no deity but God*. Muhammad's Messengership is the universe's greatest truth, as an individual he is the most noble of God's creatures, and his collective personality and sacred rank, known as *the Muhammadan Truth*, is the brightest sun of both this world and the next. Among many of the proofs in the *Risale-i Nur* which show how worthy he is of occupying such an extraordinary position, the following are but a few:

According to the rule "The cause is like the doer," an amount of reward equal to the number of the good deeds that his community has ever done or will do in the future is added to Prophet Muhammad's account. Since he illuminated the universe with the light he brought, not only jinn, humanity, and angels, but also the heavens and the earth are indebted to him. We see clearly that the supplications of the plants and animals that they offer through the tongue of potentiality and need are accepted. This shows that the prayers of millions of righteous ones among Muhammad's community must be acceptable. They have been praying to God many times a day for centuries to bestow peace and blessings on him and give him the same reward as they have earned. Furthermore, his record of good deeds also contains countless lights from his followers' recitation of the Qur'an, each letter of which brings as many as ten, a hundred or a thousand rewards.

Knowing beforehand that his collective personality—*the Muhammadan Truth*—would be like a blessed, elaborate tree of Paradise in the future, and considering him as a person to be the seed of that majestic tree, the All-Knower of the Unseen attached the greatest importance to him in His Qur'an. In His Decree He has emphasized the need for others to obey him and to gain the honor of his intercession by following his *sunna* or path and has confirmed it as the most important and serious matter of humanity.

Thus, since the truths repeated in the Qur'an have such a great value, anyone with a sound, uncorrupted nature will testify that in its repetitions can be found a powerful and extensive miracle, unless one is afflicted with some sickness of the heart or malady of the conscience due to the plague of materialism, and is therefore included under the following rule:

> A person denies the light of the sun because of their diseased eyes,
> A mouth denies the taste of sweet water on account of sickness.

TWO CONCLUDING NOTES

THE FIRST: Twelve years ago, I heard that a most dangerous and obstinate enemy of Islam had instigated a conspiracy against the Qur'an and ordered it to be translated so that "people could see its repetitiousness and understand just what it really is." He also intended to substitute a translation for the original Arabic in the canonical Prayers. However, as the *Risale-i Nur* shows decisively, an exact translation of the Qur'an is impossible. No other language can preserve the fine virtues and subtleties of the Arabic language, given how strict and precise it is in grammar and syntax. No translation can replace the Qur'an's miraculously inimitable words and phrases, which are extremely comprehensive in meaning, and each letter of which yields from ten to a thousand merits.

The *Risale-i Nur* also stymied the plan to have only translations of the Qur'an recited in mosques. But since hypocrites taught by that heretic continue to seek a way to extinguish the sun of the Qur'an in the name of Satan, I felt compelled to write the *Flower of Emirdağ*. However, since I have not met with people for a long time, I have no knowledge of the latest developments.

THE SECOND: After our release from Denizli prison, I was sitting on the top floor of the well-known Hotel Şehir. The graceful dancing of the leaves, branches, and trunks of the poplar trees in the fine gardens opposite me, each with a rapturous motion like a circle of dervishes touched by the breeze, pained my heart, which was already grieving at being parted from my brothers and finding myself alone. Suddenly I thought of fall and winter, and a kind of heedlessness overcame me. I pitied those graceful, swaying poplars and joyful living creatures so much that my eyes began to brim with tears. Since they reminded me of the deaths and separations which lie beneath the ornamented veil of the cosmic façade, the grief at a world full of death and separation took me in its grip and began to squeeze me. But then the light of the *Muhammadan Truth* came and changed that grief to joy. Indeed, I felt eternally grateful to the person of Muhammad, upon him be peace and blessings, for the help and consolation that came to me at that time, for only a single instance of the boundless grace of that light for me, as for all believers and everyone. It was as follows:

The heedlessness that had overcome me had shown me that these blessed and delicate creatures only appear in the season of summer in a purposeless and fruitless life. Their movements were not due to joy; rather they were trembling at the thought of death, separation, and the journey to non-existence. This view was deeply injurious to my passionate desire for permanence, to my love of beauty and my compassion for all creatures and living things. This way of thinking transformed the world into a kind of Hell and my intellect into an instrument of torture. But just at that point, the light that Prophet Muhammad, upon him be peace and blessings, brought as a gift for humanity lifted the veil and showed that rather than extinction, non-existence, nothingness, futility, or separation, the existence of these poplar trees had as many meanings and purposes as the number of their leaves. Moreover, it revealed that they had several duties and that their lives yielded many results, as follows:

One kind relates to the All-Majestic Maker's Names. For example, everyone applauds and congratulates an engineer who makes an extraordinary machine. By carrying out its functions properly, the machine in turn can be said to congratulate and applaud its engineer. Every created being in the universe is such a machine and congratulates and applauds its Maker.

Another instance of wisdom in things such as poplar trees is that each of them resembles a text which, when studied, reveals knowledge of God to conscious living beings. Having left their meanings in the minds of beings such as these, and having left their forms in these beings' memories, as well as on the tablets of the World of representations or "ideal forms" and the records of the World of the Unseen, they leave the material world for the World of the Unseen. In other words, they are stripped of apparent existence and gain many existences that pertain to meanings, the Knowledge that lies behind them and the knowledge of conscious beings, and the unseen realm.

Since God exists and His Knowledge encompasses all things, certainly there can be no such thing in reality, or in the world of a believer, as non-existence, eternal annihilation, or nothingness. An unbeliever's world, however, is filled with notions such as non-existence, separation, and extinction. As the famous proverb has it: "Everything exists for the one for whom God exists; nothing exists for the one for whom God does not exist."

In short, then, just as belief saves us from eternal punishment when we die, it saves everyone's particular world from the darkness of eternal extinction and nothingness. Unbelief, especially the denial of God, destroys both the individual themselves and their particular world with the fear of death, casting them into dark, hellish pits and changing their life's pleasures into pain. Those who prefer this world over the Hereafter should pay heed to this. They should either find a solution for this intractable problem or they should accept belief, thus saving themselves from a most fearful eternal loss.

> All-Glorified are You! We have no knowledge save what You have taught us. Surely You are the All-Knowing, the All-Wise.

Your brother who is in dire need of your prayers and misses you greatly,

Said Nursi

The Eleventh Matter

Hundreds of the innumerable fruits, both particular and universal, of the sacred tree of belief, one of which is Paradise, another, eternal happiness, and the other the vision of God, have been explained in certain other parts of the *Risale-i Nur*. Referring interested readers to these parts, we will set out here just a few examples of its most minor and particular fruits rather than those of its universal pillars.

One day while praying, "O my Lord! In veneration of Gabriel, Michael, Israfil and Azra'il, and through their intercession, preserve me from the evil of humans and jinn!" I felt particularly exhilarated and consoled when I mentioned Azra'il—the name of the Archangel of death and one who usually causes people to tremble with fear. "All praise and gratitude be to God!" I uttered, and began to feel earnest love for him. I will point out extremely briefly only a few of the fruits of belief in the angels, together with certain particular fruits of belief in other pillars. They are as follows:

ONE FRUIT: Everyone's most precious possession which they try their utmost to preserve is their spirit. I felt great joy at having submitted it to a powerful and trustworthy hand—Azra'il, thereby saving it from aimlessness and preventing it from being lost or annihilated. Then the angels who record human actions came to mind, and I saw that their existence yields numerous sweet fruits such as this one.

ANOTHER FRUIT: Everyone tries eagerly to preserve worthwhile sayings or deeds of theirs through prose, poetry, or film-making, thus immortalizing what they have said or done. And if their deeds are to produce everlasting fruits in Paradise, they are even more anxious to preserve them. The fact that the recording angels perch on people's shoulders to record those deeds which will gain them perpetual rewards and which people will watch as everlasting scenes in the everlasting realm, seemed so lovely and agreeable to me that I cannot describe it.

THIRD FRUIT: Then, when the worldly authorities had isolated me from everything connected with social life, keeping me away from all my books, friends, assistants and things that console me, and when I was being crushed by exile and the empty world was tumbling down all around me, one of the many fruits of belief in the angels came to my aid. It cheered up my world and lightened my life, filling it with angels and spirit beings, and making everything around me smile with joy. It showed too that the worlds of the people of misguidance weep in desolation, emptiness, and darkness.

FOURTH FRUIT: While enjoying the pleasures of this fruit, my imagination received and tasted one of the numerous fruits of belief, namely belief in the Prophets. Suddenly, my belief in all of the past Prophets so powerful as if I had actually lived among them lit up the past, expanding my belief and giving it universality. It also served to endorse the teachings of the Seal of the Prophets, upon him be peace and blessings, concerning belief to the number of the past Messengers, thus silencing the satanic ones.

Then a question occurred to me, which is also discussed in The Thirteenth Gleam, concerning the wisdom which lies in seeking refuge in God from Satan. It was as follows:

Question: Although the people of guidance are supported and strengthened by innumerable sweet fruits and benefits such as these, by the fine results of good deeds and the compassionate help of the Most Merciful of the Merciful, why is it that the people of misguidance are frequently able to defeat them? Why, at times, are twenty unbelievers able to crush a hundred believers?

The Answer: While thinking about this, I recalled the emphatic warnings of the Qur'an concerning feeble intrigues of Satan, and how it reminds us frequently that God Almighty is with the believers and sends angels to assist them. This matter has been explained in detail elsewhere in the *Risale-i Nur* and so we will allude to it here only briefly.

It may be that when a single arsonist tries to set fire to a palace, the palace can remain standing only through the efforts of a hundred men protecting it, a hundred men who have recourse to the full force of the law. For like its existence, the subsistence of the palace is possible only through the continued existence of all its parts, together with the presence of all the conditions and causes necessary for its subsistence. Its destruction and non-existence, however, may occur through the non-existence of a single condition. Just as the palace can be razed to the ground by a vandal with a single match, vast destruction and mayhem may be wrought by satanic ones among jinn and humanity with comparative ease. The basis and origin of all evil and sin is non-existence and destruction. Their apparent existence veils actual non-existence and destruction—that is, although evil and sin appear to actually exist, in truth they are the absence of good and therefore pure non-existence.

Thus the satanic ones from among jinn and humanity are able to resist a great force with what is in actual fact an extremely weak one, thus compelling the people of truth to seek refuge continuously at the Court of the Divine. For this reason, the Qur'an attaches extreme importance to the protection of the good. It offers as a source of their support ninety-nine Divine Names and orders them sternly to withstand these enemies.

This answer unveiled a great truth and the basis of an awesome matter. Paradise displays the crops of all the worlds of existence and causes the seeds sown in the world to sprout and grow into eternal plants or trees. Similarly, in order to display the grievous consequences of the innumerable terrible worlds of non-existence and nothingness, Hell burns up the products of these worlds and cleanses the universe of the filth from the world of non-existence. But this is a matter which we will discuss elsewhere.

FIFTH FRUIT: Another example of the fruits of belief in the angels concerns the "questioning angels," known as *Munkar* and *Nakir*:

I once imagined entering the grave, as one day, like everyone else, I will. As I lay there, terrified by the desolation and despair of that dark, cold, narrow pit, two blessed friends from among the species of angels called *Munkar* and *Nakir* appeared and began to converse with me. At once both the grave and my heart were broadened, illuminated, and warmed as windows were opened, one after the other, onto the world of spirits. I was filled with joy at this imaginary situation, knowing that I would experience such a thing in the future and I offered heartfelt thanks.

It was narrated that a *medrese* student who was studying Arabic died. In response to the question of *Munkar* and *Nakir*, who asked him "Who is your Lord?" he imagined for a moment that he was back in *medrese* and answered: "The word 'who' is the subject and 'your Lord' is its predicate; now ask me something difficult!" His answer made both the angels and the other spirit beings and a saintly person who was observing this incident from the world laugh, and brought a smile to the metaphorical face of Divine Mercy. God willing, the student was delivered from torment. I hope that like the late Hafiz Ali, a martyred student of the *Risale-i Nur* who died in prison while studying and enthusiastically copying the treatise known as *Fruits of Belief*, and answered the questions of *Munkar* and *Nakir* with the truths set forth in this treatise, we as students of the *Risale-i Nur* may also be graced with the ability to answer the questions to be posed by *Munkar* and *Nakir* with the powerful proofs explained in the *Risale-i Nur*.

SIXTH FRUIT: Another small benefit to be had from belief in angels concerns worldly happiness. An innocent child who had learnt his lesson of belief from a manual concerning Islamic daily life once said to another child who was weeping at the death of his little brother: "Don't cry! Be thankful, for your brother has gone to Paradise and is now with the angels. He is enjoying himself there and having a better time than we are. He is flying around like the angels and taking a look at everything." With these words he turned his friend's mournful tears into happy smiles.

Exactly like that weeping child, during this sorrowful winter I received painful news of two deaths. One was the death of my nephew, Fuad, one of the most successful high school students in the country and someone who had published the truths studied and taught by the *Risale-i Nur*. The second was the death of my sister, Alima Hanim, who died while circumambulating the Ka'ba during *Hajj*. While the deaths of my two relatives were making me weep, as did that of Abdurrahman, which is described in *Treatise of Hope and Solace for the Elderly* (that is, The Twenty-sixth Gleam), I saw in my heart through the light of belief that the innocent Fuad and that righteous woman had as their companions the angels and *houris* of Paradise, and had been saved from the perils and sins of this world. Feeling overwhelming joy instead of that dreadful sorrow, I congratulated both of them and Fuad's father, Abdülmecid, along with myself, and offered thanks to the Most Merciful of the Merciful. This has been mentioned here as a supplication for mercy for the two deceased.

All the comparisons and descriptions in the *Risale-i Nur* describe the fruits of belief that are the means of happiness in this world and the next. Compared with the happiness and pleasures of life they engender in this world, these universal and extensive fruits suggest that their belief will gain every believer everlasting happiness; indeed, it is bound to produce shoots and develop in that way. Five of these numerous universal fruits were described at the end of The Thirty-first Word as fruits of the Ascension, while five are included as examples in The Fifth Branch of The Twenty-fourth Word.

We said at the beginning that each of the pillars of belief has innumerable different fruits, and that one of the fruits of the totality of these pillars is the vast Paradise, while another is eternal happiness, and yet another, perhaps the sweetest, is the vision of God. Also some of the fruits of belief that are the means for happiness in both worlds have been described in the comparison which comes at the end of The Thirty-second Word.

SEVENTH FRUIT: Belief in Divine Decree and Destiny also yields precious fruits in this world. Evidence of this can be seen in the well-known saying "Whoever believes in Divine Destiny is secure against grief." A universal fruit of belief in Divine Destiny is explained in the fine example which is given at the end of *Treatise on Divine Decree and Destiny*, which is about two men who enter the lovely garden of a palace. I have had innumerable personal experiences which have convinced me that a lack of belief in Divine Destiny destroys the happiness of this worldly life. Whenever I consider grievous misfortunes from the perspective of Divine Destiny, I see that the misfortune is greatly lightened. I often wonder how those who do not believe in it can continue to live at all!

EIGHTH FRUIT: One of the universal fruits of the pillar of belief in the angels is mentioned in The Second Station of The Twenty-second Word as follows: the Archangel Azra'il, upon him be peace and blessings, said to God: "Your servants will be annoyed with me and complain about me when I carry out my duty of seizing the spirits of the dying."

God replied: "I will make illnesses and calamities a veil to cover your duties, so that my servants' complaints will be directed at these phenomena and not at you."

Like these veils, the duty of Azra'il is also a veil, so that unjustified complaints are not directed toward God Almighty. For not everyone can fathom the wisdom, mercy, beauty, and benefits of death: people see only its outward face and start to object and complain. It is in order that unjustified complaints are not directed to the Absolutely Compassionate One that the function of Azra'il has been veiled. In exactly the same way, the tasks of all the angels, indeed of all apparent causes, are veils that cover the hand of Power, so that the dignity and holiness of Divine Power and the all-embracing nature of Divine Mercy are preserved with regard to things whose essential beauty is not apparent and whose wisdom is not understood; they are preserved so that they do not become the target of objections, and so that those who view things superficially do not see Divine Power as something which is occupied with things that are base, trivial or cruel. For as was discussed convincingly in the *Risale-i Nur*, no cause or agent can play any essential role in the creation or control of things, and everything most evidently bears the stamp of Divine Unity. Invention and creation are particular to God exclusively; causes are merely a veil. Conscious beings like angels can do nothing but carry out certain duties with their partial, limited will-power and in accordance with the Divine purpose for their existence. This is called "acquisition."[53] What they do is a kind of worship that they offer in the form of their vital duties.

> The Dignity and Grandeur of God demand that in the view of the mind causes are veils to cover the hand of Power;
>
> While Divine Unity and Oneness demand that causes have no creative part in creation.

Just as the angels and the apparent causes employed in creational tasks are all means of preserving Divine Power from the attribution to It of defects and apparent evil that some see in things or events, the essential beauties and instances of wisdom of which are invisible or unknown; they are means of sanctifying God, of believing in and declaring His absolute freedom from any shortcoming or wrong, so too, harmful elements and satanic individuals from among human beings and jinn are employed in evil deeds and actions that pertain to non-existence so that they may assist in the preservation of Divine Power from the attribution of injustice or unjustified objections and complaints. They also help to pave the way for the glorification of God Almighty as being absolutely free of all the defects and faults in the universe. For defects and faults arise from non-existence or a lack of sufficient ability, from destruction or the failure to perform certain duties, all of which lead to non-existence and arise from acts which bring about destruction or non-existence. The defects and faults are ascribed to these satanic and evil veils; objections and complaints are directed at them, and thus they function as the means by which God Almighty is declared absolutely free from all defects.

In fact, evil and destructive works pertaining to non-existence do not need any notable power or strength: some trivial act, some insignificant power, or even the non-performance of a duty may cause great destruction

---

53 "Acquisition" denotes the volitional acts of responsible beings like humanity and jinn which yield certain results and for which they are responsible. (Tr.)

and extensive non-existence. Despite this, it is often supposed that the doers of evil have real power and ability, even though they play no role other than to cause non-existence and no power other than minor "acquisition." But since the evils arise from non-existence, the doers of evil are their agents. If they are intelligent beings, they deservedly suffer the consequences. That is to say, the perpetrators of evil deeds are their agents or doers. However, since good deeds and acts pertain to and are means of existence, those who do them are not their true doers: rather, they are the means through which Divine favor manifests itself; the wise Qur'an states that their reward too is purely a Divine favor: *Whatever good happens to you, it is from God; and whatever evil befalls you, it is from yourself* (4:79).

In short: The worlds of existence and the innumerable worlds of non-existence clash, producing fruits like Paradise and Hell. All the worlds of existence declare, "All praise and gratitude are for God!" thus declaring Him to possess all attributes of perfection to an absolute degree, while all the worlds of non-existence announce, "All-Glorified is God!" thus declaring God to be absolutely free of all defect and injustice. Angels and demons, together with instances of good and instances of evil, including the beneficent inspirations and satanic whisperings which enter the heart, all struggle against each other. And as these clashes occur, one fruit of belief in the angels is suddenly manifested, illuminating the universe. Showing us one of the lights of the verse: *God is the Light of the heavens and the earth* (24:35), it causes us to taste how sweet this fruit is.

NINTH FRUIT: Another universal fruit of belief in the angels is to be found in The Twenty-fourth and Twenty-ninth Words.

In every corner of the universe, in every realm of being and in everything, whether particular or universal, is the compassionate majesty of Lordship, which makes itself known and loved. And most certainly it is necessary to respond to that majesty, that compassion and that will to make itself known and loved with thanks and comprehensive, conscious worship, declaring them to be free of all defects. It is only the countless angels that can perform this duty on behalf of unconscious inanimate creatures and the universal elements; they are the only creatures who can represent the wise, majestic activity of the sovereignty of that Lordship everywhere on the earth, from its very core to the Pleiades and beyond.

For example, the lifeless, soulless laws of philosophy show the creation of the earth and its "natural" duties to be dark and desolate. However, Ibn 'Abbas narrates in reference to earlier Prophets of the Children of Israel that the earth sits on the shoulders of two angels called *Thawr* (the Ox) and *Hut* (the Fish). According to this narration, these angels supervise the earth. Furthermore, a substance called *sakhra*, belonging to the other world, is said to be the foundation stone of the earth and will be used in the transformation of a certain part of the earth into Paradise. This provides a perspective from which one may understand the real meaning of the narration, namely that the earth rests on the shoulders of these beings known as *Thawr* and *Hut*. Unfortunately, this figurative description came to be taken literally over the course of time, taking on a completely irrational complexion, whereas the fruit of belief in the angels illuminates the earth, its creation and duties. Since the angels travel through earth and rock and the centre of the globe in the same way that they travel through the air, neither they nor the earth have need of physical rocks, or a fish or an ox to support them!

Also, since the earth offers Divine glorifications with as many heads as there are species of beings, with tongues to the number of the members of those species, and to the number of the parts, leaves, and fruits of those members, then surely in order to consciously represent this magnificent, unconscious "natural" worship and offer it to the Divine Court, there will be an appointed angel with forty thousand heads, glorifying God with each of its forty thousand tongues, and with each tongue uttering forty thousand Divine glorifications. The Trustworthy Reporter, upon him be peace and blessings, informed us of this as a truth. This shows that the existence and extraordinary nature of angels, such as Gabriel, upon him be peace, who communicates and manifests God's relationship with humanity, the most significant result of the creation of the universe; Israfil and Azra'il, upon them be peace, who represent and watch with adoration the awesome activity of the Creator in the world of living beings, such as giving life, restoring to life, and discharging from duties through death; Michael, upon him be peace, who, in addition to watching the All-Merciful's providing for His creatures, which is the most extensive and pleasurable act of Mercy in the sphere of life, consciously represents unconscious thanks. The existence and extraordinary nature of angels like these and the immortality of their spirits are necessitated by the sovereignty and magnificence of Divine Lordship.

Their existence and that of the species to which each belongs is as certain as the existence of the sovereignty and magnificence that can be observed in the universe as clearly as the sun. Other matters concerning the angels may be approached from this perspective.

The All-Powerful One of Grace and Majesty has created hundreds of thousands of species of living beings on the earth; He has created beings with spirits in great abundance, even out of base and rotten substances, filling the cosmos with them. With regard to the miracles of His Art He causes them to declare: "What wonders God has willed! How blessed is God and how great are His blessings! All-Glorified is God!", and with regard to the gifts of His Mercy: "All praise and gratitude are for God! All thanks be to God! God is the All-Great!" Most certainly, therefore, He has created inhabitants and spirit beings appropriate for the vast heavens, beings who never rebel and perform constant worship. Not leaving the heavens empty, He has created countless different kinds of angels, far greater in number than the animal species. Some of them ride on the raindrops and snowflakes and applaud the Divine Art and Mercy in their own languages. Others ride on the moving stars and, on their journeys through space, proclaim to the world their worship in the form of the exaltation of God and the declaration of His Unity with regard to the grandeur, dignity and magnificence of Lordship.

The agreement of all the revealed Scriptures and religions since the time of Adam concerning the existence and worship of the angels, and the numerous unanimous reports in all ages of the conversations and meetings that human beings have had with angels, prove that their existence is as certain as the existence of the people of America, whom we have never seen; it is also clear that the angels are concerned with us.

Now come and experience, through the light of belief, this universal fruit: see how it fills the universe from end to end, beautifying it and transforming it into a vast mosque or place of worship. While scientific materialism and atheistic philosophy show the cosmos to be cold, lifeless, dark and desolate, belief reveals that it is full of life and light. It shows that it is conscious, familiar, and most agreeable, allowing the people of belief to experience a manifestation of the pleasures of eternal life, each according to the degree of their belief while still in this world.

In conclusion: On account of the unity in the universe which arises from God's Oneness, the same Power, the same Names, the same Wisdom, and the same Art prevail in every part of the universe, and all creatures, individually or as a species, proclaim the Creator's Unity, His absolute Control and Authority, His Creativity, Lordship, and Holiness through their tongues of disposition. In the same way, He has created the angels and populated the heavens with them, causing them to represent and offer through their worshipful tongues the glorifications which all unconscious creatures offer through their tongues of disposition. Angels never act in opposition to the Divine Command. Apart from pure worship, they do nothing in the name of creation, nor do they intervene in anything unless commanded; they cannot even intercede unless they are given permission. They manifest to the utmost degree the meaning of *Angels are but His honored servants* (21:26); and *They carry out what they are commanded* (66:6).

The Twelfth Ray

The Twelfth Ray

Quotations and selections from Said Nursi's letters to or conversations with local authorities in Denizli and Afyon

In His Name, All-Glorified is He.

WE ARE A COMMUNITY WHOSE MEMBERS ARE TIED TO ONE ANOTHER through belief. Our members show, with complete veneration, their attachment to this community five times a day through the canonical Prayers. They hasten to assist one another with their supplications and spiritual gains. Our duty is to teach the believers the Qur'anic truths of belief in a certain, verified fashion, so that both we and they may be saved from eternal annihilation and everlasting solitary confinement in the Intermediate Realm of the grave. We have absolutely no connection with any worldly political society, secret committee, or covert organization.

If we had harbored any desire to interfere in worldly affairs, it would never have remained secret. Thus, if some have accused us of plotting and scheming for ulterior motives without having actually witnessed any untoward behavior on our part over the past eighteen years, it must only be on account of their hatred for us or because of some particular grudge they hold against us.

The *Risale-i Nur* should not be attacked because of my personal faults or the faults of some of my brothers. Its source is, after all, the Qur'an, and the Qur'an is bound to the Supreme Throne of God.

Moreover, the *Risale-i Nur* has been rendering valuable services to this country and thus should not be blamed for any personal faults of ours. Indeed, attacking it may cause irreparable harm to the country, which may then be deprived of its services. Its students never think of taking part in mutinous movements like those of Sheikh Said or Menemen.[54]

In short: Just as we do not interfere in the world of the worldly, the worldly should not interfere in our service of belief and our acts which are aimed at securing eternal life in the Hereafter.

Said Nursi

* * *

In His Name, All-Glorified is He.

Gentlemen!

We know with the unshakeable certainty that two times two equals four that for us believers, death has been transformed from eternal annihilation into a discharge from duties, and that for those who follow misguidance and oppose us because we are believers and servants of the Qur'an, death is either eternal execution if they do not have certain belief in the Hereafter, or dark and everlasting solitary confinement if they believe in the Hereafter but choose to follow instead the path of vice and misguidance. Is there a more important matter for humanity in this world than salvation from eternal punishment? Since there is not, do not strive to eliminate us! Even if you oppose us, our innate feelings of humanity demand that we take pity on those who insistently follow misguidance and try to eliminate those who work for the eternal happiness of others, simply because they are certain to go to the other world and suffer on account of their wrongdoing. I am ready to prove this to everyone, including the most celebrated scientists and philosophers. I offer the Treatise on the Fruits of Belief (The 11th Ray) as a single example. Read and study it carefully, and if your heart—your carnal soul is your own affair—does not affirm what I say, then I will remain silent.

Said Nursi

* * *

54 Said Nursi refers to the provoked mutinous movements that took place in South-eastern Turkey in 1925 and in Menemen, a district of İzmir in Western Turkey, in 1930. (Tr.)

In His Name, All-Glorified is He.

They asked me: "What do you think about the Republic?" I answered: "If you look at the story of my life, you will see that I was a religious republican before any of you. I was living in retreat in an uninhabited tomb. Someone would bring me soup and I would give the vegetables to the ants in my room, content with dipping my bread in the water of the soup. Those who heard of this would ask me about it, and I would tell them: "These nations of ants and bees are like republics: I give the ants the vegetables and grains in my soup out of respect for their republicanism."

So then they said: "You are opposing the early leaders of Islam." I answered: "The Rightly-Guided Caliphs were both Caliphs and presidents of a republic. Surely Abu Bakr the Truthful, may God be pleased with him, was the president of a republic in which resided the dearest Companions of the Prophet, including the ten who were promised Paradise.[55] And it was not some meaningless title: Abu Bakr and the other Rightly-Guided Caliphs were leaders of a religious republic, the cornerstone of which was laid on true justice and the freedom of conscience and speech."

Said Nursi

* * *

In His Name, All-Glorified is He.

We have never had any intention to set up a political organization or a *tariqa*: the only thing we have tried to do is to work to save our belief. We have forged relationships with one another only through the bond of belief and the brotherhood (and sisterhood) which arises as a result of this belief. The expert report says: "There is nothing explicit or implicit in the writings of Said Nursi and the students of the *Risale-i Nur* which suggests that they have any intent to misuse religion or sacred matters, to encourage the breaching of state security or to establish a political organization. Said Nursi's treatises are both sincere and politically disinterested, and have in no way departed from the prin-

[55] It is reported from Prophet Muhammad, upon him be peace and blessings, that the following ten persons would go to Paradise: Abu Bakr, 'Umar, 'Uthman, 'Ali (the four Rightly-Guided Caliphs after the Prophet), Sa'd ibn Abi Waqqas, Zubayr ibn 'Awwam, Talha ibn 'Ubaydullah, 'Abdur-Rahman ibn 'Awf, Abu 'Ubayda ibnu'l-Jarrah, and Sa'id ibn Zayd. (Abu Dawud, "Sunna" 27; at-Tirmidhi, "Manaqib" 26.) (Tr.)

ciples of scholarship and religion. There is clearly nothing in them that exploits religion or suggests any concern with the formation of a political organization. The letters and correspondence between the students themselves and between the students and Said Nursi are in completely agreement with this general trend. The treatises expound Qur'anic verses or the true meanings of Prophetic Traditions. These are works written to explain belief in God, the Prophet, and the Resurrection using comparisons and parables. They also contain moral instructions for the elderly and for the youth of the country, using instructive incidents selected from his own life experiences."

Religion does not consist only in belief; it also includes righteous action. Is fear of imprisonment or being seen and apprehended by a government detective sufficient to prevent people from committing the kind of grievous sins and crimes which poison society, such as murder, adultery, theft, drinking, and gambling? If this were the case, there would have to be a policeman or detective stationed permanently in every house, or at everyone's side, even, so that rebellious souls would restrain themselves from committing these despicable acts. However, the *Risale-i Nur* places a permanent immaterial deterrent next to everyone—a deterrent which comes from belief and the duty to enjoin what is good and forbid what is illicit. By bearing in mind the existence of the awesome prison of Hell and Divine wrath people are able to preserve themselves from evil.

Said Nursi

* * *

Gentlemen!

Friendship, brotherly or sisterly gatherings, and sincere social relations for the sake of eternal happiness are the foundation stones of social life and an essential need of human nature; they forge a powerful and most vital bond between people, from family life to the life of the tribe, the nation, the religion, and humanity. Each of them serves as a point of support and means of consolation in the face of the assaults of material and immaterial things which cause anxiety and harm—things which prevent people from carrying out their human and religious duties and which individuals cannot fend off by themselves. Since these social relations and gatherings are not concerned with politics and exist simply for the sake of studying the truths of belief and the teachings of the Qur'an, which are certain to lead to happiness in both worlds, to accuse them of being political in nature is an act of sheer deception or willful enmity. It is not only hostile to Islam but it is also detrimental to our society and country and to humanity as a whole.

Said Nursi

* * *

Non-involvement in politics

The compassion, conscience, the truth, and the submission to that truth which are evident in the *Risale-i Nur* prevent us from becoming involved in politics. For through involvement in politics, innocent people are often wronged or afflicted with calamities, which is unjust. Some people asked me to explain what I mean by this, so I said:

In this present storm-tossed century, the egotism and racialism that are born of modern civilization, the military dictatorships which have emerged from the World War, and the mercilessness that arises from misguidance have caused such extreme tyranny and excessive despotism that if the people of truth were to defend their rights through physical force, they would either be defeated or have to act in greater tyranny and cause numerous innocent people to perish on the pretext that they are on the side of the opposing party. For those who act and attack on the basis of the feelings of egotism, racialism, and mercilessness will, on some minor pretext, strike at twenty to thirty people because of the mistakes of one or two and destroy them. If, in the cause of righteousness and justice, the people of truth strike only at the one who has struck them, they win only one in return for thirty losses, and then find themselves in a position of defeat. If, in accordance with the unjust rule of responding in kind or retaliation, the people of truth also crush twenty to thirty people on account of the errors of one or two, they will then commit a terrible injustice ostensibly in the name of truth.

This is why we, in obedience to the injunctions of the Qur'an, avoid politics like the plague and refuse to interfere in government. Adhering to this cardinal principle, we even avoid struggling for our rights, despite the fact that truth and right are on our side. Furthermore, since everything worldly is transitory and passing, since death will never disappear, since the door of the grave does not close, and since the hardships suffered for the sake of God are transformed into mercy, we with all certainty place our trust in God with patience and gratitude, and remain silent... and death does not die and the door of the grave does not close.

Said Nursi

The Thirteenth Ray

The Thirteenth Ray

Quotations and selections from Said Nursi's letters to his students

This Ray consists of the letters sent by Said Nursi to his students in 1943 and 1944. These highly valuable letters illustrate the great exertions of the *Risale-i Nur*.

In His Name, All-Glorified is He!

MY DEAR, FAITHFUL BROTHERS!

I congratulate you with all my heart and soul on the blessed Night of Power and Destiny which has passed and on the festival (*'Iyd*) yet to come, and I entrust you to the Unity and Compassion of the Most Merciful of the Merciful. Although in accordance with the well-known dictum, "Whoever believes in Divine Destiny is secure against grief," I do not see you as being in need of consolation. I believe that I have seen an indirect reference to our state in the verse: *So wait patiently for your Lord's judgment, for you are under Our Eyes (under Our care and protection); and glorify your Lord with His praise* (52:48), which gives perfect solace. It is as follows:

While we were thinking of passing a peaceful Ramadan, in forgetfulness of the world, this unimaginable and completely unendurable misfortune befell us. However, I have observed that it is pure grace for all of us—for me, for the *Risale-i Nur*, for you and our blessed month of Ramadan, and for the brotherhood which exists among us. I will describe only two or three of its many benefits for myself.

The first: The intense excitement and earnestness, and seeking refuge in God and imploring Him during Ramadan have overcome my serious illness and made me work.

The second: I had an intense longing to see all of you this year and be with you. I would have agreed to the difficulties I have now been suffering to see only one of you and to come to İsparta.

The third: All the painful events and circumstances we experienced both in Kastamonu and on the way here, and which we have been experiencing here, are suddenly changing in a most extraordinary way; contrary to all my apprehensions, a hand of grace shows itself, making me exclaim: "Good is in what God chooses." This hand of grace makes certain heedless and high-ranking worldly people read the *Risale-i Nur,* with which my mind is most occupied, with careful attention, opening up new fields for its triumphs.

While trying to endure my own pains, the pains and distress that each of you suffers were overwhelming me most. However, this calamity makes every hour of our life here into the equivalent of ten hours' worship, and since the blessed month of Ramadan makes an hour equivalent to a hundred hours in merit, every hour of us here increases to a thousand hours of worship in merit. Therefore, rather than take pity on you and weep in sorrow at your state, I congratulate you. For sincere people such as yourselves, who have been taught perfectly by the *Risale-i Nur*, know that this world is a fleeting place of trade; such people sacrifice everything for the sake of their belief and their lives in the Hereafter. I thus appreciate and applaud your steadfastness and declare: "All praise and thanks be to God for all states other than unbelief and misguidance!"

I am convinced that there are such benefits to be had, not only for me but for you, our brotherhood, the *Risale-i Nur* and our blessed Ramadan, that if the veil were drawn back from the Unseen, it would make us declare: "Thanks be to You, O God! This Divine decree is an instance of Your grace for us."

Do not blame those who were the cause of this state of affairs. The extensive and appalling plans for this calamity had long since been made, but it has struck us very lightly. God willing, it will pass quickly as well. Thus, in accordance with the message of the verse: *It may well be that you dislike a thing but it is good for you, and it may well be that you like a thing but it is bad for you. God knows, and you do not know* (2:216), do not be grieved.

Said Nursi

* * *

My dear brothers!

I am very happy to be close to you. I sometimes imagine that I am conversing with you and this consoles me. Know that if it were possible, I would proudly and happily endure all your difficulties. Because of you, I love Isparta and its environs down to its very stones and soil.

I can say that I am from İsparta in three respects. I cannot prove it historically, but I have the conviction that the ancestors of Said, who came into the world in the sub-district of İsparit (in Bitlis), went there from here. And the province of İsparta has given me such true brothers and sisters that I would happily sacrifice not only my own brother Abdülmecid and my nephew Abdurrahman, but my own self for each one of them.

I think that there is no-one on earth at this time who suffers less—in their hearts, spirits and minds—than the students of the *Risale-i* Nur. For due to the lights of certain, verified belief, the hearts, spirits, and minds of the *Risale-i Nur* students do not suffer distress. As for physical hardships, they know from the teachings of the *Risale-i Nur* that they are both transitory and trivial, and yield reward, and are a means by which the service in the cause of belief can develop in other channels, and so they meet these hardships with gratitude and patience. They prove through their behavior that certain, verified belief leads to happiness in this world too. They say "Let us see what God will do, for whatever He does, it is good," and work steadfastly to transform these transient difficulties into permanent instances of mercy.

May the Most Merciful of the Merciful increase the numbers of such brothers; may He make them the cause of pride and happiness for this country and favor them with eternal happiness in the highest floor of Paradise. Amen!

Said Nursi

* * *

In His Name, All-Glorified is He!

My dear, faithful brothers!

I congratulate you once more on the religious festival. Do not be sad that we cannot meet in person; in reality we are always together and, God willing, we will accompany each other on the road to eternity. It is my opinion that the everlasting merits and the virtues and joys of the spirit and heart that you obtain in the service of belief reduce to nothing those temporary, passing sorrows and troubles you are suffering today. Up until now there have been no people who have suffered as few difficulties as the *Risale-i Nur* students in such sacred service. Indeed, Paradise is not cheap. To save people from absolute unbelief, which destroys the life of both this world and the next, is of great importance at this time. If there are some troubles, they should be met with enthusiasm, thanks, and patience. Since our Creator, Who employs us, is All-Compassionate and All-Wise, we should meet everything that befalls us with resignation and joy, and in complete reliance on His Mercy and Wisdom.

This comes to you from your brother who, by using the first person plural in all his prayers—for example, "Deliver us; have mercy on us; preserve us,"—includes all of you in them without exception; he works in accordance with the principle of our spiritual partnership, as though we were numerous bodies with single spirit; he is more concerned with your troubles than you are yourselves; and he awaits help, steadfastness, and intercession from your collective personality.

Said Nursi

* * *

My dear, faithful brother, Re'fet bey!

Since your learned questions have become the keys to many important truths contained in *The Letters*, I cannot remain indifferent to them. A short answer to this last question of yours is as follows:

Since the Qur'an is an eternal declaration which addresses all classes of humanity and all groups of worshippers, it certainly must possess numerous meanings and levels of meaning. Some Qur'anic commentators choose only the most general or the most explicit meanings, or those which express a necessary act or a confirmed practice of the Prophet, upon him be peace and blessings. For example, some of them have understood *And in the night-time, also glorify Him* (52:49) as indicating the late-night Prayer (*Tahajjud*), which is an important *sunna*, and from the phrase *At the retreat of the stars* (52:49) they perceive an indication to the supererogatory Prayer that is performed before the morning canonical Prayer, an important practice of the Prophet, upon him be peace and blessings. However, the former sentence has numerous other meanings. My brother! Conversing with you does not cease.

* * *

My dear, faithful brothers!

Abundant heartfelt greetings! In former times in my native region we used to recite *Suratu'l-Ikhlas* a thousand times on the Day of *'Arafa*.[56] Now I am able to recite it five hundred times on the day before and five hundred times on the Day of *'Arafa* itself. Those who feel able to do so may recite them all on the same day—the Day of *'Arafa*. I cannot see you and speak to you all personally, but most of the time I am able to converse with you all while praying to God, sometimes by name.

* * *

My dear brothers!

This morning, while reciting the *tasbihat*,[57] my heart was filled with pity for Hafiz Tevfik, aware that this was the second time that troubles were beleaguering him. Then it suddenly occurred to me that I should congratulate him! With the excuse of being more precautious, he had wished to withdraw a little from his important position and his huge share in the service of the *Risale-i Nur*. But the sacredness and significance of his service led him once more to appropriate the same large share and vast merit. One should not keep aloof from spiritual honor as great as that on account of a little transient distress and hardship.

Actually, my brothers, everything passes, and when it has passed it will, if it was pleasure and enjoyment, become nothing, leaving only sighs of

---

[56] The day of *'Arafa* is the day before the religious festival. (Tr.)

[57] *Tasbihat* are the recitations of glorification, praise and exaltation of God Almighty. Those that are recited after the canonical Prayers are *subhanallah* (All-Glorified is God), *al-hamdu lillah* (All praise and gratitude are for God), and *Allahu akbar* (God is the All-Great). Each is recited 33 times. (Tr.)

regret. But if it was distress and hardship endured for the sake of sacred service, it will yield such pleasurable benefits in both this world and the Hereafter that the distress is reduced to nothing. Apart from one of you, I am the most elderly, and it is I whom troubles overwhelm most. Yet I assure you that I am content with my situation and accept it with total patience, thankfulness, and endurance. Gratitude in the face of calamities is the reward to be had for enduring them with patience and for the benefits they contain regarding both this world and the next.

* * *

My dear brothers!

With the disappearance of the obstacles which prevented the completion of the "Matters" of *Fruits of Belief*, the writing and copying of the treatises of the Light (*Risale-i Nur*) will resume, God willing. I approach this calamity from the perspective of Divine Destiny and Decree, for viewing things in this way transforms troubles into instances of mercy. As was explained in The Twenty-sixth Word—the treatise on Divine Destiny and Decree—there are two causes for every event. One is the apparent cause: people base their judgments on this and frequently do wrong or go astray as a result. The other is the truth of the matter, according to which the Divine Destiny judges: It acts with justice in all events in which humans do wrong.

For example, a person is sent to prison unjustly for a theft they have not committed. However, the Divine Destiny also sentences this person to imprisonment, but for a crime they have committed but which has remained hidden. Thus, the Divine Destiny acts justly where humans act unjustly. Bearing this in mind, there are two causes for the present suffering, the Divine purpose of which must be to sort the wheat from the chaff, the diamonds from the glass, the faithful devotees from those who vacillate in their belief, and the purely sincere from those who are unable to abandon their egoism and self-interest.

The first is that your powerful solidarity and your sincere and remarkable service as a group of students have aroused the suspicions of the worldly, including certain politicians; this is why they have wronged us in this way.

The second: Since not every individual among you could, on their own, display their worthiness for this sacred service with complete sincerity and total solidarity, the Divine Destiny considered this when apportioning our present suffering. However, the judgment of the Divine Destiny is pure mercy within pure justice, for it has caused those brothers who missed each other terribly to come together and it has transformed their hardships into worship and their losses into alms-giving. This has attracted people's attention; as a result, the treatises you copy will find a wider audience. Also, this suffering will show more effectively that worldly possessions, children, and comforts are fleeting: we will in any event leave them behind when we enter the grave. So, in order not to damage our eternal lives, we should become accustomed to patient endurance. In this way you will be heroic role models for the believers of the future; you may even be their leaders.

But there is one point that causes me to pause. If a single finger is wounded, the eye, the mind, and the heart neglect their important duties and become preoccupied with it. In the same way, our troubled lives preoccupy our hearts and spirits with their wounds. For example, just when I should have been forgetting the world, circumstances preoccupied me with a struggle against a certain secret society. I was consoled by the possibility that God Almighty might accept this state of heedlessness as a sort of intellectual striving.

I received the greetings of Ali Gül, the brother of Hafiz Mehmed, the esteemed teacher of the *Risale-i Nur*. I send greetings and prayers to him, to all his fellow villagers and to all the people of Sava, both living and dead.

* * *

In His Name, All-Glorified is He.

My dear, faithful brothers!

Your constancy and steadfastness confound all of the plans hatched by secret societies and hypocrites.

Truly, my brothers, there is no need to hide it: these heretics compare the *Risale-i Nur* and its students with certain esoteric movements. Their aim is to refute and scatter us, and so they attack us with the same kind of scheming with which they have blocked those other movements.

Firstly: They attempt to intimidate and frighten, and try to identify faults in those movements, as well as in us.

Secondly: They endeavor to find faults in their leaders and their followers which they can then publicize.

Thirdly: They try to corrupt them by tempting them with the alluring vices and pleasurable but stupefying poisons of materialist philosophy and civilization. They try to destroy their solidarity, blackening the names of their leaders with treacherous lies and discrediting their way of thought with certain principles of science and philosophy. However, the path of the *Risale-i Nur* is established on complete sincerity and the abandonment of egoism; it is based on the search to find mercy in troubles and permanent pleasures in pains, and to show the existence of grievous pains in transitory, dissolute pleasures; it is to teach that belief is the means to innumerable pleasures in this world as well, and to instruct in matters and truths that the hand of no philosophy can reach. Since its path is such, God willing, all treacherous plans hatched against it are bound to come to nothing.

* * *

My dear brothers!

Last night while I was reciting my regular invocations, some others could hear me. I wondered anxiously whether an invocation offered out loud would decrease its merit. Then I remembered a famous saying of Imam al-Ghazzali: "Sometimes doing supererogatory acts of worship in the open is better than doing it in secret." That is, if one recites loudly or performs their supererogatory acts of worship openly, without intending to show off, or obtain a worldly advantage, and if others benefit from it, are moved to imitate it or are aroused from heedlessness, or if it becomes a means of displaying the public symbols of Islam and preserving the honor of the faith, then reciting aloud or performing voluntary acts of worship openly may be much more meritorious.

* * *

My brothers!

If the short letters written before to console you, like this one, are read from time to time; if *Fruits of Belief*, particularly its last "Matters," are studied together; if any of the matters dealt with in the *Risale-i Nur* that you happen to remember are discussed, God willing, this will gain for you the honor of being students of the religious sciences. Preeminent figures such as Imam ash-Shafi'i, may God sanctify him, attached the greatest importance to this, saying, "Even the sleep of the students of (religious) sciences is counted as worship." Whatever circumstances one finds oneself in, whatever happens, should be disregarded when there is the possibility of studying truths as elevated as these. In fact we should smile happily at these troubles. As for the families of our needy friends and their responsibility to maintain them, it is a rule of the Qur'an and belief that we should consider those who are worse or poorer than ourselves in matters of hardship and poverty, and those who are more advanced in matters of belief and spirituality. Those who are able to do so are better off than eighty per cent of the people. Rather than complaining, they should offer eighty degrees of thanks. The families are entrusted to their true Provider, (in Whom we must trust). Since the reality is this, we should say *God is sufficient for us, how excellent a Guardian is He!* and offer thanks.

* * *

My brothers!

I have to explain something which occurred to me this morning. For twenty years I have been considering the viewpoints of heretical philosophers and asking myself what objections they can put forward concerning the crystal-clear truths that we have taken from the Qur'an. In truth I cannot find any weak point which either my own carnal soul or Satan and the philosophers could use as a pretext for an attack.

We are working for the sake of a truth which is unshakeable, elevated, vast, elevated, and of inestimable value—so much so that even if one were to sacrifice one's life for it, the price would still be cheap. Given this, we should indeed respond with complete steadfastness to all of the tribulations, distress, and hostilities that face us. Our enemies may also attempt to confront us with a number of deceived *hojas*, sheikhs and apparently pious people. We must preserve our unity and solidarity in the face of their attacks, and neither worry about them nor argue with them.

Said Nursi

* * *

My dear, faithful brothers!

A pious, righteous person in Kastamonu complained: "I have declined (after I entered the circle of the *Risale-i Nur*); I have lost my former spiritual state, my lights and illuminations." I told him:

"It may actually be that you have advanced, leaving behind illuminations, pleasures and spiritual unveilings which may have flattered your ego, causing the fruits of belief and good deeds which should be experienced in the Hereafter to be tasted while still in this world, thus provoking your self-centeredness. Through modesty, humility, self-abasement, and the abandonment of egoism and fleeting pleasures perhaps you have risen to a higher station." Actually, an important Divine favor lies in not allowing the person who has yet to give up their egoism to actually perceive that favor so that they do not become proud or conceited.

My brothers! Given this reality, those who think like that person, or who consider the brilliant stations that the good opinion of others give, will look at you and, when they see that the students among you who appear in the garment of humility, self-abasement, and service are common, ordinary people, they will say: "Are these the ones who have been deemed heroes of the truth ready to challenge the whole world? Who on earth *are* they? How can they be the ones who are performing the kind of sacred service that even the saints are unable to perform at this time?" If they are friends, they will experience disappointment; if they are opponents, they will find their opposition justified.

Said Nursi

* * *

My dear, faithful brothers!

The treatise on *Fruits of Belief* (The 11th Ray) is both important and extremely valuable. It is my hope that in time it will serve belief and the Qur'an considerably. You must have understood its value thoroughly, given that you have not made this place of study deprived of its lessons.

Numerous experiences have given me the firm conviction that serving belief and the Qur'an through the *Risale-i Nur* considerably lessens one's distress and gives one's heart a feeling of expansiveness. When I am not busy with reading or writing it, distress doubles and I find myself getting upset over trifling things. Although for various reasons I thought that Husrev, Hafiz Ali, and Tahiri would be suffering most, I saw that they themselves and those close to them had the greatest self-possession, tranquility, submission, and ease of heart. I asked myself why, and I now know the answer. You see, they are occupied only with their true duties and are not distracted by anything frivolous or unbeneficial. They do not question the judgments of the Divine Destiny ad Decree and they are neither bombastic nor critical, both being conditions that arise from egotism. They have honored the students of the *Risale-i Nur* and, with their self-possession, steadfastness, and inner contentment have demonstrated the moral and spiritual strength of that blessed work in the face of countless heretics. May God Almighty bless all of our brothers with true dignity and heroism on account of their utter humility and self-abasement. Amin!

* * *

My brothers!

An awesome egotism arising from heedlessness and love of this world prevails at this time. The people of truth, therefore, must abandon egotism and selfishness. If the students of the *Risale-i Nur* dissolve the ice-block of their egotism in the shared pool of their collective personality, they will not be shaken by this storm, God willing. Actually, a tried and tested method of the hypocrites is to saddle people who enjoy a certain social status with some trivial problem, thus irritating them and making them critical of one other. By tempting them to struggle with each other, they destroy their morale. Then the hypocrites are able to deal blows quite easily at those who have lost their strength and in this way destroy them. Since the students of the *Risale-i Nur* are treading the path of love, unity, and "self-annihilation in the brothers," God willing, they will bring turn the schemes of their opponents to ashes.

* * *

My dear, faithful brothers!

A spiritual guide once had so many pupils that the government saw them as a possible political threat and wanted to scatter their community. The spiritual guide told the government: "I only have one and a half followers and no more. If you like, we can put it to the test." So he pitched a huge tent and gathered together all of his thousands of pupils there. He told them: "I am going to put you to the test. Whoever is sincerely my pupil and complies with my command will go to Paradise." He began to summon them into the tent one by one. But he had had a sheep slaughtered secretly, and the sheep's blood covered the ground, the point being to pretend that the guide had killed his favorite pupil and dispatched him to Paradise.

When the thousands of followers saw the blood, they no longer obeyed the guide and began to denounce him. Only one man stepped forward, saying "May I be sacrificed for you." Then a woman stepped forward too, while the rest dispersed. The guide told the government officials: "Now you have seen for yourselves that I only have one and a half followers!"[58]

Endless thanks be to God Almighty that these troubles and hardships caused the *Risale-i Nur* to lose only one and a half of its students. Through the efforts of the heroes of Isparta and its environs, thousands have stepped forward to replace them.

* * *

Once, a non-Muslim tricked his way into being the heir to a Sufi leader and began to guide the disciples of the brotherhood. The followers under his training began to advance, but then one of them discovered that their guide had suffered a serious decline. Being perceptive, the guide told his disciple: "So you have understood." But the disciple said: "Since it was by following your guidance that I have risen to this station, I will follow you even closer from now on." He prayed to God Almighty earnestly for the salvation of his guide, who all of a sudden began to advance and, outstripping all of his disciples in spiritual excellence, became their true guide. This means that sometimes a disciple becomes the guide of his guide. What is truly good and praiseworthy is that when one sees their brother immersed in evil or sin, they do not abandon them, but rather strengthen the tie of brotherhood and try to reform the friend. This is the true characteristic of one who is loyal and faithful. The hypocrites tend to take advantage of such situations and in order to destroy the solidarity of believers, they spoil their good opinions of each other, saying: "See, those to whom you attach so much value and importance are just common, ordinary people." In any case, the misfortunes we suffer will, God willing, yield significant results which will benefit all believers. Similar incidents which befall certain other people on account of their political aspirations or for other reasons cannot yield the same results.

* * *

[58] Since women are not responsible for certain religious obligations that men are—such as the Friday congregational Prayer, and are exempt during their period and post-childbirth bleeding from the religious obligations that they do normally, the spiritual guide regarded her as a half follower. (Tr.)

Since the strange signature at the beginning of the Old Said's work *Lemeat*[59] coincides with a small change with my present circumstances and exactly with my seventieth year, I have included it here. If you consider it suitable, you can add it at the end of *Fruits of Belief* and the short letters. That strange signature consists of the following lines:

The supplicant

I am a ruined grave, in which are piled up
Sixty-nine dead Saids with his sins and sorrows.
The seventieth is a gravestone for that grave;
All together they weep at the decline of Islam.
I am hopeful that the heavens and earth of the future
Will together surrender to Islam's clear, shining hand.
For its strength lies in its belief and blessings,
It affords peace and security to all beings.

* * *

In His Name, All-Glorified is He.

There is nothing but it glorifies Him with praise.

My dear, faithful brothers!

Complaining about one another is unjust, meaningless, and harmful; indeed, it is tantamount to feeling a sort of resentment towards the *Risale-i Nur*. Beware! To consider some of the activities of the leading students to be the cause of this misfortune and to feel indignant at them is to regret having learnt the truths of belief. This is a far greater calamity than any physical misfortune. I swear that although I suffer from this misfortune twenty or thirty times more than any of you, because they have acted with pure intentions, I would not be annoyed with them even if the misfortune were ten times greater. It is also meaningless to object to events that have passed, since they are now done with and gone.

My brothers! Anxiety doubles one's misfortunes; it also plants the root of physical calamity in the heart. Worse still, it smacks of criticism of the Divine Destiny and blaming Divine Mercy. Everything has its good side: in

---

59 It was translated into English and published in *Gleams of Truth—Prescriptions for a Healthy Social Life*, Tughra Books, 2010, New Jersey. (Tr.)

all things there is a manifestation of Divine Mercy, and the Divine Destiny works with the utmost justice and wisdom. Since this is so, it is pointless to attach importance to the slight troubles we may suffer as a result of the sacred task we are performing, which concerns the whole body of believers.

* * *

My dear, faithful brothers!

Endless thanks be to the Most Merciful of the Merciful that in these extraordinary times and this strange place, through you He has allowed us to attain the esteemed honor of being students of the religious sciences and to perform important services as they do. It is related that, like martyrs, some enthusiastic and earnest students of the religious sciences who die while occupied with their studies believe themselves to be alive when in their graves and still engaged in study. Indeed, as mentioned earlier, when *Munkar* and *Nakir* asked a student who died when studying grammar and syntax, "Who is your Lord?" the student replied: "'Who' is the subject, and 'your Lord' is its predicate." He gave a grammatical answer, believing himself to still be in the religious seminary. Similarly, I believe that the late Hafiz Ali enjoys the same position of the students of religious sciences; he was busy with the *Risale-i Nur* while he was alive and is now at the degree of martyrs and their level of life. I often pray for him and for Mehmed Zühdü and Hafiz Mehmed, saying: "O God! Keep them occupied in perfect happiness and contentment until the Resurrection with the truths of belief and mysteries of the Qur'an. Amin!"

* * *

My dear and faithful brothers!

These kinds of *hadith* are allegorical: some have a general sense and are applicable to similar times, places or events in history, while others are concerned only with particular times, places or events. The one you ask about concerns the upheavals which the early Muslim community underwent in Iraq and the Hejaz. During the 'Abbasid period, numerous sectarian trends emerged, such as the Mu'tazila, the Rafida, the Jabriyya, and various heretical movements, which appeared under various guises. During these disturbances, which were harmful to the Shari'a and the Islamic creed, numerous eminent Muslim personalities, such as Bukhari, Muslim, Abu Hanifa, Shafi'i, Imam Malik,

Ahmad ibn Hanbal, Imam al-Ghazzali, 'Abdul-Qadir al-Jilani, and Junayd al-Baghdadi, emerged to put paid to dissent and opposition. Their triumph over the dissenters lasted for around three hundred years, but the followers of the misguided sects continued their secret activities and, by political means, brought down on the heads of the Muslim community the calamity of the Mongol invasion. Certain *hadiths* point to this calamity. Extrapolating from this, then, it is fair to say that since the calamity suffered by the Muslim world today is worse than all past calamities, numerous *hadiths* and a number of Qur'anic verses include references to it.

Moreover, there are *hadiths* which point to all the phases which the Muslim community will pass through. Certain particular events which happened in the course of history unveil aspects of the comprehensive meaning of the *hadiths* or their contents which indicate them. In various parts of the *Risale-i Nur* one may read interpretations of allegorical *hadiths* such as these, together with explanations as to how they should be interpreted. The basic principles used to understand and interpret them are set forth particularly in The Twenty-Fourth Word and The Fifth Ray.

* * *

My dear, faithful brothers!

I feel that it is necessary to explain a truth so that you do not accuse one another of egotism or disloyalty.

I used to see that some of the great saints who had given up egotism completely and were saved from the influence of the evil-commanding soul continued to complain bitterly about their souls. This astonished me greatly. I later understood perfectly that when the evil-commanding soul dies, its instruments are handed over to various aspects of one's temperament and sentiments, so that the meritorious struggle with the soul may continue until death. Those great saints, then, were complaining of this enemy, who is the heir to the evil-commanding soul.

Also, spiritual value, station, and virtue do not pertain to this world, thus to make themselves felt. In fact, since some of those at the highest station are not aware of the great Divine favor which has been bestowed on them, they actually consider themselves to be more wretched and bankrupt than everyone else. This shows that the wonder-workings, unveilings, spiritual pleasures, and illuminations, which most people consider to represent the zenith of spiritual perfection, cannot in reality be the means to that spiritual value or stations, or the yardstick by which they are measured. This is proved by the fact that although one hour in the life of the Companions of the Prophet, upon him be peace and blessings, was equal to a whole day in the life of other saints, or perhaps forty days' ordeal, not everyone of them was favored with the same extraordinary states or illuminations as the saints.

My brothers, be aware! Do not let your evil-commanding souls deceive you by making wrong comparisons and thinking ill of your brothers; do not allow them to make you doubt the ability of the *Risale-i Nur* to train souls.

* * *

My dear, loyal brothers!

Sami Bey told me that one of our brothers from Homa, a student called Ali, died around the same time as Hafiz Ali. Mehmed Ali, one of the heroes of Homa, also wrote to tell me about this. So in many of my prayers I have made that Ali a companion of the great martyr Hafız Ali.

Recently, a lady who is connected with us dreamt that three of our brothers had died. The interpretation of this dream is that these two Alis and Mustafa, who in prison wanted to become a follower of the *Risale-i Nur*, but was hanged, went to the Hereafter in place of all of us and were sacrificed for the sake of our well-being.

* * *

In His Name, All-Glorified is He!

My dear, faithful brothers!

The verse: *Is he who was dead (in spirit) and We raised him to life, and set for him a light by which he moves (without any deviancy) among people, is he like the one who is as one lost in depths of darkness, from which he cannot get out?* (6:122) seems to allude to the present time. Those who champion worldly life and the gratification of their physical appetites, oppressing us because we do not attach importance to their worldview and lifestyle, would have us eliminated if possible, or at least condemned to a major punishment. However, they are unable to find any legal sanction for this. As for us, we show them death, the veil which covers the gateway to eternal life, and try to bring them to their senses. We work with all our strength to save them from eternal punishment or execution or from everlasting solitary confinement in the Hereafter. Even if I am made to suffer the severest troubles because of the important treatises that have come to their attention, and even if those who saddle us with these troubles and wish for our elimination are saved from the eternal annihilation of death, both my heart and my soul would consent to these troubles. That is to say, we desire their happiness in both worlds and strive for this cause, while they wish us dead and seek pretexts to do away with us. But we do not suffer defeat at their hands, for the reality of death, as clear as the sun, visits tens of thousands of people every day and displays the decrees and announcements for tens of thousands of eternal executions or solitary confinements for the people of misguidance. Since this is the reality, we will from now on say the following, both to them, and to all other people:

We seek salvation from the eternal execution that comes with death, a specter which lies waiting for us, or from the darkness of solitary confinement in the grave, which will open its door to us and summon us to its depths without a shadow of a doubt. We also want to help you secure salvation from that awesome, inevitable calamity. Politics and worldly affairs, which in your view are the most momentous issues at hand, have little value for us. Indeed, in the view of truth, and of those not concerned with such matters directly, they are meaningless, unimportant, and without any value whatsoever. The essential human duties which we are trying to fulfill, however, are genuinely and essentially related to all people at all times. And so those who do not like this task of ours and wish to put a stop to it had better put a stop to death and close the door of the grave forever!

* * *

My dear faithful brothers!

The expert report demanded by the government concerning the *Risale-i Nur* confirms that the greatest part of it is concerns belief and is based on knowledge and true scholarship. It says that Said explains his views sincerely and earnestly, and that his power does not lie in any attempt to found a society, a *tariqa*, or a party opposed to the government, with which he has nothing to do. Rather, his power and the strength of his works stem from his strong desire and zeal to teach the needy the truths of the Qur'an.

The committee of experts, composed of two philosophers, Necati and Yusuf, and a modernist religious scholar called Yusuf Ziya, have acquitted me and all of my brothers completely of the baseless accusations leveled against us. They said: "They (i.e. the students of the *Risale-i Nur*) adhere to Said's scholarly and knowledgeable works for their belief and their afterlife. There is nothing explicit or implicit in their correspondences, their books, or treatises to suggesting any sort of conspiracy against the government."

Their only criticism is of some of my views concerning innovations in our religion, and my opinion that in our century there are many who, since the truths of Islam have not been conveyed to them, may be regarded as similar to people of the "interregnum."[60] Especially if these people are religious Christians who are victims of war, they may be saved in the Hereafter and regarded as martyrs of some sort.

Said Nursi

---

[60] People of the "interregnum" are those who live at a time or in a place where the acquisition of true knowledge about the Straight Path is impossible for them. (Tr.)

The Fourteenth Ray

The Fourteenth Ray

Quotations and selections from Said Nursi's letters to certain authorities and his students and friends

In the Name of God, the All-Merciful, the All-Compassionate.

And from Him do we seek help.

I HAVE BEEN LIVING IN SECLUSION FOR ALMOST TWENTY YEARS. DURING this long period of time, not even the slightest hint that I have had any relationship or involvement with politics has ever been established. If there had been anything irregular in my behavior it would have certainly manifested itself. Nowhere in the world are such recluses, who are preoccupied only with their lives in the Hereafter, bothered about such things.

We students of the *Risale-i Nur* do not make the *Risale-i Nur* a means of worldly advantage: even if they were to give us the whole universe on a plate, we would never misuse the *Risale* for worldly gain. Furthermore, the Qur'an severely prohibits us from becoming involved in politics. For the duty of the *Risale-i Nur* is, based on the most powerful and decisive proofs, to show and explain the Qur'anic truths of belief in the face of absolute unbelief, which destroys eternal life and transforms worldly life into a terrible poison. Since our aim is to serve the Qur'an, we cannot make the *Risale-i Nur* a tool of anything else.

We can never interfere in politics for the following reasons:

Firstly, since it would give the impression that we are misusing them as a means of political propaganda, we cannot betray the diamond-like truths of the Qur'an by reducing them to the value of fragments of glass in people's eyes.

Secondly: Compassion, truth, right and conscience—the fundamentals on which the path of the *Risale-i Nur* is established—prohibit us absolutely from political involvement and interference in the affairs of state. Imagine that there are seven or eight innocent souls—children, the sick, and the elderly—in the house of one or two irreligious people who have fallen into absolute unbelief and are deserving of blows and calamities. If blows and calamities are to descend on that house because of these one or two people, those innocent souls will also suffer. Therefore, since the results yielded by political involvement will always be doubtful, we have been forbidden absolutely from interfering in the life of society by means of political involvement, which would harm not only the state, but also the public order.

Thirdly: In order for the social life of this country and nation to be saved from anarchy during these strange times, five principles are essential: respect, compassion, refraining from what is prohibited (*haram*), security, and abandonment of lawlessness and obedience to the law. Considered from this perspective, it is clear that the *Risale-i Nur* establishes and strengthens these five principles in a most powerful and sacred fashion, thus preserving the very foundation of the public order. The clearest proof of this is that over the last twenty years the *Risale-i Nur* has helped to turn approximately a hundred thousand people into harmless, beneficial members of this nation. The provinces of Isparta and Kastamonu testify to this. This means that those who malign or place obstacles in the way of the *Risale-i Nur* are, knowingly or unknowingly, betraying Islam and the nation in favor of anarchy.

If you accuse me of opposing your government or rules, I will say this:

To reject something is one thing; not to accept it in one's heart is something else; and not to act in accordance with it is something quite different altogether. Those in authority consider only what one does, and not what one thinks, approves, or disapproves of in their heart. All governments have opponents who do not interfere in the government or public order. In fact, the Christians who lived under the rule of Caliph 'Umar, may God be pleased with him, were free to practice their own religion, even though they rejected the law of the Shari'a and the Qur'an. According to the principle of freedom of thought and conscience, and so long as they do not upset the public order, if some citizens, including, of course, the students of the *Risale-i Nur*, oppose the government on scholarly grounds, the law must not touch them.

If you act on anti-religious grounds and accuse us of being religious, I will say this:

It is a universally accepted fact that no nation can continue to exist without religion. And if that nation persists in absolute unbelief, it causes and suffers torments more grievous in this world than those of Hellfire itself. If, God forbid, a Muslim apostatizes, they fall into absolute unbelief; they cannot remain in a state of agnosticism, which would give them at least a glimmer of hope and relief. Also, they cannot be like irreligious Westerners. And in respect of the physical pleasures of life, they will fall infinitely lower than the animals, for the animals have no sense of the past and future. Because of their misguidance, the deaths of all past and future beings, and the thought that they will be separated from them eternally, overwhelm their heart with continuous anxiety. If light enters their heart and they come to believe, those innumerable friends will suddenly be raised to life. They will say through the language of their state: "We were not annihilated and we did not die.", thus transforming the former apostate's hellish pain into paradisiacal pleasure. Since the reality of the situation is thus, do not place obstacles on our path as we endeavor to serve the Qur'an and belief.

I say this to the Ministers of Internal Affairs and Justice: A man from Eğirdir, who is not a student of the *Risale-i Nur*, happened to argue with a sergeant gendarme. Because an insignificant letter of mine was found on this person, you arrested me together with a hundred and twenty other men and held us in prison for four months until we were acquitted. Most of those men are poor and were deprived of working to earn the livelihood of their families, suffering the loss of thousands of liras as a result. According to which worldly law and principle can you justify such an action? According to what worldly law and principle can innocent people be arrested and detained in prison not for a crime that they have actually committed, but for one which, according to the authorities, they may possibly commit in the future?!

My second question: The Qur'an declares *No soul, as bearer of a burden, bears and is made to bear the burden of another* (6:164). In other words, it is a universal principle of law that no one can be accused and punished for a crime that others have committed. If a person cannot be held responsible for the faults of their brother, according to which laws of justice was it deemed proper to arrest me and those poor farmers and artisans in the freezing cold simply because a letter of mine was found on one of them, or because someone somewhere had read one of my treatises which had been written to explain certain *hadiths* approximately a decade before the foundation of the Republic? According to which particular law can you justify causing these men to lose thousands of liras, purely on the basis of groundless speculation? Please tell me about these laws—if, indeed, they exist—so that we do not take any false steps.

My *third question*: If one of the many treatises contains certain sentences or paragraphs which do not conform to the law, those sentences or paragraphs may be censored, and the rest of treatise should be allowed to circulate freely. So, despite our acquittal in court, according to which principle of the government of the Republic can all the treatises be confiscated and those people who serve me in the lonely winter of my old age be arrested?

Since, in accordance with the law of freedom of conscience, the principles of the Republic do not interfere with the irreligious, surely they must not interfere with those religiously-minded people who are not involved in politics and the worldly affairs of others, who avoid disputes with the worldly and who strive usefully for the people's belief and afterlife and for the good of the country. Those who govern this country cannot ban piety and righteousness, which are as essential for this nation as food and medicine.

I consider it my patriotic duty to remind people of the following for the benefit of the country, the nation, and the public security. To offend numerous people in this way because they have some slight connection with me and the *Risale-i Nur* may turn those who are religiously beneficial for the country and its security against the government. There are more than a hundred thousand people whose belief has been saved through the *Risale-i Nur* and who have become harmless, yet highly beneficial citizens for the nation. They come from every level of society; some of them work in government departments, leading their lives in moderation and in a manner which benefits the whole of society. It is essential that these people be protected rather than offended or alienated. The authorities who act otherwise are harming public order and acting to the detriment of this country.

An important principle

It is an essential principle among the students of the *Risale-i Nur* that they try their utmost not to become involved in politics, in matters of administration, or government activities, because for them, serving the Qur'an sincerely is more important than anything else.

Furthermore, no one who enters politics in the present atmosphere of the political turbulence is able to preserve their independence or sincerity: political involvement will inevitably take advantage of their interest and corrupt the sacredness of their service. Also, the struggles and rivalries of this age, in which the severest form of tyranny and despotism prevails, will require to crush numerous innocent supporters of the opposing side on account of the error of a single individual. Those who do not act in the manner expected of them are bound to be defeated. Moreover, it will give those who have renounced their religion for the sake of the world, or who have exploited religion, the impression that the sacred truths of the Qur'an, which cannot be an instrument for any worldly advantage, are being exploited for purposes of political propaganda. Politics always divides people, while religion unites them: every class of people—supporters and opponents, officials and common people—are all equally in need of those sacred truths and should have a share of them. In conclusion, the students of the *Risale-i Nur* must avoid politics completely. They must not struggle with any section of society or involve themselves with them in any way, so that they may remain totally impartial.

Another important principle

Compassion is the basis of my way and that of the *Risale-i Nur*: it has been my cardinal principle for thirty years. For this reason, in order that no harm may come to the innocent, I avoid cursing, let alone attacking, the tyrants who persecute me. Even when I feel angry with some of those who oppress me out of vicious hatred and rancor, compassion prevents me from responding with a malediction, let alone physically. Thinking that they may have either innocent elderly parents or children who may suffer harm on their account, I do not attempt to do anything against them. Sometimes I even forgive them.

It is because of this compassion that I never interfere in affairs of government and do nothing to disturb the public order. Moreover, I have advised this so strongly to all my friends that some of the fair-minded police of three provinces have had to admit: "These students of the *Risale-i Nur* are like moral police: they preserve public order and security." In addition to thousands of witnesses to this fact, the students of the *Risale-i Nur* have confirmed it through twenty years' experience: none of these thousands of students has ever been involved in any incident recorded by the police. It is therefore completely unlawful to treat them as though they were the members of some revolutionary committee, or to malign and insult them as though they were criminals.

An important matter

Endless thanks be to God that thirty years ago, through His grace and the enlightenment of the Qur'an, I came to realize just how valueless and meaningless are the fleeting fame and glory of this world. I have since then been trying with all my strength to struggle with my evil-commanding soul in order to avoid egotism, pretension, and ostentation. This is known to all my friends. I also try to flee from people's attention, praise, and acclaim, as well as their according to me any spiritual rank. I have also been doing my best to convince my sincere friends that I have no virtue worth praising, and this I do at the cost of wounding their feelings. If there is a virtue to be praised, it belongs to the collective personality of the students of the *Risale-i Nur*. Despite this fact, I should never be held responsible for a letter which was found on someone's person or a book written in another city, neither of which I have any connection with. In the letter in question, my signature was forged, while the book has no named author. No law on earth and no decent political system would allow this.

Some significant realities

THE FIRST: Most of the Prophets appeared in the East, in Asia, while most of the philosophers emerged in the West. It is a sign of the eternal Divine Destiny that in Asia religion is dominant and philosophy is subordinate. Given this, even if those ruling in Asia are not religious, they should not interfere with those who work for religion; indeed, they should actively encourage them.

THE SECOND: The wise Qur'an is the intellect of the head of the earth and its power of thought. If, God forbid, the Qur'an were to depart from the head of the earth, the earth would go insane. It is fair to say that with its head emptied of reason, it would collide with another planet and herald an apocalypse. The Qur'an is a chain, a "rope of God" which binds the earth to the Divine Supreme Throne. It preserves the earth more than the law of general gravity. Thus, the *Risale-i Nur*, which is a true and powerful commentary on the glorious Qur'an, is a vast Divine favor which has been demonstrating its effectiveness for twenty years in this country. The government should therefore protect it and encourage people to read it.

A principle of justice

Justice, which the Justice Department should observe to the letter, requires that the rights of all who appeal to it be preserved without any discrimination and that the Justice Department work tirelessly for the sake of what is right and just. It is for this reason that, during his caliphate, Imam 'Ali, may God be pleased with him, sat together with a Jew in court and they were tried together. Also, a just chief judge saw an official display anger towards a criminal while sentencing him, and immediately dismissed him from his job. Full of regret, he remarked: "Those who give way to their feelings in this manner while executing the law have to date caused great wrongs." That is, one who executes the law should not show anger: if he does, he is acting unjustly. If he executes the death sentence with anger, he himself becomes a kind of murderer. This is what Islamic justice demands.

A reminder

In order to reduce the value of the truths explained in the *Risale-i Nur* in the eyes of the people, our secret enemies spread the rumor that I have claimed to be the *Mahdi*, or they use the *Risale* itself as an instrument for the dissemination of this calumny. My seventy-five years of life—particularly the last thirty years of it—and all the treatises of Light (*Risale-i Nur*), together with the thousands of people who have maintained sincere friendship with me, bear witness that I have never overstepped the limits of my capacity to the extent that I might even dare to make such a claim; nor have I ever made the truths of belief a means of gaining rank, status, or fame. On the contrary, the students of the *Risale-i Nur* know only too well that I have been always been ready to sacrifice whatever I have—my soul, my being, my world—in order to be able to serve people with all my strength for the sake of their belief. They also know and will testify that with regard to my evil-commanding soul I have always considered myself truly wretched, unimportant, and far inferior to my students, whose help and prayers I have always sought. And even if, on account of their excessive good opinion of me, some students accord me a rank and praise me in an exaggerated fashion—as is the age-old tradition between students and their master—is it to be considered a crime, particularly if I have never sought or accepted it?

Indifference to politics and certain other personal matters

> Those to whom some people said: "Look, those people have gathered against you, therefore be fearful of them." But it increased them only in faith, and they responded: "God is sufficient for us; how excellent a Guardian He is!" (3:173)
>
> This letter has been written according to the Divine decree *But speak to him with gentle words!* (20:44)

What follows is an answer to a question asked by many persons. As a rule, I do not like having to answer such questions, for I have bound everything related to me to reliance on God Almighty. However, since I am not left alone in my private world, I have been compelled to turn my face to worldly affairs, not for my own sake but in order to save my friends and *The Words* from the unfounded suspicions and harassment of the worldly. For this reason I am obliged to explain my state in five Points to my friends, to the worldly, and to the authorities.

THE FIRST POINT: They ask me why I have withdrawn from politics and am not involved in it at all.

The answer: The Old or Former Said was involved in politics to a certain extent; indeed, with the hope of serving religion and learning by means of politics, he tired himself out in vain. Eventually he came to see that the political route is full of doubts, pitfalls, and troubles: it was risky and unnecessary for me, and it would certainly prevent me from carrying out my most vital duties. For politics consists largely of lies, and there is always the possibility that one will unknowingly become an instrument in the hands of enemies.

Furthermore, one who enters politics is either for something or against it; they are either a supporter or in opposition. If I were the supporter of a successful political faction and participated in it, since I am not an official or a parliamentarian, working in politics would be unnecessary, useless, and meaningless for me.[61] There is no need for me to become involved in politics, so why should I participate in it in vain? If I were to become involved in politics on the side of the opposition, I would do so either with ideas or with force. If it were with ideas, there would be no need for me: the issues are all clear and everyone knows them as well as I do; discussing them over and over again is meaningless. And if I were to oppose the ruling side with force and cause trouble, it may transpire that I would possibly be committing thousands of sins for the sake of a goal whose righteousness is open to question and whose realization is, in any case, doubtful. Many people may thus suffer because of one person.

Since his conscience did not allow him to commit sins or cause the innocent to commit sins for the sake of a goal that has one in ten possibility of being realized, the Old Said abandoned politics. He also gave up smoking, reading newspapers, and having conversations about politics with others. For eight years I have neither read a newspaper nor listened to one being read, and I dare anyone to claim otherwise. The Old Said, however, would read up to eight newspapers a day!

Furthermore, for the last five years I have been under the strict scrutiny of the authorities, and so if anyone has witnessed the least sign of my involvement in politics, let them come forward and say so. For someone like me who speaks his mind openly, who has no attachment to the world, and whose basic stratagem is to have no stratagem, well, his ideas cannot remain secret for eight days, let alone eight years! If he had had any appetite and desire for politics, there would have been no need for investigation and scrutiny, for he would have shouted it from the rooftops!

The Second Point: Why does the New Said avoid politics so vehemently?

---

61 During the period of one-party rule in Turkey government officials were members of the ruling party. (Tr.)

The answer: He avoids politics vehemently in order to serve belief and the Qur'an, which is the purest, truest, most important, and most glorious service. He avoids it in order not to sacrifice unnecessarily those endeavors spent on attaining eternal life for the sake of a few years of worldly life, the length of which is in any case uncertain. He says:

> I am getting old and do not know how long I will live, and so the most important thing that I must do is to work for my eternal life. The primary means of gaining eternal life is belief, which is the key to eternal happiness, and so we must work for belief. However, since Islam wants us to work also for the benefit of people with whatever bounties God has bestowed on us, I feel obliged to serve them through learning. Service is directed either to the worldly social life of humanity or to their belief. I am unable to serve them in their worldly social life. Moreover, in such stormy times as these, it is extremely difficult to serve human worldly life as it should be served, and thus, I prefer to serve the cause of belief, which is the most important, the most necessary way, and also the safest and most sound. I leave the door of the service of belief open so that the truths of belief that I have acquired and experienced within my soul may be accessed by others. I hope that God Almighty will accept this service and make it atonement for my former sins. Apart from Satan the accursed, no one, be they believers or unbelievers, true confirmers of the Divine Message or materialists, can have the right to oppose this service. For nothing in the world can be likened to the lack of belief. There may be malevolent, satanic pleasure in wrongdoing, dissipation, transgression, and other major sins, but in unbelief there is no sort of pleasure at all. It is simply pain within pain, darkness within darkness, torment within torment.

Just consider how unreasonable it would be for someone like me—alone, with no attachment to the world, and seeking eagerly to atone for his former sins—to give up striving for eternal life and the service of belief for the sake of involvement, at my old age, in the unnecessary and perilous games of politics! Even a lunatic would be able to understand how contrary to reason and wisdom such a move would be.

If you ask why serving belief and the Qur'an prohibits me from politics, I will say this:

> The truths of belief and the Qur'an are like diamonds. Now, if I were to become involved in politics, the gullible masses would think that

> I am using them as the means of political propaganda in order to win over more supporters. As a result, they may come to regard those diamonds as mere shards of glass. My involvement in politics would therefore contribute to the devaluation of these diamonds in the eyes of the people.

Now, O worldly people! Why do you keep opposing me with such tenacity? If you say, "They call you Said-i Kurdi; you may have ethnic inclinations and aims that do not suit our interests," I would reply as follows:

> Gentlemen! The things that the Old Said and the New Said have written circulate in the public domain and are quite clear. I present them as testimony to the fact that, according to the decisive judgment of our religion, "Islam has absolutely condemned and abrogated tribalism and racism, which belong to the times of ignorance," I have always considered racism and tribalism, which is a kind of Western disease, to be like poison. It is Europe which has infected the Muslim community with this disease in order to be able to divide and rule it. My students and others who have some contact with me know that I have been trying my hardest to cure that disease.

Given this, why is it that you make every incident a pretext to harass me? According to which principle and precept of public good do you see fit to cause me distress at every turn? It is like punishing a soldier in the east of the country for a fault committed by a soldier in the west, simply on account of the fact that they belong to the same army. It is like convicting a shopkeeper in Baghdad of a crime committed by a tradesman in Istanbul, simply because they are both in the same line of business. Which conscience would allow such a thing and how does it accord with common sense?

THE THIRD POINT*:* My friends who care about my health and are astonished at my meeting every calamity with silent patience ask the following question: "How can you tolerate the difficulties and troubles that are visited on you, given that formerly you were very proud and could not endure even the least insult?"

The answer: Listen to two short anecdotes and you will receive your answer:

The first: Two years ago a director spoke insultingly and contemptuously about me behind my back. What he said was later narrated to me. For about an hour, the Old Said held sway and I was affected by what was said.

Then, through the mercy of God Almighty, the following fact occurred to me, dispelling my distress and compelling me to forgive that man. This fact occurred to me while I was addressing my soul as follows:

> If that man's insults and those faults of mine he mentioned were directed to or concerned with my evil-commanding soul, then may God be pleased with him, for he has highlighted my flaws of which I was unaware. If he was speaking the truth, he was the means of my training my soul and the reason that I was moved to save myself from arrogance. If what he said was false, then he helped to save me from ostentation and undeserved fame, which is the source of ostentation. I have not been reconciled with my soul, for I have not trained it. If someone were to tell me that there is a scorpion on my neck or in my armpit, I would be grateful to him, not offended. But if the man's insults were directed against my belief and my duty of serving the Qur'an, it would not concern me in the least, for I would refer him to the Owner of the glorious Qur'an Who employs me. He is the All-Mighty, the All-Wise. If that man meant merely to curse and insult me or destroy my character, that would not concern me either. For I am an exile, a stranger, and my hands are tied: it is not my duty to try to restore my honor myself. Rather, such an incident would concern the authorities of this village where I am a guest and under surveillance. Insulting the guest of a person concerns that person, not the guest: it is the host who must defend his guest.

Since reality is thus, my heart became easy. I said, "*I commit my affair to God (in full submission). Surely God sees the servants well* (40:44)," and imagined that the incident had not happened at all. It was only later that it became clear, unfortunately, that the Qur'an had not forgiven him.

The second incident: This year I heard about an incident. Although I only heard a brief account of it after it had happened, I was treated as though I had had some close connection with it. I had not corresponded with anyone, and if I had, I had only written extremely rarely concerning some issue of belief to a friend. In fact, I have written only one letter to my brother in four years. I try to avoid mixing with others and am also held back from doing so by "the worldly."

In any event, I am determined to exhibit the same patience and forbearance in the face of whatever befalls me as I did towards the maltreatment I was made to suffer and which I mentioned above. For what follows is what I think and say:

> If this ill-treatment, distress and oppression which are inflicted on me are on account of my faulty soul, I forgive it. I hope my soul is reformed by means of it, and that it will be atonement for my sins. I have tasted innumerable favors of God in the guest-house of the world: if I suffer its trials, I will still offer thanks. If "the worldly" trouble me because of my service in the cause of belief and the Qur'an, it does not fall to me to defend myself. Instead I refer it to the All-Mighty, All-Compelling One. If they aim to turn people against me and to impugn my undeserved fame, which is baseless and destructive of sincerity, then may God bless them! For I consider public attention and fame to be harmful for people like me. Those who have contact with me know that I have never desired respect to be shown to me; indeed, I detest it. I have even reproached a dear friend of mine many times for showing me excessive respect. If their aim in defaming me and degrading me in public is to attack the truths of belief and the Qur'an, which I try to explain, it is in vain. For it is impossible to draw a veil over the stars of the Qur'an. One who closes their eyes prevents only themselves from seeing: they cannot make the light disappear for others.

THE FOURTH POINT: "The worldly" ask me how I live and what I live on.

The answer: I live according to the principles of frugality and on the abundance which results from it. I depend upon no-one apart from the One Who provides for me and I have taken the decision not to become obliged to anyone else. One who lives daily on a hundred, or even forty, *para* (cent) surely does not become obliged to anyone.

I did not want to explain this matter: the whole issue is a disagreeable one, since it might cause me to feel proud or egoistic. But since the "worldly" question me about it suspiciously, I reply as follows:

Throughout my whole life, since I was a child in fact, it has been principle of mine not to accept anything—*Zakah* included—from the people, and not to become obliged to them for my livelihood. The people of my native region and those who have known me in other places are fully aware of this. During these five years of exile, many friends have tried earnestly to make me accept their gifts, but I have accepted nothing from any of them. If, therefore, people ask me, "So how do you manage to live?" I reply: I live frugally and on the abundance which results."

For the last six years, one bushel of wheat—enough for thirty-six loaves of bread—has sufficed me. And there is still some left: how long it will last, I have no idea.

During the last month of Ramadan, I managed with three loaves of bread and a little more than a kilo of rice; the rice finished two weeks after the end of Ramadan.

For three months on the mountain, more than a kilo of butter together with some amount of bread sufficed me and those guests who happened to visit me from time to time.

I bought this coat that I am wearing seven years ago, second-hand. Over the past five years, I have spent no more than four and a half *liras* on clothes, undergarments, shoes, and socks. Frugality, Divine mercy and the resulting abundance have sufficed.

There are numerous other examples and realities like these and the people of this village know about most of them. I mention them not out of pride but because people have compelled me to. And do not think that these instances of abundance of which I speak are a result of any goodness on my part: they were either Divine favors to those sincere friends who have visited me or a favor for the service of the Qur'an; they were either the abundant benefit resulting from frugality or they come for the sustenance of the four cats I have, who recite the Divine Names "O All-Compassionate One! O All-Compassionate One!", from which I benefit. If you listen carefully to their mournful miaowings, you will understand that they are saying, "*Ya Rahim! Ya Rahim!* "

Thinking of the cats reminds me of the hen I keep. This winter, she brought me an egg from the treasury of Mercy every day, with few exceptions. One day she brought me two eggs and I was amazed. I asked my friends "How can this be?" They replied: "Perhaps it is a Divine gift." The hen also has a young chick which she hatched in the summer. It started to lay eggs at the beginning of Ramadan and continued for forty days: whenever the mother hen stopped laying, the younger would start, thus never leaving me without eggs.

THE FIFTH POINT: Since this world is transient and life is short; since there are numerous essential duties to be done here in order to gain eternal life; since the guesthouse that is the world is not without an owner, and has a most Wise and Generous Director; since neither good nor evil will remain without recompense; since according to the verse: *God burdens no soul except within its capacity* (2:286), there is no responsibility that cannot be fulfilled; since a safe path is preferable to a harmful one; since worldly friends and status last only until the door of the grave, then surely the happiest person is the one who does not forget the Hereafter in the rush for this world. The happiest one surely is the one who does not sacrifice or destroy the Hereafter for the sake of this transient earthly life. The happiest one is surely the one who does not waste their life on trivial things, but who considers themselves to be a guest and acts in accordance with the Owner of the guesthouse, thus opening the door of the grave in safety and entering eternal happiness.

It is because of these realities that I pay no attention to the troubles and wrongs inflicted on me. I do not think that they are worth my attention and thus I do not interfere with the world.

* * *

In His Name, All-Glorified is He.

Upon you be peace, and God's mercy and blessings!

My dear, faithful brothers!

I will offer an effective source of solace in the form of three Points for prisoners and for those who help them sincerely and faithfully and supervise their food which comes from outside.

THE FIRST POINT: Each day spent in prison may gain as much reward as ten days of worship, and with regard to their fruits, may transform these transient hours into enduring hours, and a few years of punishment may be the means of salvation from millions of years of eternal imprisonment. Imprisoned believers can gain this most significant and valuable advantage by praying five times a day, by asking God's forgiveness for the sins that led to their imprisonment, and by thanking God patiently. Prison is an obstacle to certain sins; it prevents them.

THE SECOND POINT: Just as the disappearance of pleasure brings pain, the disappearance of pain brings pleasure. When thinking of past happy and enjoyable days, everyone feels regret and longing and utters a sigh of grief. When recalling past calamitous and painful days, everyone feels pleasure because they are gone, thanks God that such days are past and have left their reward, and sighs with relief. This means, an hour's temporary pain leaves an immaterial pleasure in the spirit, while an hour's pleasure leaves pain.

Such is reality. Past hours of misfortune and their pain have disappeared, while the future days of imagined distress have not yet come. Pain does not come from nothing or from that which does not exist. Therefore, it is pure lunacy to eat and drink continually today out of fear that we will probably be hungry and thirsty in the future. Similarly, it is foolish to think at this present moment of past and future pains—pains which do not exist—and, as a result, to grow impatient, to ignore one's faulty soul, and to act as though one is complaining about God. If we do not waste our precious stores of patience on worrying about the past and the future, neither of which exists, it will cause our existing pain to decrease tenfold.

This is not a complaint: During this third period of my stay in the "School of Joseph," a few days of physical and spiritual affliction and illness, which stem mainly from the despair I felt at not being able to serve the Qur'an and the like of which I had never before experienced, began to crush me. However, after Divine grace showed me this truth, I accepted my distressing illness and imprisonment. Since it is of great profit for a poor man like me, who waits at the door of the grave, to turn an hour of possible heedlessness into ten hours of worship, I thanked God.

THE THIRD POINT: There is a great reward to be had from attending compassionately to the needs of prisoners, from providing their food and soothing their spiritual wounds. Serving them the food which is sent from outside also brings the same spiritual reward as one would gain if that food were to be given away as alms. This reward is added to the records of good deeds of both the prison guards and those who contribute to it from within and outside the prison. If the prisoners are old, sick, poor, or without support or protection, the reward of such alms-giving multiplies. To gain this valuable profit, however, one must perform the daily canonical Prayers so that their service may be only for God's sake. In addition, one should hasten to help prisoners with sincerity, compassion, and cheerfulness, and in such a manner that they do not feel themselves placed under obligation to you.

A short addendum from Gençlik Rehberi (A Guide for Youth)

In His Name, All-Glorified is He!

Prisoners are in great need of the consolation that is to be had from reading and understanding the *Risale-i Nur*, especially those young people who have been sentenced to spend the prime of their lives in prison: they are as much in need of it as they are in need of bread itself.

Youth is driven by emotion rather than reason. Emotion and desire are blind: they do not see the consequences and tend to prefer an ounce of immediate pleasure to tons of future pleasure. They kill for a minute's satisfaction or revenge, and then suffer uncountable hours of painful imprisonment as a result. One hour of dissolute pleasure spent raping a woman may destroy a lifetime's happiness through the fear of prison and the enemies one has made.

Young people meet many pitfalls which cause them to transform the sweetness of life into a most bitter and remorse-laden existence. In particular, a huge and mighty state to the north is misusing the passions of its youth and shaking the very foundations of this century with its storms. It has made lawful for emotionally-driven young men the beautiful daughters and wives of upright, innocent people. By allowing men and women to mix with one another in public baths, it encourages immorality. It also allows vagabonds to use freely, and to plunder, even, the property of the rich. Everyone trembles in the face of this calamity.

During this age, all Muslim youths must act heroically and respond to this two-pronged attack with sharp "swords" such as the *Risale-i Nur*'s "Fruits of Belief" and "A Guide for Youth." Otherwise their future will be ruined, their happiness destroyed, both in this world and the next, and both worlds will be transformed into miserable realms of torment and suffering. If they abuse their energies and passions, they will end up in prison on account of their excesses, and when they grow old they will be filled with bitter regrets. But if they protect themselves with Qur'anic training and Islamic truths, some of which the *Risale-i Nur* expounds, they will become truly heroic youths, perfect human beings, prosperous Muslims and, in certain respects, masters over the rest of animate beings.

If young people in prison spend just one hour a day on the five canonical Prayers and, in addition to not committing those sins, which in any case prison prevents them from committing, choose freely to avoid those sins which are still possible, seeking God's forgiveness for the mistakes that led them to incarceration, then everyone—their country, relatives, and their future included—will benefit. By passing their fleeting ten or fifteen years of youth in such a way, they will gain an eternal, brilliant youth. The miraculous Qur'an and all revealed Scriptures proclaim this truth most clearly.

If young people show their gratitude for the delightful blessing of youth by following the Straight Path of obedience to God, the blessing increases and becomes even more pleasurable as it becomes eternal. If they are ungrateful, however, they will be pursued by calamity, pain, and grief: their youth will become like a nightmare and then disappear. They will live without purpose, harming not only themselves, but also their relatives, nation and country.

If those among prisoners who were imprisoned unjustly perform the daily canonical Prayers, they will find that each hour spent behind bars equals one day of worship. Their cells will become like a place of retreat for them. They may even be considered similar to the pious people of old who used to retreat to caves in order to devote themselves to worship. Those who are poor or old or ill and yet seek to learn the truths of belief will find that each hour spent in prison will equal twenty hours of worship. Prison will come to resemble a rest home, a place of friendliness, training, and education. Staying in prison may even bring them greater happiness than they would find on the outside, for there they would be confused and assaulted by sin. If they become educated while in prison, former murderers or those who seek revenge will be released as repentant, mature, and well-behaved people who can benefit their nation. Those who received moral and spiritual lessons from the *Risale-i Nur* in Denizli prison quickly attained this rank. The authorities who observed this said: "A fifteen-week program like this is always preferable to imprisoning them for fifteen years."

Since death will never disappear and the appointed hour is unknown, it may come at any time; since the grave cannot be closed and people enter it constantly, convoy after convoy, after a brief life, which passes swiftly; and since the Qur'an states that believers experience death as a discharge from worldly duties and that belief saves them from eternal punishment, while unbelievers experience death as a sentence of execution which leads them to everlasting torment and unending separation from their loved ones and all other creatures—for sure, the happiest people are those who thank God patiently and, benefiting from their time in prison, use the necessary moral and religious teaching to serve the Qur'an and belief on the Straight Path.

To those who are addicted to enjoyment and pleasure, I would say this. I am now seventy years old. I have come to know with utmost certainty from thousands of experiences and proofs that true enjoyment, pure pleasure, grief-free joy, and happiness are to be found only in belief and the sphere of its truths. There are many pains in a single worldly pleasure: as though delivering ten slaps for a single grape, it mars the taste of life.

To those unfortunate people who suffer imprisonment, I would say this. Since your world here is one of mourning and your life is bitter, benefit from your time in prison so that you do not have to mourn in the Hereafter and so that your eternal life may be sweet. Just as an hour's watch under severe battle conditions sometimes equals a year of worship, the hardship of each hour spent worshipping in prison multiplies and changes hardship into mercy.

* * *

In His Name, All-Glorified is He!

My fellow-prisoners and friends in religion!
I should explain to you a truth which will save you from both worldly torment and the torment of the Hereafter. It is as follows:

Let us imagine that a person has killed someone's brother or one of his relatives. One minute's pleasure to be had from revenge causes millions of minutes of distress and the anguish of prison. And the fear of revenge by the murdered person's relatives, together with the anxiety of finding themselves face to face with an enemy, removes all of the pleasure from their life. They suffer the torment of both fear and anger. There is only one solution for this, and that is reconciliation, which the Qur'an commands and truth, reality, humanity, and being Muslims require and encourage.

If there is no reconciliation, both sides suffer perpetually the torments of fear and revenge. It is because of this that Islam says: "One believer should not remain angry with another believer for more than three days." If the murder in our example was not the result of enmity or vindictive spite, and if a hypocritical troublemaker instigated the discord, it is essential to make peace quickly. Otherwise, the minor disaster becomes larger and continues. If the two sides make peace, and the murderer repents and prays continuously for the person they killed, then both sides will gain much and become like brothers. In place of the one brother who died, the wronged party will gain several brothers in religion. They will be resigned to the Divine Destiny and Decree and they will forgive their enemy. In particular, given that they have received lessons of the *Risale-i Nur*, for the sake of their own benefit and peace, and for the sake of the brotherhood engendered between them by their connection to the *Risale-i Nur*, they should give up the resentment which exists between them.

You should know that in Denizli prison all the prisoners between whom there was enmity eventually became brothers thanks to the lessons learned from the *Risale-i Nur*. This in turn caused even the irreligious and criminals to congratulate them, and all of the prisoners themselves felt relieved. I myself have seen a hundred men suffer trouble here because of one man, and refuse, out of fear, to go out to take fresh air. Such behavior on the part of that man is pure oppression. A manly believer of sound conscience cannot cause hundreds of other believers harm because of some petty error or for some minor benefit. If they make a mistake and cause harm, they should immediately repent.

* * *

In His Name, All-Glorified is He!

My dear, faithful brothers!

Today, I felt unrest and grief on your account. Just when I was feeling pain for those of my brothers whose livelihoods are constrained, a blessed memory, a truth, and certain good tidings gave me consolation. They are as follows:

The "Three Months" will begin in five days time: three blessed months which, if they are filled with worship, are truly meritorious. For if the reward for a good work at other times is tenfold, in the month of Rajab it is more than a hundredfold, in Sha'ban it exceeds three hundredfold, and in Ramadan it rises to a thousandfold. On Fridays in Ramadan it exceeds a thousand and on the Night of Power and Destiny it may even reach thirty thousand! It is certainly highly profitable, therefore, to spend these three months—which are like a sacred market for the trade of the Hereafter, an exceptional exhibition for the people of truth and worship, and a means for believers to gain a life of eighty years—in this School of

Joseph, which increases one's profits tenfold. Whatever hardships are suffered, they are pure mercy. As this is so with regard to worship, it is also thus with regard to the service of the *Risale-i Nur*, the benefits of which increase fivefold. For those who enter this guest-house and then depart from it are the means by which the *Risale-i Nur*'s lessons reach more people. Sometimes one person's sincerity yields the benefits of twenty people. The hardship and distress suffered are of no importance if the sincerity acquired through the *Risale-i Nur* spreads among the unfortunate prisoners whose disposition is inclined towards politics and who are in fact much in need of the solace that is to be found in the *Risale-i Nur*. Regarding the problem of livelihood, since these three months are a marketplace for the Hereafter, I began to feel at ease with it, understanding that being here until the Day of Festival is a great favor, for numerous other *Risale-i Nur* students will help you with your business outside.

Said Nursi

* * *

In His Name, All-Glorified is He.

My dear, truthful, faithful and compassionate brothers!

In these awesome conditions, the following complaint occurred to me: "Why do we suffer this much? How does it benefit our work?"

The answer must be as follows: Being subjected to this severe examination; being weighed on extremely sensitive scales many times so that it may be understood whether our true nature is gold or brass; being tried severely in every respect and passed through ever finer sieves three or four times so that it may become clear whether our evil-commanding souls have a share in the service we give or are playing tricks on us—all these are vitally necessary for our service, which should be purely and solely in the name of truth, so that the Divine Destiny and the Lord's grace allow it. For everyone has understood from the fact that our service has been exhibited in this arena of trial and examination before obstinate, unjust enemies who act under many pretexts that there is no trickery, egotism, malice, worldly, or personal interests in our service: it is completely sincere and has its source in pure truth. If it had remained hidden, it might have fallen foul of numerous misinterpretations and false conclusions. The mass of believers would not have had confidence in it. They would have thought: "They may be deceiving us," and the elite among them too would have had their suspicions. Imagining that we might be selling ourselves in the way that some of those who have certain spiritual ranks do in order to win public confidence, they would remain doubtful about the sincerity of our service. As it is, however, the trials and tribulations we undergo have led even the most stubborn and obdurate ones to admit the sincerity and honesty of our service. If you suffer one hardship, your profits are, God willing, a thousandfold.

Said Nursi

The Fifth Ray

The Fifth Ray

Some hadiths concerning the events to take place toward the end of time

More than forty years ago, an exposition of around twenty matters was written concerning the signs of the end of time and included as an addendum to the discussion about the Barrier of Dhul-Qarnayn and Gog and Magog in *Muhakemat*.[62] This has now been edited for the sake of a dear friend, and appears here as The Fifth Ray.

Note: In order that the purpose of the Introduction is better understood, the Matters following the Introduction should be read first.

In the Name of God, the All-Merciful, the All-Compassionate.

A subtle meaning of the Qur'anic verse *Now indeed, its portents have already come* (47:18) was written in order to protect the faith of the mass of believers and preserve it against doubt. Like the allegorical verses of the Qur'an, some of the *hadiths* about the events which, it is believed, will happen toward the end of time have profound meanings. They cannot be explained in the same way as verses which are explicit or unequivocal in meaning and content; consequently, not everyone can understand them. Rather than being explained, they are interpreted. According to the verse *None knows its interpretation*

62 This was translated into English and published as *Reasonings, A Key to Understanding the Qur'an's Eloquence*, Tughra Books, New Jersey, 2008. (Tr.)

save God and those firmly rooted in knowledge (3:7), the exact meaning of such events can only be understood after the events they indicated have actually occurred; those who are firmly rooted in knowledge say "*We believe in it; all is from our Lord,*" and disclose the hidden truths in them.

Introduction

This Fifth Ray contains an Introduction and twenty-three Matters. The Introduction consists of five points.

THE FIRST POINT

Since belief and religious responsibility are a test, a trial, and a competition, taking place within the bounds of human free will, theoretical matters concerned with them that are obscure, profound, and in need of careful study and experience cannot be obvious. Neither are they so compelling that everyone should feel they must understand or confirm them. This is because the Abu Bakrs[63] of this world may rise to the highest of the high, while the Abu Jahls[64] may descend to the lowest of the low. If there is no free will, there is no responsibility and accountability. It is because of this wise purpose that the Prophets were only rarely allowed to work miracles. Also, in this realm of responsibility, the signs of the end of the world, each of which will be recognizable only at its appointed time, are, like the allegorical verses of the Qur'an, open to interpretation. The only exception is the Prophetic Tradition that states the sun will rise in the west. This will be so clear that everyone will be compelled to affirm it; with its occurrence, the door of repentance will be closed, and professions of belief and pleas for forgiveness will no longer be accepted. Were this not so, the Abu Bakrs and the Abu Jahls would be equal in their confirmation of it. Even the return of Jesus, upon him be peace, and the realization that the person is indeed Jesus will be a matter for insight that comes from belief: when Jesus returns, not everyone will know about it or believe in his return. Similarly, fearsome fig-

63 Abu Bakr (d., 634) is the first adult to embrace Islam and the closest Companion of God's Messenger. He was also the first Caliph. (Tr.)

64 Abu Jahl, a name which means the father of ignorance, is the title which God's Messenger gave to 'Amr ibn Hisham because of his biased obstinacy in unbelief and opposition to the Messenger. He commanded the Quraysh army in the Battle of Badr, which took place in 624 between the Muslims and the Makkan polytheists. He was killed in this battle. (Tr.)

ures such as the *Dajjal* (the Antichrist) and the *Sufyan* (the *Dajjal* who will appear among Muslims) will not know themselves to be such.

THE SECOND POINT

Some of the matters of the Unseen which were revealed to the Prophet, upon him be peace and blessings, were made known in detail. The Prophet could in no way alter or interfere with these—for example, the verses of the Qur'an and the *hadiths qudsi*[65] which are explicit in meaning and content. Others, like the Traditions about certain cosmological events and future happenings, which are not included in the elements of belief, were revealed in allegorical or summarized form, and their detailed explanations were referred to the Prophet's insight and understanding. Employing his eloquence, our Prophet, upon him be peace and blessings, would explicate these through parables and in a manner commensurate with the wisdom of human responsibility. For example, when he was once conversing with some people, a deep rumbling was heard. He said: "That is the sound of a rock which has been rolling down toward Hell for seventy years and has just now come to rest in the very pit of Hell."[66] Five minutes after he had given this strange explanation, someone came and said: "O Messenger of God! Such-and-such a hypocrite has died. He was seventy years old and has gone to Hell." This showed the meaning of the Prophet's elevated, eloquent words.

NOTE: The future events that are not part of the truths of belief were unimportant in the sight of Prophethood.

THE THIRD POINT

This consists of two subtle issues.

THE FIRST: Since some *hadiths* that were uttered in the form of comparisons or allegories have come to be taken literally by ordinary people over the course of time, they do not appear to conform to reality. Although they are pure truth, they appear not to be so. For example, two angels called *Thawr* (Ox) and *Hut* (Fish),[67] who bear the earth just as certain other

---

65 A *Hadith qudsi* is a Prophetic Tradition which was revealed to the Prophet with both their meaning and wording, but not included in the Qur'an. (Tr.)

66 *Muslim*, "Janna" 31, "Munafiqun" 15; Ahmad ibn Hanbal, *al-Musnad*, 2:371.

67 For an explanation, see *The Reasonings*, pp. 54–56.

angels bear the Supreme Throne, have come to be thought of as an actual giant ox and a real giant fish.

THE SECOND: Some *hadiths* refer only to the majority of Muslims, or to the Islamic State, or to the capital of the Caliphate, but they have been understood to refer to all the people in the world. Although being particular in some respect, they have been deemed universal and general. For instance, it is related from the Prophet, upon him be peace and blessings: "A time will come when no one who utters: *Allah*! *Allah!* will remain."[68] That is, the places where God's Name is mentioned will be closed, and the call to the Prayer and *iqama* (the announcement for the start of the congregational Prayer) will be recited in, say, Turkish.[69]

THE FOURTH POINT

In the same way that, for numerous reasons and instances of wisdom, matters of the Unseen such as the appointed hour of death are kept secret, Doomsday, which is the appointed hour of the death of humankind and the animal kingdom and which marks the end of the world, has been left secret.

Indeed, if the appointed hour of death were known to people, the first half of life would be passed in absolute heedlessness and the second half in absolute terror, for every day a further step would be taken toward the gallows of death. This would destroy the wise and beneficial balance that comes from living in a state between hope and fear. Similarly, if Doomsday, which is the appointed hour of the death of the world, had been made known, the early and middle ages would have been affected only a little by the idea of the Hereafter, while the final days would have been passed in abject terror. No pleasure or value would have remained in worldly life; nor would the worship of God, as an act to be performed volitionally and in a state between hope and fear, have held any importance or wisdom. Also, if the appointed hour of the death of the world had been revealed, some of the truths of belief would have been obvious and everyone would have had to affirm them, thus negating the mystery of human responsibility and the wis-

---

68 *Muslim*, "Iman" 234; *at-Tirmidhi*, "Fitan" 35.

69 This Tradition has also been interpreted to mean that just before the end of time there will remain no one who believes in God, and that Doomsday will be visited on the heads of the unbelievers. See The Fourth Matter below. (Tr.)

dom and purpose of belief, which are bound inextricably to human choice and the exercise of free-will.

It is for numerous wise purposes such as these that matters related to the Unseen remain hidden. As a result, the believers consider both their death and their continued life and work both for this world and the Hereafter. Since they are also aware that the end of the world may occur in any age and at any time, or that the world may continue, they both work for eternal life within the transience of this world and labor to develop the world as though they were never going to die.

Also, if the time of calamities had been made known, people would have suffered from the anticipation of these in a way that would have been far worse than the calamity itself. Divine Wisdom and Mercy have therefore veiled the time of their occurrence. It is because there are these and many other instances of wisdom in most future events that the foretelling of future events has been generally prohibited. In order to avoid disrespect for and disobedience to the principle, *None knows the Unseen save God*, those who with Divine permission and teaching have given news of the Unseen other than that which concerns human responsibility and the truths of belief have done so only allusively and indirectly. Even the glad tidings about Prophet Muhammad, upon him be peace and blessings, which appear in the Torah, the Psalms and the Gospels, are veiled and obscure to a degree; consequently, some of the followers of these Scriptures have instilled different meanings to those passages and do not believe in Prophet Muhammad. However, since the wisdom inherent in the phenomenon of human responsibility necessitates that matters concerning the tenets of creed and belief be conveyed repeatedly and explicitly, the miraculously eloquent Qur'an and its glorious Conveyor, upon him be peace and blessings, tell of the matters of the Hereafter in detail, and of future worldly events only in summarized form.

THE FIFTH POINT

Since the wonders which pertain to the times of both *Dajjals*—the Antichrist who will appear in Christendom and the *Sufyan* who will appear among Muslims—have been narrated in connection with them, and as these wonders have therefore been thought to originate from their persons, the relevant narrations have become ambiguous and their true meanings have been veiled. An example is the allusion to their traveling around by plane and train.[70]

It has also been said that when the *Sufyan* dies, the devil who serves him will shout out the news to the whole world from the Obelisk in Istanbul, thus informing everyone that he is dead. That is to say, the news will be broadcast by radio, which is a wonder of the age and leaves even satans in amazement.

Also, since the strange states and alarming activities of the Antichrist's regime, and of the committee and government that he founds, have been narrated in connection with his person, their true meaning has become obscure. For example, it has been narrated that "He will be so powerful and long-lived[71] that only Jesus, upon him be peace and blessings, will be able to kill him; no one else will have the power."[72] That is, a pure, elevated, Divinely-revealed religion which will destroy his way and rapacious regime will appear among the followers of Jesus, and it is this religion which will follow the Qur'an and become united with it when Jesus, upon him be peace and blessings, descends and wipes out the irreligious hegemony of the Antichrist. In fact, a mere germ or a minor disease such as influenza can be enough to cause the death of the Antichrist himself.

Also, the commentaries and conclusions of some narrators, based on their own fallible understanding and reasoning, have been confused with the words of some *hadiths*. As a result, they have been treated as part of the *hadiths*, and the meaning of the latter has become obscured. The content of such *hadiths* does not appear to conform to reality and needs to be interpreted like allegorical *hadiths* or allegorical verses of the Qur'an.

Furthermore, since in earlier times individual opinions predominated and the collective spirit or social collectivity was not as developed as it is today, the comprehensive quality and large-scale actions of the community were ascribed to the persons who led them. In order to be worthy and fitting for extraordinary, universal attributes, those persons had to be of vast stature and possess enormous power and a strength that was a hundred times greater than was actually possible; at least this is how they were described.

---

[70] Ibn Abi Shayba, *al-Musannaf*, 7:496–497.

[71] Ibn Abi Shayba, *ibid.*, 7:496; at-Tabarani, *al-Mu'jam al-Kabir*, 11:313.

[72] *Muslim*, "Fitan" 34, 110; *at-Tirmidhi*, "Fitan" 59, 62; *Abu Dawud*, "Malahim" 14.

As this is not at all realistic, the narration becomes obscure, needing interpretation.

Moreover, although the two *Dajjals* have certain different attributes and states, people have not been able to understand which of them is referred to in the narrations that mention them without distinction; as a result, one can be confused for the other. Similarly, the states, attributes, and accomplishments attributed to the Great *Mahdi*, who will appear toward the end of time, in the narrations about the *Mahdi* do not fit the narrations referring to the earlier *Mahdis*, and so the narrations have become ambiguous. Imam 'Ali, may God be pleased with him, mentions only the *Dajjal* (the *Sufyan*) who will appear among the Muslims.

The Introduction ends here. Now we proceed with the Matters.

> For the time being, with Divine assistance, out of hundreds of narrations concerning certain future events, only twenty-three will be explained extremely concisely, as they have been circulated by heretics with the intention of corrupting the beliefs of the common people. Apart from inflicting no damage on belief, contrary to what the heretics assume, each of these narrations marks a miracle of the Prophet, upon him be peace and blessings. Since their true meaning is demonstrated and made clear, I beseech the Divine Mercy that each will be an important means of strengthening the belief of people and I entreat my All-Compassionate Lord to forgive my faults and errors.

The Second Station of The Fifth Ray

In the Name of God, the All- Merciful, the All-Compassionate.

This Station consists of twenty-three Matters.

THE FIRST MATTER

It is related: "The hand of the *Sufyan*, one of the important figures of the end of time, will be pierced."

While *God knows best*, an interpretation of this is as follows: since he is extremely wasteful, indulging in dissipated amusements, the *Sufyan* cannot preserve his belongings and they are frittered away. There is a proverb: "So-and-so has a hole in his hand," meaning that that person is very extravagant.

Thus, the *hadith* implies and warns that the *Sufyan* will provoke intense greed and ambition by encouraging wastefulness. By exploiting human weak spots in this regard, he will subjugate them to himself. The *hadith* predicts that spendthrifts will become enslaved to him, falling into his trap.

The Second Matter

It says in a narration: "A fearsome person will appear at the end of time, rising in the morning and on his forehead will be written, 'This is an unbeliever.'"[73]

While *God knows best what is right in every matter*, this may be interpreted as follows: the *Sufyan* will wear a headgear that is a mark of unbelievers, and will also compel everyone else to wear it. However, since he will compel people to adopt it by law, and given that the headgear in question is made to prostrate in worship around the heads of believers (who prostrate), it is hoped from God that it will become "Muslim," so that those who wear it unwillingly will not become unbelievers.

The Third Matter

There is a narration: "The despotic rulers at the end of time and, in particular, the *Dajjal* will have false heavens and hells."[74]

While *the knowledge is with God*, one possible interpretation is as follows: the narration indicates that prison and high schools (where boys and girls study together), which are among official buildings, (and places of amusement) will exist side by side—one being an ugly copy of Paradise's gardens where the people of Paradise will have pure servants and spouses, and the other a dungeon and torment-chamber.

The Fourth Matter

It is narrated: "A time will come when no one who utters: *Allah*! *Allah!* will remain."[75]

While *none knows the Unseen save God*, an interpretation of this is as follows: the places where people invoke God and recite His Names, together with the religious schools (*medrese*), will be closed, and a name other than *Allah* will be used in the public professions of Islam, such as the call to

---

73 *al-Bukhari*, "Tawhid" 17; *Muslim*, "Fitan" 101–103.

74 *al-Bukhari*, "Anbiya" 3; *Muslim*, "Fitan" 104, 109.

75 *Muslim*, "Iman" 234; *at-Tirmidhi*, "Fitan" 35.

the Prayer and the *iqama* (the announcement for the start of the congregational Prayer). This does not mean that all humanity will fall into absolute unbelief, for denial of God is as irrational as denying the existence of the universe. Nor is it reasonable to suppose that the majority of humankind, let alone all of them, will deny God. The majority of unbelievers do not deny God: they are in error only concerning His Attributes.

Another interpretation may be this: in order that the believers do not experience the terror of the final destruction of the world, their spirits will be taken away shortly before the end comes. Doomsday will then be visited on the heads of the unbelievers.

The Fifth Matter

There is a narration: "At the end of time, certain persons, such as the *Dajjal*, will claim Divinity and force others to prostrate before them."[76]

While *God knows best*, an interpretation is this: just as a nomad chieftain who denies the king appropriates for himself and other chieftains kingship proportionate to their power, those who come to lead the schools of naturalism and materialism imagine in themselves a sort of Lordship proportionate to their power. And to demonstrate their power, they cause their subjects to bow down worshipfully before themselves and their statues.

The Sixth Matter

It is related: "The corruption and disorder rooted in rebellion against God at the end of time will be so terrible that no one will be able to restrain their souls."[77] It is because of this that for thirteen (now fourteen) centuries, following the guidance of the Prophet, upon him be peace and blessings, the Muslim community has sought refuge in God from that corruption and disorder. "We seek refuge in God from the corruption and disorder of the *Dajjal* and from the corruption and disorder of the end of time,"[78] has been the regular invocation of the Muslim community after seeking refuge from the torments of the grave.

---

[76] *Muslim*, "Fitan" 112; *Ibn Maja*, "Fitan" 33.

[77] For similar narrations see, *Abu Dawud*, "Malahim" 14; at-Tabarani, *al-Mu'jamu'l-Kabir*, 18:220–221.

[78] *al-Bukhari*, "Adhan" 149; *Muslim*, "Masajid" 129.

While *God knows best what is right in every matter*, this narration may be interpreted as follows: the corruption at the end of time will attract souls and captivate them. People will indulge in it voluntarily, nay, eagerly. For example, in Russia, men and women bathe naked together in the public baths. And since by nature women have a strong tendency to show off their beauty, they willingly cast themselves into such corruption and are led astray. The men who are enamored of beauty are defeated by their own carnal souls and, with drunken joy, fall into the fire and are burnt. The fascinating amusements, grievous sins and innovations of that time, such as dancing and movies, draw these carnal souls around them like moths, intoxicating them. But if this occurs through absolute coercion, then will is negated and it is not considered a sin.

The Seventh Matter

There is a narration: "The *Sufyan* will be an eminent scholar, and he will fall into misguidance on account of his learning. Numerous other scholars will follow him."[79]

While *the knowledge is with God*, an interpretation is this: although, contrary to kings, he has no means of sovereignty such as power, tribal or racial support, courage, and riches, the *Sufyan* will win his position through cleverness, skillful conspiracies, and political acumen; with his intelligence he will bewitch the minds of many other scholars, causing them to confirm and support his ideas and actions. He will transform numerous teachers into his supporters and try vehemently to establish an education system that is bereft of religious instruction.

The Eighth Matter

Narrations point out that the terrible corruption and disorder of the *Dajjal* will occur among Muslims, which is why the entire Muslim community has sought refuge in God from it.[80]

While *none knows the Unseen save God*, one interpretation is as follows: the *Dajjal* who will appear among Muslims is different. In fact, like Imam

79 Ahmad ibn Hanbal, *al-Musnad*, 4:216; Ibn Abi Shayba, *al-Musannaf*, 7:491.

80 *al-Bukhari*, "Adhan" 149; *Muslim*, "Masajid" 129.

'Ali, may God be pleased with him, some exacting scholars have opined that the *Dajjal* of the Muslims is the *Sufyan*.[81] He will appear among the Muslims and will carry out his work through deception. The great *Dajjal* of the unbelievers is different. Those who are killed because of disobedience to the absolute force and tyranny of the great *Dajjal* become martyrs, while those who obey unwillingly are neither unbelievers nor sinners.

THE NINTH MATTER

In narrations, the events associated with the *Sufyan* and significant future events are depicted as occurring in the region of Damascus and in Arabia.[82]

While *God knows best*, an interpretation is this: since in the early periods of Islam the centers of the Caliphate were in Iraq, Damascus, and Madina, the narrators interpreted these events as occurring close to the centre of Islamic government, as though it was always going to remain thus, and mentioned Aleppo and Damascus. They added their interpretations to the concise predictions of the *hadith*.

THE TENTH MATTER

Narrations mention the extraordinary power of the figures who are to appear at the end of time.[83]

While *the knowledge is with God*, its interpretation is this: they are an allusion to the vast collective personality that those figures represent. Once, the Japanese Commander-in-Chief who had defeated Russia was shown in a picture with one foot in the Pacific Ocean and the other foot in the fort of Port Arthur. The immensity of the collective personality is depicted in the person who represents it, and in his pictures or the huge statues built to commemorate him. As for their extraordinarily vast power, since most of the actions they carry out are destructive and related to animal appetites, they appear to have extraordinary power. For destruction is easy: a single match can burn down a village. As for the animal appetites, since they captivate carnal souls, they are widely sought after.

---

81 Nu'aym ibn Hammad, *Fitan*, 1:246; al-Hakim, *al-Mustadrak*, 4:547.

82 Ibn Abi Shayba, *al-Musannaf*, 7:496; ad-Daylami, *al-Musnad*, 2:237.

83 Ibn Abi Shayba, *al-Musannaf*, 7:496; at-Tabarani, *al-Mu'jamu'l-Kabir*, 11:313.

THE ELEVENTH MATTER

There is a narration which says: "At the end of time one man will look after forty women."[84]

While *God knows best what is right*, this may be interpreted in two ways.

Firstly, lawful marriage will decrease at that time or, as in Communist Russia, it will almost disappear. One who flees from being tied to one woman will feel free, and become a shepherd to forty unfortunate women.

Secondly, it is an allusion to the fact that at this time of corruption and disorder, most of the men will have perished in wars, and for some reason most of the children born will be girls. Furthermore, the total freedom enjoyed by women will so inflame their lust that they will acquire superiority over their menfolk with regard to reproduction. As this will result in their causing their children to take after them, through Divine judgment, girl children will be more numerous.

THE TEWLFTH MATTER

It says in narrations: "The *Dajjal*'s first day will be a year, his second day a month, his third day a week, and his fourth day a day."[85]

While *none knows the Unseen save God*, this may be interpreted in two ways:

THE FIRST INTERPRETATION: It is an allusion to the possibility that the great *Dajjal* will appear near the North Pole or toward the north. For close to the North Pole the whole year is one day and one night. If one travels a day toward the south by train in summer, they come to a region where the sun does not set for a month. If they continue a day further toward the south by automobile, the sun is visible for a whole week. When I was a prisoner-of-war in Russia, I was close to this region. That means the narration miraculously predicts that the great *Dajjal* will attack from the north toward the south.

THE SECOND INTERPRETATION: Both the great *Dajjal* and the *Dajjal* that will appear among Muslims will have three periods of despotism. On their first day, that is, in their first period of government, they will carry out works so vast that they could not ordinarily be performed in three hundred years. On their second day, that is, in their second period of rule, they will carry out

---

84 *al-Bukhari*, "Zakah" 9; *Muslim*, "Zakah" 59.

85 *Muslim*, "Fitan" 110; *at-Tirmidhi*, "Fitan" 59; *Abu Dawud*, "Malahim" 14.

works that could not normally be carried out in thirty years. On their third day or period, the changes they will make could not under normal circumstances be brought about in ten years. On their fourth day or period, however, they will be like ordinary rulers, accomplishing nothing of importance and trying only to maintain the status quo. Of this the Prophet, upon him be peace and blessings, has informed us with great eloquence.

THE THIRTEENTH MATTER

There is a definite, sound narration which says: "Jesus, upon him be peace and blessings, will kill the great *Dajjal*."[86]

While *the knowledge is with God*, there are two aspects to this Tradition:

THE FIRST ASPECT: It could only be a wonderful person with the power of miracles and the acceptance of all men who could kill and change the way of the awesome *Dajjal*, who will preserve himself through wonders which will gradually lead him to perdition because of his haughtiness and denial—wonders such as magic, hypnotic powers, spiritualism, and the ability to make everyone fall under his spell. And thus the person who defeats him will be Jesus, upon him be peace and blessings, the Prophet of the majority of humankind, most of whose mission will concern the great *Dajjal*'s activities.

THE SECOND ASPECT: Just as the great *Dajjal* will be killed with the "sword" of Jesus, upon him be peace and blessings, it is the truly pious followers of Jesus who will kill the gigantic collective personality of materialism and irreligion that the *Dajjal* will establish. Those truly pious followers of Jesus will blend the essence of true Christianity with the essence of Islam and destroy the *Dajjal* with their combined strength, in effect killing him. The narration: "Jesus will come and follow the *Mahdi* in the obligatory Prayers,"[87] alludes to this unity, and to the sovereignty of the Qur'an and it being followed.

THE FOURTEENTH MATTER

It says in a narration: "The *Dajjal* will derive significant power from Jews. Many among the Jews will follow him willingly."[88]

---

86 *Muslim*, "Fitan" 110; *at-Tirmidhi*, "Fitan" 59, 62; *Abu Dawud*, "Malahim" 14.

87 *Muslim*, "Iman" 247; Ahmad ibn Hanbal, *al-Musnad*, 3:345, 367.

88 *Muslim*, "Fitan" 33, 124; Ahmad ibn Hanbal, *al-Musnad*, 3:224.

While *God knows best*, we can say that what is predicted by this narration has already partly taken place in Russia. The Jews, who had been persecuted by every state, gathered in large numbers in Germany, and in order to take their revenge, played a significant role in the founding of the revolutionary Communist committee. Trotsky, a most terrible individual, took over the leadership of the Russian Army, and then the government after Lenin, a leading light in the spread of Communism. In a sense, they set fire to the Russian legacy which had been achieved over a thousand years. This represents the committee of the great *Dajjal* and some of his works. They have caused similar upheavals in other countries as well, and fomented much trouble.

THE FIFTEENTH MATTER

The events connected with Gog and Magog are mentioned concisely in the Qur'an (18:98–99; 21:96), and there are some details of them in certain Prophetic Traditions.[89] Details in the Traditions are not as explicit as the concise accounts of the Qur'an which are explicit in meaning and content. As a result, they require interpretation; indeed, they need commentary since the narrators' own interpretations have been mixed in with the texts.

While *none knows the Unseen save God*, one interpretation of the events connected with Gog and Magog is as follows. Some raiding tribes in the east or north-east of Asia, which in the heavenly tongue of the Qur'an are called "*Ya'juj* and *Ma'juj* (Gog and Magog)," together with some other tribes, overran Asia and Europe several times. The narrations in question allude to the fact that they will also cause great chaos in the world in the future. In fact, even at the present moment, significant numbers of anarchists born of Communism appear among them.

Socialism emerged from the seed of libertarianism planted by the French Revolution. Destroying certain sacred values, the ideas socialism inculcated turned into Bolshevism. And because Bolshevism corrupted even more sacred moral, spiritual, and human values, the seeds it sowed will inevitably produce anarchy, which recognizes no boundaries or restrictions whatsoever. For if respect and compassion desert the human heart, intelligence and cleverness turn those with such hearts into cruel beasts: they can

89 *Muslim*, "Fitan" 1–3, "Ashratu's-Sa'ah" 1, "Dajjal" 11; *at-Tirmidhi*, "Fitan" 23, 59.

no longer be governed through politics. The ground that is the most suitable for the growth of anarchy will be those oppressed, crowded raiding tribes that are backward in respect to both civilization and government. The people who fit this description are certain tribes who caused the building of the Great Wall of China, which is one of the Seven Wonders of the World. Expounding the Qur'an's concise statements about Gog and Magog, Prophet Muhammad, upon him be peace and blessings, predicted their emergence miraculously and precisely.

THE SIXTEENTH MATTER

It says in a narration concerning Jesus killing the *Dajjal* that the *Dajjal* will have a gigantic form—he will be taller than a minaret, while Jesus, upon him be peace and blessings, will be very small in comparison.[90]

While *none knows the Unseen save God*, one interpretation is this: it is an allusion to the fact that the spiritual community of heroes that will recognize Jesus through the light of belief and follow him will be very few in number compared to the powerful scientific and military armies of the *Dajjal*.

THE SEVENTEENTH MATTER

It says in a narration: "The day the *Dajjal* appears all the world will hear.[91] He will travel the world in forty days and have an extraordinary donkey."[92]

While *God knows best*, provided that such narrations are completely authentic, they predict quite miraculously that at the time of the *Dajjal*, the means of communication and transportation will have become so advanced that an event will be heard by the entire world in a day. It will be announced by the radio and will be heard in the east and the west, and will be read about in all the newspapers. A man will travel the entire world in forty days and see the seven continents and numerous countries. These narrations thus miraculously predicted the telegraph, telephone, radio, trains and airplanes many centuries before they appeared.

Furthermore, the *Dajjal* will be heard of not by the title of *Dajjal*, but as a despotic monarch. And he will travel not to occupy lands but to cause

90 Ibn Abi Shayba, *al-Musannaf*, 7:496; at-Tabarani, *al-Mu'jamu'l-Kabir*, 11:313.

91 al-Hakim, *al-Mustadrak*, 4:573.

92 Ibn Abi Shayba, *al-Musannaf*, 7:496; at-Tabarani, *al-Mu'jamu'l-Kabir*, 11:313.

corruption and disorder and to mislead people. His mount or donkey will be either a train—one ear or head of which is an infernal firebox, and the other ear of which is a false paradise, beautifully adorned and furnished; he will send his enemies to its fiery head and his friends to the feasting head[93]—or an awesome automobile, or airplane, or... (silence!)

THE EIGHTEENTH MATTER

It says in a narration: "If my community continues on the Straight Path, it will have one day." That is, according to the verse, *a day—the measure of which is a thousand years of what you reckon* (32:5), it will have dominance and splendor for a thousand years. "If it does not continue on the Straight Path, it will have half a day."[94] That is, it will be dominant and victorious for only five hundred years.

While *God knows best*, this narration does not give news of the end of the world, but rather of Islam's victorious rule and the reign of the Caliphate. This miraculous prediction turned out to be true. For because toward the end of the 'Abbasid Caliphate its governing elite lost its way, the Caliphate (represented by Arab Muslims) lasted no more than five hundred years. But because the Muslim Community in general did not deviate from the Straight Path, the Ottoman Caliphate came to its assistance and preserved its government until the beginning of the 20th century. However, since the Ottoman politicians were unable to maintain their direction in the later periods of the state, in its true sense, the Caliphate was able to survive only five hundred years through them. With its demise, the Ottoman State confirmed the *hadith*'s miraculous prediction.

THE NINETEENTH MATTER

Narrations differ about the *Mahdi*, may God be pleased with him, who is one of the signs of the end of time and who will be from the Family of the Prophet. In fact, some scholars and saints have opined that he already appeared in the past.

While *God knows best what is right*, one interpretation of these different narrations is this: the great *Mahdi* will have numerous tasks. He will carry

---

93 *al-Bukhari*, "Anbiya" 3; *Muslim*, "Fitan" 104, 109.

94 *Abu Dawud*, "Malahim" 18; Ahmad ibn Hanbal, *al-Musnad*, 1:170.

out duties in the realms of politics, religious life, and government, and will strive for the sake of God in many different spheres of life. Similarly, since at a time of despair every century needs a sort of *Mahdi* to strengthen morale, through Divine mercy, in every age, or perhaps in every century a sort of *Mahdi* has appeared from among the descendants of the Prophet, upon him be peace and blessings, to preserve their forefather's Law and revived his Sunna. For example, like the 'Abbasid Caliph al-Mahdi[95] in the area of government, and like Gawthu'l-A'zam 'Abdu'l-Qadir al-Jilani, Shah Naqshband, the four spiritual Poles[96] and Twelve Imams[97] in the realm of religious life, many *Mahdi*-like persons have appeared and performed some of the great *Mahdi*'s tasks. Since Prophet Muhammad, upon him be peace and blessings, drew attention to these and similar persons and to their missions, the narrations about the *Mahdi* multiplied and took on various different aspects. For this reason, some of the people of truth say that the *Mahdi* has already appeared.

There is no family in the world in such solidarity, nor a tribe in such agreement, nor a community or society so enlightened, as the tribe, community and society of the Prophet's Family.

The Prophet's Family has raised hundreds of sacred heroes and produced thousands of spiritual leaders in the Muslim Community, and has been nurtured and perfected with the living essence of the truth of the Qur'an and the light of belief and honor of Islam. It is therefore completely reasonable that by reviving the Shari'a and Sunna of Muhammad, upon him be peace and blessings, and the truth of the Qur'an at the end of time, and proclaiming them and putting them into practice, they should display to the world the perfect justice and truth of the great *Mahdi*, their Com-

95 Caliph Muhammad al-Mahdi (744–785) was one of the leading Abbasid Caliphs. He was able to govern the vast Muslim state in peace and prosperity for about ten years. (Tr.)

96 It is generally accepted that the four spiritual Poles are 'Abdu'l-Qadir al-Jilani, Sayyid Ahmad ar-Rufa'i, Sayyid Ahmad al-Badawi and Sayyid Ibrahim ad-Dassuqi. Sayyid Ahmad ibn 'Ali ibn Yahya ar-Rufa'i (1120-1184), the founder of the Rufa'iya Sufi order, is one of the most renowned and celebrated saints of Islam. Sayyid Ahmad al-Badawi (1198–1275) was another leading saint in the history of Islam. The founder of the Badawiyyah Sufi order, he was born in Fez, Morocco and died in Tanta, Egypt. Sayyid Ibrahim ad-Dassuqi (1235–1277) lived in Egypt. In addition to being a great saint, he was also well-versed in religious sciences. (Tr.)

97 The twelve imams are the founders of the twelve schools of law, including Imam Abu Hanifa, Imam ash-Safi'i, Imam Malik ibn Anas, and Imam Ahmad ibn Hanbal. (Tr.)

mander-in-Chief. This is an indispensable necessity, required by the principles of human social life.

THE TWENTIETH MATTER

This concerns the sun's rising in the west[98] and the emergence from the earth of a living creature known as the *Dabbatu'l-Ard*, or "beast of the earth".[99]

The sun rising in the west will be an obvious sign of the end of the world, and because it will be an obvious heavenly event, it will mark the closing of the door of repentance, as repentance is an act of free will and reason. Therefore, the meaning of this narration is clear and requires no interpretation. However, we may add the following observations concerning the apparent cause of the sun rising in the west:

While *God knows best*, the Qur'an, which is in effect the intellect of the earth, will disappear from its head at the end of time and, as a result, the earth will go mad. With Divine leave, it will collide with another planet and its rotation will be reversed. Through Divine Will, its journey from west to east will be reversed from east to west, and the sun will start to rise in the west. Truly, if the gravity of the Qur'an, which is *the firm rope of God* that binds the earth to the sun and the ground to the Divine Supreme Throne, is broken, the tether holding the earth will come unfastened. The earth will consequently become dizzy and deranged: on account of the reversal of its usual motion, the sun will rise in the west. Through its collision with another planet, Doomsday will begin at the Divine command.

As for the *Dabbatu'l-Ard*, its existence is indicated very briefly by the Qur'an.[100] As with certain other matters, at present I have no detailed knowledge about it. I can only say this much:

While *none knows the Unseen save God*, locusts and fleas attacked the people of the Pharaoh,[101] while flocks of certain birds unknown in 'Ara-

---

98 *al-Bukhari*, "Tafsiru Sura 6" 9; *Muslim*, "Iman" 157.

99 *Muslim*, "Fitan" 39–40; *at-Tirmidhi*, "Fitan" 21.

100 *When the time for the fulfillment of the word (of punishment) about them comes, We will bring forth for them a living creature from the earth who will speak to them—that people have no certainty of faith in Our signs and Revelations* (27:82).

101 *So (in order that they might reflect and be mindful), We sent upon them floods and (plagues of) locusts and vermin, and frogs, and (water turning into) blood: distinct signs one after another. Yet they remained arrogant, and they were a criminal people committed to accumulating sins* (7:133).

bia rained down punishment on the people of Abraha, who were trying to destroy the Ka'ba.[102] Similarly, in order to bring to their senses those who fall foul of the *Dajjals'* corruption, rebel against God, and breach Divine limits, and who, through the anarchy of Gog and Magog, embark on corruption and savagery, falling knowingly and willingly into irreligion, unbelief, and ingratitude, a beast will appear from the earth to confront and annihilate them. Although *God knows best,* that beast is a species of animal. For even if it were a huge creature, it is not possible for one such animal to be everywhere at once. This means that it will be a truly terrible species of animal. As indicated by the verse ... *except that a crawling creature of the earth had been gnawing away his [Solomon's] staff (until it broke)* (34:14), it may be that the beast will be like a sort of termite which, entering every part of the bodies of humans, from their teeth to their finger-nails, will gnaw away at their bones as though gnawing wood. In reference to the believers' being saved from it on account of the blessing of belief and their refraining from vice and abuses, the verse makes the creature speak in connection with belief.

> Our Lord, take us not to task if we forget or make mistakes (2:286).
>
> All-Glorified are You. We have no knowledge save what You have taught us. Surely You are the All-Knowing, the All-Wise.

Three brief matters in addition to the previous twenty matters

The First Matter

Question: In narrations, both Prophet Jesus, upon him be peace, and the two *Dajjals* are referred to as "the Messiah;"[103] in all narrations it is said: "We seek refuge in God from the corruption and disorder of the Messiah Antichrist (*al-Masihu'd-Dajjal*)!"[104] What is the wisdom and meaning of this?

---

[102] *Have you considered how your Lord dealt with the people of the Elephant? Did He not bring their evil scheme to nothing? He sent down upon them flocks of birds (unknown in the land), shooting them with bullet-like stones of baked clay (an emblem of the punishment due to them); And so He rendered them like a field of grain devoured and trampled* (105:1–5).

[103] *al-Bukhari*, "Anbiya" 48; *Muslim*, "Iman" 273–275.

[104] *al-Bukhari*, "Adhan" 149; *Muslim*, "Masajid" 129; *Abu Dawud*, "Salah" 148–149.

The answer: While *God knows best*, the wisdom in it is this: in order to lighten their "burden" and make the Shari'a easier to practice in new conditions, at God's command, Prophet Jesus, upon him be peace, abrogated some of the burdensome ordinances of the Mosaic Law, making lawful some things that had hitherto been unlawful. Similarly, but in a spirit of rebellion against God and His Law and at the command of Satan and through his temptations, the great *Dajjal* will annul the injunctions of Christian law and by destroying the bonds that hold together the social life of the Christians, he will prepare the ground for anarchy and the advent of Gog and Magog. Likewise, the *Sufyan*—the *Dajjal* who will appear among the Muslims—will, through the intrigues and seduction of Satan and his evil-commanding soul, try to annul some of the eternal injunctions of the Shari'a of Muhammad, upon him be peace and blessings. Destroying the material and spiritual bonds of humankind, and leaving reckless, drunken, giddy souls free, he will unfasten the luminous chains of social life, such as respect and compassion. By giving people a freedom which is in reality pure despotism, by allowing them to fall on one another in a swamp of putrid lust, he will open up the way to the most terrible anarchy. There will then be no way other than the most repressive despotism to keep people under control.

THE SECOND MATTER

Question: Narrations mention the exceptional achievements of the two *Dajjals*, together with their extraordinary power and majesty. It is foretold that some unfortunate individuals will even attribute a sort of divinity to them. What is the reason for this?

The answer: While *the knowledge is with God*, their achievements will be great and extraordinary because such actions will consist mostly of destruction and the exciting of the appetite. It is because of the ease with which the two *Dajjals* carry out these extraordinary works that one narration tells us: "A single day of theirs is a year." That is, the works they carry out in one year could not normally be carried out in three hundred years. Their power appears to be superhuman for the following four reasons and perspectives:

THE FIRST PERSPECTIVE AND REASON: As the result of God's will to gradually lead them to perdition because of their haughtiness and rebellion, the agreeable things and advances that are achieved through the strength of brave armies and active peoples in their despotic, huge states will be unjustly attributed to them; this in turn will cause others to imagine that these individuals have the power of thousands of men. But by rights, the agreeable things, the honor and merits that are won through the actions of a community should be divided up among the members of that community, and any evil, destruction or losses should be attributed to the leader's imprudence, faults and lack of foresight. For example, if a battalion conquers a citadel, the gains and honor are thanks to their bayonets. However, if there are any losses on account of faulty planning and lack of foresight, this is usually the fault of the commander.

Thus, entirely contrary to this fundamental principle of truth and reality, since positive advances and agreeable achievements are attributed to such fearsome leaders, and any disagreeable developments or evil are imputed to their unfortunate peoples, it is God's will that they be gradually led to perdition due to their haughtiness and rebellion. Thus, such persons who in fact deserve public opprobrium are rather loved by all the heedless and neglectful.

THE SECOND PERSPECTIVE AND REASON: Since both *Dajjals* employ the harshest despotism, the cruelest tyranny and the maximum amount of violence and terror, they appear to have extremely vast power. Their despotism is such that under the veil of laws they interfere with everyone's conscience and sacred values, dictating everything in their lives, even down to the clothes that they should wear. I think that with a presentiment, the Muslim and Turkish lovers of freedom at the end of the previous (19th) and beginning of the last (20th) century perceived this awesome despotism and, shooting arrows at it, attacked it. But they were bitterly misled and attacked the wrong target on the wrong front. The tyranny and coercion employed by the *Dajjals* are such that they devastate a hundred villages because of one man, punishing hundreds of innocent people and ruining them by forced migrations.

THE THIRD PERSPECTIVE AND REASON: Since both *Dajjals* will win the assistance of certain secret committees which cherish an awful desire to wreak revenge on Islam and Christianity, and use women's liberation as a screen, and since the *Dajjal* that appears among the Muslims will deceive even certain secret lodges and win their support, they will be seen as having tremendous power. Also, it can be understood from the spiritual unveilings of some saints that the *Dajjal* called *Sufyan* who will come to lead the

Muslim government will have a capable, intelligent, and hardworking grand vizier (prime minister) who is not fond of show and who attaches no importance to personal rank and glory. He will also have a bold, forceful, steadfast, and energetic commander-in-chief who does not condescend to fame-seeking. The *Sufyan* will subjugate that vizier and commander to himself. Taking advantage of the fact that they give no importance to show, he will have their exceptional accomplishments attributed to himself, as well as the reforms and advancements achieved by the army and government, driven as they are by the severe need arising from the changes brought about by the World War; he will have it announced and spread everywhere by his adulators that he possesses an awesome and extraordinary power.

THE FOURTH PERSPECTIVE AND REASON: The great *Dajjal* will have spellbinding, charismatic qualities, while the *Dajjal* who appears among the Muslims will also have hypnotic powers, but in one eye only. By announcing that "The *Dajjal* will be blind in one eye,"[105] Prophetic Traditions draw our attention to their eyes. That is, one of the great *Dajjal's eyes* will be blind, while one eye of the other *Dajjal* will be blind in comparison to his other eye. That is, since both will be absolute unbelievers, they will in effect have only one eye, and that eye will be restricted to this world; they will have no eyes with which to see the Hereafter or the consequences of their actions. I once had a vision of the *Dajjal* who is to appear among the Muslims. I observed with my own eyes that he had a spellbinding hypnotic power in one of his eyes, and I understood that he would be an absolute denier of the Religion of Islam. He will attack religious values with an audacity and insolence that stem from absolute denial. But since the common people will not know the truth of the matter, they will suppose that he possesses extraordinary power and courage.

Also, since a glorious, heroic nation will have a successful, famous, fortunate, and cunning leader at the time of their defeat, without considering his secret and fearsome true nature, they will applaud him for their love of heroism; they accept him as their leader and ignore his iniquities. However, it can be understood from narrations that through the light of belief and the Qur'an in their spirits, the heroic army and religious nation will see the truth and try to repair the terrible damage done by that leader.

---

105 *Muslim*, "Fitan" 104, 105; Ahmad ibn Hanbal, *al-Musnad*, 3:201.

THE THIRD MATTER

This consists of three incidents, each full of lessons.

THE FIRST INCIDENT: Once, God's noblest Messenger, upon him be peace and blessings, pointed out to 'Umar, may God be pleased with him, a child among a group of non-Muslim children and said: "That is his very image!" 'Umar said: "Then I will kill him!" But God's Messenger declared: "If that is the *Sufyan*, you cannot kill him. And if he is not, he cannot be killed by killing his image."[106]

This narration indicates that at the time of his rule, the *Sufyan*'s image will appear in a number of ways, and that he will be born among non-Muslims in Muslim lands.[107] It is strange that although 'Umar, may God be pleased with him, felt so strongly on this matter that he was ready to kill a child who looked like the *Sufyan*, he [i.e. 'Umar] will be one the *Sufyan* most admires, appreciates, and praises highly.

THE SECOND INCIDENT: Many people narrate that the *Dajjal* who will appear among the Muslims is highly curious about the meaning of the *Suratu't-Tin* (Chapter 95), which begins with *By the fig and the olive*, and will ask about it.

It is strange that the verse, *No, indeed, man is unruly and rebels* (96:6) in the following *Sura—Suratu'l-'Alaq*, beginning with *Read in the Name of your Lord Who creates*, alludes to the time and person of the *Sufyan*, and also indicates in the succeeding verses (9–10) that he will rail with overweening vanity against the mosques and the people who perform the canonical Prayers. In other words, that man, whose successes will lead him to perdition, perceives that a short *Sura* is concerned with him, but falls into confusion and knocks instead on the door of its neighbor.

THE THIRD INCIDENT: It says in a narration: "The *Sufyan* will appear in the vicinity of Khorasan."[108]

While *none knows the Unseen save God*, an interpretation of this narration is as follows: when the noblest Messenger, upon him be peace and blessings, gave this news, the Turks, who were the most courageous, numerous, and powerful people of the east and who were to form the hero-

---

106 *Muslim*, "Fitan" 95; *at-Tirmidhi*, "Fitan" 63.

107 *Muslim*, "Fitan" 33; Ahmad ibn Hanbal, *al-Musnad*, 3:224.

108 *at-Tirmidhi*, "Fitan" 57; *Ibn Maja*, "Fitan" 33.

ic army of Islam, were around the region of Khorasan and had not yet made their homeland in Anatolia. By mentioning the region where they were found at that time, the *hadith* could indicate that the *Sufyan* would appear among the Turks.

It is exceedingly strange that the *Sufyan* will, even though for a short time, try to use Turkism and the Turkish nation, which for seven hundred years has been a honorable, flashing diamond "sword" in the hand of the Qur'an and Muslim religiousness, against some of the public symbols of Islam. But he will not be successful and will withdraw. It is understood from the narrations that the heroic army will take its reins from his hand.

None knows the Unseen save God.
And God knows best what is right.

The Fifteenth Ray

The Fifteenth Ray

The Radiant Proof

This consists of two "Stations."

This lesson is a treatise which is, on the surface, slight; however, in reality, it is powerful, extensive, and of great importance. It is a paradisal fruit of the Qur'an and of belief, having been produced from a combination—at the degrees of certainty based on knowledge and certainty based on vision or observation—of my life of reflective thought and the immaterial life of the *Risale-i Nur*, which is based on investigation and verification.

The first station

This is a concise summary of The Twentieth Letter. It consists of three parts.

Part One

In the Name of God, the All-Merciful, the All-Compassionate.

And from Him do we seek help.

THE STUDENTS OF THE RISALE-I NUR ARE TRYING THEIR BEST TO TEACH the lessons of the Light wherever they are. However, the young and elderly people who read the newspapers, which write about the attacks of Communist Russia with its awful denial of God, are in greater need of its definitive, powerful instruction about belief in God's Existence and Unity. I was thinking of writing a brief summary of the lesson that the following magnificent pronouncement of God's Existence and Unity teaches—a pronouncement which should be recited ten times after every morning Prayer:

> There is no deity but God, One, having no partners; His is the Sovereignty and to Him belongs all praise; He alone gives life and causes to die, and He is the All-Living and dies not; in His hand is all good; He has full power over everything; and to Him is the homecoming.

This pronouncement of Divine Unity contains eleven glad tidings and eleven proofs of belief. I will briefly point out the proofs and refer their further explanations and the glad tidings they bring to The Twentieth Letter and other relevant parts of the *Risale-i Nur*.

THE FIRST PHRASE: *THERE IS NO DEITY BUT GOD*

The proof here is the treatise called *The Supreme Sign*, the Seventh Ray. *The Supreme Sign* points out thirty-three vast, unanimous, universal proofs in the totality of all beings. Pointing to innumerable arguments in each universal proof, firstly with the words of the heavens and stars, then with the sentences of the earth, the animals, and plants, then with the messages of the totality of the universe and all its contents, and through the realities of coming into existence within time, contingency, and change, it proves the Existence and Unity of the Necessarily Existent Being as clearly as the light of day. Those who seek unshakeable belief and an unbreakable sword to combat irreligion and anarchy should refer to *The Supreme Sign*.

THE SECOND PHRASE: *(HE IS)* ONE

An extremely brief indication of the proof in this phrase is as follows:

In every aspect of the universe, unity is apparent. For example, the universe displays unity inasmuch as it is an entirely well-organized city, a magnificent palace, a meaningful, materialized book, and an embodied Qur'an, every verse, letter, and dot of which is miraculous. Similarly, since the palace's lamp and fiery cook (the sun) is one and the same, and its calendar-lamp (the moon)[109] is one, and its water-bearing sponges (clouds) are of the

---

[109] The calendar-lamp is the moon. The Qur'an declares: *They ask you (O Messenger) about the new moons. Say: "They are markers for the people to determine time periods and for the Pilgrimage."* (2:189) (Tr.)

same formation and nature, and since hundreds of thousands of other things it contains are all one and the same, it proves decisively that the owner, organizer, ruler, and author of the city, palace, book, and mighty embodied Qur'an is Existent, One and Single.

The Third Phrase: *He has no partners*

An extremely brief indication of the proof in this is as follows:

The source, master, and basis of *The Supreme Sign* is the mighty verse, *Say: "If there were, as they assert, deities apart from Him, surely they would seek a way to the Master of the Supreme Throne (the dominion of the creation)* (17:42)." This is itself a supreme sign. That is, if God had had any partners or other agents who had a part in creation or intervened in Lordship, the order of the universe would have been destroyed. However, the perfect order in everything, whether big or small, particular or universal, from the wing of the tiniest fly and the cell of the pupil of the eye to the innumerable birds which fly through the air and the solar system, provides decisive and indubitable evidence for the impossibility and non-existence of any such partners. It also testifies self-evidently to the Existence and Unity of the Necessarily Existent One.

The Fourth Phrase: *His is the Sovereignty*

What follows is an extremely concise indication of the comprehensive proof found in this phrase:

We see with our eyes that there is a veiled, All-Powerful, All-Knowing Director and Controller Who makes the face of the earth an arable field, Who every spring sows the seeds of hundreds of thousands of species of plants, all mixed together in that vast field. Then He harvests them in perfect order, and without any confusion distributes from this field sustenance and rations to hundreds of thousands of animal species according to their needs with the hand of Mercy and Wisdom. He performs these acts throughout His vast, rich dominion, and particularly on the face of the earth. Therefore, those who do not recognize this All-Wise and All-Compassionate Director, Controller, and Owner are compelled to deny the earth together with its produce, as the foolish Sophists have done.

THE FIFTH PHRASE: *TO HIM BELONGS ALL PRAISE*

This is a brief indication of the very extensive proof in this phrase:

We see with our eyes and understand clearly with our minds that an All-Compassionate, All-Munificent Provider and Bestower of bounties governs, supervises, and maintains this city of the universe, this quarter of the earth, these barracks of humans and animals. For in order to encourage conscious beings to praise and thank Him exclusively in return for His bounties, He makes the earth into a merchant ship and a railway train that brings provisions; He makes spring into a wagon filled with hundreds of thousands of types of foods and packets of conserves called breasts, conveying them to the needy living creatures whose rations have been exhausted by the end of winter. Anyone with a modicum of intelligence would affirm that this is the work of an All-Compassionate Provider. However, one who does not affirm this but deviates into denial is a foolish, harmful creature who will be compelled to deny all the regular bounties and specified foods on the face of the earth, which are the means for praise and thanks.

THE SIXTH PHRASE: *HE ALONE GIVES LIFE*

An extremely brief indication of the proof in this phrase:

It is explained convincingly in The Tenth Word and in certain other parts of the *Risale-i Nur* that every spring on the earth a glorious army comprising hundreds of thousands of different species, each of which has infinite members, is revived. Their lives and whatever they need are given to them with perfect order and regularity, thus displaying hundreds of thousands of examples and signs of the supreme Resurrection. All of these innumerable different creatures are raised to life in perfect balance and order without forgetfulness, error, and confusion, despite the fact that they are all intermingled. Those hundreds of thousands of species of creatures with their innumerable members, all different in respect to their forms, art, and livelihoods, are brought into being from droplets of seminal fluid, which are all similar; or from seeds buried in the earth which resemble one another; or from the tiny eggs of flies which are all similar; or, in the case of the birds of the air, from fluid or eggs, which are either the same as or only a little different from one another. The person, therefore, who does not conclude that it is an All-Living and Self-Subsistent One, an All-Knowing Giver of life and Creator Who has inscribed on the page of the earth and the spring hundreds of thousands of different "books," all together, one within the other, without error, perfectly, and Who acts and performs works with infinite care and wisdom—that person is surely obliged to deny both themselves and all the living creatures that each spring are attached to the string of time throughout the animated earth and space. Indeed, such a person must be the most foolish and wretched of living creatures.

THE SEVENTH PHRASE: *AND CAUSES TO DIE*

A very brief indication of the proof contained in this phrase is as follows:

When hundreds of thousands of species of plants are being discharged in fall from their duties under the name of death, the registers of the actions of each species and all their members, and the list of the contents of everything they have done and everything they will do the following spring—their seeds, which are their spirits of a sort—are all entrusted in their places to the hand of Wisdom of the All-Majestic Preserver. Whoever, therefore, does not recognize the All-Wise Creator, the All-Living and Undying One, He Who inscribes the life-history of the fig-tree, details of which would fill a large volume, in its miniscule seeds—each of which is like an immortal spirit and bears all the laws "governing" the tree's life—that person cannot be called foolish; rather, they are more abject than the devils who stoke up the fire of Hell, and will be condemned to eternal execution.

Just as it is clearly impossible that the universal, comprehensive, and wise acts mentioned above, which comprise numberless wonders and miracles and mark the proofs in the phrase discussed, could exist without the One Who performs them, so too, to attribute them to blind, deaf, impotent, unconscious, lifeless, confused, or disorderly material causes is inconceivable and unjustifiable, a thousand times over. For this would require that every particle of earth should possess infinite power and wisdom, together with an extraordinary universal craftsmanship in order to give form to all plants and flowers and to endow them with the necessary equipment. Furthermore, as is explained in "He: A Point of Divine Unity" in The Thirteenth Word, every molecule of air would have to possess the ability to know all speeches made or uttered by beings and all the words spoken on the radio and telephone, and then convey them to other molecules. Not even a demon could cause anyone to accept such a fantastic idea. Therefore, the just due for unbelief and denial, which is so far from reason and truth that it constitutes an insult and onslaught against all beings, could only be terrible Hell, the punishment of which is pure justice.

THE EIGHTH PHRASE: *HE IS THE ALL-LIVING AND DIES NOT*

An extremely brief indication of the proof in this phrase is as follows:

For example, just as the innumerable tiny suns reflected in the foams on the surface of a rough sea or on a flowing river point and testify to the existence of the same, single sun in the sky, so too, by their disappearance from the foams that go and which are replaced by new ones, they bear witness to the permanence of the same, single sun. Similarly, the creatures on the surface of the constantly changing sea of the universe, throughout ever-renewed, limitless space, in the field of minute particles or atoms, and in the river of time, which holds all events and transitory beings in its embrace and flows together with them, move on continuously and speedily and then die together with their apparent causes. Every day, every year, a universe dies and a new one replaces it. Since the produce of traveling worlds and flowing universes is continuously harvested in the field of atoms, then certainly, just as the foams and tiny suns reflected in them point to a perpetual sun by their disappearance and re-appearance, the deaths of these numberless creatures and endless products (to be replaced by new ones), their being discharged in perfect orderliness together with their apparent causes, testify with the clarity and certainty of the sun itself to the necessary Existence and Unity of an All-Living, Undying One: an Eternal Sun, an All-Permanent Creator, a Most Pure and Holy Commander. All beings testify to this truth a thousand times more clearly and definitely than the existence of the universe can.

By now you must certainly have understood just how deaf, foolish, and offensive is the person who does not hear or pay heed to these loud voices and powerful testimonies which fill the universe.

THE NINTH PHRASE: *IN HIS HAND IS ALL GOOD*

A brief indication of the proof contained in this phrase is as follows:

We see that each sphere or realm of beings in the universe, each level, each individual, and bodily member, and even each cell of each body, has a store or depot containing reserve supplies of sustenance and a field or treasury that produces and protects all the body's requirements. For at exactly the right time, in perfect order and balance, and with perfect wisdom and graciousness all these needy beings are given their requirements by a hidden hand, outside their power and will.

For example, mountains contain all the minerals and chemicals necessary for human beings and other living creatures, as well as all the things necessary for life. Just as they are perfect stores and treasuries which are operated at someone's command and organization, so too the earth is an arable field, a harvest, a kitchen, producing with perfect order and regularity the sustenance of all those living beings through the Power of an All-Wise Provider. Indeed, in the same way that human beings and all organs and limbs of their bodies have treasuries and stores, and even a minute cell has a tiny depot, this world is the store of the world of the Hereafter—the world of Islam and true humanity, which produces the good, the beauty and the lights that are the field and depot of Paradise, while all evils, which yield all ugliness and kinds of unbelief, and which come from non-existence and pollute the thoroughly good worlds of existence, are a storehouse of Hell. And the store of the heat of the stars is Hell, while the treasury of lights is Paradise. Thus, alluding to all those infinite treasuries, the phrase *In His hand is all good* demonstrates a most brilliant proof.

This phrase, together with the statement *His are the keys of the heavens and the earth* (39:63), indicates to anyone who is not totally blind an infinitely extensive, wonderful proof of Divine Lordship and Unity. For example, consider just a few of these numberless treasuries and stores as follows: Just as with His command of "Awake!" and with the key of His Will, an All-Wise Director and Controller Who holds the keys of seeds and grains—tiny stores containing all the necessary equipment and the plans and programs of huge trees or radiant flowers—opens up in perfect balance and order the minute door of a seed, so too with the key of the rain, which is the treasury of the earth, He opens without error all the seeds, the tiny stores that contain the "seminal fluid" of plants, as well as the tiny storehouses of droplets of semen and eggs; these then receive the command to develop and act as the origin of animals, of birds, and flying insects. If you want to understand that the One Who opens all these treasuries and storehouses also opens up with the hand of Wisdom, Will, Mercy, and Choice all the treasuries and depots, physical and non-physical, universal and particular, in the universe, each with its particular key, consider your own heart, mind, body, and stomach, each of which is a storehouse for you, and your garden and spring, which is the flower of the earth, and its flowers and fruits. See how they are opened by a hidden hand with perfect order, balance, mercy, and wisdom, each with a different key that comes from the workbench of *"Be!" and it is*. That hidden hand produces pounds—sometimes hundreds of pounds—of food from a minute box weighing less than an ounce and presents them to living creatures as a feast. Is it at all possible that blind force, deaf nature, aimless chance, or lifeless, ignorant, impotent causes could have a part in such a boundless, orderly, knowing, and discerning act? Is it possible that they could play any kind of role in such a totally wise, completely chance-free art, in such accurate, perfectly balanced disposals, and in such completely just acts of administering, raising, and maintaining? Could any being that does not see and administer all beings together at once, or does not hold under their command minute particles together with the planets and stars, intervene in this disposal and government, which is in every way wise, miraculous, and balanced?

As the verse *Almost bursting with fury* (67:8) states, Hell boils over with anger at the person who does not recognize the All-Compassionate Director and Controller, the All-Wise Lord, in Whose hand is all good and with Whom are the keys of all things, and who as a result deviates into denial: it boils up in fury, declaring through the tongue of mute eloquence: "He deserves my boundless torments and is never worthy of compassion."

THE TENTH PHRASE: *AND HE HAS THE FULL POWER OVER EVERYTHING*

An extremely concise indication of the proof in this phrase is as follows:

As soon as every conscious creature that comes into this guest-house of the world opens its eyes, it sees that a Power holds in its grasp the entire universe and that within that Power is infinite, eternal, all-embracing Knowledge, Which never confuses anything, as well as a most precise Wisdom and Favoring, Which never act aimlessly or without balance. Just as the Power employs a single particle in numerous tasks, turning it this way and that, like an ecstatic Mevlevi dervish, it also causes the globe of the earth to travel the distance of twenty-four thousand years in a single year, according to the same law. At the same time and according to the same law by which It sends to humans and animals the produce of the seasons, It employs the sun as a shuttle or spinning-wheel, making it move around its center ecstatically and in a way that produces a powerful gravity, employing the planets—the army of the solar system—in various tasks with perfect order and balance. At the same time and according to the same law of Wisdom, that same Power inscribes on the page of the face of the earth the "books" that are hundreds of thousands of species, one within the other, without error or confusion, thus displaying thousands of examples of the supreme resurrection of the dead. At the same time, that Power transforms the page of the air into a tablet for writing and erasing. Employing all the atoms of air, which are like the nibs of pens or the dots that make up writing, in the tasks specified for them by Will and Command, It endows all of them with such ability that each receives all words and speech as though it knows them, and broadcasts them without confusion. It employs each as a miniscule ear and a tiny tongue, proving that the element of air is a "throne" for Divine Will and Command.

Thus, as indicated in this brief indication, the One Who makes the universe into a well-ordered city, a perfectly-built and organized apartment-building and guest-house, and a miraculous book or Qur'an, holds in His Grasp with the balance of Knowledge and arrangements of Wisdom all the levels, realms, and groups of creatures from the universe as a whole to minute particles, directing and controlling them. He is the All-Merciful and All-Compassionate One Who displays His Wisdom and Mercy within His Power and makes known His Existence and Unity within His absolute Lordship as clearly as the sun. So, those who do not recognize that All-Merciful and All-Compassionate One through belief in return for His making Himself known, who do not love Him through worship in return for His making Himself loved, and do not offer Him thanks or praise in return for His bounties—these demons in human form who, instead of recognizing Him and trying to love Him, or thank and praise Him, foster a sort of enmity toward Him through denial; they are minor Nimrods and Pharaohs and are certainly deserving of infinite torment.

THE ELEVENTH PHRASE: *AND TO HIM IS HOMECOMING*

This means that just as beings will leave for His Presence and proceed to the eternal world—the Hereafter—and the everlasting realm of happiness, so too is He the refuge of all the creatures in the universe. All the chains of material causes end in Him and rest on His Power. They are all merely veils for the acts of His Power—veils for preserving the Dignity and Majesty of His sacred Power against unbecoming complaints. They have no part whatever in creation. Were it not for His Will and Command, nothing, not even a particle, could move or act. A very brief indication of the proof in this phrase is as follows:

FIRSTLY: We refer to The Tenth Word and its addenda, The Twenty-Ninth Word, The Seventh Matter of Fruits of Belief (The Eleventh Ray), The Third Ray (The Treatise of Supplication), and to the treatises of the *Risale-i Nur* concerning belief, the fact that the Resurrection will occur and that the Hereafter and eternal life will be brought about as indubitably and clearly as the coming spring. Truly, these treatises have proved this pillar of belief in such a way, with so much evidence that they compel even the most obstinate deniers to affirm that the existence of the Hereafter is as certain as the existence of this world.

SECONDLY: One third of the miraculously eloquent Qur'an concerns the Resurrection and the Hereafter and it builds all its claims on them. Therefore, all of the Qur'an's miraculous aspects and the evidence that proves that it is God's Word also testify to the existence of the Hereafter. Similarly, all of the miracles which bear witness to the Prophethood of Muhammad, upon him be peace and blessings, and all other evidence of his Prophethood and proofs of his truthfulness also testify to the reality of the Resurrection and the Hereafter. Throughout his life one of this noblest being's most constant claims concerned the Hereafter; in the same way, all the other twenty-four thousand Prophets, upon them be peace, also gave humankind glad tidings of everlasting happiness in an eternal realm, proving it with countless miracles and clear evidence. Therefore, all the miracles and evidence that proved their Prophethood and truthfulness also bear witness to the Hereafter and eternal life, which, after the Existence and Unity of God, was their constant and most important doctrine. Furthermore, all the evidence that prove the other pillars of belief also testify to the reality of the Resurrection and the opening up of the realm of happiness.

THIRDLY: In order to display His Perfections, His Power and His Lordship, an All-Majestic Maker, an All-Gracious and Beautiful Creator, an All-Perfect God has created the universe with all its atoms, planets, parts and levels, and makes each work at a task, indeed, at numerous tasks, continuously and with perfect wisdom. Also, in order to display the endless, perpetual manifestations of His Names, He sends convoy after convoy, indeed, world after renewed traveling world, and the tribes of creatures, to the guest-house of this world and the arena of trial, which is worldly life. Having recorded all their images, deeds, and states for the movies of the Hereafter with the cameras that have been set up in the World of representations or "ideal" forms and belong to the Intermediate Realm (between the material and immaterial realms), He discharges them from their duties to be followed by other tribes, convoys, and flowing or traveling worlds for the same tasks and in order that they should be mirrors to the manifestations of His Names. Is it therefore at all possible that there should be no realm of reward and punishment, no Resurrection and Last Judgment, for human beings, who with consciousness and intelligence should respond in this fleeting world to all the purposes of the Creator, and should, with all their capacity, love Him and make Him loved, recognize Him and make Him known, and who endlessly pray to Him for everlasting happiness in the Hereafter, and who, on account of having intelligence, suffer infinite pains and long for eternal life, which is pure pleasure, with all their being, spirit, and capacities? God forbid! A hundred thousand times, God forbid!

Since this brief indication is found in detail together with its proofs in relevant parts of the *Risale-i Nur*, we refer you to them and cut this long story short here.

> All-Glorified are You! We have no knowledge save what You have taught us. Surely You are the All-Knowing, the All-Wise.

Part Two: A brief summary o the meaning of Suratu'l-Fatiha

This is a short exemplary lesson for the students of the *Risale-i Nur*:

While reciting *Suratu'l-Fatiha* during a canonical Prayer, it occurred to me that one drop from its ocean and a single gleam from the seven colors in the light of its sun should be expounded briefly. Actually, we have written some very sweet and beautiful indications from this sacred treasure trove in a part of The Twenty-Ninth Letter, particularly in the imaginary journey taken in "the *Nun* (we) of *Na'budu* (we worship)," and The Eight Symbols (*Rumuzat-i Thamaniya*), and Signs of (the Qur'an's) Miraculousness *(Isharatu'l-*

I'jaz), which is a key to the interpretation of the Qur'an, and in certain other parts of the *Risale-i Nur*. However, I felt obliged to write down my reflections during the Prayer, but only about how *al-Fatiha*, that very sweet summary or extract of the Qur'an, indicates the pillars of belief and its proofs in the form of an extremely brief summary and in the manner of Part One above. So, referring the phrase *In the Name of God, the All-Merciful, the All-Compassionate* to two or three treatises of the *Risale-i Nur*, I begin with *All praise and gratitude are for God:*

In the Name of God, the All-Merciful, the All-Compassionate.

All praise and gratitude are for God, the Lord of the worlds; the All-Merciful, the All-Compassionate; the Master of the Day of Judgment. You alone do We worship, and from You alone do we seek help. Guide us to the Straight Path—the path of those whom You have favored, not of those who have incurred (Your) wrath nor of those who are astray.

THE FIRST PHRASE: *ALL PRAISE AND GRATITUDE ARE FOR GOD*

A very brief indication of the proof of the truths of belief in this phrase is as follows:

Purposeful bestowals and bounties, which are the cause of praise and thanks, including in particular the sending of pure, clean, nutritious milk to infants from a place between blood and excrement, along with purposeful gifts and presents, and merciful benefactions and feasts, fill up the earth, indeed, the universe. The price one must pay for these is to say "In (and with) the Name of God" when one begins (to consume them); "All praise and gratitude are for God" at the end, and in the middle to perceive the act of bestowing in the bounty, and through it to recognize one's Lord. Consider your own self, your stomach, and your senses! See how many things, how many bounties they need! See how much food and pleasure they seek for the price of praise and thanks. See this and then compare all living creatures with yourself. Thus, the endless praise offered verbally and through tongues of innate disposition in response to these all-embracing bestowals shows as clearly as daylight the Existence and universal Lordship of One Who is Worshipped and Praised, an All-Compassionate Bestower of bounties.

THE SECOND PHRASE: *THE LORD OF THE WORLDS*

A very short indication of the proof contained in this phrase is as follows:

We see with our own eyes that in the universe there are not thousands but millions of worlds, small universes, mostly one within the other. Although the conditions for the administration and maintenance of these are all different, they are organized, maintained, and administered so perfectly that the universe, like a single page, and all of these worlds, each like a line, is constantly in His view, and is written, renewed, and changed with the Pen of His Power and Destiny. At every instant, attestations both particular and universal—unending testimonies to the number of minute particles and the beings formed out of them—come in view to the necessary Existence and Unity of the Lord of the worlds Who administers these millions of worlds, these traveling universes, with an infinite Knowledge, Wisdom, and a limitless all-embracing Mercy within an infinite Lordship. A person who does not perceive and confirm, who does not understand and see this Lordship, Which maintains and administers with the same law and the same wisdom all beings from the field of atoms to the solar system and the Milky Way, and from the cells of the body to the storehouse of the earth, and to the universe in its entirety—such a person certainly makes themselves deserving of endless torment and gives up any right to be pitied.

THE THIRD PHRASE: *THE ALL-MERCIFUL, THE ALL-COMPASSIONATE*

An extremely brief indication of the proof in this phrase is as follows:

The existence and reality of a boundless mercy is as clearly apparent in the universe as the light of the sun. As certainly as light testifies to the existence of the sun, this all-embracing mercy bears witness to an All-Merciful and All-Compassionate One behind the veil of the Unseen.

An important part of mercy is provision, and for this reason the All-Merciful is also called the All-Providing. Provision points to an All-Compassionate Provider so clearly that anyone with an iota of consciousness is compelled to affirm Him. For example, He sends food to all living beings, particularly to the helpless and young, throughout the earth and the atmosphere, in an extremely wonderful fashion that is beyond their will and power, from seeds, droplets of fluid and grains of earth, all of which resemble each other. He drives birds to seek food for their frail, flightless chicks in the nests at the tops of trees and to bring it to them. He subjugates the hungry lioness to her cubs so she does not eat the meat she finds but gives it to them instead. He sends sweet, nutritious, pure white milk, like the water of *Kawthar* from the taps of breasts to the offspring of humans and the young animals, without it being polluted by other bodily secretions, and complements it with the tenderness of mothers to help them. In a similarly wonderful fashion, He causes appropriate sustenance to hasten to all the trees, which need a certain sort of food, and so He bestows an extensive table of "foods" on humans to satisfy their physical and non-physical senses, their minds, hearts, and spirits. It is as though the universe consists of hundreds of thousands of tables laden with every different kind and variety of food, all enfolded one within the other like the petals of the rose and the leaf sheaths of the maize. With multifarious tongues, particular and universal, and as numerous as the tables and the foods and bounties they bear, the universe indicates to anyone who is not completely blind an All-Merciful, All-Compassionate, and All-Munificent Provider.

If it is said: The calamities, ugliness, and evils in this world are contrary to that all-embracing Mercy and contaminate it.

The answer: Complete and satisfactory answers have been given to this highly complex question in various parts of the *Risale-i Nur*, such as The Treatise on Divine Destiny (and The Twenty-sixth Word). Referring you to them, here we make only a brief reference as follows:

Every element, every species of being, every creature has numerous duties, particular and universal, and each of those duties yields numerous results and fruit. These results and fruit are in most cases beneficial, beautiful, good, and merciful. Only a few of them, which are apparently ugly and harmful, visit or happen to those lacking the necessary capacity to receive the good in them and use them for good, and those who act wrongly or those who deserve punishment and disciplining, or those who have the potential to yield numerous fruits of good in order that they could develop them. There is in appearance a minor evil and ugliness in them; they appear to be lacking in mercy. But if in order that the minor evil should not exist an element or universal being would be prevented by Mercy from performing its duty, then all its other good and beautiful results would not come into existence. Since the non-existence of a good is evil and the destruction of beauty is ugly, evil, ugliness, and mercilessness would occur to the number of these results. Thus, hundreds of instances of evil and mercilessness would be committed just so that one evil should not occur, and this would be entirely contrary to the wisdom, benefit, and mercy of Lordship. For example, such universal elements as snow, cold, fire, and rain have hundreds of benefits and good purposes. If through their own selection or misuse, careless or imprudent people cause themselves harm because of these elements—for instance, if they put their hands in the fire and then say there is no mercy in the creation of fire, the innumerable good, beneficial, and merciful uses of fire will contradict and silence them.

Furthermore, selfish human desires and lowly emotions, which are blind to consequences, cannot be the criteria, measure, or balance with which to evaluate the laws of Mercy, Sovereignty, and Lordship that are in force in the universe. Everyone sees things according to the color of their own mirror. One who is cruel and dark of heart sees the universe as weeping, ugly, dark, and devoid of justice. But if they were to look at the universe through the eye of belief, they would see it as a macro-human, smiling with mercy and clothed, like a *houri* (maiden) of Paradise, in seventy thousand beautiful garments, one covering the other, sewn from mercy, goodness and wisdom. They would see that humankind is a miniature universe, and each individual human being a miniature world. They would exclaim with all their heart and spirit: "*All praise and gratitude are for God, the Lord of the worlds; the All-Merciful, the All-Compassionate; the Master of the Day of Judgment!*"

THE FOURTH PHRASE: *THE MASTER OF THE DAY OF JUDGMENT*

What follows is a very short indication of the proof in this phrase:

FIRSTLY: All the proofs set forth at the end of The First Station which testify to the truth of "And to Him is homecoming" and to the Resurrection and the Hereafter also testify to the extensive truth of belief which "the Master of the Day of Judgment' indicates.

SECONDLY: As stated at the end of The Tenth Word, just as the perpetual Lordship, Mercy, Wisdom, Grace, Beauty, Majesty, and Perfection of the Maker of this universe, together with all of His other Attributes and Names, certainly demand the Hereafter, the Qur'an also testifies to the eternal life in the abode of the Hereafter with thousands of its verses and proofs. Prophet Muhammad, upon him be peace and blessings, and all of the other Prophets also indicate the same truth with their revealed Books or Scriptures, each of which is replete with innumerable proofs. The person, therefore, who does not believe in the everlasting life of the Hereafter casts themselves into a sort of Hell in this world—a Hell that arises from unbelief and causes them to suffer constant torment. As is described in *A Guide for Youth*, through their decay, death, and separation, all past and future events and beings continuously rain down endless pain on the unbeliever's heart and spirit, causing them to undergo the torments of Hell before actually going there.

THIRDLY: "The Day of Judgment" (*Yawmu'd-Din*) alludes to a vast and powerful proof of the Resurrection. However, there is no need here to indicate the proofs contained in it, as various parts of the *Risale-i Nur* have proved, with hundreds of powerful arguments, that the morning and spring of the Resurrection and Supreme Gathering will come as certainly as day follows night and spring follows winter.

THE FIFTH PHRASE: *YOU ALONE DO WE WORSHIP AND FROM YOU ALONE DO WE SEEK HELP*

Before indicating the proof contained in this sentence, I should relate briefly a true journey of the imagination which is described in The Twenty-Ninth Letter. It was as follows:

As explained in various parts of the *Risale-i Nur*, in particular in *Isharatu'l-I'jaz* (Signs of Miraculousness), a key of the Light to the interpretation of the Qur'an, and *Rumuzat-i Thamaniya* (The Eight Symbols), when I discovered four or five miraculous predictions at the end of *Suratu'l-Fath* and an historical miracle in the verse, *So this day We will save only your body* (10:92), together with gleams of miraculousness in many of the Qur'an's words and points of miraculousness in even some of the Qur'an's letters, when reciting *Suratu'l-Fatiha* during the canonical Prayer, this question occurred to me: Why, instead of the first person singular has *we* been preferred in the verse, *You alone do we worship and from You alone do we seek help*?

Suddenly a broad highway opened up through the door of that "*Nun*" (we), taking me on a journey in the imagination. I understood at the degree of certainty based on vision or observation the great significance and vast benefits of performing the canonical Prayers in congregation, and that this single letter is a miracle. It was as follows:

While performing a canonical Prayer in congregation in Bayezid Mosque in Istanbul, I uttered: "*You alone do we worship and from You alone do we seek help.*" I looked and saw that the congregation in the mosque was reciting the same verse and its members were all participating in the supplication of "Guide us!" which follows it, thus corroborating my supplication.

Then another vision appeared and I saw that all the mosques in Istanbul had become one huge Bayezid Mosque. All their congregations were exclaiming: "*You alone do we worship and from You alone do we seek help,*" like me, setting their seals on my affirmations and entreaties and saying "Amin!" to them.

Then, as I felt that they were taking on the form of intercessors for me, another vision appeared in my imagination. I saw that the world of Islam assumed the form of a huge mosque, with Makka and the Ka'ba as the *mihrab*, the niche in the mosque where the imam stands. All the rows of Muslims performing the Prayer were in circles facing that sacred niche. Like me they too were saying "*You alone do we worship and from You alone do we seek help. Guide us to the Straight Path!*" Each was praying in the name of all and affirming the same cause, and in so doing making all of the others intercessors for themselves.

Then, as I was thinking "The cause and path of such a vast community cannot be wrong and its prayers are surely not rejected—this rebuffs any Satanic doubt," and while observably affirming the vast benefits of performing the Prayers in congregation, another vision presented itself to me. I saw that the universe was a huge mosque in which each of the numerous nations of creatures was performing the Prayer in a manner particular to its way of life and existence and through the tongue of innate disposition. Responding with extensive worship to the all-embracing Lordship of the All-Worshipped One of Majesty, each nation was confirming the testimonies and affirmations of Divine Unity presented by all the others.

While observing this, yet another vision came into view. I saw that just as the macro-human that is the universe was exclaiming: "*You alone do we worship and from You alone do we seek help,*" with the tongue of its disposition, with its constituent parts proclaiming it through the tongue of capacity and innate need, and conscious beings uttering it verbally, all thus displaying their worshipful servanthood before the Creator's compassionate Lordship, so too were all of the atoms, faculties, and senses of my body displaying the same, each expressing through the tongue of need and submission their dependence on the Creator's Lordship. Thus, they too showed that they were acting in accordance with the Divine Will and Command and were at every instant in need of their Creator's grace, mercy, and assistance. Having observed in amazement both the sacred mystery of performing the Prayers in congregation and the beautiful miracle of the *Nun*, I left my journey through the same door of the *Nun* by which I had entered. "*All praise and gratitude are for God!*" I exclaimed. Thereafter, I became accustomed to reciting the verse, *You alone do we worship and from You alone do we seek help*, on account of those three congregations and all these companions of mine, great and small.

Now we have completed the introduction and come to our main topic. It is a brief indication of the proof contained in *You alone do we worship and from You alone do we seek help*:

FIRSTLY: We see with our own eyes that in the universe, and especially on the earth, there is an awesome, continuous and regular Divine activity, within which a compassionate, organizing, nurturing, and absolute Lordship responds with perfect wisdom and favor to the pleas for help and entreaties made actively or verbally or through the tongue of innate disposition. Also, within this active response of Lordship, sound intellects and the eye of belief see, and all the revealed Scriptures and Prophets show, that the manifestations of an absolute Divinity and the attribute of being universally worshipped respond to the thousands of forms of worship offered by all beings—animate creatures in particular—and most importantly to both the innate worship of human beings and the worship they perform through their will.

SECONDLY: All of the three congregations signified by the *Nun* of *na'budu* and described above are engaged together in their different innate or voluntary acts of worship. This is without doubt a grateful response to God's being the All-Worshipped One and an indubitable, boundless testimony to the existence of an All-Holy Object of Worship. Furthermore, the *Nun* of *nasta'in* ("we" in the "we seek help") signifies that the three congregations mentioned above—that is, every group and every individual from among the whole of the universe and the congregation of the atoms of a living body—pray to Him and ask Him for help both by act and by disposition. This testifies beyond all doubt to the existence of an All-Compassionate Director and Organizer Who hastens to help them, and Who responds to their prayer with acceptance. For example, as explained in The Twenty-Third Word, the wonderful, unexpected acceptance of the three sorts of prayers of all the creatures on the earth clearly testifies to an All-Compassionate Lord and Answerer of prayer. Actually, we see before our eyes that grains and seeds ask their Creator through the tongue of innate need to become shoots and trees and that their prayer is accepted. Similarly, we also see that the prayer for sustenance and all of their other necessities which living creatures perform through the tongue of innate need is also accepted. At exactly the right time, unconscious creatures are made to hasten to their calls for help. This testifies clearly to the existence of an All-Munificent Creator.

Thus, together with the two kinds of prayer mentioned—the prayer performed through the tongue of innate capacity and the prayer performed through the tongue of innate need—the acceptance of the verbal prayers uttered by humans, and in particular the wonderful acceptance of the prayers of the Prophets and distinguished ones, attests to the proof of Divine Unity contained in *From You alone do we seek help.*

The Sixth Phrase: *Guide us to the Straight Path*

An extremely brief indication of the proof in this phrase is as follows:

Just as the shortest path between two places and the shortest of lines drawn between two points is the straightest and most direct, so too the straightest and most direct of spiritual paths is the shortest and easiest. For example, all the comparisons in the *Risale-i Nur* that are made between the ways of belief and unbelief decisively demonstrate that the way of belief and Divine Unity is extremely short, direct, straight, and easy, while the ways of unbelief and denial are not only exceedingly dangerous, but also extremely lengthy, circuitous, tangled, and difficult. That is to say, unbelief and the association of partners with God are not acceptable in this wise universe where everything is led along the straightest, easiest, and shortest path, while the truths of belief and Divine Unity are as necessary and essential as the sun.

Also, the shortest, safest, easiest, and most beneficial way in human morality and conduct is the way established by the Straight Path and following the moderate, middle way between extremes.

For example, if the power of reason is divorced from wisdom, which is the middle way, and deviates from moderation, it falls into either of two extremes: harmful demagogy and wiliness, or calamitous stupidity and foolishness. It suffers all kinds of difficulties on these long and tortuous paths. Similarly, if the power of anger—the power of self-defense—does not follow the path of courage or gallantry, which is the middle way, it goes to either the extreme of the most injurious, oppressive fury and tyranny or to the opposite extreme of an abased, painful cowardice and timidity. As a consequence of deviating from the straight path, it has to suffer the continuous torments of the conscience.

And if the power of animal appetites or lusts loses the safe middle way of chastity, it goes to either the extreme of a calamitous, shameful debauchery and immorality or to the opposite extreme of frigidity or lack of physical desires. It deprives itself of the pleasure inherent in bounties and suffers the torments of that spiritual sickness.

Thus, of all of the paths of personal and social life, the straight path is the easiest, shortest, and most beneficial. Whereas the ways that are followed when the straight path is lost are lengthy, harmful, and full of calamities.

Consequently, while *Guide us to the Straight Path* is a comprehensive example of prayer and worship, it also indicates a proof of Divine Unity, instruction in wisdom, and moral training.

THE SEVENTH PHRASE: *THE PATH OF THOSE WHOM YOU HAVE FAVORED*

An extremely brief indication of the proof contained in this phrase is as follows:

FIRSTLY: The verse, ... *those whom God has favored—the Prophets, and the truthful ones (loyal to God's cause and truthful in whatever they do and say), and the witnesses (those who see the hidden Divine truths and testify thereto with their lives), and the righteous ones (in all their sayings and deeds, and dedicated to setting everything right)* (4:69), provides the answer to the question: "Who are those whom He has favored?" With this answer, which explains the four groups of people among humankind who represent the Straight Path, the verse also indicates the leaders of these groups. By "the Prophets" Prophet Muhammad, upon him be peace and blessings, is being referred to as the leader of the Prophets; by "the truthful" the one who is primarily meant is Abu Bakr the Truthful; by "the witnesses" 'Umar, 'Uthman and 'Ali are being referred to; and by "the righteous ones" a mention of Hasan, the son of 'Ali, is being made. Thus by predicting that Abu Bakr, 'Umar, 'Uthman, 'Ali, and Hasan would be Caliphs after the Prophet, and that 'Umar, 'Uthman and 'Ali would bear witness to the truthfulness of Islam by being martyred, the verse displays a gleam of miraculousness.[110]

SECONDLY: The truth of Divine Unity, which these most elevated, truthful, and upright groups of humankind have claimed and taught with all their strength since the time of Adam, employing innumerable proofs, miracles, wonders, evidence, and illuminations, and whose evidence has been affirmed by the majority of humankind, is most certainly as clear as the sun. With hundreds of thousands of miracles and proofs, these preeminent members of the human race have proved and unanimously agreed on absolute truths, such as Divine Unity and the necessary Existence of the Creator. This forms a most indubitable proof. For the human race is the most important fruit of the universe, appointed on this earth to rule and develop it; and the most elevated of living creatures and possesses the most comprehensive capacity. And these four groups are humankind's most truthful and confirmed guides, and its leaders in perfection. Therefore, do those who do not recognize or who choose to deny a truth in which these perfected individuals believe, proving its existence with evidence taken from the universe and

110 Abu Bakr, 'Umar, 'Uthman and 'Ali, may God be pleased with them, were the four leading Companions of Prophet Muhammad, upon him be peace and blessings. Abu Bakr was his closest, loyal Companion and was elected as Caliph after him. 'Umar, who was universally famous for his justice, uprightness, and insightfulness; 'Uthman, to whom the Prophet gave two of his daughters in wedlock, one after the death of the other, was known for his chastity, compassionateness, and generosity; 'Ali married the Prophet's beloved daughter Fatima and was the father of the Prophet's descendants, and was famous for his bravery, profound knowledge, and sagacity. All these were elected Caliphs after Abu Bakr. Hasan was the eldest son of 'Ali and together with his younger brother Hussein, were the two most beloved grandsons of the Prophet and the Prophet's descendants came from them. Hasan was elected Caliph after 'Ali, but resigned six months later in favor of Mu'awiya. Abu Bakr, 'Umar, 'Uthman, and 'Ali, and according to many, Hasan, are known and loved as the Rightly-Guided Caliphs. (Tr.)

all of the beings within it, unanimously and at the degrees of certainty of knowledge, certainty of vision, and certainty of experience—do these wretched individuals in their obdurate unbelief not perpetrate an infinite crime? Are they not deserving of infinite punishment?

The Eighth Phrase: *Not of those who have incurred (Your) wrath nor of those who are astray*

A concise indication of the proof contained in this phrase is as follows:

Based on unanimous reports and certain events, facts, and observations, human history and the sacred revealed Scriptures inform us in a clear, definite manner of the following:

As established by thousands of events, the Prophets, the people of the Straight Path, were given miraculous help from the Unseen; what they sought was given to them exactly, while their disbelieving enemies were visited with wrath and heavenly blows. This demonstrates beyond all doubt that the universe and humankind within it have such an All-Wise, All-Just, All-Favoring, All-Munificent, All-Glorious, All-Mighty, and All-Overwhelming Disposer and Lord—One Who, as history records, bestowed victory and salvation on many Prophets such as Noah, Abraham, Moses, Hud and Salih, upon them be peace, while dealing terrible heavenly blows on numerous oppressive and disbelieving peoples such as the 'Ad and the Thamud, and the people of the Pharaoh, as punishment in this world for their rebellion against the Prophets.

Since the time of Adam, upon him be peace, two mighty conflicting currents have come down to us. One is that of the Prophets and their righteous, believing followers, who have followed the Straight Path and have been favored with true happiness in this world and will be favored with it in the next. Since they act straightforwardly and uprightly along the way of the Straight Path in accordance with the true beauty, order, and perfection of the universe, they are favored with both the gifts of the universe's Owner and happiness in this world and the next. Being the means of humankind's rising to the level of the angels or even higher, through the truths of belief they attain a sort of Paradise in this world and bliss in the Hereafter, thus helping others to attain these too.

As for the second current, since it strays from the Straight Path and goes to either extreme, making reason into an instrument of torment, it casts humanity down to a degree lower than that of the animals. Moreover, in addition to being visited with the blows of Divine wrath in this world as a result of their wrongdoing, because reason makes humankind related with all beings, they see the universe as a place of general mourning and as the slaughterhouse of living creatures, which are constantly falling into nothingness; they see it as the most ugly and confused, and this causes their spirits and consciences to suffer a perpetual Hell in this world, ensuring that they are condemned to everlasting torment in the next.

Thus, the last verse of *Suratu'l-Fatiha*, *The path of those whom You have favored, not of those who have incurred (Your) wrath nor of those who are astray*, informs us of these two mighty currents. It is also the source, basis, and teacher of all the comparisons between belief and unbelief in the *Risale-i Nur*. Since the treatises of the *Risale-i Nur* expound this verse with hundreds of comparisons, we refer you to them for further explanation, and make do here with this brief indication.

THE NINTH PHRASE: *AMIN*

An extremely brief indication of this is the following:

The *nun* (we) in *na'budu* (we worship) and *nasta'in* (we seek help) indicates to us the three great congregations (mentioned in The Fifth Phrase), particularly the congregations of those who believe in Divine Unity in the mosque of the world of Islam and of the millions performing Prayers all at the same time: it includes us among them and, since both we and they recite the same words, it opens the way for all of us to receive a share of each other's prayer, affirmation, and intercession. In return, through the word "Amin," we join in and support the prayers of that congregation of believing worshippers, confirming what they say, and offering up a plea that their intercession and requests for help may be accepted. Thus, it transforms our individual worship, prayers, and entreaties into universal, extensive worship, enabling us to respond to universal Lordship. That is to say, through the mystery of the brotherhood and sisterhood of belief and Islamic unity, through the bonds of the unity of the congregation of millions in the mosque of the Muslim world at the time of the canonical Prayers, and by means of spiritual communication, the "Amin" at the end of *Suratu'l-Fatiha* acquires universality and may become millions of "Amins."[111]

All praise and gratitude are for God, the Lord of the worlds.

All-Glorified are You! We have no knowledge save what You have taught us; surely You are the All-Knowing, the All-Wise.

Part Three

In the Name of God, the All-Merciful, the All-Compassionate.

And from Him do we seek help

INTRODUCTION

It was *Suratu'l-Fatiha* of the five daily canonical Prayers and the first part of the declaration of testimony of belief—*I bear witness that there is no deity but God*—which urged me to write Part Two of this Ray. I have now been prompted to write this Third Part by the second phrase of the declaration of belief, that is *I bear witness that Muhammad is the Messenger of God*, and by the following sublime verses at the end of *Suratu'l-Fath*, which contain five miraculous predictions.

---

[111] Thus, if, according to the degree of each, an ordinary person receives a tiny share like a seed from this sacred truth, a perfected person who has advanced spiritually may receive a share like the palm-tree. But a person who has not advanced should not intentionally recall these meanings while reciting the *Fatiha*,* lest it impair their sense of the Divine presence. When they advance to such a station, these meanings will, in any case, make themselves clear.

* We asked our Master what was meant by "intentionally" in the footnote above, and we are writing here exactly the answer we received:

"I consider that to dwell on the comprehensive, elevated meanings of the *Fatiha* and *tashahhud*, not intentionally but indirectly, and not in detail – which causes a sort of heedlessness of the Divine presence – but concisely and briefly, dispels heedlessness and imparts a brilliance to the worship and invocations. This demonstrates completely the high value of the Prayer, the *Fatiha*, and the *tashahhud*. What is meant by "not recalling intentionally" in the footnote is that sometimes to be busy with the detailed meanings themselves causes one to forget the Prayer, lessening the sense of the Divine presence. But I feel that to dwell on them indirectly and concisely yields great benefits."

Signed in the name of the *Risale-i Nur* students,

Ceylan

> He it is Who has sent His Messenger with the Divine guidance and the Religion of truth that He may make it prevail over all religions. God suffices for a witness. Muhammad is the Messenger of God; and those who are in his company are firm and unyielding against unbelievers, and compassionate among themselves. You see them (constant in the Prayer) bowing down and prostrating, seeking favor with God and His approval and good pleasure. Their marks are on their faces, traced by prostration. This is their description in the Torah; and their description in the Gospel: like a seed that has sprouted its shoot, then it has strengthened it, and then risen firmly on its stem, delighting the sowers (with joy and wonder), that through them He fills the unbelievers with rage. God has promised all those among them who believe and do good, righteous deeds forgiveness (to bring unforeseen blessings) and a tremendous reward. (48:28–29)

The details, explanations, and documented proofs concerning these verses can be found in The Nineteenth Letter—Miracles of Muhammad—and in the Arabic *al-Hizbu'n-Nuri*. Here I will write briefly and concisely, under the title of Indications, a summary of *al-Hizbu'n-Nuri* and a sort of translation of the part of the declaration of God's Unity or belief, *Muhammad is the Messenger of God*, which I constantly recite after the Prayers and which was written in Arabic.

FIRST INDICATION

Prophet Muhammad, upon him be peace and blessings, who responded with universal worship and teaching to the manifestation of the Lordship of the Owner of the universe and His perpetual Divinity and infinite bounties, is as necessary for the universe as the sun. For he is the supreme master of humankind and its greatest Prophet, the pride of the world, and the one honored with the Divine address: "Had it not been for you, I would not have created the worlds."[112] The Muhammadan Truth—the truth he has as Muhammad—was the reason for the world's creation, and is its result and most perfect fruit. Also, the realities connected with the universe, such as its true perfections, its consisting in enduring mirrors held up to the All-Beautiful and Gracious One of Majesty, the manifestations of His Names, the duty-bound works of His wise, purposeful Acts, and His most meaning-

112 'Aliyyu'l-Qari, *al-Asraru'l-Marfu'a*, 385.

ful missives, its bearing the seed of a permanent world, and the fact that it will result in the Hereafter and a realm of happiness for which all conscious creatures yearn—all these realities connected with the existence of the universe are realized through the Supreme Truth possessed by Prophet Muhammad and his mission as God's Messenger. Since this is so, the universe testifies most powerfully and decisively to his Messengership. Moreover, in order to be saved from non-existence, nothingness, eternal execution, and absolute annihilation, all of humankind, indeed all conscious beings in general, and the Muslims, and the world of Islam in particular, constantly and earnestly seek the eternally permanent life with all the powers of their comprehensive natures, with the tongues of all their capacities, and with all their prayers, worship, and entreaties. Since it is the Messengership of Muhammad, upon him be peace and blessings, and the Muhammadan Truth which most powerfully give definite glad tidings of eternal life, this both testifies to the Messengership of Muhammad and the Muhammadan Truth and confirms that he is the pride of humanity and the noblest of creatures. Furthermore, in accordance with the rule: "The cause is like the agent or doer," the equivalent of all the good deeds done every day by hundreds of millions of believers are recorded in Muhammad's record of good deeds, and the single person of Muhammad, upon him be peace and blessings, reaches a degree (of perfection) commensurate with that which comes from the reward given in return for the universal worship and effulgence of billions of righteous worshippers. This is another most powerful testimony to the Messengership of that noble being, upon him be peace and blessings.

SECOND INDICATION

The following indicates more than twenty testimonies, on which I reflect during my regular recitations:

> Muhammad is the Messenger of God, ever truthful and trustworthy in his declarations and promises, through the testimony of his sudden appearance with a perfect Religion, religious life, and Shari'a, despite being unlettered, and with the firmest belief, creed, and worship, and with the most elevated call, supplications and prayers, and with the most encompassing message, and with complete steadfastness and fruitful, unequaled wonders.

THE FIRST TESTIMONY: This is a proof of Muhammad's Messengership which comes from eleven of his attributes and states that are mentioned in the expressions above.

- It is an unequaled attribute of Prophet Muhammad that although he did not know how to read or write, he appeared suddenly and without experience with a Religion which has left in amazement the learned people and philosophers over fourteen centuries and has won first place among the revealed religions.
- It is also unequaled that Islam, which emerged from his reports, words, actions, and conduct, has at all times educated and trained the spirits, souls, and minds of hundreds of thousands of millions of people, and propelled them to spiritual advancement.
- Moreover, another unequaled attribute of his is that he appeared with a Shari'a so sublime that for fourteen centuries it has ruled one-fifth of humankind with its just laws, leading them to material and spiritual progress.
- Also, that person, upon him be peace and blessings, appeared with a faith, creed, and conviction so elevated that all the people of truth have been illuminated and nurtured by his degree of belief and all have affirmed unanimously that his belief was the highest and strongest.
- Furthermore, the fact that the opposition of his numerous opponents at that time never caused him the slightest anxiety, doubt, or suspicion about his message and mission also shows that he is unequaled in strength and universality of belief.
- His worship of God and his servanthood to God were such that they encompassed all degrees and dimensions of worship and servanthood. Without imitating anyone, he observed the subtlest points and dimensions of worship, fulfilling his duty of worship perfectly, even at times of the greatest disturbance and dangers. This was also one of his incomparable attributes.
- He displayed such excellence in offering prayers, supplications, and entreaties to his Creator that up to the present no one has ever been able to reach the level he reached, despite fourteen centuries of successive and mutually supportive thoughts and learning. For

example, in the supplication *al-Jawshanu'l-Kabir*, which takes as intercessor a thousand and one Divine Names, he so describes and acquaints us with his Creator that nothing like it has since existed. In short, he is also unequaled in his knowledge of God.

- He called people to Islam with such steadfastness and declared his Messengership with such boldness that although his people, his uncle, the great powers of the world, and the followers of the former religions all opposed him and were hostile against him, he did not show the least fear or hesitation; rather, he challenged them all and accomplished his task successfully. This too was an unparalleled attribute.

These eight wonderful, unparalleled attributes form a very powerful proof of his veracity and Prophethood. They also show that there is complete certainty concerning his utter seriousness and conviction, and his perfect trustworthiness and truthfulness. Every day in the *tashahhud* the world of Islam, in millions of tongues, declares: "Peace be upon you, O Prophet, and also God's mercy and blessings." It declares its submission to his Prophethood, and confirmation of the glad tidings of eternal happiness that he brought. Saying gratefully and with a sense of obligation: "Peace be upon you, O Prophet!" in the face of the sure way which leads to eternal life, which all humankind seeks with a profound yearning, every member of Muslim community visits him in spirit and congratulates him in the name of hundreds of thousands of millions, indeed, billions of people.

THE SECOND TESTIMONY: This is one of twenty universal testimonies and contains many others within it.

> Muhammad is the Messenger of God, ever truthful in his declarations and promises, and trustworthy, through the testimony of all truths of belief to his absolute truthfulness…

That is, the truths of the six pillars of belief and their realization in life decisively testify to the Messengership of Muhammad, upon him be peace and blessings. For the collective personality of his life as Messenger, the basis of all his claims, and the essence of his Prophethood are these six pillars. Thus, all the evidence that testifies to the truth and realization of the pillars of belief prove that Muhammad, upon him be peace and blessings, is certainly God's Messenger and that he was truthful in his claims. The proofs of the other pillars of belief for the truth of the Hereafter are set forth in *Fruits of Belief* and the Addenda of The Tenth Word; and every pillar together with its proofs forms a proof of his Messengership.

THE THIRD UNIVERSAL TESTIMONY: This is a testimony that contains thousands of other testimonies.

> Muhammad is the Messenger of God, ever truthful in his declarations and promises, and trustworthy, through the testimony of his person, upon him be peace and blessings, which is corroborated by his hundreds of miracles and perfections and by his excellent character.

That is: this person, upon him be peace and blessings, was proof for himself as brilliant as the sun. Through his hundreds of miracles and perfections and through his most elevated character and morality he testifies to his own Messengership and truthfulness most powerfully.

In the treatise entitled *Miracles of Muhammad*, around three hundred of his miracles have been proved based on sound narrations. For example, as declared explicitly in the verses, *And the moon split* (54:11), and *When you threw, it was not you who threw; but God threw* (8:17), the moon split in two at the movement of a single finger of his hand;[113] with the same hand he cast a handful of dust at an attacking enemy army, which then turned back and fled, blinded by the dust.[114] Water flowed forth in five springs from the five fingers of the same hand, providing enough to drink for a whole army of thirsty men, who testified to this miracle. This amazing event was repeated twice more in other places.[115] Also, small pebbles glorified God in the palm of that same hand, as though they were human, saying: "All-Glorified is God!"[116] Hundreds, indeed, according to verifying scholars, around a thousand miracles such as these are related in sound narrations, some of which appear in a number of reports from a number of reliable persons.

Also, according to friend and foe alike, Prophet Muhammad had praiseworthy attributes and a most excellent character;[117] it is also agreed

---

113 *al-Bukhari*, "Manaqib" 27; *Muslim*, "Munafiqun" 43–48.

114 *Muslim*, "Jihad" 81; Ahmad ibn Hanbal, *al-Musnad*, 1:303.

115 *al-Bukhari*, "Manaqib" 25; *Muslim*, "Fadail" 6, 7.

116 al-Bukhari, *al-Tarikhu'l-Kabir*, 8:442; al-Bazzar, *al-Musnad*, 9:431.

117 The fourth Caliph 'Ali, who was a hero of courage, says: "When we were frightened at war, we took shelter behind God's Messenger, upon him be peace and blessings." Histories re-

unanimously and confirmed to the degree of certainty based on experience by all the people of truth who have attained spiritual perfection through following him and attained the truth with certainty of observation that the attainments of Prophet Muhammad, upon him be peace and blessings, were of the very highest order. The historic spiritual and intellectual achievements of the Muslim world, attained through reliance on the Religion he communicated, as well as the truths of mighty Islam itself, form another proof of his extraordinary perfections. This surely means that this person, upon him be peace and blessings, testifies in a most brilliant and universal fashion to his own Messengership.

THE FOURTH TESTIMONY: This comprises numerous powerful testimonies.

> Muhammad is the Messenger of God, ever truthful in his declarations and promises, and trustworthy, through the testimony of the Qur'an, with all its innumerable truths and proofs.

That is, with its innumerable truths and proofs, the Qur'an of miraculous exposition testifies to the Messengership and truthfulness of Muhammad, upon him be peace and blessings.

The Qur'an is miraculous in forty respects and has illuminated fourteen centuries, governing through its unchanging laws one-fifth of humankind. Also, from the time of its revelation, it has challenged all of its opponents to produce its like, or even an approximation of its shortest *sura*, yet no one has ever dared, or been able to produce anything like it. Furthermore, and as explained convincingly in *The Supreme Sign*, the Qur'an's six aspects are luminous and cannot be penetrated by doubts: its being God's Word is endorsed by six supreme levels of proof, and is based on six unshakeable truths. Also, the Qur'an is recited with enthusiasm and respect at every moment by hundreds of millions of tongues, and is inscribed most reverently in the hearts of thousands of memorizers. The belief and testimony of all Muslims are based on the Qur'an's testimony to all the truths of belief and Islam and all the sciences of belief and Islam flow forth from it. Just as it affirms all the previous revealed Scriptures (in their original forms as being God's Words), so too the Qur'an is affirmed by them. Thus, with all its truths and all the proofs of its being God's Word, the mighty Qur'an testi-

---

cord that even his enemies confirmed that Muhammad, upon him be peace and blessings, was the most courageous of people.

fies to the veracity and Messengership of Muhammad, upon him be peace and blessings,.

THE FIFTH, SIXTH, SEVENTH AND EIGHTH UNIVERSAL TESTIMONIES

> Muhammad is the Messenger of God, ever truthful in his declarations and promises, and trustworthy, through the testimony of *al-Jawshaul-Kabir* with the sacredness of its indications, the *Risale-i Nur* with the strength of its proofs, the past with the unanimity of its signs indicating a future Prophet, and the future with the confirmation of thousands of its events.

That is to say, *al-Jawshanu'l-Kabir*, which indicates a thousand and one Divine Names explicitly or allusively, is a wonderful supplication that in one respect proceeds from the Qur'an. It is superior to all the other supplications written or compiled and recited by those who have advanced in knowledge of God. It is an invocation that the Archangel Gabriel advised the Messenger to read during a war. Thus, all the truths it contains and all of its perfectly accurate descriptions of the Lord testify to the Messengership and truthfulness of Muhammad, upon him be peace and blessings. In addition, with its one hundred and thirty parts, the *Risale-i Nur*, which is based on the Qur'an and establishes all the truths of Muhammad's Messengership rationally and logically, teaches matters that are philosophically abstruse and complex in the most reasonable and easy fashion, as though they were clearly observable or discernible with eye. Thus, the *Risale-i Nur* is also a universal proof of the Messengership and truthfulness of Muhammad, upon him be peace and blessings.

Also, the past—before his birth—was a universal witness to his Messengership, for numerous extraordinary incidents known as *irhasat* that occurred before the beginning of his Prophethood and which are related in the histories and books of his biography narrated through reliable channels testify to his Messengership soundly and reliably. These are of many different sorts. Some of them will be mentioned below, while others are related in the form of sound narrations in The Nineteenth Letter (Miracles of Muhammad) and in various historical works.

For example, close to the time of the Prophet's birth, upon him be peace and blessings, stones rained down from the claws of a flock of *ababil* (a kind of bird unknown in Arabia) on the heads of the troops of Abraha, the Yemenite governor of Abyssinia, who had come to destroy the Ka'ba;[118] on the night of Prophet Muhammad's birth, the idols in the Ka'ba all toppled over,[119] and the palace of the Persian Emperor Khusraw was destroyed.[120] The fire of the Zoroastrians, which had been burning continuously for a thousand years in their fire temples, was also extinguished that night.[121] Bahira the monk[122] and Halima as-Sa'diya reported that clouds shaded Muhammad when he was a young boy.[123] Numerous incidents such as these foretold his Prophethood before he actually declared it himself.

Also, there were numerous events that he predicted would occur in the future, that is, after his death. Some were predictions concerning his Family and Companions and Muslim conquests. Around eighty of these are mentioned in The Nineteenth Letter (Miracles of Muhammad), together with their authentic sources, on the basis of historical documentation and the Prophet's biography. All of these predictions—for example, the martyrdom of 'Uthman, may God be pleased with him, while reading the Qur'an;[124] the martyrdom of Husayn, may God be pleased with him, at Karbala;[125] the conquests of Syria,[126] and Iran,[127] and Istanbul;[128] the emergence of the 'Abbasid dynasty[129] and its eventual destruction at the hand of Genghis and Hulagu[130]—have turned out to be true. And so, with other predictions of his that either have come true or are yet to come true in order to prove the veracity of Prophet Muhammad, upon him be peace and blessings, the future—the time after his death—testifies also in powerful and universal fashion to Muhammad's Messengership and the truthfulness of his claim.

---

118 Ibn Hisham, *as-Siratu'n-Nabawiyya*, 1:168–173; Ibn Sa'd, *at-Tabaqatu'l-Kubra*, 1:91–92.

119 al-Bayhaqi, *ad-Dalailu'n-Nubuwwa*, 1:19; as-Suyuti, *al-Hasaisu'l-Kubra*, 1:81.

120 al-Bayhaqi, *ibid.*, 1:19, 126; Abu Nu'aym, *ad-Dalailu'n-Nubuwwa*, 139.

121 al-Bayhaqi, *ibid.*, 1:19, 126; Abu Nu'aym, *ibid.*, 139.

122 *at-Tirmidhi*, "Manaqib" 3; al-Hakim, *al-Mustadrak*, 2:672.

123 Ibn Sa'd, *at-Tabaqatu'l-Kubra*, 1:112; Qadi 'Iyaz, *ash-Shifa*, 1:368.

124 al-Hakim, *al-Mustadrak*, 3:110; Qadi 'Iyaz, *ash-Shifa*, 1:339.

125 Ahmad ibn Hanbal, *al-Musnad*, 3:242, 256; al-Hakim, *al-Mustadrak*, 3:197.

126 *al-Bukhari*, "Fadailu Madina," 5; *Muslim*, "Hajj" 496–497.

127 *al-Bukhari*, "Jihad" 157; Ahmad ibn Hanbal, *al-Musnad*, 5:86–87.

128 Ahmad ibn Hanbal, *al-Musnad*, 4:335; al-Bukhari, *al-Tarikhu'l-Kabir*, 2:81; al-Hakim, *al-Mustadrak*, 4:468.

129 Ahmad ibn Hanbal, *al-Musnad*, 1:209; al-Bayhaqi, *ad-Dalailu'n-Nubuwwa*, 6:517.

130 al-Munawi, *Faydu'l-Qadir*, 4:4; Ibn 'Ashur, *at-Tahrir wa't-Tanwir*, 8:423.

THE NINTH, TENTH, ELEVENTH, AND TWELFTH TESTIMONIES

> Muhammad is the Messenger of God, ever truthful in his declarations and promises, and trustworthy through the testimony of Muhammad's Family to his truthfulness through the power of their belief at the degree of certainty based on experience, and of his Companions with their perfect belief at the degree of certainty based on vision or observation, and of the purified scholars with the power of their investigations and verifications at the degree of certainty based on knowledge, and of the spiritual poles with their agreement on his Messengership based on their verified illuminations and unveilings.

That is to say, among the universal testimonies to Muhammad's truthfulness in his claim and veracity are included the following:

The ninth: The members of the Family of Muhammad, upon him be peace and blessings, are foremost in being honored with the Prophet's description: "The scholars of my community are like the Prophets of the Children of Israel"[131] (in the mission they shoulder and perform, apart, of course, from receiving Revelation). They are also mentioned together with the Prophets of the Family of Abraham, upon him be peace and blessings, when God's blessings and peace are called upon them. With their absolutely certain belief based on experience, their spiritual unveilings, illuminations, and visions, with their wonder-working and the extraordinary guidance they have given the Muslim community, the great saints, spiritual poles, and imams among this Family, such as 'Ali, Hasan, Husayn and the rest of the Twelve Imams from the Prophet's Family,[132] and individuals such as Ghawthu'l-A'zam 'Abdu'l-Qadir al-Jilani, Ahmad ar-Rufa'i, Ahmad al-Badawi, Ibrahim ad-Dassuqi, and Abu'l-Hasan ash-Shadhili[133]—all of these ratified through their belief and testimonies the veracity of Muhammad, upon him be peace and blessings, and his Prophethood.

---

131 al-Munawi, *Faydu'l-Qadir*, 4:384.

132 The Twelve Imams are: 'Ali ibn Abi Talib, Hasan son of 'Ali, Husayn son of 'Ali, 'Ali Zaynu'l-'Abidin son of Husayn, Muhammad al-Baqir son of 'Ali Zaynu'l-'Abidin, Ja'far as-Sadiq son of Muhammad al-Baqir, Musa Kazim son of Ja'far as-Sadiq, 'Ali ar-Riza son of Musa Kazim, Muhammad at-Taqiy son of 'Ali ar-Riza, 'Ali an-Naqiy son of Muhammad at-Taqiy, Hasan al-Askari son of 'Ali an-Naqiy, Muhammad al-Mahdi son of 'Ali an-Naqiy. (Tr.)

133 Shaykh Hasan ash-Shadhili (1195–1258): One of the leading, most celebrated saints of Islam. He lived in Tunus and died during his last journey to Makka for pilgrimage. He founded the Shadhiliyah, one of the most important Sufi brotherhoods. (Tr.)

The tenth: Despite being illiterate Bedouins in the beginning, the Companions of the Prophet, regarded as the most elevated and esteemed group after the Prophets, drew on the light of Muhammad, upon him be peace and blessings, and in a short time came to govern with justice a very wide area of the Middle East and Northern Africa, ruling a Caliphate that stretched from Spain to China. They defeated the world-powers of the time and became masters, teachers, judges, and just administrators of the then advanced, educated, and civilized nations, turning that century into an age of happiness. After scrutinizing every aspect of the Prophet's conduct, and through the power of the many miracles they witnessed with their own eyes, they abandoned their former enmities and the ways of their forefathers, with many of them—Khalid ibn Walid[134] and Ikrima ibn Abi Jahl[135] for example—giving up the tribalism of their fathers. They embraced Islam with theirs hearts and souls and, in a truly devoted and self-sacrificing fashion, believed in the veracity of Muhammad, upon him be peace and blessings, and his Messengership to the degree of certainty based on vision or observation. This is an unshakeable, universal testimony.

The eleventh: Based on thousands of categorical arguments and definite proofs, thousands of punctilious scholars, including particularly the top-level religious scholars who are described as the purified, truthful ones, and brilliant philosophers such as Ibn Sina (Avicenna)[136] and Ibn Rushd (Averroes),[137] have, while each following their own way, believed in the

---

134 Khalid ibn Walid (592?–642) is one of the most famous, invincible generals of human history. He was the commander in Makkan army who caused the Muslims' setback at the second stage of the Battle of Uhud in 625. He embraced Islam after the Treaty of Hudaybiya in 627. He victoriously fought against the apostate dissidents after the death of the Prophet, defeated the Byzantines in Yarmuk, and conquered Syria and many cities in Anatolia. (Tr.)

135 Ikrima ibn Abi Jahl (d., 635), the son of Abu Jahl, was, like his father, one of the most refractory and bitterest enemies of Islam and God's Messenger, upon him be peace and blessings. He became a Muslim after the conquest of Makka. He was martyred at the Battle of Yarmuk. (Tr.)

136 Abu 'Ali ibn Sina (Avicenna) (980–1037): One of the foremost philosophers, mathematicians, and physicians of the golden age of Islamic tradition. In the West he is also known as the "Prince of Physicians" for his famous medical text *al-Qanun* ("Canon.") In Latin translations, his works influenced many Christian philosophers, most notably Thomas Aquinas. (Tr.)

137 Ibn Rushd, Muhammad ibn Ahmad (1126–1198 ce) was a master of early Islamic philosophy, Islamic theology, Maliki law and jurisprudence, logic, psychology, Arabic music theo-

veracity of Muhammad, upon him be peace and blessings, and his Messengership at the degree of certainty based knowledge. Theirs is such a universal testimony that no one can oppose them unless their intelligence is the combination of all these great thinkers, or perhaps even greater.

The *Risale-i Nur* may be counted among the last of these innumerable witnesses.

The twelfth: Based on illumination, vision, and unveiling or spiritual discovery, the spiritual "poles," who are among the most profound of the veracious ones and each of whom has drawn into the circle of his instruction a significant part of the Muslim community, causing them to advance spiritually with their extraordinary guidance and wonder-working—all of these poles have discerned in their spiritual progress that Muhammad, upon him be peace and blessings, was the Messenger of God, that he was absolutely truthful in his claims, and that his veracity was of the very highest degree. Their unanimous and mutually supportive testimony to his Prophethood forms such a confirmation that no one who has not yet attained a degree of perfection as elevated as all of them together is able to annul it.

THE THIRTEENTH TESTIMONY: This consists of four universal, definite, and extremely extensive proofs:

> Muhammad is the Messenger of God, ever truthful in his declarations and promises, and trustworthy through the testimony of the past with the agreed predictions of seers, certain classes of spirit beings, and gnostics, and through the testimony of the glad tidings of Muhammad's Messengership of the previous Messengers and Prophets in the previous holy Scriptures.

A brief explanation of the above passage will be given here; a more detailed account, including relevant chains of transmission, can be found at the end of Miracles of Muhammad (The Nineteenth Letter).

There are sound narrations, some of which are based on several chains of reliable narrators, in the histories and books of *Hadith* and biography, which report that the most prominent and famous among humankind in past

---

ry, and the sciences of medicine, astronomy, geography, mathematics and physics. He lived in Spain, and died in Morocco. He was known in the West by his Latinized name, Averroes. He has been described as the founding father of secular thought in Western Europe. He wrote about 70 works in different fields of science. (Tr.)

times, in particular the Prophets and the gnostics, seers, and certain jinn, unanimously, explicitly, and repeatedly foretold the coming of Muhammad, upon him be peace and blessings. The most powerful and certain of these thousands of predictions are detailed in The Nineteenth Letter titled *Miracles of Muhammad*. Referring the reader to that treatise, here let us just give a brief indication:

Out of hundreds of verses in the revealed Scriptures—the Torah, the Psalms, and the Gospels—twenty verses that are almost explicit with regard to the Prophethood of Muhammad, upon him be peace and blessings, are mentioned in The Nineteenth Letter (Miracles of Muhammad). Husayn al-Jisri[138] discovered a hundred verses alluding to Muhammad's Prophethood in these Books, despite the numerous corruptions and alterations the Jews and Christians had made in them, and recorded them in his book.

According to a sound narration transmitted by numerous reliable narrators, the seers, and in particular Shiqq and Satih, who by means of jinn and spirit beings were able to give information about the Unseen,[139] explicitly predicted the appearance of a Prophet in the Hijaz, and that he would destroy the Persian Empire. Similarly, Ka'b ibn Lu'ayy, a gnostic and one of the Prophet's forefathers, together with many other gnostics and saints of the time, such as the rulers of Yemen and Abyssinia, Sayf ibn Dhi Yazan and Tubba, clearly predicted the Messengership of Muhammad, upon him be peace and blessings, proclaiming it in their poetry.[140] The most significant and veracious of these are included in The Nineteenth Letter. One of those kings even said: "I would prefer to be a servant of Muhammad than to rule this kingdom."[141] Another said: "If I had lived long enough to see him, I

---

138 Husayn al-Jisri (1845–1909) was born and mainly lived in Lebanon. He was well versed in Islamic sciences, and had an interest in natural sciences. He founded a *madrasa* where both kinds of sciences were taught. His thoughts greatly resembled those of Said Nursi about both religious and contemporary issues. His most famous work is *Risalati Hamidiya*. (Tr.)

139 Before Islam, God allowed some of jinn and other kinds of spirit beings to rise to the heavens in order to listen to the conversations of angels. They conveyed what they heard to seers, who are today called mediums. However, when the Qur'an began to be revealed, God no longer permitted jinn and other kinds of spirit beings to eavesdrop on angels. (Tr.)

140 See Ibn Hisham, *as-Siratu'n-Nabawiyya*, 1:29–30, 124–129, 158, 190–192; Ibn Sa'd, *at-Tabaqatu'l-Kubra*, 1:158–159; Ibn Kathir, *al-Bidaya wa'n-Nihaya*, 2:244; al-Bayhaqi, *ad-Dalailu'n-Nubuwwa*, 1:126–130, 2:12; Abu Nu'aym, *ad-Dalailu'n-Nubuwwa*, 90, 97–98, 125–128. (Tr.)

141 *Abu Dawud*, "Jana'iz" 58; Ahmad ibn Hanbal, *al-Musnad*, 1:461.

would have been his cousin."[142] By this he meant that he would have been a self-sacrificing servant and minister to him, like 'Ali ibn Abi Talib was. The histories and books of the Prophet's biography have included all these prophecies, showing that the gnostics affirmed the veracity of Muhammad, upon him be peace and blessings, and his Messengership with a powerful, universal testimony.

Also, like these gnostics and soothsayers, spirit beings called *hatif*, which are heard but not seen, made explicit predictions about Muhammad's Messengership. Moreover, by foretelling his Prophethood, many other creatures and objects even affirmed his Messengership and his truthfulness: animals that were sacrificed to idols and, with the inscriptions on them, the idols themselves and gravestones bore witness, testifying through the tongue of history.

THE FOURTEENTH TESTIMONY: The following, originally written in Arabic, indicates the powerful testimony of the universe:

> Muhammad is the Messenger of God, ever truthful in his declarations and promises, and trustworthy through the testimony of the universe to the all-embracing Messengership of Muhammad, upon him be peace and blessings, with all its aims and the Divine purposes in it, for the realization of these aims and the Divine purposes in it, the establishment of its value and the performance of its duties, the manifestation of its beauties and perfections, and the realization of the wisdom in its truths are dependent upon the existence of humankind and the Messengership of Muhammad, upon him be peace and blessings, as his Messengership revealed these and was the means of their realization. Had it not been for his Messengership, this perfect universe, this great and eternally meaningful book, would have existed for nothing: its meanings would have vanished and its perfections would have been totally diminished, which is impossible for numerous reasons.

In The Supreme Sign (The Seventh Ray), the above passage is interpreted in the following way:

Just as the universe indicates its Maker, Author, and Inscriber—the One Who has created it, organized it, and Who administers it, and the One Who, in decorating, determining, and planning it, directs and maintains it as

[142] Ibn Kathir, *al-Bidaya wa'n-Nihaya*, 2:166; *Tafsiru'l-Qur'an*, 4:145; al-Qurtubi, *al-Jami' li-Ahkami'l-Qur'an*, 16:145.

though it were a palace, a book, an exhibition hall, or an art gallery, there also must be an elevated herald, a truthful discoverer, an exacting master, and a faithful teacher who will understand the Divine purposes in creation and make them known. This demands the existence of one who will teach the instances of the wisdom of Lordship that are inherent in the universe's changes and transformations, and who will announce the results of its dutiful motions, proclaiming its innate value and the perfections of the beings within it. This herald, discoverer, master, and teacher will also answer incredible questions, such as: From where do these beings come? Where are they going? Why are they coming here? Why do they stay only a short while and then depart? In this way he will interpret the meanings of that macro-book and the phenomena of its creation and operation, all of which indicate its Creator and Director. Thus, the universe testifies to the veracity of Muhammad, upon him be peace and blessings, in a powerful and universal fashion; it was he who performed these duties better than anyone, and he was the highest and most loyal official of the Creator of the universe. The universe thereby affirms: "I bear witness that Muhammad is the Messenger of God."

Through the light which Muhammad, upon him be peace and blessings, brought, the nature, value and perfections of the universe come to be known, and the duties, results, and value of the beings within it, together with the fact that they are dutiful officials of the Creator, can be perceived. From the top to the bottom, the universe has proved to be a collection of Divine missives full of meaning, an embodied Qur'an of the Lord, and a magnificent exhibition of the All-Glorified One's works. It would otherwise have become a desolate, confused ruin—a terrifying place of mourning, crumbling under the veils of the darkness of decay, death, non-existence, and nothingness. It is in consequence of this truth that the perfections of the universe, the wise changes and transformations in it, and its eternal meanings all declare in powerful fashion: "We bear witness that Muhammad is the Messenger of God!"

THE FIFTEENTH TESTIMONY: The following, originally written in Arabic, consists of numerous sacred testimonies. It indicates the sacred testimony to the Messengership of Muhammad, upon him be peace and blessings, which issues from the acts of the Lordship and deeds of the Mercifulness of the Necessarily Existent One, Who directs and controls the universe, and through Whose Will, Command, and Power all change and transformation occur, as well as all motion and rest, all life and death throughout the universe, from the minutest particles to the planets.

> Muhammad is the Messenger of God, ever truthful in his declarations and promises, and trustworthy through the testimony of the universe's Owner, Creator, Director, and Controller to the Messengership of Muhammad, upon him be peace and blessings, with the deeds of His Mercifulness and acts of His Lordship. Included among the deeds of His Mercifulness are the facts that God sent down the miraculously eloquent Qur'an to Muhammad, that He displayed a great variety of miracles through Muhammad's hand, that He helped and protected Muhammad in all circumstances and perpetuated the Religion and all its truths, and that God raised Muhammad to a position of high respect and honor, favoring him above all creatures; all of this is visible and observable. Among the acts of His Lordship are that God made Muhammad's Prophethood a spiritual sun in the universe, He made the Religion that Muhammad brought the source and index of all the perfections of His servants, God made his Truth a comprehensive mirror to the manifestations of His Divinity and God entrusting Muhammad with duties as indispensable for the existence of creatures in the universe as mercy, wisdom, and justice, and as necessary as food and water, and air and light.

Details of this most certain, extensive, and sacred testimony can be found in the *Risale-i Nur*; here we will give only a brief and concise meaning of it.

We see clearly that out of His general Acts and Deeds in the universe, in accordance with His Justice, Wisdom, Mercy, Favoring, and Protection, and as a usual practice of His Lordship, God Almighty protects the good and rains down blows on the wrongdoers and the mendacious.[143] Thus, as demanded by "the acts of His Mercifulness:"

- He revealed the miraculously eloquent Qur'an to Muhammad, upon him be peace and blessings;

---

143 Being devoid of a universal vision which can comprehend events with all their causes and results, we may not be able to discern Divine Justice in every event in the universe. While God Almighty executes absolute justice in the world with regard to people's deeds connected with the worldly life—everyone gets whatever they deserve according to the Divine laws of the worldly life—He usually defers to the Hereafter the recompense of "religiously" good or bad deeds, even though He helps the true believers who follow His Path carefully and act in accordance with the Religion that He sent and the laws of the worldly life He has established. (Tr.)

- He bestowed on him nearly a thousand miracles of varying sorts;
- He protected him with the utmost compassion in all dangerous circumstances and situations, even by means of a pigeon and a spider;[144]
- He gave him complete success in all his duties;
- He has perpetuated his Religion together with all its truths,
- and caused it to prevail over the earth and humankind.
- By granting Muhammad a position of honor above all creatures, a permanent rank of acceptance superior to all the pre-eminent of humankind and, as agreed by friend and foe alike, the highest character and qualities, God Almighty made one-fifth of humankind his community. All of these testify most decisively to his veracity and Messengership.
- We also see from the point of view of "the acts of Lordship" that the Director and Controller of this world has made the Messengership of Muhammad, upon him be peace and blessings, a sun in the universe, and as explained convincingly in the *Risale-i Nur*, He has dispelled all kinds of darkness with it and shown its luminous truths, and made all conscious beings, indeed the whole universe, rejoice at the glad tidings of eternal life.
- He has also made his Religion a source and index of the perfectibility of all the acceptable people of worship and a sound program for their acts of worship.
- Again, as demonstrated by the Qur'an and *al-Jawshanu'l-Kabir*, He has made the Muhammadan Truth or the Truth of Muhammad, upon him be peace and blessings, which is his collective, spiritual personality, a comprehensive mirror held up to the manifestations of His Divinity.
- Furthermore, as indicated by the above-mentioned truths, and by the fact that every day for fourteen centuries he has gained the equivalent of all the good deeds of all his community, and by his works and the traces of his deeds in human social and spiritual life He has made him the highest leader, master, and authority of humankind.

---

144 Ahmad ibn Hanbal, *al-Musnad*, 1:348; 'Abdu'r-Razzaq, *al-Musannaf*, 5:389; at-Tabarani, *al-Mu'jamu'l-Kabir*, 11:407; 20:443.

- Moreover, God Almighty sent Muhammad to the aid of humankind with sublime, sacred duties, and has made human beings as in need for his Religion[145] with all its truths as they are for mercy, wisdom, justice, food, air, water, and light.

And so, given that God Almighty has offered sacred testimony to the Messengership of Muhammad, upon him be peace and blessings, with the twelve universal, decisive proofs which have so far been mentioned and summed up in the fifteenth testimony, is it at all possible that the Messengership of Muhammad, upon him be peace and blessings, which has been supported by these twelve testimonies of the universe's Owner, Who is not indifferent to the ordering of the wing of a fly or the petal of a flower—is it at all possible that this Messengership should not be a sun of the universe?

Each of the fifteen universal testimonies mentioned comprises numerous testimonies, and through the tongue of miracles the third one even comprises nearly a thousand, thus proving the proclamation "I bear witness that Muhammad is the Messenger of God" most powerfully and definitively, and demonstrating its reality, value, and importance, so that five times a day in the *tashahhud*—the seated section of the Prayer—the world of Islam announces this fact to the universe with hundreds of millions of tongues. Also, billions of believers have accepted and affirmed without hesitation that the Truth of Muhammad, upon him be peace and blessings, which is the basis of that proclamation, is the original seed of the universe, the reason for its creation, and its most perfect fruit. Furthermore, the universe's

---

[145] In my old age and wretchedness, I perceived a millionth of the spiritual provision which Muhammad, upon him be peace and blessings, brought. If I had been able, I would have thanked him by calling God's blessings and peace on him with millions of tongues. It was like this:

> I suffer greatly from separation and decay, but the world and the things that I love in it leave me and depart. I know that I too will depart. And it is only by hearing from Muhammad, upon him be peace and blessings, the glad tidings of eternal happiness and everlasting life that I am saved from that severe pain and soul-searing despair and I find complete solace. In fact, when I say: "Peace be upon you, O Prophet, and God's mercy and blessings!" in the seated section *of* Prayers, I am both paying allegiance to him, and declaring my submission and obedience to his mission, and offering him congratulations on his duty, and expressing a sort of thanks and response to the glad tidings he brought of eternal happiness. All Muslims offer these greetings five times every day.

Owner, all-exalted is His Majesty, has made that spiritual collective personality of Muhammad, upon him be peace and blessings, the loudest herald of the sovereignty of His Lordship and the accurate discloser of the talisman of the universe and the riddle of creation; He has made him a shining exemplar of His Favor and Mercy and an eloquent tongue of His Compassion and Love; He has made him the most powerful bringer of the glad tidings of everlasting life and happiness in the eternal realm, and He has made him the final and greatest of His Messengers.

One who is not content with a truth such as this or who does not attach any importance to it should understand what a great error, foolishness, and crime they are committing and what a terrible loss they are suffering.

Thus, as indicated in Part Two, just as *Suratu'l-Fatiha* offers decisive proofs for the truth of Divine Unity which is expressed in the profession: "I bear witness that there is no deity but God," which is recited in the *tashahhud*, so too, this Third Part sets forth powerful evidence for the reality of Messengership as professed in the phrase: "I bear witness that Muhammad is the Messenger of God," which is also recited in the *tashahhud*, and stamps it with innumerable confirming signatures.

O Most Merciful of the Merciful! In veneration of Your noblest Messenger, upon him be peace and blessings, favor us with his intercession, enable us to follow his Sunna, and make us neighbors to his Family and Companions in the eternal realm of happiness! Amin. Amin. Amin.

> O God! Bestow blessings and peace on him, and on his Family and Companions, to the number of the letters of the Qur'an, both those recited and those written. Amin.
>
> All-Glorified are You! We have no knowledge save what You have taught us; surely You are the All-Knowing, the All-Wise.

The Second Station

In the Name of God, the All-Merciful, the All-Compassionate

And from Him do we seek help

One of the truths contained in the last verse of *Suratu'l-Fatiha*, which compares the people of guidance and the Straight Path with the people of misguidance and rebellion, and which is the source of all the comparisons in the *Risale-i Nur*, is also expressed in a most wonderful fashion by the following verse of *Suratu'n-Nur*:

> God is the Light of the heavens and the earth. The example of His Light is like a niche wherein is a lamp; the lamp is in a crystal, and the crystal is shining as if a pearl-like radiant star, lit from the oil of a blessed olive tree that is neither of the east nor of the west. The oil would almost give light of itself though no fire touches it. Light upon light! God guides to His Light whom He wills. God strikes parables for people. God has full knowledge of all things. (24:35)

and by the verse:

> Or their deeds are like veils of darkness covering up an abysmal sea down into its depths, covered up by a billow, above which is a billow, above which is a cloud: veils of darkness piled one upon another, so that when he stretches out his hand, he can hardly see it. For whomever God has appointed no light, no light has he. (24:40)

The first verse was the main reason for the name "*Nur*" (light) being given to the *Risale-i Nur* (The Treatises of Light). The traveler in The Supreme Sign (*Ayatu'l-Kubra*) questioned the entire universe and all beings in order to seek, find and learn about their Creator. They came to know Him through thirty-three ways and decisive proofs to the degrees of certainty based on knowledge and certainty based on vision or observation. This untiring, insatiable traveler also journeyed through the centuries and the various levels of the heavens and earth with their mind, heart and imagination, inspecting the entire world as though it were a single city. Having their reason dwell now on the Qur'an and now on philosophy, and gazing at the most distant levels through the powerful telescope of imagination, the traveler saw truths as they are in reality and in part informed us of them in The Supreme Sign.

Now, of these many worlds and levels that the traveler entered on their journey of the imagination, which was representational in nature and completely in conformity with reality, only three are explained here in brief in order to illustrate just one aspect of the comparison at the end of *Suratu'l-Fatiha*. It concerns the power of reason. The other visions of the traveler and other comparisons may be found in the relevant parts of *Risale-i Nur*.

THE FIRST EXAMPLE IS SIMILAR TO THE FOLLOWING

The traveler, who has come into the world only to find their Creator and attain knowledge of Him, addresses their reason thus: "We have asked everything about our Creator and have received perfectly satisfying answers. Now, as expressed in the proverb: "In order to learn about the sun one has to ask the sun itself," we will make a further journey in order to gain knowledge of our Creator through the manifestations of His sacred Attributes, such as Knowledge, Will and Power, and through His visible works and the manifestations of His Names." And so the traveler enters the world. Then in the manner of the people of misguidance—those who represent the second current or way mentioned at the end of *Suratu'l-Fatiha*—they embark on the ship of the earth. They put on the spectacles of the science and philosophy that do not follow the wisdom of the Qur'an, and look in accordance with the program of the geography that does not map out the Qur'an. They see the following:

The earth is traveling in an infinite void seventy times faster than a cannon-ball, covering a twenty-thousand-year distance in one year. It has taken upon itself millions of species of wretched, helpless living beings. The traveler realizes that if the earth were to confuse its way for even a minute, or were to collide with a stray star, it would break up and scatter throughout space, pouring all these wretched creatures into nothingness and non-existence. Perceiving the awesome calamity of the current indicated in the verse, *Not of those who have incurred Your wrath, nor of those who are astray*, and the suffocating gloom of the *veils of darkness covering up an abysmal sea down into its depths*, the traveler exclaims: "Alas! What have we done? Why did we get on this terrible ship? How are we to be saved?" Then smashing the spectacles of blind philosophy, the traveler joins the current of *Those whom You have favored (with true guidance)*. Suddenly the wisdom of the Qur'an comes to their aid, giving their reason a telescope that shows the exact truth of everything. "Look now!" it says. The traveler looks and sees the following:

The Name "the Lord of the heavens and earth" rises like a sun in the sign of *He it is Who has made the earth subservient to you (like a docile animal), so go about through its shoulders and eat of His provision* (67:15).[146] The Lord

[146] This verse is miraculous in meaning. It likens the earth to an animal which has been subservient to humankind for its benefits, although it travels very speedily in space. Its *shoulders* are its uplands or mountains, where provision for human beings are found deposited. (Tr.)

has made the earth like a well-organized and secure ship, filling it with living beings together with their provision, and causing it to journey around the sun in the ocean of the universe to attain numerous benefits and instances of wisdom, bringing the produce of the seasons to those who are in need of provision. The Lord has appointed the two angels *Thawr* (Ox) and *Hut* (Fish) as captains of the ship; they steer it on its voyage for the enjoyment of the All-Majestic Creator's creatures and guests, through the magnificent domain of the Lord. The traveler understands that this indicates the truth of *God is the Light of the heavens and the earth*, and thus makes known their Creator through the manifestations of this Name that is the Light. With all their heart and spirit the traveler exclaims: "*All praise and gratitude are for God, the Lord of the worlds*," and joins the group of *Those whom You have favored.*

THE SECOND EXAMPLE

The second example of what the traveler sees on their journey through the worlds is as follows:

Leaving the ship of the earth, the traveler enters the world of animals and humankind. They look at that world through the spectacles of the natural science that is devoid of spirit, and sees the following:

These innumerable living creatures have endless needs and are under constant attack from countless harmful enemies and pitiless events, while having a capital with which they can only meet a thousandth, nay, a hundred thousandth of their need. Their power too is perhaps a millionth of what is required to combat these harmful things. Feeling a connection with them on account of being an intelligent being and out of compassion for their fellow beings, the traveler pities them in their terrible plight and feels so sorry for them that they suffer hellish pain. They begin to regret a thousand times over ever having come to this wretched world when suddenly a flash of Qur'anic wisdom comes to their aid, giving them the telescope of *Those whom You have favored*, and saying: "Look!" The traveler looks through it and sees that through the manifestation of *God is the Light of the heavens and the earth*, numerous Divine Names, such as the All-Merciful, the All-Compassionate, the All-Providing, the All-Bestowing, the All-Munificent, and the All-Preserving are each rising like the sun in the signs of verses like: *No living creature is there but He holds it by its forelock* (11:56); *How many a living creature there is that does not carry its own provision in store but God provides for them, and indeed for you* (29:60); *Assuredly We have honored the children of Adam (with many distinctions)* (29:70), and *The virtuous and godly ones will indeed be in (the Gardens of) perpetual bliss* (82:13). Filling the world of humankind and animals with mercy and bounties, they transform it into some sort of temporary Paradise. The traveler now understands that these verses ensure that the All-Munificent Host of this spectacular, instructive guest-house is perfectly known. The traveler repeats a thousand times, *All praise and gratitude are for God, the Lord of the worlds*!

The Third example

What follows is the third example of the hundreds of observations of the traveler during their journey:

The traveler who wants to know their Creator through the manifestations of His Names and Attributes then says to their mind and imagination: "Come! Leaving our bodies behind on the earth, we will ascend to the heavens like the spirits and angels. We will ask the inhabitants of the heavens about our Creator." Their spirit mounts their imagination, their mind mounts their thought, and together they ascended to the heavens. They take astronomy as their guide and look with the view of the philosophy that does not heed the Religion, and the current of *Those who have incurred Your wrath* and *Those who are astray*. The traveler sees the following:

Thousands of heavenly bodies and fiery stars, each a thousand times larger than the earth and moving a hundred times faster than a cannon-ball, are spinning around unconsciously, lifelessly, aimlessly. If one of these bodies happens to lose its way for even a second, it will collide with another unconscious body in that infinite space, causing utter confusion and chaos, like Doomsday.

In whichever direction they look, the traveler is filled with terror and dismay: they are sorry a thousand times over that they have ascended to the heavens. Their mind and imagination are extremely upset and bewildered. The mind and imagination exclaim: "Our duty is to see and point out fine truths. We no longer want to observe or know such infernally ugly and tormenting spectacles; we withdraw from this task!" Then suddenly, through the manifestation of *God is the Light of the heavens and the earth*, numerous Names such as "the Creator of the heavens and the earth", "the Subjugator of the sun and moon", and "the Lord of the worlds" each rise like a sun in the signs of verses such as *And We have adorned the lowest heaven (the heaven of the world) with lamps* (67:5); *Do they, then, never observe the sky above them, how We have constructed it and adorned it?* (50:6), and ... *then He directed (His Knowledge, Will, Power, and Favor) to the heaven, and formed it into seven heavens* (2:20). They fill all the heavens with light and with angels, transforming it into a huge mosque and military encampment. The traveler enters the current of *Those whom You have favored*, and is saved from that of *Those who are astray* and *veils of darkness covering up an abysmal sea down into its depths*. The traveler sees a well-organized, beautiful, and magnificent land, as wonderful as Paradise itself. Observing that its inhabitants are making known the All-Majestic Creator, the value of the traveler's mind and imagination increases a thousand times over, and so does their task.

Referring to the *Risale-i Nur* the other observations of the traveler, which are comparable with these three, and the knowledge of the Necessarily Existent One which is acquired through the manifestations of His Names, here we will mention only certain brief indications. Like that traveler through the world, we will try to become acquainted very briefly with the Creator of the universe through the works and manifestations of Knowledge, Will, and Power, which are three of His seven sacred Attributes. For a detailed explanation, we refer you to the relevant parts of *the Risale-i Nur*.

Proofs of Divine Knowledge

The following piece, which is originally in Arabic, is an excerpt from my regular recitation. It expounds three of the thirty-three ranks of "God is the All-Great" (*Allahu akbar*). It serves to open up a way to discern and observe the manifestations of Divine Knowledge, Will, and Power in the universe and to acquire belief in them at the degree of certainty based on vision or observation. It also leads to the affirmation of the Existence and Unity of the Necessarily Existent One at the degree of certainty which is based on knowledge through these three Attributes.

In the Name of God, the All-Merciful, the All-Compassionate.

Say: "All praise and gratitude are for God, Who has neither taken to Himself a child, nor has a partner in the sovereignty (the dominion and ownership of the whole creation), nor (being exalted above all want or insuffi-

> *ciency) has He a guardian against neediness and weakness. And exalt Him in His immeasurable greatness* (17:111)."
>
> God is the All-Great, greater than all things in power and knowledge, for He knows all things with an all-encompassing Knowledge, indispensable to His Essence.[147] Nothing can be hidden from or escape It due to Its omnipresence and all-inclusiveness, and due to the fact that Existence demands universality and the light of Knowledge encompasses the entire realm of existence.
>
> Whatever is observed in the whole of creation, such as precise, measured orderliness ad balanced arrangement, an orderly measure and appropriate balance, all-inclusive and purposeful wisdom, all-embracing and particular favors, well-ordering decrees and fruitful determining, the appointed final ends and fixed, regular provisions, skillful precision and faultlessness, and pleasing, ornate care and attention (that is given to all things), as well as the absolutely perfect order, harmony, arrangement, precision, balance, and measure, as well as distinction with absolute ease—all these testify to the all-encompassing Knowledge of the Knower of the Unseen and of all things. *Should He Who creates not know? He is the All-Subtle, the All-Aware* (67:14). If the beauty of the art in one's work indicates one's consciousness to the extent of the infinitesimal light of a firefly on a pitch-dark night, humanity's creation indicates its Creator's Knowledge to the extent of the sun's splendor at noon.

Just as Mercy shows Itself as clearly as the sun through the wonders of provision and proves decisively the existence of an All-Merciful and Compassionate One behind the veil of the Unseen, so too, through the instances of wisdom and fruits of order and balance in things, Knowledge, Which is mentioned in hundreds of Qur'anic verses and Which, in one respect, is the chief of the seven sacred Attributes of the Divine Being, manifests Itself like the light of the sun, making known with certainty the Existence of One Knowledgeable of all things. The comparison between the ordered and measured arts of humans that indicate their consciousness and knowledge and their fine creation, indicating the Knowledge and Wisdom of their Creator, is like the comparison between the tiny glow of the firefly on a dark night and the encompassing light of the sun at noon.

---

147 *To God applies the most sublime description*: Knowledge is indispensable to the Divine Being like its encompassing light being indispensable to the sun.

THE SACRED CONVERSATION DURING THE PROPHET'S ASCENSION

Now, before explaining the proofs of Divine Knowledge, we will briefly mention the sacred conversation which took place during the Prophet's Ascension, which indicates that, on account of their being the manifestations of the Attribute of Knowledge, all living and non-living creatures make their Lord known to us. Being an envoy on behalf of all living beings and in the meaning of giving the greeting on behalf of all creatures, Prophet Muhammad, upon him be peace and blessings, said on that night: "All appreciative and grateful worship (performed by all living creatures through their lives) is God's; and so too is the congratulating and admiring worship (particular to and performed by all the living beings, especially through their seeds or eggs); and all the sanctifying and submissive worship (performed by all conscious beings); and all the conscious, adoring, and enthusiastic worship (performed by believing and knowledgeable humans, jinn, and angels)." Thus he presented their gifts to their Creator.

That is, with the four phrases mentioned above, that is, with *at-tahiyyat, al-mubarakat, as-salawat, at-tayyibat,* he offered up to God the appreciative, grateful, congratulating, admiring, sanctifying, submissive, adoring, and enthusiastic worship of the four main groups of living beings, which are based on the manifestations of Eternal Knowledge. It is for this reason that this recitation, in its broad meaning of this sacred conversation which occurred during the Ascension, has become an obligatory part of the *tashahhud* for all Muslims. A detailed explanation of that sacred conversation can be found in the *Risale-i Nur*, but we will expound one meaning of it in the form of four very brief indications.

The first is *at-tahiyyatu li'llah.* Its brief meaning is as follows:

For example, if a master craftsman makes a wonderful machine with their profound knowledge and miraculous intelligence, everyone who sees it applauds and congratulates them, offering them both material and immaterial gifts in the form of appreciative commendation and praise. The machine too, by displaying the master craftsman's purposes, as well as their wonderful, subtle art, skill, and knowledge, and by working perfectly in exactly the way desired, applauds and congratulates the craftsman through the language of its existence, in effect offering its maker immaterial gifts. Similarly, all living beings in the universe, individually and as different species, are in every respect miraculous, wonderful machines. In full appreciation and through the language of their existence and lives, humans, jinn and angels verbally applaud their All-Majestic Maker, Who sees the relationship of everything with each other and knows all the things necessary for the life of each, conveying them to each at the right time; it is He Who makes Himself known through the profound and subtle manifestations of His all-encompassing Knowledge. They declare: "*at-Tahiyyatu li'llah* (All appreciative and grateful worship is for God)." In the spirit of worship they offer the price of their lives directly to their Creator, Who knows all creatures together with all their states. On the night of the Ascension, in the name of all living creatures, Prophet Muhammad, upon him be peace and blessings, said: "All appreciative and grateful worship is for God!" when greeting the Necessarily Existent One in His Presence, and offered appreciative thanks, gifts, and greetings from all species of living beings.

Just as with its order and balance, an ordinary well-designed and well-working machine undoubtedly demonstrates the existence of a meticulous, skilful craftsman, so too do each of the numberless living machines which fill the universe display a thousand and one miracles of Knowledge. Thus, by being the manifestations of Knowledge, living beings testify to the necessary Existence of their eternal Maker and to His being the All-Worshipped One. If we compare the testimony of a machine to its maker or craftsman to the feeble glow of a firefly, their testimony to the Necessarily Existent One is as brilliant as the light of the sun.

The second sacred word from the Ascension is *al-mubarakat*.

According to a *hadith*, the canonical Prayers are the believer's ascension[148] and are honored with the manifestation of the supreme Ascension of Prophet Muhammad, upon him be peace and blessings. And since the traveler throughout the universe (in The Supreme Sign) finds that their Creator possesses the Attribute of the All-Knowing of the Unseen in every world, we will accompany the traveler and enter the broad world of blessed things, which make those who see them utter: "May God bless them! How great are God's blessings!" Like the traveler, we will observe the world of "blessed beings," primarily the innocent, blessed infants of beings with spirits, and the seeds of living creatures, which are the tiny containers of the

---

148 as-Suyuti, *Sharhu Sunan-i Ibn Maja*, 313; al-Munawi, *Faydu'l-Qadir*, 1:497.

programs of their lives; through studying them we will attempt to know our Creator to the degree of certainty based on knowledge through the miraculous, subtle manifestations of His sacred Attribute of Knowledge.

We see with our own eyes that through the Knowledge of an All-Wise and All-Knowing One, all these innocent, new-born infants and blessed tiny treasuries and containers—both collectively and individually—awaken suddenly and proceed to realize the aim of their creation. They cause those who observe them with the eye of truth to exclaim: "May God bless these a thousand times over! What limitless wonders God has willed!"

For example, all seeds, eggs, sperm and grains, both individually and collectively, demonstrate visibly through the following fifteen languages the marvels of their Maker's skills and His miraculous Knowledge, making known the One All-Knowing of the Unseen, their Necessarily Existent Maker as clearly as the sun:

- They have a precise, measured orderliness and balanced arrangement established by Knowledge;
- that order is based on a perfect measure balance, which is the result of clear skill;
- the balance is established and continues through constant reordering;
- the reordering is effected through a constant measuring and balancing;
- the measuring and balancing occur together with perfect distinguishing and nurturing, demonstrating the intentional differentiation of each being from its fellow beings;
- this differentiation and nurturing take place within the acts of ornamentation and artistic adorning;
- ornamentation happens within the giving of wise, appropriate, and perfect forms and members;
- this giving of form takes place in order to satisfy the tastes of those desirous of sustenance, and to bring about differences in the flesh and edible parts of those edible creatures and fruits;
- these differences are realized through miraculous and multifarious designs and embroideries, which reflect Knowledge;
- the designs and embroideries are combined with pleasing smells and delicious tastes which are all different;

- all of these occur together, but with perfect order and absolute discernment,
- and with the utmost speed and in absolute abundance,
- yet without any fault or error;
- this wonderful reality is the same throughout the whole of time.

It is because of these extensive and brilliant testimonies of animate creatures to their Maker that on the night of the Ascension, when speaking on behalf of all creatures, Prophet Muhammad, upon him be peace and blessings, said "*al-mubarakat* (all congratulating and admiring worship [particular to and performed by all living creatures, especially through their seeds or eggs)" when he greeted the Necessarily Existent One.

The third word is *as-salawat.*

Prophet Muhammad, upon him be peace and blessings, uttered this sacred word during his supreme Ascension, and hundreds of millions of believers offer it to the Divine Court at least ten times every day when they perform the *tashahhud* during the canonical Prayers, which are known as the "ascension of the believers." In fact they proclaim it to the universe. The truths of the Ascension have been expounded in The Thirty-First Word in a powerful and decisive fashion, even to obdurate, materialist deniers, whom it in part addresses. Here, very briefly, we will take a look at the strange world of the various kinds of conscious beings and beings with spirits, which illustrates the extensive meaning of this third word of the Ascension. In so doing we will try to understand by means of the manifestation of His eternal Knowledge the perfect Mercy and Compassion of our Creator, and the vastness of His Power and all-encompassing Will in the context of His Existence and Unity.

We see in this world that all beings with spirit are aware, be it consciously and rationally or otherwise, that despite their absolute impotence and weakness, they have innumerable adversaries and harmful things ranged against them, and that despite their limitless poverty and want they have endless needs and desires. Since their power and capital are not sufficient to meet even a thousandth of these, they cry out and weep with all their might, and through the discourse of their natures they implore and entreat. Each one of them with its own particular voice and language offers invocations, entreaties, prayers of a sort, and appeals to the Court of the One Who is All-Knowing and All-Powerful. We observe clearly that an All-Wise, All-Powerful, and All-Knowing One Who perceives all the needs of those crying out, understands their troubles and plight and hears their pleas and innate petitions, coming to their aid and performing all that they wish. He transforms their laments into smiles and their cries into thanks. This wise, knowing, compassionate help makes known, in a truly brilliant fashion through the manifestations of Knowledge and Mercy, One Who answers prayers and helps, One Who is the All-Munificent and All-Compassionate. During his Supreme Ascension, Prophet Muhammad, upon him be peace and blessings, said: "All sanctifying and submissive worship (performed by all conscious beings), and all conscious, adoring, and enthusiastic worship (performed by believing and knowledgeable humans, jinn, and angels) is for God," while offering to Him exclusively all the supplications and worship of the world of beings with spirits. The Community of Prophet Muhammad recites these expressions during the Prayers, which are lesser ascension.

The fourth sacred word is *at-tayyibat li'llah*!"

The sacred word *at-tayyibat* (all conscious, adoring and enthusiastic worship) refers to the good words, deeds, and worship of humans, jinn, angels, and other kinds of spirit beings, who are people of knowledge of God and belief, and who, with universal consciousness, beautify the universe with their good words, deeds, and acts of worship. They are always turned to the world of beauties and understand fully the infinite beauties of the eternal, absolutely Beautiful and Gracious One and the perpetual beauties of His Names which adorn the universe; they respond to them with passion, ardor, and universal adoration. As this word was offered to the Creator during the Ascension in the spirit of radiant belief, extensive knowledge of Him, and praise and laudation, together with the fragrant scents they produce, the Muslim Community repeats it during the *tashahhud* every day without tiring.

The universe is the mirror of an infinite, perpetual Beauty and Grace, and consists of Its manifestations. All the beauty and perfections of the universe come from that eternal Beauty and become beautiful and increase in value through their connection with It. The universe would otherwise be a ruin, a house of sorrows. What that connection means is understood through the knowledge and affirmation of humans, angels, and spirit beings, who are the heralds and announcers of the sovereignty of God. In order to broadcast everywhere the beautiful, sweet praise and laudation of those heralds of the One Whom they worship, and to send them up toward the Sublime Throne and offer these good words to the Divine Court, it is quite possible that the element of the air has been given a truly strange and remarkable state whereby its atoms, like dutiful soldiers, are miniscule tongues and ears.

Thus, just as through their belief and their worship, humans and angels make known the All-Majestic, All-Worshipped One, so through making each of those announcers a microcosm connected to the entire universe through the comprehensive capacities, wonderful faculties, and subtleties of knowledge that He has given them, the All-Majestic, All-Wise One makes Himself known in brilliant fashion. For example, by creating numerous amazing machines in a space the size of a walnut in the human head – namely faculties such as memory, imagination, and thought – and by making memory into a large library, God shows Himself as clearly as the sun through the manifestation of His Eternal Knowledge.

THE FIFTEEN ARGUMENTS FOR DIVINE KNOWLEDGE MENTIONED ABOVE

We will now indicate a very brief meaning of that which is mentioned above under the title of Proofs of Divine Knowledge. Originally in Arabic, it is a comprehensive proof of the all-encompassing Knowledge and consists of fifteen arguments. We will give a brief explanation of them.

The first of the fifteen arguments: *a precise, measured orderliness and balanced arrangement*

That is, the measured orderliness and balanced arrangement observed in all creatures testify to an all-encompassing Knowledge. In everything—from the totality of the universe, which is like a well-built, well-organized palace, with the solar system and the atmosphere around us, the element of the air, the atoms of which display an amazing order in the broadcasting of words and sounds, and with the earth, where every spring hundreds of thousands of different species are raised with perfect order and regularity, down to the organs, the bodily systems, the cells and atoms of all living beings—there is a perfectly balanced orderliness and arrangement which can only be the work of a profound, comprehensive, and infallible knowledge. This testifies to an all-encompassing Knowledge in an extremely clear and decisive manner.

The second argument: *an orderly measure and appropriate balance*

In all the creatures in the universe, in everything, be it particular or universal, from the celestial bodies of space to the red and white corpuscles in the blood, there is a most orderly measure and appropriate balance or harmony. This testifies self-evidently and decisively to an all-encompassing Knowledge. We see, for instance, that the organs, members, and bodily systems of a fly or human being, even the cells of the body and the red and white corpuscles in the blood, are positioned in such a way that they are in complete harmony with one another, with a balance and measure so fine that it is in no way possible that one who lacks infinite knowledge could have given them these positions.

The existence of so perfect a balance and so regular and unfailing a measure in all animate and inanimate creatures, from the minute particles to the planets of the solar system, most brilliantly testifies to an all-encompassing Knowledge. This means that all the proofs of Knowledge are also proofs of the Existence of the All-Knowing One. Since it is impossible that there should be an attribute without the thing it qualifies, all the proofs of Knowledge form a powerful and most conclusive proof of the necessary Existence of the Eternal All-Knowing.

The third argument: *all-inclusive, purposeful wisdom*

In all the creativity and activity in the universe, and in all the changes, in the restoring to life, in the employing of beings in duties and their being discharged from them, in all individual creatures and species there are functions, benefits and purposes which are so deliberate that there is no room for chance. We see that one who does not possess all-encompassing knowledge could in no way claim to be their creator or maker. For example, although it is only a piece of flesh, the tongue, which is one of about a hundred members of the body of a human individual, himself or herself only one of innumerable animate creatures, is the means for hundreds of instances of wisdom, results, fruits, and uses through its basic duties. Its duty of tasting foods consists in recognizing all the different flavors and informing the body and the stomach of them and in being an exacting inspector of the kitchens of Divine Mercy. Its duty of speech lies in its being an accurate interpreter and telephone exchange for the heart, spirit, and mind in the function of speech. With these two basic duties, the tongue testifies most brilliantly and decisively to an all-encompassing knowledge.

If through its purposes and fruits a single tongue provides such evidence, innumerable languages and living and non-living beings testify to an infinite Knowledge with the clarity and certainty of the noonday sun. They announce that there is nothing at all outside the bounds of the Knowledge of the One All Knowing of the Unseen, and outside His Wisdom and Will.

The fourth argument: *all-embracing, particular favors*

The favors and instances of compassion and protection bestowed on all living creatures in the world of conscious beings, on every species and individual, particularly and appropriately, point self-evidently to an all-encompassing Knowledge and provide innumerable testimonies to the necessary Existence of an All-Knowing Gracious One, Who knows those who receive the favors and their needs.

> [NOTE: The explanation of the words of the Arabic piece, which is the essence of my regular invocation and which I call The Summary of Summaries, indicates the truths which the *Risale-i Nur*—which has its source in the Qur'an—has taken from the gleams of Qur'anic verses and particularly the proofs for Knowledge, Will, and Power. The scholarly proofs, which the Arabic words indicate, are expounded intensely. This means that each of these scholarly proofs explains an indication and a fine point made by numerous Qur'anic verses.]

To return to our main topic, we see clearly that there is an All-Knowing and All-Compassionate One, Who knows us and all other beings with spirits, and, in knowing them, protects them compassionately. He also knows all their needs and pleas, and knowing these, comes to their aid with His favors. One of numberless examples: the favors bestowed on human beings generally or particularly, and which come in the form of provision, medicines, and the minerals that one needs, point most clearly to an all-encompassing Knowledge and provide testimonies to the existence of an All-Merciful and All-Compassionate One to the number of foods, medicines, and minerals provided. Wise and purposive works, such as the feeding of humans, and particularly of the weak and infants, the conveying of the nutrients needed for each cell and organ of the body from the kitchen of the stomach, and the fact that mountains are like pharmacies and stores for all the minerals that are necessary for humanity—all of these are possible only through an all-encompassing Knowledge. Aimless chance, blind force, deaf nature, lifeless, unconscious causes, and the simple, pervasive elements could in no way have a part in maintaining, administering, preserving, or organizing the universe, all of which reflect knowledge, percipience, wisdom, compassion, and grace. Apparent "natural" causes are employed merely within the bounds of the Knowledge and Wisdom of the absolutely All-Knowing One, at His command and with His permission, as a veil to cover the dignity of Divine Power.

The fifth and sixth arguments: *well-ordering or organizing decrees and fruitful determining*

All things, particularly plants, trees, animals, and humans, are given forms so wise, well-ordered, well-measured, and proportioned thanks to the principles of Divine Decree and Destiny, which are two sorts of eternal Knowledge, that they are full of art, cut out with skilful artistry, sewn in a way entirely appropriate to the stature of each, and fitted perfectly. These point individually and collectively to an infinite Knowledge and testify in countless ways to an All-Knowing Maker.

Out of innumerable examples, consider a single tree and a human individual. We see that this fruit-bearing tree and that human being, with many members or limbs, have been delimited both outwardly and inwardly by unseen compasses and a subtle pen of Knowledge, and that each of their members has been given perfectly ordered fitting forms in order that they may yield the required fruits and results and perform the duties required by the purpose of their creation. Accordingly, since this could be possible only through an infinite Knowledge, they testify—to the number of plants and animals—to the necessary Existence and limitless Knowledge of a Maker and Giver of form, an All-Knowing Determiner, Who knows the interrelationships of all things and keeps them in view, and knows how to wisely define, individually and collectively, each and all of the trees and human beings with their outsides and insides through the compasses and pen of the decree and determining of His eternal Knowledge.

The seventh and eighth arguments: *the appointed final ends and fixed, regular provision*

Due to important instances of wisdom, the appointed final ends or hours of death and the amount of the provision that a living being will consume throughout its life are kept hidden and appear to be unspecified. However, the final end of the life of every living being is determined in the notebook of eternal Divine Decree and Destiny: it can be neither brought forward nor delayed. Similarly, there are numerous proofs which show that the provision of every living being is also appointed and determined, being inscribed on the tablets of Decree and Destiny. For example, it is through the wise law of the All-Knowing Preserver that a huge tree dies and leaves its seed behind, which is in one sense its spirit, to continue its duties in its place. Likewise, milk, the sustenance of infants and young, begins to be produced from between blood and excrement in the intestines and flows forth from breasts into their mouths, pure and clean. This rejects decisively the interference of chance and shows clearly that such a phenomenon occurs through the compassionate law of an All-Knowing and All-Compassionate Provider. These two small examples can, in comparison, be applied to all living creatures and beings with spirits.

This means that in reality both the appointed hour of death is specified and determined and that the provision of each living being has been determined and recorded in the notebook of Destiny. But for most important instances of wisdom, both the appointed hour and provision are kept behind the veil of the Unseen and appear to be unknown, unspecified, and apparently bound to chance. For if the appointed hour of death had been as clear to people as the rising and setting of the sun, the first half of life would be spent in absolute heedlessness and would be lost by not working for the Hereafter, while the second half would pass in terrible terror, with people feeling that every day they were taking another step toward the gallows of death, causing the calamity of their demise to increase a hundredfold. For this and other reasons the calamities that are to be visited on people and the final destruction of the world, which is its appointed hour of death, have mercifully been left unknown behind the veil of the Unseen.

As for provision, since after life it is the greatest treasury of bounties, the richest mine of thanks and praise and the most comprehensive source of worship, prayer, and entreaty, it has apparently been left vague and appears to be bound to chance. For in this way the door of seeking provision through the intercession of continuously seeking refuge at the Divine Court, through petitioning and entreating, and praise and thanks, is not closed. If, indeed, provision had been clearly specified, its nature would have been changed completely. The doors of thankful, grateful petitions and prayers, indeed of humble worship, would have been closed.

The ninth and tenth arguments: *skillful precision and faultlessness, and pleasing, ornate care and attention*

That is, in every being, particularly in all the beautiful creatures that display the manifestations of an eternal Beauty and Grace on the earth in spring, including particularly the flowers, fruits, small birds, and flies, and in particular the shining flying insects—in their creation, forms, and organs, one can see such miraculous skill and precision, such wonderful art, faultlessness, and excellence, and so many sorts of shapes and tiny mechanisms which show their Maker's miraculous proficiency that they cannot but decisively indicate a truly comprehensive Knowledge, and—let there be no mistake in the expression—an extremely skilful Faculty of Knowledge, testifying that it is impossible for random chance or unconscious, confused causes to have a part in them. The phrase, "pleasing, ornate care and attention" means that these fine creatures are adorned in a way so pleasing, ornamented in a way so sweet, and possessed of a beauty of art so attractive that it is obvious that their Maker works through infinite Knowledge. He knows the best way in everything, and wills to display to conscious beings the beauty of perfect craftsmanship and the perfection of that beauty. He creates and shapes the most insignificant flower and tiniest fly with the greatest care, skill, and art, and imbues them with the greatest importance. This attentive adorning and beautification self-evidently indicate a limitless and all-encompassing Knowledge; they testify in countless ways to the necessary Existence of an All-Knowing and All-Beautiful Maker.

The eleventh argument, which in fact comprises five universal arguments:

> The absolutely perfect order, balance, measure, and distinction with absolute ease; and the creation of things with firmness and precision despite their absolute abundance, and with absolute balance and measurement despite absolute speed, and with perfect beauty and art despite their infinite extent, and with complete congruence despite the infinite distances, and with complete distinction despite the fact that they are all intermingled.

This argument is a better form of the proof which appears at the end of the Arabic piece above, but because of severe illness, only five or six of the proofs it contains will be indicated briefly.

FIRSTLY: We see throughout the earth that amazing living mechanisms are made, some instantaneously and some in a minute or two, in an orderly and measured fashion with each being different from its fellows; this is done with the greatest ease, arising from a perfect Knowledge and Skill. This indicates an infinite Knowledge and testifies to the perfection of that Knowledge proportionately to the ease resulting from the skillful knowledge in art.

SECONDLY: Perfect and utterly artistic inventions that exist in the greatest profusion and multitude without the least confusion point to a limitless Knowledge within an infinite Power, and testify in countless ways to One Who is absolutely Knowing and Powerful.

THIRDLY: Inventions that possess perfect balance and measure, despite the absolute speed with which they are created, point to a limitless knowledge and testify in countless ways to an absolutely Knowledgeable and an absolutely Powerful One.

FOURTHLY: The making of innumerable living beings on the broad face of the earth with the greatest skill, adornment, and beauty of art, despite their wide extent, indicates an all-encompassing Knowledge Which confuses nothing, Which sees all things together, and for Which nothing is an obstacle to anything else. Also, those living beings testify individually and collectively that they are the artifacts of One Who is All-Knowing of all things, an absolutely Powerful One.

FIFTHLY: The coming into being of the members of a species which are far from each other, with one in the east, one in the west, one in the north, and one in the south, in the same way, and in resemblance with one another but with distinct individuality. This can only be only through the infinite Power of One Who is absolutely Knowing and absolutely Powerful, Who governs the entire universe and, through His infinite Knowledge, encompasses all beings together with all their states, thus indicating an all-encompassing Knowledge and testifying to One All-Knowing of the Unseen.

SIXTHLY: A great multitude of living mechanisms are created in confusing circumstances and dark places. For example, seeds are made to germinate and grow under the ground, without confusion, despite their similarity and all being mixed up together, in a miraculous fashion, without neglecting any single one of any sort, together with all their distinguishing features. This indicates, as clearly as the sun, eternal Knowledge and testifies as clearly as daylight to the creativity and Lordship of One Who is absolutely Powerful and absolutely Knowing. A more detailed exposition of this may be found in the *Risale-i Nur*, and so here we cut a long story short.

Now we discuss the matter of "Will," which is in The Summary of Summaries:

Proofs of Divine Will

> God is the All-Great—greater than all things in power and knowledge, for He is the All-Willing. Whatever He wills occurs; whatever He does not will does not occur. For every creature with its own specific essence, particular attributes, individual nature, and distinctive identity and form, is created with the finest and most precise order within a limitless number of possibilities and confused probabilities, amid intervening and mutually opposing elements that flow chaotically like floods, and in the midst of its numerous fellows which resemble one another, a further cause of disorder. Also, every creature is subjugated to a precise, perfect, and regular order, and all its members and organs are appointed and attached to it with a sensitive, exact balance, and measure. Furthermore, each living creature is given a well-proportioned, beautiful, and unique face, and all its different members and organs are created living and with perfect art from simple, lifeless matter. For example, a human being is created with a hundred different organs from a droplet of fluid; a bird is made with numerous different members and organs from a simple egg and clothed in a miraculous form; and a tree is produced or is made to grow from a tiny seed comprising simple, lifeless carbon, nitrogen, hydrogen, and oxygen, together with its branches and twigs and various other members and parts; it is then dressed in an orderly, fruitful form. This proves that all of the facts mentioned are possible only through the Will, Choice, Volition, and Judgment of the Almighty and All-Glorified One. Similarly, the correspondence in physical structures and basic systems among the members of a species shows that their Maker is One and Unique. Also, the fact that each member is different and distinguishable from others demonstrates that the One and Unique Maker does whatever He wills and judges however He wills.

All of this is a universal proof of the Divine Will, which comprises many arguments. Also, all the above-mentioned proofs of Divine Knowledge are also proofs for the Divine Will. Every creature displays the manifestations and works of Knowledge and Will one within the other. The indubitable testimony of a single creature to Divine Will shows that all creatures testify to the Divine Will, Which encompasses all things, with a certainty as clear as the sun, and that they comprise countless proofs of the necessary Existence of an All-Powerful, All-Willing One.

All the proofs for the Divine Knowledge mentioned above are also proofs for the Divine Will, since both operate together with Divine Power. One cannot exist without the other. In the same way that all the correspondences and conformities between the bodily organs of the members of a species indicate that their Maker is One and the same, the wise and purposeful differences and distinction in their facial features indicate definitely that their One and Unique Maker has absolute Will, doing whatever He wills, however He wills. He creates everything with Will and Choice, and for certain purposes.

The discussion about Divine Will ends here. I had intended to write many more important points in this regard, but since my mind has been exhausted on account of illness, it must be postponed to another time.

Divine Power

> God is the All-Great, greater than all things in power and knowledge, for He is All-Powerful over all things with an absolute, all-encompassing Power Which is essential and intrinsically indispensable to the All-Pure and Holy Essence. Therefore it is impossible and inconceivable that this Power should have an opposite which could intervene in It. Furthermore, that Power is absolutely free of gradation: equal before It are atoms and stars, the part and the whole, the particular and the universal, the seed and the tree, the universe and humanity, as confirmed by the perfect order, balance, measurement, harmony, distinction, and precision that are observable, together with or despite the absolute ease, abundance, speed, and intermingling. This is because of the existential facts such as luminosity and transparency—the Divine Power is free of matter and the dimension of things with which the Power deals is immaterial, luminous and transparent—and reciprocity and interrelation among things, and the exact balance, order, and obedience in creation. This is also because of the assistance of Divine Unity, the ease coming from the unity of the source, and because of the manifestation of Divine Oneness or Uniqueness. This is also because His existence is absolutely

> necessary and He exists by Himself; because He is absolutely free of matter and totally different from the created, and also because He is unrestricted, indivisible, and uncontained by space. This is also because nothing impedes Him; rather, (like the veins in our bodies or metal wires that conduct electricity or other subtle forces,) the things which are supposed to form obstacles and impediments actually serve as a means of facility (although He has no need for any help in conducting or executing His commands). Whatever He creates has the same quality of art—the atom, the part, the particular, the seed, and the human are in no way less beautiful or less artful than the star, the whole, the universal, the tree, and the universe. Whoever creates the latter creates the former. Also, in relation to the large universals that encompass the particulars and the wholes that encompass the parts, the individual parts and particulars which are encompassed are like, for example, a seed in which a huge tree is inscribed with miniature letters, or like the drops milked or squeezed from what encompasses them. So there is no doubt that the large entities and universals are in the grasp of the Creator of the small, encompassed things and particulars which they encompass: He includes or inserts the universal into the particular with the scales of His Knowledge, and filters the particular from the universal with the principles of His Wisdom. The copy of the "Qur'an of glory" which is inscribed in an atom with particles of ether is not less in eloquence or marvels of art than the copy of the "Qur'an of grandeur" written on the pages of the heavens in the ink of stars and suns. Similarly, in relation to the Power of the universe's Creator, a rose is not less in eloquence or beauty of art than a pearl-like star; nor is an ant inferior to an elephant or a germ to a rhinoceros. Also, the absolutely perfect speed and ease in the creation of things cause the people of misguidance to confuse creative formation with self-formation, which entails endless impossibilities and is beyond all probability and assumption. While the utmost and perfect speed and ease in the creation of things lead the people of right guidance to the certainty that stars and minute atoms are the same in relation to the Power of the Creator of the universe, all-exalted is His Majesty! And there is no deity but He, and He is the All-Great.

Before proceeding to explain briefly this piece concerning the supreme matter of Divine Power, I deem it necessary to express a truth. It is as follows:

The existence of Divine Power is more certain than the existence of the universe. Indeed, every single creature is an embodied word of Divine Power: they all demonstrate the existence of that Power to the degree of certainty based on vision. They testify in countless ways to the Absolutely

Powerful One, the One qualified by that Power. There is no need to prove that Power with further proofs. What is left to be done is to prove an awesome truth concerning Divine Power, declared in the verse, *Your creation and your resurrection are but as (the creation and resurrection) of a single soul* (31:28). This truth is a most formidable foundation of the Resurrection and Supreme Gathering, one of the most important bases of faith, and a most necessary means to understanding numerous matters of belief and Qur'anic truths. Since not everyone has been able to find a way to reach it by means of reason, some people have remained bewildered concerning Divine Power or have even denied It.

The basis in question or the foundation, the means, and truth, is the very meaning or content of the above verse. That is to say: "O humans and jinn! The re-creation and raising to life of all of you on Judgment Day is as easy for My Power as the creation and resurrection of a single individual!" Divine Power creates spring as easily as It creates a single flower. The particular and the universal, the small and the large, the many and the few are also the same for that Power. It turns planets as easily as It turns atoms.

The above passage explains a most conclusive, powerful proof of this awesome reality. It comprises nine steps, the very foundation of which is indicated by the following:

> God is the All-Great, greater than all things in power and knowledge, for He is All-Powerful over all things with absolute, all-encompassing Power, essential and intrinsically indispensable to the All-Pure and Holy Essence. Therefore, it is impossible and inconceivable that that Power should have an opposite which could intervene in It. Furthermore, that Power is absolutely free of gradation: equal before It are atoms and stars, the part and the whole, the particular and the universal, the seed and the tree, the universe and humanity.

That is, Almighty God's Power is absolute in the sense that It is able to do everything, for It encompasses all things. It is essential to the Necessarily Existent One; in terms of logic, It is intrinsically indispensable to Him and it is impossible that It should be separated from Him. Since the All-Pure and Holy Essence has such indispensable Power, Its opposite—impotence—could certainly in no way intervene in It. Impotence could in no way blight the All-Powerful Essence. Since the existence of degrees in a thing is through the intervention of its opposite—for example, the degrees and levels of heat exist through the intervention of cold and the degrees of beauty through the intervention of ugliness—impotence, the opposite of this essential Power, can in no way approach It. Therefore, there can be no degrees or grades in that absolute Power. Since there can be no degrees in It, stars and atoms are equal before that Power and there is no difference for It between the part and the whole or between an individual and a species. Thus, it is equally easy for that Power to revive a seed, a huge tree, or the entire universe; it is as easy for that Power to revive a single human individual and all beings with spirits at the Resurrection. There is no difference between the great and the small, the many and the few. Conclusive proofs of this truth are the perfect art, order, harmony, balance, distinction, and abundance that we see in the creation of things together with or despite the absolute speed and ease with which they are created.

THE FIRST STEP: *....as confirmed by the perfect order, balance, and measurement, harmony, distinction, and precision that are observable, together with or despite the absolute ease, abundance, speed, and intermingling.*

This step has already been explained above.

THE SECOND STEP: *This is because of the existential facts such as luminosity and transparency—the Divine Power is free of matter and the dimension of things with which the Power deals is immaterial, luminous and transparent—and reciprocity and interrelation among things, and the exact balance, order, and obedience in creation.*

A detailed explanation of this paragraph can be found in the final part of The Tenth Word, The Twenty-Ninth Word, and The Twentieth Letter; here we will expound it very briefly.

Because the sun is a light-diffusing object, through the Power of the Lord, its light and image enter the whole surface of the sea and all its bubbles or foams as easily and at the same instant as they enter a single fragment of glass. Given this, it is as easy for the absolutely matter-free Power of the Light of Lights to create and rotate the heavens and stars as it is to create flies and atoms and rotate them: neither causes It the least difficulty.

Also, on account of the quality of *transparency*, the sun's light and image are present with the same ease in a single transparent thing—in a tiny mirror or in the pupil of the eye, for example—in the same way that, through the Divine Command, the same light and image are reflected on all shining things, transparent objects, drops of water, and on the surface of the entire sea. Similarly, since the inner faces or immaterial dimensions and natures of things are transparent and shining, the absolute Power creates the entire animal kingdom with the same ease as It manifests Itself in the creation of a single individual: there is no difference between the many and the few, the great, and the small.

Also, on account of the quality of *balance*, if two walnuts of equal weight were put on a pair of absolutely precise scales which were large enough to weigh mountains, and a little seed was added to one of the walnuts, it would raise one of the pans as high as the peak of a mountain and lower the other to the bottom of the valley with the same ease. If, instead of two walnuts, two mountains of equal weight were placed in the pans, and a walnut was added to one, it would raise one pan to the skies while lowering the other to the valley bottom. Experts in theology (*Kalam*) say: "Contingency means the equality of two possibilities." That is, if there is nothing to necessitate their existence or non-existence, the things whose existence and non-existence are not intrinsically necessary are equal in regard as to whether they exist or not. The few or the many, the big or the small are the same in regard to this contingency and equality. Thus, creatures are contingent, and since they are contingent, their existence and non-existence are equal. This being so, it is as easy for the limitless eternal Power of the Necessarily Existent One to give existence to all contingent beings as it is to give it to a single contingent being. Thus, the fact that the eternal Divine Power gives existence to all contingent beings as easily as giving existence to a single contingent one destroys the balance of non-existence or removes the equality between the existence or non-existence of contingent beings in favor of their existence; this Power clothes every contingent thing with an appropriate being. When the being's duties of life are completed, the Power removes its garment of external existence and dispatches it to apparent non-existence; however, in fact this is an existence that resides within the sphere of His Knowledge. This means that if things are attributed to the Absolutely Powerful One, the creation of spring becomes as easy as that of a single flower, and the raising to life of all humankind at the Resurrection is as easy as raising to life a single soul. But, if they are attributed to "natural" causes, a flower becomes as difficult to create as spring and a fly as difficult as all living beings.

Also, due to the *order* or *orderliness* in creation, it is as easy to set in motion a large ship or an airplane merely by pressing a button with one's finger as it is to work the mainsprings of a clock by turning the key with one's finger. Similarly, since all things, be they universal or particular, large or small, many or few, have each been given an immaterial mold, a particular measure and proportions, and particular limits through the principles and laws of God's eternal Knowledge and Wisdom and the universal manifestations and specific principles of the Divine Will, they act within the bounds of the order established by the Divine Knowledge and are bound to the laws of the Divine Will. Therefore, rotating the solar system and causing the ship of the earth to move around its annual orbit through His infinite Power is as easy for the absolutely Powerful One as making blood circulate in a body, as making the red and white corpuscles move around in the blood, and making the tiny atoms in the corpuscles move in absolute order and for wise purposes. From a droplet of fluid He creates a human being, together with its wonderful organs, on the pattern of the universe without the least difficulty. This means that if attributed to the eternal, infinite Power, the creation of the universe is as easy as the creation of a single human being. But if not attributed to that Power, it would be as difficult to create a single human being together with its wonderful organs, members, and senses as it would to create the entire universe.

On account of the principles of *obedience* and *compliance*, with the command of "Forward march!" a commander impels a private to attack; with that very same command, he can, with similar ease, drive forward an entire army into battle. In the same way, all creatures, save for those endowed with free will, are absolutely obedient to the laws of the Divine Will: they are thousands of times more obedient than dutiful soldiers and subservient to the Lord's commands of creation and life with innate eagerness, and they always act within the limits set by the eternal Knowledge and Wisdom. Thus, it is as easy for the Divine Power to create an entire army of living beings in springtime and to assign them their duties as it is to clothe an individual living being with existence through the command: "Come into existence out of non-existence and begin your duty of life!" in a manner determined by Divine Knowledge and in a form specified by Divine Will. This means that if everything is attributed to that Power, the creation of the entire army of atoms and battalions of stars is as easy as the creation of a single atom and a single star. If attributed to "natural" causes, however, the creation of an atom in the pupil of an animal's eye or brain, together with its ability to perform a range of amazing duties, would be as difficult as the creation of an entire army of animals.

THE THIRD STEP: *This is also because of the assistance of Divine Unity, the ease coming from the unity of the source, and because of the manifestation of Divine Oneness or Uniqueness.*

That is, on account of his independent sovereignty over all of his subjects and the fact that all his subjects obey his commands alone, it is as easy for a ruler to govern a large empire comprising many nations as it is to govern the people of a village. Because of the unity of the source from which the laws or rules issue, the members of the nation, like the soldiers of an army, obey the ruler without confusion and the laws are easily executed. However, if the government were left to various rulers, confusion would reign, and governing a single village would be as difficult as governing an entire country. And since the obedient nation is dependent on the single ruler, relying on his power and the strength of his army with its equipment stores, each member of the army may take an enemy king captive and perform works far exceeding his own individual strength. His connection with the ruler secures for him an extremely formidable power, so that he may perform great tasks. But if this connection is severed, he loses that vast power and can perform works only to the extent of his own petty strength and the arms and ammunition on his back. If he were required to perform all the works that he carried out in reliance on the power of his connection with the ruler, he would have to have in his possession the strength of the entire army, together with all of the stores of arms and ammunition belonging to the ruler.

In the same way, since the All-Powerful Maker and Monarch of all eternity is the unique, all-independent Sovereign over the whole creation, He creates the universe as easily as He creates a city, He creates spring as easily as He creates a garden, and He raises to life all the dead at the Resurrection as easily as He creates the leaves, flowers, and fruits of the trees of an earthly garden in spring. He creates a fly easily on the pattern of a large eagle and an individual human being on the pattern of the universe. By contrast, if attributed to "natural" causes, a germ would be as difficult to create as a rhinoceros, and a piece of fruit would be as difficult as a huge tree. It would even require that every atom which performs amazing tasks in the body of a living creature should be given an eye that sees all things and knowledge that knows all things in order to perform those subtle, perfect, and vital duties.

Also, there is absolute ease in the unity of the source. For if an army is equipped from one source, from one factory, then it becomes as easy to equip all of the troops as it is to equip a single soldier. However, if numerous different hands interfere in the provision of the army's equipment, with different items being supplied from different factories, then a single soldier's equipment could be prepared only with a thousand difficulties, and, due to the interference of various authorities, it would be as difficult to equip one solider as it would a thousand. Also, if the command of a thousand soldiers is given to a single officer, in one respect it becomes as easy as that of a single soldier, whereas if it is left to ten officers or the soldiers themselves, commands become confused and contradictory, and are carried out only with great difficulty, if at all.

Yet if all things are attributed to the Single One of Unity—the One Who has absolute authority over creation both as a whole and individually—they become as easy as a single thing; if they are attributed to causes, a single living creature becomes as difficult to create as the entire earth, or even impossible. This means that ease or facility in unity is at the degree of necessity—such that it makes the existence and government of a thing necessary. And the difficulty that arises from the interference of numerous hands amounts to impossibility.

If the alternation of day and night with the gradual, precisely calculated lengthening and shortening of each, or the movement of the planets and the alternation of the seasons of the year, are left to a single organizer or authority, that unique and all-independent Commander simply orders the earth, which is His soldier, to "Rise up, rotate, and travel!" Out of the joy and delight it feels at being the addressee of this royal command, with two motions like a Mevlevi dervish in ecstasy, it easily becomes the means of the daily and annual changes and the apparent, imaginary movements of the sun, thus demonstrating the complete facility that unity engenders. But if the alternations and movements in question were left not to the single Commander but to the many different causes and the caprices of the planets, the sun and the earth, and the earth were told: "Stop where you are and do not move!", every night and every year the earth, the sun and the planets, and even thousands of huge galaxies that may somehow be connected with the solar system, would have to cross countless light years so that these heavenly and earthly results—such as the seasons and the alternation of day and night—might come about. This would be so difficult as to be impossible.

The phrase, *because... of the manifestation of Divine Oneness or Uniqueness* indicates an extremely subtle, profound, and extensive truth. A detailed explanation and proof of it can be found in the *Risale-i Nur*; here we will outline just a single point by means of a comparison.

By illuminating the entire earth at the same time, the sun provides an example of Divine Unity, (which is marked by the all-encompassing manifestation of God's Names throughout the universe all at the same time,) while through its image and seven-colored light that appears in each and every transparent thing that faces it, such as mirrors, it forms an example of Divine Oneness or Uniqueness, (which the particular manifestation of God's Names on things individually indicates). If the sun had knowledge, power, or will, and the fragments of glass and drops and bubbles of water in which the tiny suns appear had the necessary capacity, through the law of Divine Will, a real sun with all its attributes would be present in each and every thing at the same instant. Its simultaneous presence in all things over the face of the earth would cause no deficiency in its power to be present in or near a single thing with all its manifestations; through the Command and Decree of the Lord's Power it would be the cause of truly extensive manifestations, thus demonstrating the extraordinary ease in oneness or uniqueness.

Similarly, just as in manifesting His Unity, the All-Majestic Maker is all-present and all-seeing everywhere through His Knowledge, Will, and Power, Which encompass all things simultaneously, so in manifesting His Oneness or Uniqueness, He is present together with His Names and Attributes in all things individually—the animate in particular—so that with the greatest of ease He creates in an instant a fly on the pattern of an eagle and a human being on the pattern of the universe. He creates living creatures in a way so miraculous that if all causes were to gather together, they could not make even a nightingale or a fly. And just as the One Who creates the nightingale is the One Who creates all birds, the One Who creates a human being is the One Who creates the whole universe.

THE FOURTH AND FIFTH STEPS: .... *This is also because His existence is absolutely necessary and He exists by Himself; because He is absolutely free of* *matter and totally different from the created, and also because He is unrestricted, indivisible, and uncontained by space.*

Only one or two points of this passage will be explained here in brief.

The absolutely All-Powerful One has the rank of absolutely necessary existence, which is the most formidable, stable, and powerful of all ranks of existence. His existence is also eternal, beyond all time and space. Furthermore, He is absolutely free of matter and totally different from the created in both essence and nature. Thus, in relation to His Power, the creation and management of the stars are as easy as the creation and management of minute particles; the resurrection of the dead is as easy as bringing about spring, and raising to life all the dead at the Resurrection is as easy as raising to life a single soul. For a thing the size of a fingernail which belongs to a species at the levels of existence that are powerful may hold and manipulate a mountain from an insubstantial level of existence. For example, a mirror or faculty of memory from the level of powerful, external existence may hold a hundred mountains or a thousand books respectively from the level of existence of the World of representations or "ideal" forms, which is weak and insubstantial, and thus have disposal over them. Therefore, however inferior in respect of power the "ideal" or representational existence is to the level of external, physical existence, the created, accidental existences of contingent beings are infinitely more inferior and weaker than the eternal, necessary Existence. Consequently, through a minuscule manifestation of It, that sacred Existence can manipulate a world from the worlds of contingent beings. Regrettably, my illness and certain other important reasons do not permit me to go into further explanations, so we refer the reader to an elaboration of this lengthy truth and its fine points in the relevant parts of the *Risale-i Nur* and to another time.

THE SIXTH STEP: *This is also because nothing impedes Him; rather, (like the veins in our bodies or metal wires that conduct electricity or other subtle forces,) the things which are supposed to form obstacles and impediments actually serve as a means of facility (although He has no need for any help in conducting or executing His commands).*

That is, owing to a manifestation of Divine Will and a law of the Divine Command of creation and life, which science calls "the knot or nucleus of life," the unconscious, hard branches and twigs of a huge tree do not form obstacles or impediments to the necessary substances and foods which go to its fruit, leaves, or flowers from that nucleus of life, which is the tree's mainspring and stomach; rather, they facilitate the operation. Similarly, all things that are supposed to form obstacles to the creation of the universe cease to be obstacles in the face of the manifestation of Will and the operation of the Lord's Command and become a means of facility. Consequently, the eternal Power creates the universe and all the species of creatures on earth as easily as It creates a single tree. Nothing at all is difficult for It. If all these acts of creation are not attributed to that Power, then the creation and manipulation of that single tree would be as difficult as the creation and manipulation of all trees, indeed, of the whole earth. For then, everything would form obstacles and obstructions. If all causes were to gather together, they could not send the necessary sustenance to the fruits, leaves, branches, or twigs in an orderly, regular fashion from the stomach or the mainspring of the tree's "knot or nucleus of life"—which is a manifestation of Divine Command and Will—unless all the parts of the tree, even all its atoms, possessed sight, all-encompassing knowledge, and extraordinary power, and were able to comprehend the entire tree together with all its parts and atoms in order to know and assist them.

So, climb these six steps and see what difficulties—indeed, impossibilities—there are in unbelief and associating partners with God and how unreasonable, illogical, and precluded they are. Then see what ease and what reasonable, acceptable, and decisive truths there are in belief and the way of the Qur'an and how the existence of things becomes necessary through this easiness and truth. Understand this, and say: "All praise and gratitude are for God for the favor of belief!"

The illnesses and difficulties I have been suffering have caused the remaining part of this important step to be postponed.

THE SEVENTH STEP: *Whatever He creates has the same quality of art; the atom, the part, the particular, the seed and the human are in no way less beautiful or less in art than the star, the whole, the universal, the tree, or the universe.*

> (NOTE: The basis, source and sun of the truths contained in these nine Steps are the following verses from *Suratu'l-Ikhlas*: *Say: "He—[He is] God, [Who is] the Unique One of Absolute Oneness. God—[God is He Who is] the Eternally-Besought [Himself in need of nothing]."*. They are brief indications of the gleams of the manifestation of God's being the One, the Unique Who has concentrated manifestations of His

> Names and Attributes on things individually, and His being the Eternally-Besought, while He is in no need of anything at all.)

After giving a very brief explanation of this seventh step, we refer the reader to a more detailed discussion of the subject in the *Risale-i Nur*.

An atom which performs amazing duties in the eye or brain is not less with regard to the beauty of art and wonders of creation than a star; nor is a part less than its whole. For example, the brain and eye are not inferior to a human body of which they are parts. Nor is a particular individual less with regard to the beauty of art and the wonders of creation than a species; nor with its wonderful organs, senses, and faculties is a human being inferior to all the animate species; nor, in respect of perfect craftsmanship and its being a store or resembling a complete list of contents, a program, and memory bank, is a seed inferior to the mighty tree which grows from it; nor, with respect to their perfect creation and their wonderful, comprehensive organs and faculties, placed there to perform thousands of amazing duties, is a human being—the microcosm—inferior to the whole universe. This means that the One Who creates the atom must be able to create the star. And the One Who creates an organ like the tongue can, self-evidently, create a human being easily. And the One Who creates a single human being so perfectly can undoubtedly create all animate beings with perfect ease, as He does before our very eyes. And the One Who creates a seed to resemble a list, an index, a notebook of the laws of creation and life, as a "knot or nucleus of life," is certainly the Creator of all trees. And the One Who creates the human being to resemble a sort of seed of the universe and as its comprehensive fruit, favoring them with the manifestations of His Divine Names and making them a mirror to these Names—the One Who makes the human being connected to the entire universe and appoints them as the vicegerent on earth most certainly has such Power that He is able to create the universe as easily as He creates a single human being and to set it in order. This being the case, whoever is the Creator, Maker, and Lord of the atom, the part, the particular individual, the seed, and the human being must also be the Creator, Maker, and Lord of the stars, all species, all universals, all trees and, indeed, the entire universe. It cannot be otherwise.

THE EIGHTH STEP: *Also, in relation to the large universals that encompass the particulars and the wholes that encompass the parts, the individual parts and particulars which are encompassed are like, for example, a seed in which a huge* *tree is inscribed with miniature letters, or like the drops milked or squeezed from what encompasses them. So there is no doubt that the large entities and universals are in the grasp of the Creator of the small, encompassed things and particulars which they encompass: He includes or inserts the universal into the particular with the scales of His Knowledge and filters the particular from the universal with the principles of His Wisdom.*

That is, in relation to the large wholes and universals which encompass them, the individual parts and particulars which are encompassed are like a seed in which a huge tree has been inscribed in miniature letters. Thus, the encompassing universals must be within the grasp of the Creator of the particulars and completely under His disposal so that, with the scales of His Knowledge and Its fine pens, He can include that huge all-encompassing book in hundreds of miniscule sections or notebooks; that is, He can insert a huge tree in its numerous seeds. Or in relation to the encompassing wholes or universals, the encompassed parts or particulars are like drops that have been "milked" from what encompasses them. For example, a melon seed is a drop milked from the totality of the melon or a point in which the whole book of the melon is inscribed, for the seed contains its index, list of contents, and program. Since this is so, the encompassing wholes and universals must be within the hand of the Maker of those particulars, drops, and points, so that He can milk or filter the individuals, drops, and points from them in accordance with the subtle principles of His Wisdom. This means that the One Who creates the seed and the individual must be the One Who creates the whole and the universals, as well as the other much greater universals and types that encompass the latter; it could not be otherwise. This being the case, the One Who creates a single soul is able to create all of humankind. And the One Who raises to life one dead person is able to raise to life all jinn and humans at the Resurrection, and will indeed raise them to life. So see how most definitely and brilliantly true is the verse: *Your creation and your resurrection are but as (the creation and resurrection) of a single soul* (31:28).

THE NINTH STEP: *The copy of the "Qur'an of glory" which is inscribed in an atom with particles of ether is not less in eloquence or marvels of art than the copy of the "Qur'an of grandeur" written on the pages of the heavens in the ink of stars and suns. Similarly, in relation to the Power of the universe's Creator, a rose is not less in eloquence and beauty of art than a pearl-like star; nor is an ant inferior to an elephant or a germ to a rhinoceros. Also, the absolutely perfect speed and ease in* *the creation of things cause the people of misguidance to confuse creative formation with self-formation, which entails endless impossibilities and is beyond all probability and assumption. While the utmost and perfect speed and ease in the creation of things lead the people of right guidance to the certainty that stars and minute atoms are the same in relation to the Power of the Creator of the universe, all-exalted is His Majesty! And there is no deity but He, and He is the All-Great.*

> (I wanted to explain this last step at length, but regrettably I have been prevented by my extreme distress, weakness, and the serious illnesses I have suffered as a result of being poisoned. I have therefore been compelled to be content with a brief indication.)

If a Qur'an of mighty stature was written on an atom with miniscule particles of ether, and if another mighty Qur'an was written in stars and suns on the pages of the heavens and the two were compared, the microscopic Qur'an written in particles would certainly not be inferior in respect of wonders and miraculous art than the vast Qur'an gilding the face of the heavens; indeed, in some respects it would be superior.

In the same way, in relation to the Power of the universe's Creator, the rose is not inferior to the planet Venus, nor is the ant inferior to the elephant in respect of the originality and extraordinariness of their creation. Also, as regards their creation, a germ is more wonderful than a rhinoceros and the bee is superior to the date-palm. This means that the One Who creates the bee can create all animals. The One Who raises a single soul to life can raise to life all humans at the Resurrection and gather them together in the place of the Supreme Gathering, as surely He will. Nothing at all is difficult for Him, for before our eyes every spring He creates hundreds of thousands of samples of the Resurrection with the greatest ease and speed.

What is meant by the final sentence of the piece in question is that since the people of misguidance do not know the unshakeable truths of the above "steps," and since creatures come into existence with the greatest ease and speed, they imagine their formation and creation by the infinite Power of the Maker to be self-formation, believing that they come into existence of themselves. In so doing, they open for themselves the door to superstitions, which are impossible in every respect and which no sound mind or imagination could accept. For example, their assertion requires that every single atom of every living creature should have infinite power and knowledge, an eye that sees everything, and the capability to execute every art and skill. By not accepting a single God, they are bound to accept deities to the number of particles in existence, and thus deserve to be cast into the lowest of the low reaches of Hell.

As for the people of guidance, the powerful truths and proofs in the "steps" above give to their sound hearts and straight minds a very firm conviction, a powerful belief, and a sound affirmation at the degree of certainty based on knowledge. Consequently, they believe without doubt and with the utmost contentment of the heart that in relation to the Divine Power there is no difference between the stars and the atoms or between the smallest and the largest; all these amazing things occur before our very eyes and every marvel of art confirms the declaration of the verse,

> Your creation and your resurrection are but as (the creation and resurrection of) a single soul,

and testifies that it is pure truth and reality. And through the tongue of their beings they declare: "God is the All-Great!" We too declare: "God is the All-Great!" along with them. And with all our strength and conviction we affirm the verse's claim, and we testify with innumerable proofs that it is pure truth and reality.

> All-Glorified are You! We have no knowledge save what You have taught us; surely You are the All-Knowing, the All-Wise.
>
> O God! Bestow blessings and peace on the one whom You sent as a mercy to all the worlds, and all praise and gratitude are due to God, the Lord of the worlds.

Introduction to the Turkish translation of The Damascus Sermon, which was originally in Arabic

In His Name, All-Glorified is He!

And there is nothing but it glorifies Him with praise.

Peace be upon you and God's mercy and blessings!

My dear, faithful brothers (and sisters)!

> With a presentiment, the Old Said sensed the truths expressed in this Arabic sermon, which, at the behest of scholars in Damascus, he delivered in 1911 at the Umayyad Mosque in front of a congregation of approximately ten thousand people, including a hundred religious scholars. He gave the glad tidings of certain agreeable developments in the future with complete certainty as though they were going to be realized shortly. However, two World Wars and twenty-five years of absolute despotism delayed their realization; it is only now that the signs of their realization are beginning to appear in the world of Islam. Therefore, this important lesson was not simply some old, outdated sermon, rather, it is a new, true lesson which instructs its listeners regarding certain social and Islamic matters which were addressed not to the relatively small congregation in the Umayyad Mosque, but rather to a congregation of more than a billion in the great mosque of the Muslim world. If you consider it appropriate, you may publish its translation.

Question: It is appropriate here to answer a most important question. Many have asked both myself and the students of the *Risale-i Nur*: "Why do you give such great importance to the *Risale-i Nur*, and how does it give such conviction and contentment to its students that they have not been defeated by the many obdurate philosophers and people of misguidance who oppose them? By preventing to an extent the publication of numerous true and valuable books on belief and Islam, and by promoting worldly pleasures and vices, they deprive many youths and others of the truths of belief. But despite their most violent and vicious attacks on the *Risale-i Nur* and their lying propaganda to destroy it and to scare people away from it, the *Risale-i Nur* is spreading its message in an unparalleled way. Six hundred thousand copies of its treatises have already been written out by hand with untiring enthusiasm and published by his students, and they are read with perfect eagerness. What is the reason for this?"

THE ANSWER: In response we say the following:

The *Risale-i Nur* is a true commentary on the wise Qur'an that emanates from its miraculousness. It demonstrates that in misguidance there is a sort of Hell in this world, while in belief there is a kind of Paradise. It shows the severe pains in sins, evil deeds, and forbidden pleasures, and proves that pleasures akin to those in Paradise are to be found in good deeds and virtues, and in the truths of the Shari'a. Thus, it saves the sensible among those who have fallen into vice and misguidance. At this time there are two terrible realities:

THE FIRST: Since human emotions, which are blind to the consequences of things and prefer an ounce of immediate pleasure to tons of future joy, have come to prevail over mind and reason, the only way to save the dissipated from their vices is to show them the pain which underlies their apparent pleasures and thus defeat their emotions. As indicated by the verse, *They choose the present, worldly life over the Hereafter* (14:3), although they are believers and aware of the diamond-like bounties and pleasures of the Hereafter, many people tend to prefer worldly pleasures, which are like pieces of glass destined soon to shatter over them. Therefore, the only way to save the people of faith from following the people of misguidance on account of this reality and love for the world is by showing them the hellish torments and pains present in the way of misguidance. This is the method the *Risale-i Nur* follows. For at this time, in the face of the obduracy coming from absolute unbelief and the misguidance caused by scientific materialism or scientism and the addiction to vice, only one in ten or even twenty can be turned away from vice and encouraged to give it up by proving the existence of Hell and its torments, after having given them certain amount of knowledge of God the Almighty.

However, even after they have received this instruction, it is still possible that such people will say: "God is the All-Forgiving and the All-Compassionate, and Hell is a long way off," and continue in their dissipation. Their hearts and spirits are defeated by their emotions.

Thus, by showing through most of its comparisons between belief and unbelief the grievous and terrifying results in this world of unbelief and misguidance, the *Risale-i Nur* causes even the most stubborn and arrogant people to feel repugnance with regard to those inauspicious, illicit pleasures, thus leading them to repent. The short comparisons in the Sixth, Seventh, and Eighth Words, and the long one in The Third Station of The Thirty-Second Word frighten the most dissipated and misguided person away from the way they are following, leading them to accept what is taught. As an example, I will relate briefly the states that the Verse of Light (24:35) showed me on a journey of the imagination, which were in fact reality. Those who desire a detailed account of it may refer to the end of *Sikke-i Tasdik-i Gaybi* ("The Confirming Stamp of the Unseen").

During that imaginary journey I saw the animal kingdom in need of provision, and I looked upon it through the prism of materialist philosophy. Their weakness and impotence in the face of their innumerable needs and severe hunger showed that kingdom to be a most miserable and painful one. Since I was looking with the eyes of the people of misguidance and heedlessness, I cried out. Then suddenly I saw through the telescope of Qur'anic wisdom and belief that the Divine Name the All-Merciful had risen in the sign of the All-Providing like a shining sun, gilding that hungry, wretched animal world with the light of its mercy.

Then I saw within the animal world another wretched realm which was enveloped in darkness and where the young were struggling in their need and powerlessness. It was enough to make anyone feel pity. I regretted having looked with the eyes of the people of misguidance. Suddenly, belief gave me different spectacles and I saw the Name the All-Compassionate rise in the sign of affection and tenderness. It changed that painful world into a joyful one in such a beautiful and lovable fashion and illuminated it in such a way that my tears of complaint and sorrow were transformed into tears of rejoice and thanks.

Then the world of humanity appeared to me as though on a cinema screen. Looking again through the telescope of the people of misguidance, I saw that world to be so dark and terrifying that I cried out from the depths of my heart. Humans have desires and ambitions that extend to eternity; they have thoughts and conceptions that encompass the entire universe and earnest desires and yearnings for eternal life, everlasting happiness, and Paradise. They have innate capacities and powers that are unrestricted and left free. Also, despite their weakness, impotence, and very brief life, they have innumerable needs and purposes, and are exposed to the attacks of countless adversaries and the blows of endless calamities. Under the perpetual threat of death, they are leading a brief and tumultuous life in wretched circumstances. Striving for their livelihood in misery and suffering from the continuous blows of death and separation—a most painful and terrifying state for the heart and conscience—they are heading straight for the grave, which appears to the misguided to be the door to everlasting darkness. I saw that they are being cast individually and in groups into that well of darkness.

On seeing the world of humanity under such layers of darkness I was just about to cry out with my heart, spirit, and mind, indeed, with all my faculties and even all the particles of my being, when the light and power of belief issuing from the Qur'an smashed these spectacles of misguidance, providing me with a different means of vision. I saw God's Name the All-Just rise like the sun in the sign of the All-Wise, the Name the All-Merciful in the sign of the All-Munificent, the Name the All-Compassionate in the sign of the All-Forgiving, the Name the All-Resurrecting in the sign of the All-Inheriting, the Name the All-Reviving in the sign of the All-Favoring, and the name the All-Nurturing in the sign of the Sovereign. They lit up that entire dark world of humanity, within which there are many other worlds. They dispelled these hellish states and, opening up windows from the luminous worlds of the Hereafter, scattered light over the world of humanity. I uttered: "All praise and gratitude be to God; thanks be to God!" to the number of particles in existence! I saw and knew to the degree of certainty arising from vision that in belief there is a sort of Paradise in this world too, while in misguidance there is a kind of Hell.

Then the realm of the earth appeared. On that journey of the imagination, the dark, hypothetical rules of the philosophy and laws of the science which do not obey the Religion presented an appalling world to my imagination. Voyaging through space on the ship of the extremely ancient earth—which travels in a year the distance that it would take a human being twenty-five thousand years to walk, with a movement seventy times faster than a cannon-ball, and being a structure that could break up at any moment with the innermost parts being in constant flux and turmoil—wretched humankind appeared to be trapped in a most desolate darkness. I became dizzy and almost lost self-control. I flung the spectacles of philosophy to the ground, smashing them. Then, suddenly, I looked with a view illuminated by the wisdom of the Qur'an and belief. I saw the Names the Creator of the heavens and earth, the All-Powerful, the All-Knowing Nurturer, God, the Lord of the heavens and earth, and the Subjugator of the sun and moon rise like suns in the signs of Mercy, Grandeur and Lordship. They illuminated that dark, desolate, and terrifying world with such brilliance that the earth appeared to the eye of my belief as a perfectly well-ordered, subservient, pleasant, and safe vessel in which the provisions of everyone have been stored. I saw it as a ship or an airplane or a train which has been prepared for trade and enjoyment, carrying beings with spirits through the Lord's realms around the sun, bringing the produce of spring, summer, and fall to those in need of sustenance. I exclaimed: "All praise and gratitude be to God to the number of the atoms of the earth for the favor of belief!"

It has thus been proved with many examples and analogies in the *Risale-i Nur* that the people of vice and misguidance suffer a hellish torment in this world too, while on account of the manifestations of belief, the people of faith and righteousness can taste paradisiacal pleasures through the stomachs of Islam and humanity. They are able to benefit, each according to the degree of their belief. But in these stormy times, the currents numb the senses and scatter human attention to peripheral, futile matters and engulf them, anesthetizing their senses, obliterating sound reasoning and reflection. As a result, the people of misguidance are temporarily unable to totally perceive their spiritual torment, while the people of guidance are overwhelmed by heedlessness and cannot truly appreciate the pleasures of right guidance.

THE SECOND TERRIBLE REALITY OF THIS AGE: Compared with today, in former times there was little misguidance that arose from absolute unbelief and blind faith in science, and little obstinacy that emanated from stubborn, willful unbelief. For this reason, the teaching and arguments of the Muslim scholars of those times were enough to dispel any unbelief arising from doubt. Since almost everyone believed in God, most people would give up misguidance and vice after being taught about God and warned about Hellfire. But now there are a hundred absolute unbelievers in one small town, when in the past there was only one. Those who go astray due to blind faith in science and learning, obstinately opposing the truths of belief, are a hundred times greater in number in relation to former times. As these obstinate deniers oppose the truths of belief with the arrogance of the Pharaoh, there must be a sacred truth that will utterly destroy the foundations of their unbelief in this world with the strength of an atomic explosion, halting their aggression and bringing some of them to belief.

Endless thanks be to God Almighty that with its numerous comparisons and the remedies it provides for the ills of this time, the *Risale-i Nur*, which comprises some gleams of the Qur'an of miraculous exposition, vanquishes even the worst of those obstinate deniers with the diamond sword of the Qur'an. By indicating the proofs and arguments for Divine Unity and the truths of belief that exist to the number of the atoms of the universe, for twenty-five years it has not been defeated in the face of the severest attacks; indeed it has been victorious. With its comparisons of belief and unbelief, of right guidance and misguidance, the *Risale-i Nur* self-evidently proves these truths. For example, if one looks at the proofs and gleams in The Second Station of The Twenty-Second Word, The First Station of The Thirty-Second Word, the "Windows" of The Thirty-Third Word, and the eleven proofs of The Staff of Moses (*Asa-yi Musa*), and if other comparisons are considered in their light, it can be understood that it is the truths of the Qur'an that are manifested in the *Risale-i Nur* which will smash and destroy absolute unbelief and obdurate misguidance at this time.

Said Nursi

In His Name, All-Glorified is He!

The Second Chapter from The Twenty-Ninth Gleam

Why belief is the greatest blessing for humankind

This chapter concerns the phrase *All praise and gratitude are for God.*

In this short treatise, out of endless benefits and lights of belief which lead people to declare *All praise and gratitude are for God*, only nine will be expounded.

In the Name of God, the All-Merciful, the All-Compassionate.

First Point

First of all, the following two things should be pointed out:

- Philosophy (which does not obey the Religion) is a pair of dark glasses which shows everything to be ugly and frightful. On the contrary, true religious belief is a transparent, clear, radiant pair of spectacles which shows everything to be beautiful and lovable.
- Because they are connected with all creatures, having a sort of transaction with all things, and are by nature compelled to meet, converse and be neighborly with the things that surround them, humans have six sides or aspects: left, right, front, back, above and below.

On wearing either of the two pairs of spectacles mentioned, humans can see the creatures and circumstances that are on these sides.

The right side: What is meant by this side or aspect is the past. When the past is viewed through the spectacles of irreligious philosophy, it appears to be a vast, dark, terrifying, overturned graveyard, whose doomsday already seems to have come to pass. It is doubtless that this sight causes humans great terror, fear and despair.

However, when this side is seen through the spectacles of belief, even if this realm appears to have been overturned, there has been no loss of life. Instead one understands that its crew and inhabitants have been transferred to a better, light-filled world. The graves and pits are considered to be underground tunnels, dug to lead to another, light-filled world. This means that the rejoice, relief, contentment and peace of mind which belief affords humans is a Divine favor which makes them utter thousands of times over: "All praise and gratitude are for God!"

THE LEFT SIDE: The left side represents the future. Now when the future is viewed through the spectacles of philosophy, it appears in the form of a vast, dark, frightening grave which is going to rot us and make us food for snakes and scorpions. But when viewed through the spectacles of belief, it appears in the form of a banquet prepared for humans by God Almighty, the Creator, the All-Merciful and the All-Compassionate, complete with all manner of the finest and most delicious foods and drinks. And it makes them utter thousands of times: "All praise and gratitude are for God!"

ABOVE: When someone uses the spectacles of philosophy to look upwards toward the heavens, they feel an awful dread and terror at the extremely rapid and varied movements of the billions of stars and heavenly bodies, racing like wild horses around in endless space. However, when a believer looks at them, they see that just as army maneuvers are carried out under the supervision and on the orders of a commander, the stars are light-diffusing lamps that adorn the world of the heavens. Consequently, rather than feeling terror and dread at those horses racing, they are filled with friendliness and love. It is surely little to say "All praise and gratitude are for God!" thousands of times in return for the bounty of belief, which depicts the world of the heavens in such a benign way.

BELOW: When someone uses the eye of philosophy to gaze at the earth below his feet, he sees that it resembles an animal left unbridled to wander aimlessly around the sun, or a scuppered boat without a captain, and they are struck with terror and anxiety. But when they look through the prism of belief, they see it as a ship of the All-Merciful, taking humankind on a pleasure cruise around the sun under the command of God Almighty, with all necessary food, drink and clothing on board. And so they begin to utter "All praise and gratitude are for God!" wholeheartedly for this great bounty which issues from belief.

THE FRONT: If a person who indulges in philosophy looks at this side, they see that all living creatures, whether humans or beasts, are disappearing convoy by convoy and with great speed. That is to say, they are going to non-existence and ceasing to be. Since they know that they too are condemned to the same end, they almost lose their mind with grief. But for a believer who views the same thing with the eye of belief, the people traveling on this side are not going to the world of non-existence; rather, they are being transferred from one pasture to another, like nomads. They are migrating from a transitory realm to an eternally permanent one; from the farm on which they have labored to the office where they collect their wages; from a place of hardship and difficulty to one of ease and mercy. And so they view this aspect with pleasure and gratitude.

Apparent difficulties which emerge along the road, such as death and the grave, are in fact means of happiness with respect to their results. For the road which leads to the light-filled worlds passes through the grave, and the greatest happiness comes as the result of the worst, most grievous disasters. For example, Prophet Joseph, upon him be peace, attained the happiness of being vice-ruler of Egypt only after he had been thrown into a well by his brothers and put in prison on account of the slander of Zulaikha.[149] Likewise, a child coming into the world from its mother's womb attains happiness in this world only as a result of the tiresome, crushing difficulties he or she suffers along the way.

THE BACK: When one looks through the prism of philosophy at those who come from behind, they can find no answer to the question: "Where have they come from and where are they going? And why did they come to the realm of this world?" Naturally the questioner remains in a torment of bewilderment and doubt. But if they look through the prism of belief, they will understand that human beings are observers that are sent to the world

---

[149] According to certain Muslim historians, Zuleykha is the name of the wife of the minister, who bought the Prophet Joseph as a slave. She sought to enjoy herself by him, but when Prophet Joseph rejected her, she ordered him to be imprisoned. See the Qur'an, 12:23–35. (Tr.)

by the Eternal Sovereign to contemplate and study the amazing miracles of Power displayed in the exhibition of the universe. After having received their grades in accordance with the level at which they grasp the value and grandeur of those miracles of the Power and the extent to which they point to the Grandeur of the Eternal Sovereign, human beings will return to the realm of the Eternal Sovereign. And so they will say, "All praise and gratitude are for God!" for the favor of belief which has led them to this blessing of understanding.

Since the praise offered in saying, "All praise and gratitude are for God!" for the favor of belief, which thus removes the above-mentioned layers of darkness, is also a blessing or favor, it also requires praise and thanks. This in turn requires the offering of praise and thanks a third time, which in turn requires them a fourth time, and so on, forming an infinite chain of praise that is born of a single uttering of the phrase: "All praise and gratitude are for God!"

SECOND POINT

We should say, "All praise and gratitude are for God!" for the bounty of belief which illuminates these six sides, for in addition to being a great favor or blessing on account of dispelling the darkness of the six sides and therefore warding off evil, belief is also a bounty and a favor in respect of the fact that it illuminates these sides and thus attracts benefits. Therefore since humans are by nature civilized, they are connected with all the creatures on the six sides, and have the possibility of benefiting from these sides through the favor of belief.

Thus according to a meaning of the verse, *To whatever direction you turn, there is the "Face" of God* (2:115), humans find enlightenment on whichever of the six sides they are. In fact, a believer has a life which in effect extends from the foundation of the world to its end. This life of theirs benefits from the light of a life which extends from pre-eternity to post-eternity. Also, thanks to belief, which illuminates the six sides, the present narrow time and space in which humans find themselves are transformed into a spacious world. This extensive world becomes like their house, while the past and the future become like present time for their spirit and heart: the distance between them disappears.

THIRD POINT

Since belief provides points of support and assistance, it requires the response "All praise and gratitude are for God!"

Humanity needs a source of support or reliance because of their impotence and the multiplicity of their adversaries, so that they may seek refuge in that source to repel those who are ranged against them. Likewise, because of the abundance of their needs and their extreme innate poverty, they are in need of a source of assistance from which they may seek help, so that through it they may meet their needs.

O humankind! Your one and only point of support or reliance is belief in God. The only source of assistance for your spirit and conscience is belief in the Hereafter. Therefore, one who is unaware of these two sources suffers constant fear in their heart and spirit, and their conscience is continually tormented. However, the person who relies on the first point and asks for help from the second experiences numerous pleasures and instances of friendliness in their heart and spirit: as a result they become consoled and their conscience finds rest and satisfaction.

FOURTH POINT

The light of belief removes the pain which arises from the imminent vanishing of lawful pleasures by showing that similar pleasures always exist and will come again in the future. Furthermore, by indicating the source of bounties, it ensures that those bounties continue eternally and do not diminish.

Also, by showing the pleasure of the union with pleasures similar to them, it removes the pain of separation and parting. That is to say, a single pleasure contains many pains due to the thought of separation, while belief removes them by calling to mind the recurrence of that pleasure. There are further pleasures in the renewal of pleasure. If the tree from which a fruit is taken is unknown, the pleasure restricted to the fruit disappears when it is eaten up, which causes sorrow. But if the tree is known, there is no pain when the fruit ceases to exist, for there are other fruits which can be picked from that tree to take its place.

In fact, renewal itself is a pleasure. For what causes the human spirit the greatest distress are the pains that arise from separation. The light of belief removes the pains of separation from pleasures through their replacement by similar ones, and through the hope of attaining them.

FIFTH POINT

The light of belief shows the things that humans imagine to be strange and hostile to them, or to be lifeless and lost as though orphans among creatures, as friends and siblings, as living, and as glorifiers of God. That is to say, a person who looks with the eye of heedlessness supposes the beings in the world to be harmful like enemies, and they take fright: they see everything as alien. For in the view of misguidance, there are no bonds of brotherhood between the things of the past and those of the future: there is only an insignificant, partial relationship between them. Consequently, the brotherhood of the people of misguidance is only like a minute out of thousands of years.

In the view of belief, all bodies are living, familiar and friendly with one another. Belief also shows each of them to be glorifying its Creator through the tongue of its being. It is in this respect that all bodies have a sort of life and spirit appropriate to each. Therefore there is nothing fearful or frightening about bodies when they are viewed in the light of belief; instead there is friendliness and love.

The view of misguidance considers human beings, powerless as they are to secure their demands and aspirations, as ownerless and without protector; it sees them grieving and sorrowful, like weeping orphans because of their impotence. By contrast, the view of belief sees living creatures not as orphans but as officials charged with certain tasks, as servants charged with the duty of glorifying and extolling God.

SIXTH POINT

The light of belief depicts this world and the Hereafter as two tables filled with numerous varieties of bounties: believers benefit by accessing them with the hand of belief, with their inner and external senses, and their spiritual faculties. Seen through the prism of misguidance, the sphere of benefit for living beings diminishes and is restricted to material pleasures. Seen through the prism of belief, however, it expands to a sphere which encompasses the heavens and the earth. Truly, believers consider the sun to be a lamp hanging in the roof of their house, and the moon to be a night-light. For this reason, the sun and the moon are bounties and examples of Divine grace for them, and the sphere from which believers benefit is broader than the heavens. Through the eloquence of its verses, *He has made the sun and the moon constant in their courses, and so serviceable to you* (14:33), and *He has made all that is in the heavens and all that is on the earth of service to you* (31:20), the miraculously eloquent Qur'an points to these wonderful favors and blessings which arise from belief.

SEVENTH POINT

It is known through belief that God's Existence is a great favor that surpasses all others; it is a source, a fountain, which contains endless varieties of favors, innumerable sorts of blessings and uncountable kinds of gifts. It is therefore incumbent upon humans to repay this debt by offering praise and laudation for the favors of belief to the number of particles in creation. Some of these favors have been pointed out in various parts of the *Risale-i Nur* where belief in God is discussed.

One of the favors for which praise and thanks should be offered by saying *al-hamdu li'llah* ("All praise and gratitude are for God!")—by mentioning the word *hamd* (praise) with the definite article *al*, in the form of *al-hamdu*, meaning "all praise"—is the favor of God's being the All-Merciful. God's Mercifulness refers to, and is the source of, favors and bounties as numerous as the living beings which need and are favored with mercy. For a human being in particular is connected with all living creatures, and because of this, he or she becomes happy on account of their happiness and is saddened by their pains. Thus a favor enjoyed by a single individual is a favor also for their fellows.

God has another important Attribute, namely Compassion. His being the All-Compassionate comprises, and is the source of, bounties as numerous as the children and young favored with their mothers' tenderness, and therefore deserves praise and laudation accordingly. A person with conscience who feels sorrow and pity at the weeping of a motherless, hungry child, surely feels pleasure on seeing a mother's compassion for her children: they are pleased and happy with it. Thus pleasures of this sort are all favors and require praise and thanks.

Another of the bounties or favors which requires praise and thanks to the number of all the varieties and instances of wisdom contained in the universe is Divine Wisdom or God's being the All-Wise. For just as a person's soul is favored with the manifestations of Divine Mercy and their heart with the manifestations of Divine Compassion, their intellect also derives pleasure from the subtleties of Divine Wisdom. Therefore they require endless praise and laudation through the loud utterance of "All praise and gratitude are for God!"

Also, Divine Preservation or God's being the All-Preserving is another favor for which praise should be offered with an "All praise and gratitude are for God!" so great that it would fill all space with its sound—it should be offered as many times as there are manifestations of the Divine Name the All-Inheriting, as there are descendants who continue to live after the death of their forebears, as there are beings in the next world, and as there are actions of humans which are preserved so that they may receive their rewards in the Hereafter. For the continuation of a favor is more valuable than the favor itself; the permanence of pleasure is more pleasurable than the pleasure itself; eternal permanence in Paradise is superior to Paradise itself, and so on. Consequently, with all the bounties it contains, Almighty God's Attribute of Preservation is far greater than, and far superior to, all the bounties which exist throughout the universe. Thus this Attribute requires an "All praise and gratitude are for God!" so great that it would fill the world. You can compare the rest of the Divine Names and Attributes with the four mentioned here, and since in each there are endless bounties or favors, each requires endless praise and thanks.

Likewise, Prophet Muhammad, upon him be peace and blessings, who is the means of attaining the favor of belief, which has the authority to open all the treasuries of bounties, is also such a favor that humankind owes him the debt of extolling and applauding him throughout eternity.

Similarly, the favors of Islam and the Qur'an, which are the concentrated form and source of all varieties of bounties, both material and spiritual, require and deserve infinite praise.

EIGHTH POINT

All praise and gratitude be to God that, as established by the mighty Qur'an with all its chapters and sections, all its pages and lines, and all its words and letters, this cosmic book known as the universe praises and extols Him, the All-Pure and Holy One, through making manifest His Attributes of Beauty and Grace and Perfection. It is as follows:

According to its capacity, however great or small, each embroidery of this cosmic book praises and extols its Embroiderer, Who is the One and Eternally Besought, through manifesting His Attributes of Majesty. Also, through displaying His Attributes of Beauty and Grace, each inscription in this book extols its Inscriber, Who is the All-Merciful and the All-Compassionate. Besides, on account of being favored with and mirroring the manifestations of the Divine All-Beautiful Names, all the inscriptions, points and embroideries of this book praise and extol the All-Pure and Holy One through lauding, glorifying and exalting Him. Furthermore, each ode in this book extols and glorifies its Composer, Who is the All-Powerful and the All-Knowing.

The supplicant

I am a ruined grave, in which are piled up
Seventy-nine dead Saids with his sins and sorrows.
The eightieth is a gravestone to his grave;
All together they weep at the decline of Islam.
Together with my gravestone and moaning grave of dead Saids,
I am advancing toward my abode of tomorrow.
I am fully certain that the heavens and earth of the future
Will together surrender to Islam's clear, shining hand.
For its strength lies in the blessing of belief,
It affords peace and security to all beings.

Index

H

I

J

K

L

M

N

Q

R

S

T

U

V

W

Y

Z

Index of God's Names and Attributes